The
RAF
in Action

The RAF
in Action
From Flanders to the Falklands

Robert Jackson

BLANDFORD PRESS
POOLE · DORSET

First published in the UK 1985 by Blandford
Press, Link House, West Street, Poole, Dorset,
BH15 1LL.

Copyright © 1985 Robert Jackson

Distributed in the United States by
Sterling Publishing Co., Inc.,
2 Park Avenue, New York, N.Y. 10016.

British Library Cataloguing in Publication Data

Jackson, Robert, *1941–*
   The RAF in action—from Flanders to the Falklands.
   1. Great Britain. *Royal Air Force*—History
   I. Title
   358.4′00941   UG635.G7

ISBN 0 7137 1419 0

Third Printing
Printed by Arcata Graphics
Kingsport, TN.

Typeset by Graphicraft Ltd Hong Kong
Printed in Great Britain by BAS Printers, Over
Wallop, Hampshire

Contents

Part I 1918–1939

1 Combat over Flanders, 1918   6
2 The RAF in Russia, 1918–20   13
3 The Middle East, 1918–30   16
4 The 'Exclusive Flying Club'   25
5 Re-armament and the Approach of War   37

Part II 1939–45

6 Before the Storm   45
7 Flames over Norway   51
8 *Blitzkreig*: The Battle in the West, May–June 1940   55
9 The Battle of Britain   63
10 The Middle East, 1940–41   72
11 The Atlantic and Western Europe, 1941–42   80
12 North African Victory   88
13 Air operations in the West, January 1942–May 1944   94
14 From Sicily to the Balkans, 1943–45   102
15 Air operations in the West, 1944–45   108
16 The Far East, 1941–45   124

Part III 1945–85

17 The RAF and the Atlantic Alliance, 1945–68   133
18 RAF Action Overseas, 1948–71   142
19 The RAF, 1968–84   148
20 Fortress Falklands—the Last Battle?   154

Index   158
Acknowledgements   160

Frontispiece
**A Hawker Hart with the majestic peak of Nanga
Parbat (Devil Mountain) in the background,
circa 1932**

Opposite
**The Harrier GR. 3, together with the Royal
Navy's Sea Harriers, rendered unparalleled
service during the Falklands conflict.**

5

1

Combat over Flanders

1918

The weather was fine and the visibility good. A total of 23 tons of bombs were dropped by night and 17 tons by day. Enemy aircraft were active south of the Somme, and enemy two-seaters were employed in low flying and firing at our troops. Several large formations of E.A. scouts were also encountered at a height. Two hostile balloons were shot down, and one hostile machine was brought down in our lines by infantry, in addition to those accounted for by aerial combat.

So ran the terse words of Royal Air Force Communiqué No. 1, dated 1 April 1918. There was nothing to indicate that the Royal Flying Corps and the Royal Naval Air Service, both of which had issued separate communiqués on the previous day, had ceased to exist or that the Royal Air Force

Combat over Flanders–1: a German pilot falls from his blazing Albatros D.V.

had been born overnight of their amalgamation.

Neither was the change of identity of much interest to the thousands of officers and men who made up the new Service. They were too busy fighting.

A few days earlier, at 04.45 on 21 March 1918, the Germans had launched a massive offensive on the Western Front, hurling 56 divisions—many of them released from service in the East following the armistice with the Russians—against the fronts of the British Third and Fifth Armies. Despite all the preliminary warnings, the attack, which was launched in thick mist, achieved total surprise, and by noon the German spearheads had smashed their way through the British defences.

As soon as the mist began to clear, the Royal Flying Corps threw every available fighter and bomber into the assault on the densely-packed enemy columns. Large-scale air battles flared up between the bomber escorts and enemy fighters, particularly on 23 March when 28 German aircraft were shot down for the loss of five British—although 28 more British machines were lost in the course of the day through battle damage. The next day, 42 German machines were destroyed and one Sopwith Camel pilot of No. 43 Squadron, Captain J.L. Trollope, set up a record by shooting down six between dawn and dusk.

Although the low-level air attacks inflicted severe casualties on the advancing Germans the pace showed no sign of easing at the end of March. There was intense air fighting on 1 April; during the day, seven aircraft failed to return from patrol and another from reconnaissance; two others were shot down while bombing Bapaume; twelve were damaged by anti-aircraft fire and crashed on landing; and 24 more were wrecked in various other ways. In fact, the first of April, 1918, followed the pattern of the endless days

that had gone before it; aircraft going down in flames, faces missing from the mess-tents, exhausted crews, many of them unable to keep down any food except brandy and milk, snatching a few hours' nightmare-torn sleep before the dawn. To these men, hurling themselves into action day after day in support of the greatest fighting retreat in the history of the British Army, 1 April had no special significance other than that they had lived through it.

There was to be no respite, no easy transition period for the new Service. The German offensive continued; by this time the fog had lifted and the RAF was able to operate at maximum effort, with aircraft of every type ranging low over the front and attacking the enemy with light bombs and machine-gun fire. There was bitter fighting on 12 April,

Combat over Flanders–2: a blazing Nieuport 27C–1 photographed from an accompanying aircraft during its death plunge.

when the RAF flew more than 3,200 hours on operations. Some crews were in action for five and a half hours between dawn and dusk. There were several big air fights, and Captain H.W. Woollett of No. 43 Squadron, flying a Camel, shot down six enemy aircraft before nightfall. The British air activities contributed greatly to the overall defence, which proved too strong for the Germans. Although they made several determined efforts to extend their front during the week that followed, the British line stood firm and the enemy offensive finally petered out. There now followed a lull of four days in the fighting; during this period the RAF kept up its attacks on the enemy rear areas and lines of communication, while reconnaissance aircraft kept the German positions under constant surveillance.

On 21 April, two RE.8s of No. 3 (Australian) Squadron were photographing the lines west of Hamel when they were attacked by fifteen gaily-coloured Fokker Triplanes and Albatros D.IIIs. Their predicament was seen by Captain A.R. Brown, leading eight Camels of No. 209 Squadron, who at once went to their assistance. The Camel pilots were soon fighting for their lives. One of them, 2nd Lieutenant W.R. May—a newcomer to the squadron, carrying out his first operational patrol—exchanged fire with one enemy aircraft and then turned for home, as

he had orders to avoid combat if possible. Suddenly, machine-gun bullets crackled past his aircraft; looking round, he saw an all-red Fokker Triplane hard on his tail. Roy Brown saw it too, and dived down to intervene. The three aircraft sped low over the front-line trenches in line astern. Brown, some Australian machine-gunners of the 5th Division and some Lewis gunners attached to a nearby Field Artillery battery all fired at the red Triplane simultaneously; it staggered, went down on an even keel and landed heavily two miles inside the British lines. The pilot, slumped in the cockpit, was dead; Manfred von Richthofen, after 80 victories in the air, had fought his last battle. Brown and the Australians each claimed the credit for shooting him down, sparking off a controversy which will probably never be satisfactorily resolved.

That month of April 1918 was a bitter,

bloody time. When it began, the RAF had 1,232 front-line aircraft serving with the squadrons in Flanders; by the time it ended, 1,000 of them had been destroyed—a total that included 195 missing in action, 696 wrecked, and 141 burnt or abandoned following forced landings in no-man's land. But, for the first time in history, the advance of an army had been broken by tactical air power used on a massive scale, and air attacks had accounted for a considerable proportion of the 348,000 casualties suffered by the Germans in their last great offensive of the 1914–18 War.

Offensive operations by the Royal Air Force against the enemy's lines of communication proved, as never before, the value of bomber aircraft in causing chaos deep in the Germans' rear areas. Some 600 tons of bombs were dropped by the RAF in April, and the results obtained encouraged the British Government, in May, to form an Independent Force for an extended and sustained bombing offensive against German industrial targets, primarily munitions factories. Commanded by Major-General Sir Hugh Trenchard, the new force officially came into existence on 6 June 1918 and was based on the existing VIII Brigade, RAF, which had been carrying out bombing operations with a variety of aircraft for several months. Originally, the Brigade structure underwent very little change; the Independent Force continued to operate five squadrons in two wings, the 41st Wing comprising Nos 55, 90 and 104 Squadrons for day-bombing and the 83rd Wing comprising Nos 100 and 216 Squadrons, which were reserved for the night-bombing role. Later, in August 1918, the Independent Force's strength was boosted by the addition of four more squadrons: Nos 97, 115 and 215 with Handley Page 0/400s, and No. 110 with de Havilland DH.9As. No. 100 Squadron also began con-

The Avro 504 was in use as a trainer at the end of World War One and in this role served in the RAF until 1933. This example crashed after stalling on the approach to land at Netheravon in 1919.

version to 0/400s in August. In addition, the Independent Force had one fighter-escort squadron, No. 45, which was equipped with Sopwith Camels; Trenchard, however, would not allow it to operate in its intended role until it re-equipped with Sopwith Snipes and, as these did not arrive until after the Armistice, No. 45 Squadron's activities were restricted to patrols in the front-line area.

Some idea of the effectiveness of the Independent Force, RAF—the first air formation in the world designed specifically for the strategic bombing role and as such the forerunner of RAF Bomber Command—may be gleaned from Trenchard's own despatch, published as a supplement to *The London Gazette* on 1 January 1919:

The total weight of bombs dropped between the 6th June and the 10th November was 550 tons, of which 160 tons were dropped by day and 390 tons by night. Of this amount no less than 220¼ tons were dropped on aerodromes. This large percentage was due to the necessity of preventing the enemy bombing machines attacking [the Independent Force's] aerodromes and in order to destroy large numbers of the enemy's scouts on their aerodromes, as it was impracticable to deal with them on equal terms in the air. I think this large amount of bombing was thoroughly justified when it is taken into consideration that the enemy's attacks on our aerodromes were practically negligible, and not a single machine was destroyed by bombing during the period 5th June to 11th November.

Trenchard's despatch lists forty-one other targets, including industrial centres such as Mannheim and Frankfurt, which were at-tacked by the Independent Force before the Armistice, and continues:

It must also be remembered that of the 109 machines which were missing, the majority dropped bombs on targets before landing. The amount of bombs dropped by these machines is not included in the above figures ...
... A large amount of photographic reconnaissance was done by individual machines at a great height. This work was nearly always successfully carried out, and only one photographic machine was lost during the whole period of operations. Photographs have proved time and time again the efficiency of the work of the bombing machines. Captured correspondence testified to the great moral effect of the bombing attacks on Germany.
It was apparent by the end of June that the enemy was increasing the number of fighting machines opposed to us. These machines were presumably being provided from squadrons he had withdrawn from the Russian front and re-equipped for home defence work. In September and October our day-bombing squadrons had to fight practically from the front line to their objective, and from there home again. In several cases they had to fight the whole way out and the whole way back. This necessitated the most careful keeping of formation in order to avoid undue casualties, as once the formation was split up the enemy's machines could attack individual machines at their leisure. When our machines were in formation he generally concentrated on the rear machines, occasionally making attacks on the machines in front.

Trenchard made the point that, although the weather in the summer months was extremely favourable for long-range bombing operations, it could hardly have been worse from September onwards:

Day after day, attempts were made to reach the long-distance targets, but the wind was generally too strong; or, if there was no wind, heavy rain and fog prevailed by day and dense mist by night, which lasted often until ten or eleven o'clock the next morning. Often the nights were perfect, but dense white mist completely obliterated the ground, making it impossible for machines to ascend.

Twenty-two years later, the crews of Bomber Command, flying to targets in Nazi Germany, were to experience exactly the same problems. Long-range navigation, particularly by night, had not advanced a great deal, nor would it do so until the advent of radar aids.

Despite all the problems, the Independent Force was really getting into its stride by November 1918 and plans were being laid for attacks on Berlin itself. In September, a new Group, No. 27, had begun to form at RAF Bircham Newton under the command of Lieutenant-Colonel R.H. Mulock. It was to consist of two wings, Nos 86 and 87, and was to be equipped with a new four-engined heavy bomber, the Handley Page V/1500. One squadron, No. 166, had begun to equip with the type when the Armistice intervened. Two other squadrons, Nos 167 and 274, also received V/1500s, but of the 36 aircraft built most were used for trials work and the type was relinquished when the squadrons using it disbanded in 1919–20.

Returning to the early days of the Royal Air Force, the Service was involved in more heavy fighting during May 1918, when the Germans launched another, although smaller, offensive in the south, on the river Aisne. This was a hitherto quiet sector, defended by four British divisions which had been sent there to rest after the fierce battles in the north, and were supported by a single RAF reconnaissance squadron, No. 52, equipped with RE.8s. The surprise enemy assault wiped out two of the British divisions and only timely intervention by French reserves prevented a massive breakthrough. As it was, the Germans penetrated as far as the Marne and eight RAF squadrons were rushed south on 3 June to carry out ground attack operations. The battle raged throughout July and, in the course of air operations, RAF aircraft—RE.8s—were used for the first time to drop supplies of ammunition to hard-pressed ground forces.

Many skilled and veteran pilots on both sides, who had survived for months in an environment where the life expectancy on average was less than three weeks, lost their lives in that hectic summer sky. One of them was Major Roderick Dallas, the Australian

CO of No. 40 Squadron, which was equipped with SE.5s. Despite being badly wounded in April on a ground-attack sortie, Dallas soon returned to action and by the end of May his personal score had risen to 39 enemy aircraft destroyed. On 1 June 1918, Dallas set out on one of his habitual lone patrols, intending to lurk in the sun over the front line and trap an unsuspecting enemy observation aircraft. He never returned but the wreckage of his aircraft was found later near the village of Lieven. Later, a German account told the story of Dallas's last minutes. It appeared that he had dived down to attack a solitary Fokker Triplane, unaware that two more were cruising several thousand feet higher up, waiting for just such a moment. Dallas must have died instantly, his body shot through by a score of bullets.

Another pilot who flew with No. 40 Squadron was Major Edward Mannock, vc, dso, mc, who became the top-scoring pilot of the RFC/RAF with at least 74 enemy aircraft destroyed. In the summer of 1918, he was commanding No. 85 Squadron, which had recently moved to France with SE.5As, and on 26 July, a cloudy, rainy day, he set out on patrol with Lieutenant D.C. Inglis. The two of them surprised an enemy two-seater and shot it down, but on the flight home they encountered intense ground fire over the front line and both aircraft were hit. Inglis managed to land a few yards inside the British lines but 'Mick' Mannock fell in flames to his death.

Some survived everything the enemy could throw at them only to die needlessly as the result of an accident. One such was Major

Airships were used by the RAF's coastal patrol units at the end of World War One. The upper photograph shows a C-Type, *C-5* which had an endurance of more than 24 hours; the lower photograph shows a C*-Type, *C*7*. Both are at Longside.

James B. McCudden, who had shot down 58 enemy aircraft, mostly while serving with No. 56 Squadron. His decorations included the vc, dso, mc and mm. After a four-month rest spell in England, McCudden was ordered back to France to take command of No. 60 Squadron. On 9 July 1918, he crossed the English Channel in his SE.5A and landed at a French airfield to refuel before continuing to No. 60's base. He took off again a few minutes later but as he was climbing away his engine suddenly died. Observers on the ground saw the nose of his machine go down as McCudden looked ahead for somewhere to land.

One of the cardinal rules of flying is that you never turn back towards the field if your engine fails on take-off; too much height and airspeed are lost in a turn. It was a rule that McCudden had drilled into his pupils during his months as an instructor. But on this occasion, astonishingly, McCudden did turn back. Witnesses saw his machine bank, then it stalled and fell, starting to go into a spin. There was not sufficient height to recover. A few seconds later, Major McCudden lay dead in the wreckage.

A few—very few—fighter pilots seemed to bear charmed lives. One such was Captain W.A. 'Billy' Bishop, the Canadian CO of No. 85 Squadron, who by the end of his combat career had destroyed 72 enemy aircraft and

been awarded the vc, dso and mc. In June 1918, Bishop's score stood at 47 and did not look like going much higher for his superiors, deciding that his luck would not last for ever, decided to send him back to England in a fortnight's time. During that fortnight, Bishop flung himself into the bitter air fighting over the Lys with complete disregard for his own safety. In a period of twelve days, representing a total of only 36 and a half hours' flying time, he destroyed a further 25 enemy machines. On 17 June, his last day of action but one, he shot down three aircraft in 30 minutes, using only 55 rounds of ammunition. His terse combat report described the action:

10.25 am. Staden and Hooglede. 18,000 feet. (i) Between Staden and Hooglede, 18,000 feet at 10.25 am, I turned back a two-seater

Royal Air Force Order of Battle on the Western Front, April 1918.

IX (GHQ) Brigade: Hogg

Ninth Wing: Freeman

Sqn	CO	Aircraft	Sqn	CO	Aircraft
25	Duffus	DH.4	29	Dixon	Nieuport Scout and one S.E.5a
27	Hill	DH.4			
62	Smith, F.W.	Bristol Fighter	32	Russell	SE.5A
73	Hubbard	Camel	57	Hiatt	DH.4
79	Noel	Dolphin	60	Moore	SE.5A
80	Bell	Camel	65	Cunningham	Camel
			74	Caldwell	SE.5A
			98	O'Malley	DH.9

Fifty-Fourth Wing: Small

Sqn	CO	Aircraft
58	Tyssen	FE.2b (Night Flying)
83	Gower	FE.2b (Night Flying)

I Brigade: Pitcher

First (Corps) Wing: Gossage

Sqn	CO	Aircraft
2	Snow	FK.8 and two Bristol Fighters
4	Saul	RE.8
5	Gardner	RE.8
13	Garrod	RE.8
16	Portal	RE.8 (Canadian)
42	Gould, R.G.	RE.8

Tenth (Army) Wing: Maclean

Sqn	CO	Aircraft
3	Collishaw	Camel
4	McClaughry	Camel (Australian)
18	Howard	DH.4
19	Pretyman	Dolphin
22	McKelvie	Bristol Fighter
40	Dallas	SE.5A
41	Bowman	SE.5A (from Reserve, 11 April)
46	Mealing	Camel
64	Smythies	SE.5A
208	Draper	Camel
210	Bell	Camel

II Brigade: Becke

Second (Corps) Wing: Blake

Sqn	CO	Aircraft
3	Brown, R.S.	RE.8 (Australian)
7	Sutton	RE.8
10	Murray	FK.8 and two Bristol Fighters
21	Gould, L.T.N.	RE.8

Eleventh (Army) Wing: Van Ryneveld

Sqn	CO	Aircraft
1	Barton Adams	SE.5A and one Nieuport Scout
6	MacLaren	DH.9
9	Butler, C.H.	Camel
19	Pretyman	Dolphin
20	Johnston	Bristol Fighter

III Brigade: Higgens

Twelfth (Corps) Wing: Mitchell

Sqn	CO	Aircraft
12	de Courcy	RE.8 and one Bristol Fighter
13	Garrod	RE.8
15	Stammers	RE.8 and one Bristol Fighter
59	Mackay	RE.8

Thirteenth (Army) Wing: Playfair

Sqn	CO	Aircraft
3	Barker	Camel
11	Morton	Bristol Fighter
22	McKelvie	Bristol Fighter
41	Bowman	SE.5A
43	Miles	Camel
46	Mealing	Camel
49	Gould, J.R.	DH.4
56	Brown	SE.5A and one R.E.8
60	Moore	SE.5A
64	Smythies	SE.5A
70	Edwards	Camel
102	Baker	FE.2b (Night Flying)

V Brigade: Charlton

Fifteenth (Corps) Wing: Edwards I.A.E.

Sqn	CO	Aircraft
8	Leigh-Mallory	FK.8
35	Holt	FK.8 and two Bristol Fighters
52	Morison	RE.8
53	Henderson	RE.8
82	Jackson	FK.8

Twenty-Second (Army) Wing: Holt

Sqn	CO	Aircraft
5	Goble	DH.4
23	Bryant	Spad
24	Robeson	SE.5A
48	Shield	Bristol Fighter
54	Maxwell	Camel
84	Douglas	SE.5A
101	Hargrave	FE.2b (Night Flying)

who was approaching our lines, finally closing to seventy-five yards. After twenty rounds he burst into flames.

10.50 am. Sailly-sur-Lys. 4,000 feet.

(ii) Over Sailly-sur-Lys, 4,000 feet at 10.50 am, seeing one Albatros I zoomed into the edge of a cloud. Albatros passed cloud and I secured position on tail. After twenty rounds he burst into flames.

10.55 am. Laventie (near). 2,000 feet.

(iii) After attacking (ii) I saw a two-seater EA quite low. I dived at him from the east but he turned and got east of me. After second burst of twenty rounds he fell in a turning dive, then crashed between Laventie and main road.

Bishop's last day in action was even more dramatic. Patrolling near Ypres, he saw and attacked three Pfalz fighters, one of which he quickly destroyed. As the others turned to attack him, two more Pfalz dropped out of the clouds and a turning fight developed. Two of the Pfalz suddenly broke towards Bishop, who saw his chance and dived between them. The Pfalz tightened their turns in an effort to get on his tail and collided, whereupon the other two turned away towards their own lines. Bishop went after them, opening fire on one from 200 yards. It went down in flames; the other escaped into a cloud. Next day, Bishop left France for good. He had destroyed 72 enemy aircraft in just over a year of air combat. No other fighter pilot in the 1914–18 War had achieved as much in such a comparatively short time and in this top-scoring bracket only one other— the Frenchman, René Fonck—was destined to survive the conflict.

In contrast to the murderous air battles over Flanders, operations elsewhere by the Royal Air Force may have seemed routine, almost dull. Nowhere was this better illustrated than in the work carried out by the squadrons of the former Royal Naval Air Service, particularly those whose task it was to protect friendly shipping in the North Sea and the English Channel. Yet it was vital work, for in the early months of 1918, the U-boat threat, although not as great as it had been in 1917, was still considerable. U-boat commanders, finding it increasingly difficult to attack well-protected convoys, adopted new tactics, lying close inshore to mount attacks on individual ships once the convoy had dispersed.

To counter this move, the RAF stepped up its offshore patrols, operating a miscellany of aircraft from a chain of coastal bases stretching from the Humber to the Irish Sea. The squadrons involved in this task laboured under considerable hardship; quite apart from the vagaries of the weather, the equipment they used was obsolescent and far from suited to the demands of sustained operational flying. Early in 1918, for example, two hundred Airco DH.6 aircraft, first produced as two-seat primary trainers in 1916, were pressed into service as anti-submarine patrol aircraft. Thirty-four coastal defence flights were equipped with them and they were flown as single-seaters, carrying a 100-pound bomb-load. It is not on record that they destroyed any U-boats, but their presence in the vicinity of a convoy may have acted as a deterrent.

In all, the maritime patrol aircraft of the RNAS and RAF carried out 117 attacks on enemy submarines, a further thirteen attacks being made by airship. They resulted in the destruction of some six U-boats; 25 more were damaged. To keep the U-boats penned up in their bases, minefields were laid in the Heligoland Bight; the Germans constantly tried to clear these with the use of mine-sweeping trawlers and these were attacked whenever possible by Curtiss H.4 and Felix-stowe H.12 flying-boats, usually from Great Yarmouth. Since German aircraft and airships maintained patrols over the trawlers, air encounters were not infrequent; in May 1918, for example, a Felixstowe flying-boat fought an engagement with Zeppelin *L.62* over the minefields and registered some hits, driving the airship away. *L.62* subsequently blew up, although the cause may have been a sabotaged bomb-load rather than the action of the British aircraft.

The closing months of World War One were of tremendous significance for the development of British naval air power. On 17 July, the aircraft carrier HMS *Furious* sailed from Rosyth, accompanied by the First Light Cruiser Squadron, and headed out into the North Sea. The *Furious* was the Royal Navy's first true aircraft carrier, with a continuous flight deck broken only by her funnel and superstructure, and she had accommodation for fourteen aricraft. On 19 July 1918, *Furious* made history by launching the first air strike from a ship at sea. Two flights of Sopwith 2F1 Camels—six aircraft in all—took off from her flight deck and set course for the German airship base at Tondern. Each aircraft carried two 50-pound bombs. They took the Germans completely by surprise, destroying a huge hangar and the two airships inside, *L.54* and *L.60*. However, only two of the RAF pilots involved— Captains W.F. Dickson and B.A. Smart— regained the carrier; three of the others had to land in Denmark because of bad weather and the fourth crashed into the sea and was drowned.

Another spectacular success was regis-

tered on 11 August 1918 by another naval Camel pilot, Lieutenant Stuart Culley. Launched from a lighter towed behind the destroyer HMS *Redoubt*, he succeeded in intercepting the Zeppelin *L.53* at a height of over 19,000 feet above the Heligoland Bight. He fired all his ammunition into the airship's vast bulk and *L.53* caught fire, crashing to the sea far below. Exploits such as these reinforced the Admiralty's strongly-held viewpoint that their aircraft and crews, over which they had lost all control on the formation of the RAF, should be returned to them but it was to be another twenty years before a Fleet Air Arm administered solely by the Royal Navy became a reality.

If the RAF's coastal defence squadrons were suffering from outdated equipment in April 1918, the Service's home defence squadrons were in an even worse state. By

The *R.24*, a rigid airship built by Vickers. Together with two more, the *R.23* and *R.25*, it entered RAF service in the last year of World War One, but saw little active service.

Collapsing an RAF C-Type airship by 'ripping' the envelope, a difficult operation that required a large ground crew.

this time, however, attacks on British targets by Zeppelins and aircraft were beginning to tail off; the last big airship raid on Britain had taken place in October 1917 and after that the number of Zeppelins venturing into British skies seldom exceeded five at one time. They were occasionally intercepted; on 12 April 1918, for example, Zeppelin *L.62*—part of a five-strong raiding force—was attacked by an FE.2b of No. 38 Squadron and only escaped after the airship's gunners wounded the FE's pilot, Lieutenant C.H. Noble-Campbell, in the head.

FEs and BE.2cs still equipped the bulk of the RAF's home defence units but some were by now receiving the more modern Sopwith Camel and Bristol Fighter and these types formed a strong part of the 84 fighters that took to the air on the night of 19/20 May 1918 to intercept 43 Gotha and Staaken R.VI bombers that set out to attack London. About fifteen of the raiders reached the primary target. The anti-aircraft defences fired 30,000 shells at the bombers and the fighters destroyed six of the enemy. A seventh made a forced landing at Clacton with engine trouble and an eighth crashed in Belgium. It was the last, and greatest, attack by German aeroplanes to take place during the 1914–18 War; the last airship attack occurred on the night of 5/6 August, when Zeppelin *L.70* was shot down by Major Egbert Cadbury and Captain Robert Leckie, flying a DH.4.

The spring of 1918 saw a growing RAF involvement in the fighting on the Italian front. The first RFC squadrons had been sent out in the autumn of 1917 to bolster the Italians, who had suffered a series of reverses

Major G.H. Scott, AFC, leaving the *R.34* after the Transatlantic Flight.

in their campaign against the Austrians; early air reinforcements included No. 28 Squadron with Camels and No. 34 with RE.8s, which were followed by two more Camel squadrons, Nos 45 and 66. The operational task here, although not under the same constant pressure as that on the Western Front, was far from easy; the Austrian and German squadrons on the Italian front included some very skilled and determined airmen and the difficulties were compounded by the weather. Flying in open cockpits over the treacherous mountain regions of northern Italy became a nightmare and several pilots were lost when their engines froze and they crashed into the mountain sides.

One of the leading RAF fighter pilots on the Italian front was Major W.G. Barker of No. 28 Squadron, who scored 41 victories in this sector to add to the five he had already claimed over Flanders. His squadron was involved in a particularly hectic period of fighting in June 1918, when the Austrians launched a major offensive, in the course of which Barker shot down one of Austria's greatest air aces, Major Linke, within sight of the latter's own airfield. By the time the 24-year-old Canadian was posted back to the Western Front to command No. 201 Squadron, which was equipped with the latest Sopwith 7F.1 Snipe fighters, his decorations included the DSO and Bar, MC and two Bars, the Croix de Guerre and the Italian Cross of Valour. Barker's command of 201 Squadron was short-lived. For some time, his superiors had been thinking about grounding him before his luck ran out; in the end, they decided to give him a safe posting in England.

So, on the morning of 27 October 1918, Bill Barker took off in his Snipe and set course for the English Channel, his ultimate destination being Hounslow. Over the forest of Mormal, however, he spotted a Hanoveraner two-seat reconnaissance aircraft at 21,000 feet and attacked it, killing the German gunner and eventually shooting down the Hanoveraner after expending a good deal of ammunition. Almost immediately, Barker was himself attacked by a Fokker D.VII and wounded in the thigh. The Snipe went into a spin and when Barker recovered he found himself in the middle of a formation of fifteen Fokkers. He at once attacked them, damaging two and shooting down a third before he was wounded again in the other thigh. The Snipe entered a second spin and this time Barker blacked out for a few seconds, regaining consciousness to find himself surrounded by another fifteen Fokkers. He shot down one of them, then a bullet shattered his left elbow and he again lost consciousness. When he recovered he was attacked by fifteen more German fighters; by this time his aircraft was smoking badly and, convinced that it was about to catch fire, Barker dived at the nearest Fokker with the intention of ramming it. At the last instant he changed his mind and opened fire; the German fighter went down in flames.

Breaking off the unequal combat, Barker managed to nurse his crippled aircraft down to a crash-landing in the Allied lines. His epic fight earned him the last air VC of World War One. While he lay in hospital, recovering from his wounds on 11 November 1918, the guns on the Western Front were finally silenced.

2

The RAF in Russia
1918-20

In the summer of 1918, while the conflict in western Europe still raged, contingents of British, French, Japanese—and, later, American—troops landed on Russian soil. Ostensibly, their purpose was to guard Allied war stores from capture by the Germans in a Russia that was now torn by civil war, but it was not long before they became directly embroiled in the bitter struggle between the embryo Bolshevik armies and the so-called 'White' Russian forces loyal to the Tsar.

In both North and South Russia, Allied land operations were supported by small RAF contingents. In September 1918, a Royal Air Force flight of eight DH.4s arrived by sea at the north Russian port of Archangel'sk and quickly moved up to a primitive airfield at Bakaritsa to operate in support of Allied operations on the river Dvina. At Bakaritsa, the RAF personnel discovered several Nieuport 17s and Sopwith One-and-a-Half Strutters, still in crates, part of a batch supplied to Imperial Russia the previous year and, apparently, overlooked by the Bolsheviks, who had recently been driven out of the area. These aircraft were quickly assembled and, together with the DH.4s, were used to form two squadrons, Nos 2 and 3 (numbers which bore no relation to those of normal RAF units). No. 2 Squadron was commanded by Major Charles R. Carr, RAF, and the other by an expert Russian airman named Alexander Kazakov, who had been CO of the 19th Squadron, Imperial Russian Air Corps.

The two squadrons went into action in November 1918 against the Bolshevik units that were pressing the Dvina Force. Loading their aircraft onto sleighs, the mixed Anglo-Russian force dragged them through the snow for two days, beating off attacks by groups of Reds.

Late in November, the pilots received a welcome addition to their equipment in the shape of six Sopwith Camel fighters, and it was while flying one of these that Kazakov, in January 1919, shot down the first Bolshevik aircraft—a seaplane—to be destroyed by the Allied Expeditionary Force. Enemy aircraft, in fact, were very scarce in this sector, a fact

that enabled the Allied pilots to carry out their task, albeit with poor equipment and under difficult conditions, in fairly routine fashion. The few machines that were available to the Reds in the north—mainly ex-Imperial Air Service types flown over by a handful of defecting pilots—were quickly neutralized in attacks on the enemy aerodromes. One such attack was carried out on the Red airfield at Puchega on 17 June 1919 by five DH.9 bombers, three of them from Captain Kazakov's No. 3 Squadron, escorted by two Sopwith Snipes, a Sopwith Camel and a Nieuport 17. One of the Snipe pilots, Major Carr, flew back and forth over the enemy airfield for twenty minutes, destroying four enemy aircraft and killing several personnel. He was later awarded the Distinguished Flying Cross. Two other RAF officers won the DFC for service in North Russia prior to the Allied withdrawal in September 1919: Flying Officer Lloyd Mason for ground attack work on the Dvina and Vologda fronts while flying a Snipe and Flight Lieutenant Oliver Bryson for a series of successful raids flying a DH.9 who later flew a Snipe on the Dvina and Pinega rivers.

In south Russia, the situation was somewhat different. Here, although British officers attached to a military mission served with front-line White units in an advisory capacity, there was no commitment of regular British units, as there was in the north. The sole exception was in the case of the RAF, which deployed No. 47 Squadron from Amberkoj in Greece to Ekaterinodar in April 1918 and No. 221 Squadron from Mudros to Petrovsk in December 1918; the latter unit was accompanied by 'A' Flight of No. 17 Squadron. The function of Nos 221 and 17 Squadrons, both of which were equipped with DH.9s, was to bomb the Bolshevik bases on the Caspian and to provide air support for the Royal Navy, which was operating a small armada of vessels in the area. By May 1919, following a series of limited air-sea actions against the Bolsheviks, the whole of the Caspian was in Allied hands with the exception of Astrakhan.

No. 47 Squadron, commanded by

Lieutenant-Colonel Raymond Collishaw—a redoubtable Canadian who had a score of 68 enemy aircraft destroyed on the Western Front to his credit—consisted of three flights, two equipped with DH.9 and 9A bombers and the third with Sopwith Camel fighters. The aircraft were war-weary at the time of their arrival in Russia; this was especially true of the Camels, which were ex-RNAS aircraft from Mudros. The poor state of the aircraft was demonstrated during the flight over the steppe from Ekaterinodar to the Squadron's advanced base at Beketovka; two of the Camels had to make forced landings with engine failure, a third just managed to creep in with fuel pump trouble and the oil pressure pump of a fourth fell off in flight. The Squadron's first task, two days after its arrival, was to carry out a reconnaissance beyond Tsaritsyn. It was made by four Camels led by Major Marcus Kinkead, 'A' Flight commander. One Camel, flown by Captain Marion Aten, became separated from the rest and was attacked by a Nieuport fighter, which missed and overshot; Aten dived after it and opened fire at 50 yards, seeing the Nieuport dive into the bank of the Volga and explode. It was No. 47 Squadron's first victory in Russia.

The Squadron was in action again the following day, escorting a formation of 'A' Flight DH.9s in a raid on the Bolshevik HQ at Tsaritsyn. Everything went according to plan, the HQ being destroyed by 112-pound bombs. Two enemy fighters, a Spad and a Fokker Triplane, came up to intercept but the Spad was immediately shot down by the escorting Camels and the Fokker broke off the engagement. Later that week, 'B' Flight's Camels were in action against a flotilla of gunboats which had been sighted on the Volga; the aircraft attacked with 20-pound bombs, causing little damage. As they climbed away, they were attacked by six Spads and Nieuports, two of which were shot down. All the Camels returned to base, although some had sustained damage.

In May 1919, a month that saw the 10th Red Army smashed by the Whites, No. 47 Squadron was ordered to step up its operations and destroy as many enemy aircraft as possible in support of the White advance on Tsaritsyn. During the first ten days of May they destroyed seven enemy aircraft.

Several of the Red squadrons in the area were based on Urbabk airfield, and during the second week in May this was attacked by a formation of White DH.9s escorted by the Camels of 'B' Flight. The bombing attack did very little damage, and the Reds came up in strength to intercept with a mixed formation that included Nieuports, Spads, an Albatros and a Sopwith One-and-a-Half Strutter, the whole led by an all-black Fokker D.7. The black Fokker destroyed two DH.9s, then circled overhead while the rest of his squadron engaged the Camels. The British pilots got the best of the encounter, shooting down five enemy aircraft, but all the Camels were damaged and Kinkead was forced to land on the bank of the Volga with a shot-up engine. He was picked up by Captain Bill Daley who shot down his pursuer.

At the end of May, No. 47 Squadron carried out a series of ground-attack operations in the Tsaritsyn area; three enemy fighters were also shot down. Then, on the morning of 14 June, 'B' Flight was ordered to attack a strong force of Red cavalry which was advancing to the relief of Tsaritsyn from the north. Five Camels led by Major Kinkead found the cavalry passing through a ravine and made repeated strafing attacks on the congested mass of men and horses, inflicting severe casualties and effectively halting the relief column.

So far, No. 47 Squadron had escaped without serious casualties, but on 20 June this record was marred by a tragic accident. It happened when a DH.9 of 'A' Flight, one of several which took off to attack enemy troops north of Tsaritsyn, was forced to turn back with engine trouble. As it approached to land at Beketovka, the observer stood up to look over the pilot's shoulder and the bomb toggle near his seat got caught in the pocket of his flying jacket. A bomb dropped away and exploded on the ground a few feet under the aircraft, blowing off its wings. The fuselage plummeted to earth and the remainder of the bomb-load went off. The two officers, both Canadians, were killed instantly.

The Squadron flew intensively during the summer weeks of 1919, the aircrew earning two DSOs and three DFCs in July alone. The first of the Squadron's pilots to be cited for the award of the DFC was Flying Officer S.G. Frogley, who, on 15 July, flying a DH.9, led a highly successful attack on a flotilla of about 40 Bolshevik vessels bringing reinforcements to Kamyshin, an action that played no small part in the capture of the town by the Whites.

Two days later, another pilot, Flying Officer Edward J. Cronin, was also cited for the award of a DFC for particularly daring reconnaissance work on the Kamyshin front.

One of the most dramatic incidents of the Squadron's service in South Russia took place on 30 July, when two DH.9s were sent out to make a reconnaissance of the Chorni-Yar area on the Volga. The leading aircraft was hit by machine-gun fire and its pilot, Flying Officer William Elliot, forced to land about five miles behind enemy lines. Red cavalry patrols tried to capture the aircraft and crews, but Elliot's observer kept them at bay with bursts of machine-gun bullets while Elliot set fire to the DH.9. His predicament, meanwhile, had been spotted by the pilot of the other machine, Flight Lieutenant W.F. Anderson, who landed alongside and picked up the two men despite the fact that his own petrol tank had been hit and holed. Anderson flew the badly overladen aircraft back to base with his gunner, Observer Officer John Mitchell, clinging to a wing strut and plugging the hole in the DH.9's tank with his thumb. He and Anderson were awarded the DSO and Elliot received a bar to his DFC.

Enemy fighters, including the all-black Fokker, continued to oppose the RAF operations, although many of the Red aircraft had now been withdrawn for service on other fronts. In August, the Fokker and a Nieuport attacked an RE.8 observation aircraft over the Volga and were at once engaged by two escorting Camel pilots, Flight Lieutenants Aten and Burns-Thompson. After a dogfight lasting several minutes both enemy aircraft were shot down and a third Nieuport was also destroyed by Aten. It later emerged that the pilot of the black Fokker had destroyed at least a dozen White aircraft; his RAF opponents were convinced that he was a German mercenary.

During the White Russian retreat to Tsaritsyn, the pilots of No. 47 Squadron flew up to four patrols each day; the Camels of 'B' Flight shot down ten enemy aircraft during the first fortnight of August. During this period, Beketovka was strafed by a formation of Red aircraft while the Squadron was absent on operations; six men were killed but one of the attackers, a Pfalz, was shot down by machine-gun fire. On 27 August, three more No. 47 Squadron pilots won the DFC. They were Flying Officer Norman Greenslade, MC, Flying Officer H. E. Simmons, MC, and Flying Officer J.R. Hatchett, all DH.9 pilots who had been detailed to attack a large flotilla of enemy vessels on the Volga at Chorni-Yar. They pressed home their attacks at water level through a heavy barrage of gunfire, inflicting considerable casualties.

In September, No. 47 Squadron moved up to Kotluban, and from this base it continued its attacks on the enemy's lines of communication. It was now the sole RAF squadron operating in South Russia, No. 221 having disbanded on 1 September. Another DFC was earned on 25 September, when Flying Officer Howard Mercer, MC, flying a DH.9, bombed a Bolshevik flotilla at Dubovka. The vessels were heavily armed but Mercer braved the fire to attack on four separate occasions in the course of the day. This exploit followed a highly successful attack by DH.9s on 17 September which destroyed a barge carrying eight enemy seaplanes.

Raymond Collishaw had arrived at Kotluban from base HQ on 14 September. During the next few days he took part in three patrols, flying a Camel, shooting down two enemy aircraft and killing a considerable number of enemy troops in a strafing attack before a bout of typhus brought a halt to his operational flying for a time. A week after his departure, a patrol by Kinkead, Daley, Fulford and Burns-Thompson ran into seven enemy Spads, one of which got on Fulford's tail and wounded him in the shoulder. The enemy aircraft was shot down by Kinkead and all the Camels returned to base.

Early in October, it was decided to withdraw the RAF commitment in South Russia, although No. 47 Squadron was given permission to remain as a purely volunteer unit. The whole of 'A' Flight, about 90 men, elected to stay in Russia, as did most of 'B' and 'C' Flights. The Squadron now lost its identity, becoming known simply as 'A' Detachment, RAF. Its ground-attack work continued, and October brought more awards for its pilots. On the 2nd, 'Tommy' Burns-Thompson received a DFC for a daring attack on a Red gun battery near Katchalinskaya, and on the 12th Kinkead was awarded the DSO for leading 'B' Flight in an attack on an enemy cavalry division near Kotluban. Two days earlier, two more RAF aircrew—Flying Officer A.H. Day and Observer Officer Roger Addison, MC, both in DH.9s—had won the DFC for their part in an attack on a heavily-armed convoy of 40 Bolshevik vessels which had broken through the Volga defences north of Tsaritsyn; on the 15th, another enemy flotilla was dispersed by a flight of DH.9s led by Flying Officer S.G. Frogley, who was awarded the DSO.

Air combats during this period were infrequent, the pilots being occupied mainly with attacking enemy troops and transport, but, on 9 October, Collishaw, now recovered from his illness, destroyed an Albatros D.V. twenty miles north of Tsaritsyn. He reported that it was 'evidently flown by a much practised German pilot.'

By the last week in October, the Red forces were advancing on all fronts. No. 47 Squadron was earmarked to carry on the fight in support of General Mai-Maevsky's White Volunteer Army, engaged in bitter fighting around Kharkov, but both men and machines were swept up in the chaos of retreat and the RAF Detachment was disbanded, the crews making their way to Rostov. They were finally evacuated in March 1920, after destroying their remaining aircraft.

The departure of No. 47 Squadron was not quite the end of the RAF's involvement in the Russian Revolution and its immediate aftermath. In the summer of 1919, a Royal Navy task force entered the Baltic to operate in defence of the neutrality of the Baltic States, which were being subjected to the ravages not only of the Bolsheviks, but also of mercenary German 'Free Corps' units. The primary task of the British naval force was to keep the Russian Baltic Fleet penned up in its base at Kronshtadt, at the eastern end of the Gulf of Finland.

A Royal Air Force contingent commanded by Squadron Leader D.G. Donald and equipped with a miscellany of aircraft that included Sopwith Camels and One-and-a-Half Strutters, Short Seaplanes and Griffins, was transported to the area by the seaplane carriers *Vindictive* and *Argus* and placed ashore in Estonia, where rudimentary advanced bases were established at Biorko, Koivisto and Sidinsari. Air operations began within a week of the aircraft being disembarked in July; operational patrols were flown by the Camels, but no enemy aircraft were sighted.

During their early operations, the RAF aircraft were employed mainly on reconnaissance and anti-submarine work from their principal base at Biorko, but, on 30 July, the naval force commander, Admiral Cowan, decided to mount an attack on Kronshtadt to try to inflict some damage on Russian submarines, the principal threat to his own warships, that were berthed there. The aircraft involved in the attack were five Short seaplanes, three Camels, two Strutters and a Griffin, the strength being dictated by the fact that there were only eleven pilots available, and five of these were seaplane pilots. The two-seater Sopwith Strutters were flown off the *Vindictive*, since the airstrip at Biorko was still not level enough for use by machines carrying a full bomb-load.

The aircraft arrived over Kronshtadt at first light and released ten 112-pound and six 65-pound bombs on the depot ship *Pamyat Azova* and a neighbouring dry dock. The

crews reported five direct hits and two large fires started. All the British aircraft returned safely, although they had to run through heavy gunfire from the ships and batteries defending the anchorage. This was particularly unpleasant for the seaplane crews, as their aircraft would not climb higher than 4,000 feet.

During August 1919, eight daylight and two night bombing raids were carried out in addition to the routine seaplane patrols, and several sorties were made against enemy kite balloons which were being used to observe the movements of the British ships. The Bolsheviks usually managed to haul them down in time, but one—over Krasnaya Gorka—was surprised by a Camel and shot down in flames.

On the night of 17/18 August, Squadron Leader Donald's small force of aircraft made a diversionary attack on Kronshtadt in conjunction with a raid by fast torpedo-boats. The bombing attack was timed to begin before the boats arrived within sound of the anchorage and was to last until they reached the harbour entrance. The position of all Russian warships in the anchorage had been exactly plotted by air reconnaissance. Individual aircraft were detailed to attack the guard ship anchored in the harbour entrance, gun crews and searchlights on the breakwater and to cover the withdrawal of the torpedo-boats after the operation, the pilots having orders to do their utmost to draw enemy fire and searchlights away from the boats. All available aircraft—four Short seaplanes, two Strutters, a Griffin and a Camel—were to take part.

The aircraft approached the harbour from different directions, arriving overhead at 01.30 and releasing their small bomb-loads. The diversion was a complete success, all guns and searchlights in the harbour being fully occupied with the aircraft right up to the moment when the boats reached the entrance. Having expended their bombs— sometimes attacking at mast height—the pilots went on circling over the anchorage to draw the enemy fire. One searchlight was put out of action by machine-gun fire from a Short seaplane, while the Sopwith Camel made several low-level strafing attacks on searchlight and gun crews. One torpedo-boat, caught in the beam of a searchlight, was saved from a tricky situation by the gunner of a Sopwith Strutter, who knocked out the light with a short burst of machine-gun fire. The torpedo attack was a complete success; subsequent air reconnaissance showed that the *Pamyat Azova* and two battleships had been sunk, leaving only a handful of submarines and destroyers to oppose the British naval presence. Squadron Leader Donald's

aircraft continued to operate over Kronshtadt regularly during September 1919.

Seaplane patrols accounted for most of the operational flying during the month, but there were also five day and three night bombing raids, two attacks on enemy ships and a number of balloon-strafing missions. Camels were used for the daylight raids, as they had a greater operational ceiling than the other types, but even at 15,000 feet the anti-aircraft fire was very accurate and one Camel was shot down. Over 70 bombs of various sizes were dropped on Kronshtadt in the course of the month. The seaplane patrols were maintained during October, despite unfavourable weather conditions; three daylight raids were carried out on Kronshtadt and there were three actions with enemy surface craft, including one in which two seaplanes fought it out with an enemy destroyer in a snowstorm. On 14 October, the principal bombing target was shifted from Kronshtadt to two fortresses which were holding up the left flank of a White Russian advance on Petrograd; more than 300 bombs were dropped in five days. One Camel was shot down and its pilot killed; a seaplane was also shot down, but the crew was picked up unhurt by an Estonian destroyer.

Weather conditions at the end of October were very severe, and great difficulty was experienced in starting the water-cooled seaplane engines. These difficulties increased in November, when the temperature was never higher than 25°F during the day and more often about 16°F.

Ice was now forming rapidly on the Gulf of Finland and, on 25 November, the airfield and seaplane base were evacuated, the aircraft being re-embarked on HMS *Vindictive*. A few days later, there was an unexpected warm spell and seaplane patrols were flown from the carrier until 11 December, when Kronshtadt was reported to be completely frozen in. There were no further air operations against the Russians; on 2 February 1920, Estonia signed a peace treaty with the Bolshevik Government and the British presence in the Baltic was withdrawn.

During their five months of active service in the Baltic, the RAF aircraft had flown a total of 837 operational hours. Of the 55 aircraft employed, 33 had been lost: three were shot down, nine force-landed in the sea, seven crashed on take-off and fourteen deteriorated beyond repair owing to the climatic conditions. Four pilots were killed and two wounded.

The Royal Air Force would return to Russia again. In 1941, two squadrons of Hurricanes were shipped to Murmansk. But on that occasion, they came as allies.

3

The Middle East
1918~30

The spring of 1918 saw the Royal Air Force engaged in three separate theatres in the Middle East: Macedonia, Mesopotamia and Palestine. In Mesopotamia, the Royal Flying Corps' effort had been sustained entirely by No. 30 Squadron, operating Martinsyde S.1 and assisted by some RNAS aircraft, until August 1917, when it was joined by No. 63 Squadron with RE.8 army co-operation aircraft. This unit, however, did not become fully operational until November because of technical difficulties with its aircraft and continuing sickness among its personnel. British operations against the Turks in Mesopotamia were now continuing on three fronts—the Tigris, Euphrates and Diyala—and a major offensive was planned to take place on the Euphrates front early in 1918. Shortly before it began, a third RFC squadron, No. 72—equipped with Martinsyde G.102s—also reached Mesopotamia. 1 April, 1918, saw all three squadrons operating a variety of aircraft; in addition to their Martinsydes, BE.2s and RE.8s, they also had a small number of Bristol Scouts, which had been rushed to the front to combat the still very active Fokkers, Albatros and Halberstadts that equipped the German units in the area, and de Havilland DH.4 bombers. While flying one of the latter, Lieutenant-Colonel Tennant, commanding the RAF units in Mesopotamia, was shot down and captured by the Turks; he was subsequently rescued by a British armoured car detachment.

During the first week of April, No. 72 Squadron received a number of SE.5As and used these to good effect on the 7th when the pilots carried out a successful ground-strafing mission in support of a cavalry attack south of Kirkuk. Soon afterwards, No. 72 Squadron's 'B' Flight, which was still equipped with Martinsydes, was detached in support of 'Dunsterforce', which had been formed under the command of Major-General L. C. Dunsterville to co-operate with Russian troops—many of whom, ironically, were Bolsheviks—who were fighting the Turks in the Baku area. The two Martinsydes involved caused considerable havoc

among the Turkish ground forces until both aircraft were destroyed; their pilots survived and fought on alongside the infantry. The most important task of the RAF in Mesopotamia during the summer of 1918, however, was air reconnaissance; constant air patrols made it impossible for the Turkish forces to move unobserved, while extensive photographic coverage enabled the Allies to produce accurate maps of their lines of advance.

Meanwhile, Macedonia—where an Anglo-French expeditionary force had landed at Salonika to form another front against the Turks, assisted by the Serbian army—had been the scene of some fierce air fighting. The two RFC squadrons in this area, Nos 17 and 47, were equipped with a mixture of BE.2cs and BE.12s, and both suffered heavy losses in 1917 at the hands of a German unit designated Flieger Abteilung 30. The latter was commanded by a near-legendary pilot named Rudolf von Eschwege, whom the Bulgarians nicknamed 'Bjelomorsko Orel'—the Eagle of the Aegean

Bristol Fighter of No. 6 Squadron over Iraq in the early 1920s.

Sea. By the time of his death in November 1917, von Eschwege had destroyed twenty Allied aircraft.

To combat his activities, a composite squadron was formed from RNAS Sopwith One-and-a-Half Strutters and aircraft drawn from the two RFC squadrons. These aircraft carried out many attacks on the enemy's aerodromes and lines of communication during 1917, but losses were heavy and the RNAS/RFC combination never gained air superiority; the scales were tilted even further against it when the single-seat fighter element of Flieger Abteilung 30, the Kampfeinsitzer Kommando, and Jasta 25, the latter operating on the Monastir front, exchanged their Fokker E.IIIs for Albatros D.IIIs. It was only when the first few SE.5s arrived in Macedonia towards the end of 1917 that the RFC was able to meet the enemy on equal terms.

By April 1918, the British had at last succeeded in establishing a degree of air superiority, but the RAF in Macedonia was still badly lacking in bombers. Lieutenant-General G.F. Milne, commanding the British element of the expeditionary force, had been asking for bombing aircraft since the previous September, but it was August 1918

Bristol Fighter of No. 6 Squadron at Mosul, 1925.

before he got any. The overall result was that, whereas RAF squadrons on other fronts were assigned to specialist roles such as scouting, reconnaissance or bombing, Milne's small band of pilots had to be jacks-of-all-trades, carrying out a variety of operational tasks in the course of a single day.

Important though the campaigns in Mesopotamia and Macedonia undoubtedly were, the decisive front against the Turks lay in Sinai, between the Suez Canal and Palestine. Here, land operations were supported by the 5th Wing of the RFC, whose strength in the summer of 1917 was twenty BE.2cs and 2es, two Bristol Scouts and nine Martinsydes divided between Nos 14 and 17 Squadrons, with five more BE.2cs on attachment to Colonel T.E. Lawrence's forces in Arabia. Following the appointment of General Sir Edmund Allenby as the British commander on the Sinai front in June 1917, two more squadrons were added to strength: No. 111 with Bristol Fighters and Vickers Bullets (and later SE.5s) and No. 113 with RE.8s.

With the aid of the Bristol Fighters, the RFC managed to establish air superiority in readiness for Allenby's coming offensive in southern Palestine, most of which had been photographed during the preceding weeks by the BEs. Allenby wanted the Turks to believe that the main attack would once again be directed against Gaza whereas, in fact, Beersheba was the objective, and his preparations were completed by 30 October 1917. On that date, a German reconnaissance aircraft was shot down by a Bristol Fighter of No. 111 Squadron and its crew captured;

they had in their possession photographs and sketches showing the British positions and the line of the attack. Had they got back to base, this information would have enabled the Turks to meet the assault; as it was, they were taken completely by surprise and Beersheba fell with 2,000 prisoners. The Turks retreated in confusion, harassed by artillery fire and air attack, and Jerusalem was captured on 9 November.

In 1918, the British forces, depleted by the transfer of some divisions to the Western Front to help meet the threat of a major German offensive following the collapse of the Eastern Front, pushed on to occupy the territory between Jerusalem and the River Jordan, and from there towards Amman in conjunction with the Arab advance in the desert. Throughout these operations, the Palestine Brigade of the RFC and, later, RAF remained at full strength; the Order of Battle now comprised Nos 14, 111, 113, 142, 145 and No. 1 (Australian) Squadrons, which by now were receiving a constant flow of reinforcements from Britain via Egypt.

Allenby bided his time, waiting until the fierce heat of the summer months had dispersed before launching his last and most masterly offensive on 19 September 1918. It was preceded by bombing attacks on several important enemy communications centres, the RAF making good use of a solitary Handley Page 0/400 which had been flown out from England, originally at the request of General Milne in Macedonia. Telephone exchanges were primary targets, and for several hours after the offensive began the Turkish and German commanders were in complete ignorance of what was happening. They were unable to rely on air reconnaissance because their main airfield at Jenin was constantly patrolled by flights of SE.5As, which dropped small bombs and pounced on anything that tried to take off. During the early stages of the British attack, RE.8s of No. 113 Squadron laid a smoke-screen—the first time that aircraft had been used for this purpose. Elsewhere, Bristol Fighters, SE.5As and DH.9s were used to strafe columns of Turkish troops and transport, streaming back through narrow defiles towards Nablus. The commander of the enemy forces, General Liman von Sanders, later paid tribute to the effectiveness of these attacks: 'The British air squadrons,' he wrote, 'relieved every half-hour, flew very low and continuously bombed, and they covered the roads with dead men and horses and shattered transport.'

Every possible line of Turkish retreat had been carefully studied by air reconnaissance before the start of the offensive, and by the early morning of 20 September, General

DH.9As of No. 8 Squadron at Hinaidi, Iraq, *circa* 1925.

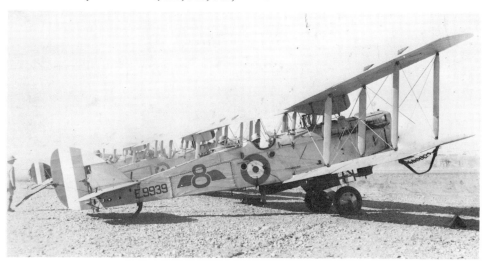

17

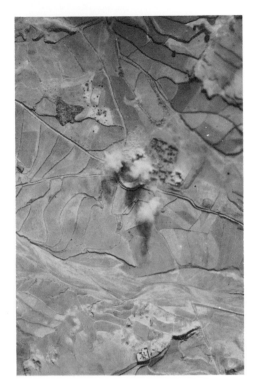

Policing the Empire: a bombing attack on a dissident village on the North-West frontier.

Allenby knew that the Turkish Eighth Army on the right flank, near the sea, was pulling back in a state of confusion. He therefore threw the weight of his assault against it and the retreat had become a rout by the evening. This Turkish disaster made the position of the Turkish Seventh Army completely un-tenable, all its lines of retreat except one having been cut by British armoured cars and cavalry.

Soon, the Seventh Army had joined the remnants of the Eighth in a panic-stricken rout, columns of men and material jamming the road that ran south of Nablus to cross the Jordan at Jisr ed Damiye. For a considerable distance, this road ran through a deep defile, the Wadi el Far'a, and shortly after dawn on 21 September, two patrolling Bristol Fighters reported that the Wadi was choked by a dense mass of Turkish troops and transport.

It was now that the RAF squadrons unleashed their full fury on the luckless Turks. For an hour, from 11.00 until noon, the Bristol Fighters of No. 1 (Australian) Squadron, the DH.9s of No. 144 and the SE.5As of Nos 111 and 145 roved back and forth above the wadi, carrying out 88 bombing and 84 machine-gun attacks in which they dropped nine and a quarter tons of bombs and expended 56,000 rounds of ammunition. The slaughter was frightful. When the last aircraft droned away, the wadi was clogged with corpses, lying in heaps amid dead and dying horses and shattered transport. Some days later, when British forces inspected the carnage, they counted 100 guns, 55 lorries, four staff cars, 912 wagons and twenty water carts; the dead were numbered in thousands and no-one ever bothered to establish an exact total. The utter destruction of the Turkish armies in Sinai had been accomplished in 60 minutes for the loss of two aircraft, destroyed by ground fire.

East of the Jordan, the Turkish Fourth Army was under severe pressure from irregular Arab forces under Prince Faisal, aided by Colonel Lawrence and supported now—in addition to a pair of RE.8s of 'X' Flight, No. 14 Squadron—by two Bristol Fighters and a DH.9. A German air squadron was operating in the area and the Arabs had suffered several bombing and strafing attacks, but the tables were soon turned when the Bristol Fighters shot down two German two-seaters and a Pfalz in a single air engagement. The air support had a profound effect on the Arabs' morale and they were soon co-operating fully with British forces that were moving against the Fourth Army, which was now being attacked from the air by the squadrons which had blocked the Wadi el Far'a.

On 28 September, the Turkish Fourth Army surrendered and the forces of Allenby and Faisal marched together on Damascus on 1 October. At the end of October, Turkey sought an armistice, bringing the long struggle in the Middle East to an end. Nowhere else, in four years of war, had sustained air attack played such a vital part in achieving final victory.

The Royal Air Force ended the 1914–18 War a formidable fighting machine, with 95 squadrons on the Continent, 55 operational and 199 training squadrons in the United Kingdom and 34 more in the Middle East

The Handley Page Hinaidi was used as a VIP transport between Iraq and India.

and India. By the beginning of April 1919, however, the number of squadrons on the Continent had dwindled to 44 and at the end of October there was only one. The wholesale decimation of the Royal Air Force began in earnest in January 1920, by which time the total personnel strength of the Service stood at 29,730 officers and men; a little over a year earlier, the figure had been 304,000. In a matter of months, the Aircraft Disposal Company Ltd, formed under government authority, had disposed of material amounting to £5,700,000; this included 10,000 aircraft, 30,000 engines and thousands of tons of ancillary equipment. By March 1920, the Order of Battle of the Royal Air Force had been reduced to eight squadrons in India, seven in the Middle East and one at home.

The battle waged by the Air Staff—and by one man in particular—to save the Service from complete extinction is dealt with in a later chapter. In the context of Middle East operations, the turning point came on 12 March 1921, when a conference was held in Cairo under the presidency of Winston Churchill, who was then Secretary of State for the Colonies, with the Chief of Air Staff, Air Chief Marshal Sir Hugh Trenchard, at his right hand. The conference was attended by the civil and military administrators of the British protectorates and mandates throughout the Middle East, and to them Churchill and Trenchard proposed a novel scheme: that the policing of troubled areas, particularly in Mesopotamia and the North-West Frontier of India, be carried out by designated squadrons of the Royal Air Force, reducing ground forces to the necessary minimum.

The scheme was adopted without question and it was decided to implement it initially in Mesopotamia (re-named Iraq in September 1921) and Jordan. The RAF assumed responsibility for internal and external security in these two countries in 1922. At that time, there was only one fighter squadron in the whole of the RAF, No. 1, and this was based in Iraq together with three army co-operation units, but with the RAF's new peace-keeping role the garrison in Iraq was quickly raised to eight squadrons by forming three new ones and transferring one from Egypt. Five of these were stationed at Hinaidi; they were No. 1 (Snipes), No. 6 (Bristol Fighters), No. 30 (DH.9As), No. 45 (Vickers Vernons), and No. 70 (Vickers Vimys, exchanged for Vernons in November 1922). No. 8 Squadron with DH.9As was at Basra, No. 55 with DH.9As at Mosul and No. 84 with DH.9As at Shaibah.

The air policing method was simple enough in principle. If a local political officer

Wapitis of the Risalpur Wing, *circa* 1930. The photograph well illustrates the rugged terrain over which the North-West Frontier squadrons had to operate.

or the police reported a disorder that was beyond their control, the offenders would be summoned to appear for trial in a court of law. If they refused, or continued their criminal activities, a warning would be dropped telling them that unless they submitted, their village would be bombed and subsequently blockaded by air until the required submission was forthcoming. An aircraft would duly appear over the now-deserted village on the stated date and bomb it, and in the days that followed further light attacks would be made, possibly with delayed-action bombs scattered around the area of the village. Almost without fail, this method produced a submission within a short time; the villagers, already living at poverty level, could not afford to have their routine interrupted for long. Once the offenders had surrendered, a small force of police or troops, supported by medical personnel, would be flown in to restore order, tend to the sick and wounded and help restore the bombed village to habitable standard. After the system had been in force for some time, a mere threat of action was usually all that was needed to persuade offenders to turn themselves in.

Sometimes, however, the RAF squadrons in Iraq were called upon to deal with more

An example of RAF humour (the kind that could be sent home, anyway) of the 1920s.

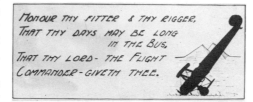

serious disturbances. At the end of 1922, the Turks—now beginning to recover from their earlier defeats and humiliation under the energetic leadership of Mustapha Kemal—began to create trouble among the tribes in Kuristan and the Mosul Vilayet, and in September 1922, they established an outpost on Iraqi territory 40 miles from Kirkuk. This was attacked by RAF aircraft and the Turks expelled. The British build-up to the operation was well planned and executed, with a reinforcing detachment of DH.9As from No. 30 Squadron being sent up to Kirkuk the previous June, when British Intelligence began to get an inkling of what was happening, and during the following weeks supplies and spares, including W/T equipment, were delivered by air. Nevertheless, the local Kurdish leader, Kerim Fattah Beg—known as 'KFB' to the RAF—refused to be deterred by the show of force, and in August his insurgents were threatening the town of Sulaimaniya. Since a relief column of British troops and levies was unable to break through, the decision was taken to evacuate British subjects and pro-British officials from the town by air, carried out successfully over a period of six hours by 24 DH.9s, two Vickers Vernons and three Bristol Fighters of No. 6 Squadron, the latter being already at Sulaimaniya.

To help restore order in Iraq's northern province, the British authorities removed a remarkable and colourful leader named Sheikh Mahmoud from prison in India, where he had been interned since May 1919. At that time, he had held the post of Gover-

Hawker Harts of No. 11 Squadron. The Squadron re-equipped with Harts in 1932 and used them until 1939, when they were replaced by Blenheim Mk Is.

nor of Southern Kurdistan, a British Government appointment, but he had been deposed after leading an unsuccessful uprising. He was now re-instated on a promise of good behaviour, but Mahmoud, who had a vision of a united and independent Kurdistan, was soon plotting with his Turkish neighbours and by early 1923, the British received intelligence that a general uprising was planned. It was to start with an attack on Kirkuk, which was garrisoned by a small contingent of Assyrian levies supported by a few RAF armoured cars and the Bristol Fighters of No. 6 Squadron.

As a first step, the RAF airlifted reinforcements into the Kirkuk area. This was carried out by ten Vickers Vernons of Nos 45 and 70 Squadrons. In 48 hours, beginning on 21 February 1923, they made 28 round trips, carrying two British officers, 320 men of the 14th Sikhs and 30,000 rounds of ammunition. Next, Sheikh Mahmoud's headquarters at Sulaimaniya were bombed, forcing him to retreat into the mountains and carry

on a guerrilla campaign, and in April, 6,000 British and Indian troops, supported by local levies and aircraft, marched up from Mosul and drove out Turkish infiltrators who had been supporting Mahmoud. In May, the infantry pushed on to occupy Rowanduz, a town on the vital strategic road linking Turkey and Persia. Throughout the operation the ground forces depended almost entirely on air supply. The variety of goods delivered by the RAF is reflected in an extract from the list: 1,000 boots, 3,000 pairs of socks, 100 pounds of boot repair materials, 4,000 shirts, 500 pairs of shorts, 500 puttees, 1,400 bars of soap, 270 tins of dubbin, 500 fathoms of rope (needed for bridging a river), 1,000 horseshoes, 7,000 horseshoe nails and 1,200 nosebags—and all this in addition to regular supplies of food and ammunition. The brunt of the airlift was borne by the Vickers Vernons, with their greater load-carrying capacity.

Mahmoud gave up his plans for a general uprising, at least for the time being, and was once more bound over to keep the peace. It was not long before the promise was broken. In May 1924, a riot in Kirkuk between Assyrian levies and Moslems had to to be put

down by British troops, and Mahmoud chose to use the incident as a pretext for declaring a '*Jihad*', or Holy War, against Britain and the Assyrians. Sulaimaniya was again bombed and what was left of it was occupied by British forces in July, and once again the Sheikh sought refuge in the hills. In 1925, he was soundly defeated, but in the summer of 1926 his supporters tried to lauch an attack in the Sulaimaniya area. The Vernons of No. 45 Squadron hurriedly flew up servicing personnel and spares for No. 1 Squadron, which was still equipped with Sopwith Snipes, and these aircraft succeeded in breaking up the rebel assembly with some accurate ground-attack work. Sheikh Mahmoud eventually made his final submission to the British in 1927, but in 1930—by which time Iraq had become an independent state—he once again tried to establish himself as ruler of an independent Kurdistan. The Iraqi army moved against him and defeated him, and Mahmoud at last went into exile for good.

Policing work by the RAF squadrons in Iraq continued, and in January 1928 another major emergency arose when areas of southern Iraq and Kuwait were threatened by the Akhwan, a fanatical Islamic group. An air and ground operation was mounted against them, the units involved being known as Akforce; its primary task was to deny the use of waterholes to the raiders and then to throw the raiders back across the Persian border. Akforce HQ was established at Ur, and the DH.9As of Nos. 55 and 84 Squadrons were detached to desert airstrips at Busaiya and Sulman to operate in conjunction with armoured car sections. Air supply was undertaken by No. 70 Squadron, which had now begun to replace its Vernons with Vickers Victorias. Fuel for the DH.9As was the main commodity transported by No. 70 Squadron, each Victoria carrying 56 four-gallon drums on a typical sortie. By the time the operation ended with the withdrawal of the raiders on 29 May, the Victorias had

Spit, Polish—and Sand. Inspection of squadrons and personnel at Abu Sueir, Egypt, by the AOC, Air Vice-Marshal Swanne, on 30 April 1925.

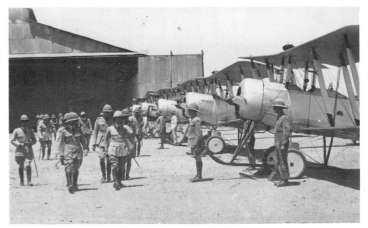

airlifted 1,192 passengers and 517 tons of freight, the crews flying in appalling conditions of extreme heat often accompanied by dust storms.

The structure of the RAF in Iraq, meanwhile, had undergone some changes. No. 1 Squadron had disbanded on 1 November 1926, to re-form at Tangmere in February 1927 with Armstrong Whitworth Siskins as part of the fighter defence of the United Kingdom. No. 8, re-equipped with Fairey IIIFs, had moved to Aden in February 1927; No. 30 was still at Hinaidi, but No. 45 had gone to Heliopolis in Egypt in April 1927. No. 55 Squadron still shared Hinaidi with No. 30, and No. 84 Squadron was at Shaibah, where it was to remain throughout the inter-war years. No. 14 Squadron, equipped with DH.9As until December 1929, when it exchanged them for Fairey IIIFs, was at Amman in Jordan, where it carried out several police actions against tribal raiders.

In 1932, the RAF squadrons in Iraq were active in support of the Iraqi Army, which was under heavy pressure from rebel Barzan tribesmen under Sheikh Ahmed. In April, No. 70 Squadron's Victorias undertook many supply-dropping operations, and in June these aircraft—accompanied by the Victorias of No. 216 Squadron, on detachment from Egypt—airlifted 562 men of the 1st Northamptonshire Regiment from Ismailia to Hinaidi in an operation to restore order in northern Iraq, where there was trouble among the Assyrian minority. Twenty-five Victorias were involved, and the operation was completed in 36 sorties. In the event, the troops were not called upon to go into action; the Assyrian levies surrendered their arms peaceably and the British contingent was flown back to Egypt. Another

Vickers Vernon J7143 of No. 70 Squadron, with air ambulance insignia, pictured at Abu Sueir in 1924.

big airlift, this time involving Assyrian refugees, was carried out by the Victorias in September 1933; in all, 790 people, mostly women and children, were flown from the north, where they had suffered fearful massacres at the hands of Moslem factions and the Iraqi Army, to Hinaidi.

By 1934, the bomber-reconnaissance squadrons in Iraq were equipped with Westland Wapiti aircraft, and on 15 January four of these aircraft from 84 Squadron set out on a 10,630-mile flight to Singapore and back, supported by two No. 70 Squadron Victorias carrying personnel and spares. The Wapitis returned to their base at Mosul on 17 February. Long-range exercises of this kind were also a regular feature in the life of a relative newcomer to Iraq, No. 203 Squadron, which had been based at Basra since March 1929 and was equipped with Short Rangoon flying boats. In September and

How they did things in the desert: salvaging the engine of a wrecked Bristol Fighter in Egypt.

Crashed Avro 504s at Abu Sueir, 1925.

Crashed DH.9As in Egypt in 1924–25. Frequently, aircrews escaped unhurt, or with only minor injuries, from fearsome crashes.

October 1934, three of the Squadron's Rangoons cruised from Basra to Melbourne to represent the RAF at the centenary celebrations of the State of Victoria; they returned to Basra after a round trip of 19,000 miles, having experienced no technical trouble of any kind.

In 1935 the 'resident' RAF squadrons in Iraq all received new aircraft. No. 30 re-equipped with the Hawker Hardy general-purpose biplane; Nos 55 and 84 received Vickers Vincents; and No. 70 exchanged its ageing Victorias for Vickers Valentias. No. 203 also received Short Singapore IIIs, which it was to retain until 1940. In January-February 1937, Nos 84 and 203 Squadrons flew to Singapore to participate in inter-Service exercises, supported once again by the faithful 70 Squadron. A similar exercise took place in January 1938, the month in which No. 30 Squadron began to re-equip with Bristol Blenheim Mk 1s. By the spring of 1939, Nos 55 and 84 Squadrons had also received Blenheims and all the RAF land-based units in Iraq except No. 84, which was still at Shaibah, were now based at Habbaniyah, a big new airfield 60 miles south-west of Baghdad. They were still there in September 1939, when, for the second time in a quarter of a century, the British Empire and its Commonwealth went to war.

Elsewhere within the British sphere of influence during the inter-war years, the effectiveness of the aircraft as a peace-keeping instrument was well demonstrated in 1919 in Somaliland, where for seventeen years the Dervish leader, Mohammed bin

Abdullah Hassan—better known as the 'Mad Mullah'—had been fomenting unrest. A force of twelve DH. 9s under the command of Group Captain Robert Gordon and known as 'Z Force' was shipped out to Berbera in HMS *Ark Royal*. In three weeks of sustained operations alongside the Camel Corps and the King's African Rifles, they succeeded in overthrowing the Mullah completely.

In India, there were two resident RAF Squadrons—Nos 31 and 114—at the time of the 1918 Armistice. Both were re-equipped with Bristol Fighters in 1919, and in June that year the RAF's strength in India was boosted by the arrival of three more squadrons, Nos 20 and 48 with Bristol Fighters and No. 99 with DH.9As. Another squadron, No. 97 arrived in August with twelve DH.10s. All six squadrons were incorporated in an India Group, with its HQ at Raisina (later New Delhi)

Before this structure was established, however, the RAF in India had become involved in operations along the North-West Frontier. Bombing and reconnaissance operations against rebel tribesmen had been a frequent undertaking ever since No. 31 Squadron had first come to India at the end of 1915, but now, in May 1919, a serious threat to India's security erupted when the ruler of Afghanistan, Amir Amanullah—beset by warring factions within his own country—tried to unite the Afghans by declaring war on India. The threat was removed by a single aircraft, a four-engined Handley Page V/1500 bomber which had flown out to India from England earlier that year carrying Major-General Geoffrey Salmond, the AOC RAF Middle East (see chapter four). On 24 May 1919, the V/1500,

piloted by Lieutenant R. Halley, flew to Kabul and dropped several bombs on the Amir's palace. As an official dispatch put it rather succinctly a few weeks later: 'There is little doubt that this raid was an important factor in producing a desire for peace at the headquarters of the Afghan Government.'

In the autumn of 1919, all RAF units in India were engaged in a fierce struggle against one of the most warlike of the tribes on the Frontier, the Mahsuds, and while these operations were in progress the squadrons underwent some organizational changes. On 1 April 1920, No. 48 was re-numbered No. 5 Squadron, while Nos 97 and 99 became 60 and 27 Squadrons respectively. Between them, the handful of squadrons in India had the formidable task of policing some 27,000 square miles of some of the world's most barren and inhospitable terrain, peopled by several millions of the world's hardiest, cruellest and most experienced guerrilla fighters. For this purpose, the RAF had, in the summer of 1922, 70 aircraft—on paper. The reality was different. Of that total, only seven were airworthy; the remainder were grounded either through a critical shortage of spares or because they were so worn out that no power on earth would induce them to fly. The problem was so serious that Air Vice-Marshal Sir John Salmond was sent out to India to investigate matters and he subsequently reported that the RAF in India at that time (August 1922) was non-effective as a fighting force. Steps were taken to set matters right but it was to be *six years* before they were fully implemented and the India squadrons provided with better equipment.

Meanwhile, they carried on as best they could with whatever material was available and it says much for the skill and dedication of the RAF ground crews, working often in conditions of appalling heat, that the RAF was never unable to meet the Army's request for tactical support in its operations along the Frontier. Sometimes, operations were undertaken solely by the RAF units, and as a result the authorities in India came to rely more on air action that was independent of costly, and often unwieldy, movements on the ground.

There was a good example of this policy in March 1925, when sixteen DH. 9As of Nos 27 and 60 Squadrons were flown up to the outpost airstrip at Miramshah, 120 miles from Kohat, under the command of Wing Commander R.C.M. Pink, OC No. 2 (Indian) Wing, for operations against Mahsud tribesmen in South Waziristan. Operations HQ were at Tank and the Bristol F.2Bs of No. 5 Squadron were flown there from

Kohat to support the DH.9s. For seven weeks, beginning on 9 March, the DH.9As carried out sustained bombing operations against the Mahsud strongholds in the mountains, each bombing raid usually being followed by strafing attacks. On 1 May, the rebel leaders sought an honourable peace and the short air campaign that became known as 'Pink's War' came to a close. The cost to the RAF had been one DH.9A of No. 27 Squadron, which was shot down by ground fire on 21 March; the crew, Flying Officers N.C. Hayter-James and E.J. Dashwood, received fatal burns and died shortly afterwards, despite attempts by tribesmen to save them.

In October 1928, the long awaited increase in the RAF's strength in India at last became reality with the arrival of two more squadrons, Nos 11 and 39, the former equipped with Westland Wapitis and the latter with DH.9As. No. 39 did not retain its 'Ninaks' for long; by February 1929, it too had re-equipped with Wapitis. The two squadrons had barely had time to settle in when a new crisis developed in November.

It began when a rebellion broke out against the ruler of Afghanistan on 14 November. Thousands of tribesmen went on the rampage throughout the country's southern provinces and the British Legation, situated two and a half miles outside Kabul, was trapped between Loyalist and rebel forces. On 17 December, the British Minister, Sir Francis Humphreys, sent a signal asking for the urgent evacuation of all women and children from the Legation and, on the following day, a Vickers Victoria of No. 70 Squadron was flown from Hinaidi, arriving at Quetta via Karachi. While this aircraft carried out altitude tests, a DH.9A of No. 27 Squadron was despatched to drop a message and a Popham Panel, a device used for visual Morse signalling, in the Legation grounds, but its engine was hit by ground fire and it had to make a forced landing before its mission could be completed. A second aircraft was successful, and with the aid of the Popham Panel the Legation staff signalled to further DH.9A reconnaissance aircraft that no landings should be attempted. On 22 December, however, the Legation's radio facilities—which had been channelled through a station in Kabul and cut off when the rebels captured it—were restored, and Humphreys signalled that he wished the evacuation to start the next day.

On 23 December, the Victoria evacuated 21 women and children from Kabul's Sherpur aerodrome, while three DH.9As brought out 390 pounds of luggage. On Christmas Eve, the Victoria flew out another seventeen people, while eleven DH.9As of Nos 27 and 60 Squadrons each brought out one passenger. On 27 December, a second Victoria and a Handley Page Hinaidi—Air Vice-Marshal Sir Geoffrey Salmond's VIP aircraft—also joined the airlift, and by 1 January 1929 the

number of people evacuated, including all the women and children from the various European legations in Kabul, had risen to 134. Six more No. 70 Squadron Victorias arrived from Iraq during January and, with the help of these reinforcements, the RAF successfully evacuated a total of 586 civilians and 41 tons of baggage by the time the operation ended on 25 February. In all, the RAF aircraft had flown 57,438 miles—about half of which were logged by the Victorias—through very severe winter weather and at altitudes of up to 10,000 feet in mountainous terrain to achieve their objective.

Punitive air operations against dissident tribesmen continued regularly throughout the 1930s, during which time the RAF strength in India remained at eight squadrons. In October 1930, the RAF pre-empted a big incursion by 6,000 Afridi tribesmen by mounting sustained bombing attacks on their villages over a ten-day period; this operation became known as the 'Peshawar Incident'. There was a six-week period of intensive bombing in August and September 1935, when the squadrons flew virtually non-stop to quell a rebellion among the Mohmad tribes. Then, in the autumn of 1936, long unrest between the Hindu and Moslem peoples of the North-West Frontier's Tochi Valley area flared into open rebellion when

Hawker Hart K3958 of No. 142 Squadron flying over units of the Royal Navy in Alexandria harbour in 1936.

one Mirza Ali Khan, self-styled Faqir of Ipi, declared himself to be 'Champion of Islam' and called for a *Jihad* against the British. Army operations were assisted initially by Nos 5 and 27 Squadrons, both of which were equipped with Wapiti Mk IIAS, and by the end of the year all the RAF squadrons in India were committed. Air operations reached a peak in April 1937, the squadrons taking it in turn to bear the brunt of the air offensive, and continued on and off for a year. The RAF's tactics were simple enough; they involved bombing any village suspected of sympathizing with the Faqir, and culminated in a series of heavy attacks on selected targets in May 1938. By this time, the local tribes had had enough of the Holy War and they expelled the 'Champion of Islam', who, although he never again stirred up a major rebellion, continued to make trouble on the North-West Frontier until his death in 1960.

The fight against the Faqir was the last major operation undertaken by the RAF squadrons in India during what might be termed the 'biplane era'. In July 1938 No. 11 Squadron began to re-equip with Blenheim Mk I bombers, but re-equipment of its sister units was painfully slow; Nos 39 and 60 Squadrons did not receive Blenheims until a year later and the other units in India were still using biplanes when the Japanese War engulfed the east.

4

The 'Exclusive Flying Club'

On 28 July, 1918, a Handley Page 0/400 bomber took off from Manston in Kent and set course out over the Channel. Captained by Major A.S.C. MacLaren, the aircraft, serial number C9681, reached Cairo on 7 August after a laborious journey across Europe and the Mediterranean. To MacLaren fell the honour of completing the first-ever flight from England to Egypt, and of laying the basis for the record-breaking long-range flights between various points of the British Empire for which the Royal Air Force was to become justly famous in the years between the wars.

With Captain Ross Smith at the controls, C9681 flew on from Cairo to Baghdad on 29 November and continued its journey from Iraq to India on 4 December, eventually arriving at Calcutta. To all but the most sceptical, the 0/400's flight had proved that it was possible to set up an air route between Britain and the Far East, and on 13 December 1918, Major MacLaren set out from Martlesham Heath to make a through flight to India. On this occasion, the aircraft was a Handley Page V/1500, a new and operationally untried type originally conceived for the bombing of Berlin from bases in England. This particular example, J1936, was named *Old Carthusian* in honour of Charterhouse, where both MacLaren and his second pilot, Captain Robert Halley, had been educated. The aircraft also carried two fitters, Flight Sergeant A.E. Smith and Sergeant W. Crockett, a rigger, Sergeant W. Brown, and a VIP passenger, Brigadier General Norman McEwen, who was on his way to take command of the Royal Air Force in India.

The V/1500's flight turned out to be an adventurous one. The first leg, to Catania in Sicily, was dogged by bad weather, and MacLaren was forced to make two precautionary landings before reaching his destination. Then, on the other side of the Mediterranean, two engines failed and the aircraft had to land in the desert 50 miles west of Mersa Matruh. Repairs were made by an RAF ground party from Aboukir, and the flight resumed on 31 December, the V/1500 arriving at Baghdad on 9 January 1919 after

overcoming several obstacles, including a storm. The next serious trouble occurred on the leg from Bandar Abbas to Karachi, when the port rear engine seized. MacLaren made an emergency landing on a strip of beach near a fishing village. With little possibility of spares arriving before the intense heat warped the aircraft's structure, MacLaren and Halley decided to risk a take-off on three engines after unloading everyone else except Sergeant Brown, who was needed to sit in the tail as ballast. The take-off was accomplished successfully and, despite continual engine trouble and a fractured oil pipe, *Old Carthusian* scraped in over high ground to land

in darkness at Karachi airstrip. She had covered 5,560 miles in a flying time of 72 hours 41 minutes at an average speed of 77 mph. All her crew members were decorated, MacLaren receiving the OBE.

The flight of the V/1500, although dramatic, had scarcely served to underline the

In the 1920s, individual RAF crews made numerous attempts to set up new records. In March 1924, Sqn Ldr A.S.C. MacLaren, Fg Off W.N. Plenderleith and Sgt R. Andrews set out to fly round the world in a Vickers Vulture amphibian. Their aircraft, G-EBHO, is seen here at Abu Sueir. The attempt ended in failure when the aircraft was damaged in heavy seas near Petropavlovsk, Kamchatka, after covering 13,000 miles.

The Fairey IIIF, widely used by the RAF in the 1920s, pioneered long-distance routes and created several records in Africa and the Middle East.

reliability of the long-range aircraft available to the RAF. In fact, the V/1500, experimental as it was, had been the wrong machine for the job; the Handley Page 0/400 was a far better proposition, and in May 1919 the Air Ministry proposed that two squadrons of these well-tried machines be used to carry on a regular weekly mail service between Cairo and India. The opening of an Egypt-India route, the Air Ministry pointed out, would make air reinforcement much easier in times of unrest, of which there was plenty along India's turbulent North-West Frontier. New airfield facilities would have to be developed at a cost of some £100,000, which the Air Ministry claimed would be a small price to pay for effective communications with the outposts of the Empire.

The Treasury thought otherwise. The war was over and slashing economy cuts were in the air. Besides, the Treasury stated with some justification, out of 51 0/400s of Nos 58, 214 and 216 Squadrons, deployed from France to Egypt between April and October 1919, no fewer than fifteen were destroyed accidentally en route, with the loss of eight crew members. It was not a very sound safety record with which to launch the Air Ministry's desired mail service.

In fact, an experimental mail service was started in India on 24 January 1920, with the DH.10s of No. 97 Squadron operating between Karachi and Bombay, but it was abandoned after only a few weeks on the grounds that it could not be justified economically. So was another air mail service between Cairo and Baghdad, started in February 1920 on the initiative of Lieutenant-Colonel A.T.

Wilson, the Civil Commissioner in Mesopotamia. Air mail was eventually flown between Cairo and Baghdad in the summer of 1921, but this was a spin-off from the need to provide rapid air reinforcement to Mesopotamia (Iraq). The route was a hazardous one; it was 850 miles long and two-thirds of it passed over an arid desert plateau that reached up to 2,000 feet above sea level. As a preliminary to air operations, the whole route was marked out by ground parties, who mapped emergency landing strips at intervals of twenty miles. The task took two months, the ground parties often working under appalling conditions and relying entirely on air supply for their survival. The route was officially opened on 30 June 1921, when two DH.9As of No. 47 Squadron flew from Baghdad to Heliopolis, and on 9 July another No. 47 Squadron DH.9A flew in the opposite direction, carrying Air Vice Marshal Sir Geoffrey Salmond as passenger. On 28 July, a batch of mail left Baghdad in a DH.9A, was transferred to an 0/400 at Heliopolis and reached London on 9 August. A further consignment of mail had already left London on 4 August, and this arrived in Baghdad on the 17th.

Three squadrons, Nos 30, 47 and 216, were tasked with flying the mail. Nos 30 and 47 were both equipped with DH.9As and based at Helwan, Egypt; No. 216 operated 0/400s until October 1921, when it re-equipped with DH.10s. The Kantara-based squadron had the job of flying the fast long-distance leg of the route, for which the DH.10 was much more suitable than the 0/400; cruising at 110 mph, it could make the Cairo-Baghdad run in about ten hours, carrying two passengers. However, the aircraft had some unpleasant handling character-

istics, including a tendency to swing on take-off, and its 400 hp Liberty engines suffered continual problems through faults in the fuel system; both these shortcomings combined to create a number of accidents. The DH.9A was much more reliable, but far slower; with several fuel drums lashed to its bomb racks it trundled along at 90mph, and then had to make two refuelling stops en route.

Nevertheless, during their first year of operations, the three squadrons carried four and a quarter tons of mail and 140 passengers between Cairo and Baghdad, and there were no longer any doubts about the value of the service they offered. The volume of mail carried increased sharply after January 1922, when No. 216 Squadron exchanged its trouble-plagued DH.10s for Vickers Vimy aircraft; shortly afterwards, Nos 30 and 47 Squadrons were withdrawn from the mail service and their places taken by Nos 45 and 70 Squadrons, which were equipped with Vickers Vernons. The Vernon, a military version of the Vimy Commercial, was the first true RAF transport aircraft and could carry up to eleven passengers. It was slow—70 mph—and unaerpowered, and its wooden airframe suffered severe warping problems in the desert climate, but apart from that it proved well suited to its task, and its effectiveness improved at a later date when it was re-engined with 450 hp Napier Lions.

Not unnaturally, the crews who flew the Baghdad Mail were drawn from the most experienced in the Royal Air Force, and some later rose to high command. They included Squadron Leader Arthur T. Harris, who was to become C-in-C of Bomber Command in the 1939–45 War, Flight Lieutenants Ralph Cochrane, Robert Saundby and Basil Embry, all of whom were to reach Air Officer rank. They were part of what was probably then the most closely-knit and elite team in the RAF.

Nos 70 and 216 Squadrons re-equipped with Vickers Victoria aircraft in 1926, which gave a new boost to the mail route. Powered by two 450 hp Napier Lion engines, the Victoria carried up to twenty passengers. No. 70 Squadron, now based at Hinaidi, was the first to re-equip and, when the Cairo-Baghdad mail service was taken over by Imperial Airways at the end of 1926, this unit continued to be based in Iraq as a bomber-transport squadron until the outbreak of World War Two. In the same role, No. 216 Squadron remained at Heliopolis until 1941, equipped successively with Vickers Vernons and Valentias and then Bristol Bombay transports. The third squadron, No. 45, was employed on police duties in Egypt and Palestine from 1927, its DH.9As being re-

placed by Fairey IIIFs in 1929 and the latter by Hawker Harts in 1935.

From the mid–1920s, RAF operations in Africa were characterized by a series of record-breaking long-distance flights, which enabled the aircrew involved to acquire a vast amount of navigational experience over difficult terrain. The first such flight began on 25 October 1925, when three DH.9As led by Squadron Leader A. Coningham set out from Cairo for Kano, Nigeria on the start of the round trip that lasted until 17 November. There was an even more spectacular enterprise beginning on 1 March 1926, when four Fairey IIID aircraft left Cairo for Cape Town in a formation led by Wing Commander C.W.H. Pulford. They reached Cape Town without incident, returned to Cairo and subsequently flew on to Plymouth, having covered a total distance of 13,900 miles in a flying time of 180 hours 30 minutes. None of the aircraft involved had experienced any technical difficulties.

A further flight to South Africa was carried out in the early spring of 1927. It began on 30 March, when four Fairey IIIFs led by Wing Commander C.R. Samson flew from Heliopolis to Nairobi, where they were joined by four DH.9s of the South African Air Force under the command of Major Meintjes. The eight aircraft flew on to Pretoria, where the DH.9s stayed; the Fairey IIIFs went on to Cape Town before returning to Cairo. This kind of joint long-range exercise was to become a regular feature of RAF and SAAF operations during the inter-war years.

Although individual RAF crews and aircraft took part in many of the long-distance record attempts that were a feature of aviation development in the 1920s and 1930s, most truly significant long-range operations were mounted to develop navigational techniques or to test new equipment under arduous conditions. On 17 October 1927, for example, four Supermarine Southampton flying boats of the RAF's Far East Flight (later to become No. 205 Squadron) left Felixstowe under the command of Group Captain Cave-Brown-Cave on the first leg of a long-range flight that was intended primarily to test the strength of the Southampton's hull under prolonged operational conditions. On 15 December, the flying boats reached Bombay in sixteen stages and, on 27 December, they set off for Singapore, arriving on 28 February 1928 after thirteen stops en route. Between 21 May and 15 September 1928, the four Southamptons, still in formation, made the Singapore-Sydney round trip in 29 stages, and finally, from 1 November to 10 December, they made a tour of various points in the Far East including Manilla, Hong Kong, Tourane and Bangkok before returning to their base at Singapore. During the whole of the journey, since leaving England, they had covered 27,000 miles.

While this epic flight was in progress, another took place which, in its own way, was every bit as significant and certainly indicative that long-range operations by the RAF were now being treated as fairly routine. On 29 September 1928, a Blackburn Iris flying boat (serial N158) left Lee-on-Solent for Africa, captained by Wing Commander C.L. Scott and carrying the Secretary of State for Air, Sir Philip Sassoon, on a tour of inspection. This same aircraft, a year earlier, had taken part in a 'Baltic Tour' with three other flying boats.

The Iris reached Aboukir on 2 October after calling at Marseilles, Naples and Athens. From Aboukir, Sassoon continued his tour of RAF bases in Egypt in a Fairey IIIF, accompanied by Air Commodore (later Air Chief Marshal Sir) Arthur Longmore, and between 5 and 8 October he visited Khartoum together with Air Vice Marshal Webb Bowen. Continuing his busy schedule, he flew to Amman and Baghdad in a Westland Wapiti and then went on to Basra, where the Blackburn Iris was waiting for him. The Iris took him on to Karachi, and from there he flew to Jodhpur in a Handley Page Hinaidi, arriving on 16 October. A DH.9A took him on to Ambala and Lahore, and a Bristol Fighter ferried him up to Peshawar. Then it was on to Quetta, where the Hinaidi was waiting to take him back to Baghdad and subsequently to Aboukir, where he once again boarded the Iris for the final stage of the flight to Calshot via Benghazi, Malta,

Naples, Marseilles and Ushant. Sir Philip arrived home on 13 November after an absence of six weeks; only two decades earlier, a similar journey would have taken a year or more.

From 1929, the RAF was much preoccupied with the development of non-stop long-range flying, and to this end the Fairey Aviation Company designed a special Long-Range Monoplane, a two-seater in which every available cubic foot of space was crammed with fuel. In this machine, on 24 April 1929, Squadron Leader A.G. Jones-Williams and Flight Lieutenant N.H. Jenkins set out from Cranwell in a bid to establish a world non-stop flight record. They failed, but landed at Karachi on 26 April after covering a distance of 4,156 miles in 50 hours 48 minutes. Three years later, these two airmen were to lose their lives in a tragic accident when their Fairey Monoplane crashed in the Atlas Mountains near Tunis on another long-range flight.

The distance record that Jones-Williams and Jenkins had set out to beat in 1929 had then been held by Charles Lindbergh; this was beaten in July 1931 by two more Americans, Russell Boardman and John Polando, who set up a non-stop record of just over 5,000 miles on a flight from New York to Constantinople. On 6 February 1933, the RAF set out to better this; the aircraft, once again, was a Fairey Long-Range Monoplane, and the crew consisted of Squadron Leader O.R. Gayford and Flight Lieutenant E. Nicholetts. Their aircraft, K1991, was

equipped with three altimeters, an auto-pilot which had been tested by various RAF units—particularly No. 7 Squadron, which operated Vickers Virginias in the long-range bombing role—and roller bearings on the wheels to assist take-off at an all-up weight of 17,000 pounds. Extra 1,000-gallon fuel tanks had also been fitted into the wings. K1991 left Cranwell and touched down at Walvis Bay, South-West Africa, on 8 February after a non-stop flight of 57 hours 25 minutes, having covered a distance of 5,309.24 miles at an average speed of 93 mph. On 12 February, the aircraft flew on to Cape Town, where a new Napier Lion engine was fitted before the flight back to England.

The non-stop distance record set up by Gayford and Nicholetts stood until 1938, when it was beaten by two Vickers Wellesley long-range bombers of the RAF Long-Range Development Flight, a remarkable aircraft for its day, the Wellesley had its origins in Air Ministry Specification G. 4/31. In 1938, five Wellesley aircraft—L2637, '38, '39, '80 and '81 —were specially converted for the LRDU. Powered by modified Pegasus XXII engines, they were stripped of all military equipment and fitted with extra fuel tankage. In July 1938, a detachment of four aircraft under the command of Squad-

ron Leader R.G. Kellett flew from Cranwell to Ismailia via the Persian Gulf in preparation for an attempt on the world record for the greatest distance flown in a straight line. On 5 November, three of them (L2638, '39 and '80) took off from Ismailia to fly direct to Australia. L2639 was obliged to land at Keopang, on the island of Timor in the Netherlands East Indies, but the other two flew on in deteriorating weather to reach Darwin after covering a straight-line distance of 7,162 miles in 48 hours.

The RAF also succeeded in establishing a number of altitude records in the 1930s. In

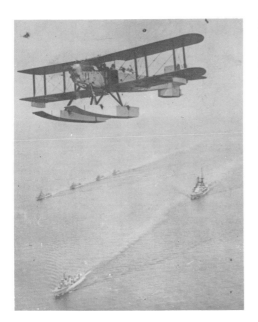

Fairey IIIC floatplane over units of the Home Fleet at Spithead, *circa* 1921. The battleship in the centre is HMS *Barham*.

March 1933, an expedition financed by Lady Houston and led by Squadron Leader Lord Clydesdale set out to fly over the summit of Mount Everest, the highest point on earth, in a Westland Wallace and a Westland PV. 3 aircraft which had been fitted with specially-modified 525 hp Pegasus IS. 3 engines. Both aircraft bore civil registrations: G-ACAZ (PV. 3) and G-ACBR (Wallace).

A reconnaissance flight was made on 15 March by two of the expedition's members, Flight Lieutenant D.F. McIntyre and Mr. S.R. Barnett; they reached an altitude of 31,000 feet, and a similar reconnaissance was carried out the next day by Clydesdale and Lieutenant-Colonel L.V.S. Blacker, the expedition photographer. The actual flight over Everest was made on 3 April by both machines, the Westland PV. 3 being crewed by Clydesdale and Blacker and the Wallace by McIntyre and Barnett. Blacker described the conditions:

The pilot swung the machine skilfully again towards the westward into the huge wind force sweeping down over the crest; so great was its strength that, as the machine battled with it and struggled to climb upwards against the downfall, we seemed scarcely able to make any headway in spite of our 120 mph air speed. We were now for a few minutes in the very plume itself, and as we swung round, fragments of ice rattled violently into the cockpit.

Inspiring though the Everest mission undoubtedly was, a much more significant high-altitude flight from the operational point of view was carried out three years later from Farnborough, one of its objectives being to assess the ability of a pilot to withstand prolonged high-altitude flying with a view to future reconnaissance tasks. The aircraft involved was the Bristol Type 138A, which had been specially developed for the task, and the pilot who set out to establish a new altitude record in it was Squadron Leader F.R.D. Swain. Taking off from Farnborough on 28 September 1936, and fitted with a special pressure suit made of rubberized fabric and a helmet with a large double plastic faceplate, Swain succeeded in reaching a record height of 49,944 feet. The Italians captured the altitude record in 1937, only to lose it again when the 138A reached a new altitude of 53, 937 feet on 30 June that year, the pilot on this occasion being Flight Lieutenant M.J. Adam.

Often, in those times of stringent Service economies, the RAF was forced to rely on the generosity of private individuals in its record-breaking pursuits. Nowhere was this fact more in evidence than in the development of high-speed flying between the wars, and particularly in the RAF's response to the challenge of the celebrated Schneider Trophy. The trophy—or La Coupe d'Aviation Maritime Jacques Schneider, to give it its correct title—had originated in 1912, when Schneider had first offered the 25,000-franc trophy, together with a similar sum of money, to be competed for by seaplanes of any nationality over a course of at least 150 nautical miles in length. The contest was interrupted by the 1914–18 War and afterwards underwent a considerable change in that its participants were now government-sponsored Service teams rather than wealthy private individuals, who had dominated the event prior to 1914. Britain won the Trophy in 1922, but the following year it was captured by the US Navy and in 1924 one of the British entries, a Gloster-Napier floatplane, sank during trials and the other, designed by Supermarine, was not ready in time.

Three British aircraft were prepared for the 1925 race—two Gloster-Napier IIIs and a Supermarine-Napier S.4, all powered by 700 hp Napier Lion engines. All three were designed to Air Ministry Specification 2/25; the S.4, designed by Reginald J. Mitchell, was to be piloted by Captain H.C. Biard, who had won the 1922 event. The S.4 made its first flight at Southampton on 25 August 1925 and was shipped with the other two competitors to Chesapeake Bay, Baltimore, where the race was to be held. Already, flown by Biard, the aircraft had set up a new seaplane world speed record of 226.6 mph on 13 September, and it was the firm favourite to win. Unfortunately, on 22 October—the day before the race—the S.4 developed wing flutter in a turn and went out of control. It plunged into the sea and was a total loss; Biard narrowly escaped with his life.

There were no British entries in the 1926 Schneider race, which was won by an Italian team. However, with the 1927 event in mind, the Air Ministry had issued Specification 6/26, calling for a Napier Lion-powered seaplane capable of a speed of 265 mph at 1,000 feet and a touch-down speed of less than 90 mph. This requirement was met by two companies, Supermarine and Gloster; the former put up an improved version of the S.4, the S.5, just as Gloster's earlier Mk III seaplane was redesigned and uprated to become the Mk IV. Three aircraft of each type were built.

For the first time, the British entry in the 1927 race was to be an all-RAF affair, and a unit known as the High Speed Flight was formed for the occasion, although this did not achieve official status until April 1928. Meanwhile, two S.5s had been shipped to Venice, where the 1927 contest was to be held; the aircraft differed slightly from one another in that one, N219—which was to be flown by Flight Lieutenant O.E. Worsley—had a direct-drive Lion VIIB engine, while the other, N220 (Flight Lieutenant S.N. Webster) had a geared version of this powerplant. In the event, it was Webster's S.5 that won the race with an average speed of 281.49 mph, with Worsley's aircraft coming second. None of the other competitors completed the course. During the contest, which was held on 26 September, Webster also set up a 100-kilometre closed circuit world seaplane speed record of 283.66 mph.

There was no contest in 1928, but high-speed development work was carried on at Felixstowe by the High Speed Flight under Flight Lieutenant D. d'Arcy Greig, and it was he who, in the course of the year, set up a new British seaplane speed record of 319.57 mph in one of the S.5s. Then, in February 1929, the Air Ministry once again decided to field a team for that year's Schneider Trophy race. At the Supermarine Aviation Works, Reginald Mitchell's team set about developing a new aircraft, the S.6, which was somewhat larger than the earlier S.5 and powered by a 1,900 hp Rolls-Royce 'R' racing engine, while the Gloster Aircraft Company produced the Gloster-Napier VI, powered by a 1,400 hp Lion VIID engine. Both S.6s and one of the two Glosters were entered for the race, but the Glosters were withdrawn because of engine problems. One of the S.6s, flown by Flying Officer H.R.D. Waghorn,

29

A Short Singapore III flying boat, probably of No. 203 Squadron on detachment from Basra, seen at Ismailia in October 1936.

went on to win the contest with a speed of 328.63 mph, and on 12 September, one of the other High Speed Flight pilots, Squadron Leader A.H. Orlebar, flew this aircraft (N247) to a new world seaplane record speed of 357.7 mph.

The Schneider Trophy contest was now held every two years, mainly because of economic considerations, and early in 1931 the British Government announced that it was not prepared to subsidize RAF participation on grounds of cost. The news was received bitterly by everyone involved because Britain had won two consecutive contests and, if she won a third, she would keep the coveted Trophy permanently. In the end, it was that great patriot Lady Houston—who was later to finance the Everest expedition—who stepped into the breach with an offer of £100,000. Time was short, so instead of initiating a new design, Mitchell first of all modified the two existing S.6s by fitting them with enlarged floats and redesignating them S.6As, and then built two new machines, based on the existing airframe but incorporating much more powerful 2,350 hp Rolls-Royce 'R' engines. The new aircraft were designated S.6B.

Suddenly, the British found themselves with no competitors; the Italians could not produce an aircraft in time, and the French entry had crashed during trials, killing its pilot. Nevertheless, Britain allowed the 'race' to go ahead and on 13 September 1931, Flight Lieutenant J.W. Boothman flew S.6B S1595 over the seven laps of the 50-kilometre course at an average speed of 340.08 mph. That same afternoon, Flight Lieutenant G. H. Stainforth set up a new world speed

record of 379.05 mph in the other S.6B, S1596. Later, on 29 September, Stainforth pushed up the absolute world speed record to 407.5mph.

Both S.6Bs are preserved today, one (S1595) in the Science Museum and the other (S1596) at Southampton. They had brought the Schneider Trophy back to Britain for all time; but more important by far, they had made a contribution to the development of high-speed aerodynamics and high-powered engines that, within a decade, would help the nation to survive her hour of greatest peril.

The four years of World War One marked history's greatest technological leap forward in terms of military hardware. Yet, almost before the guns had ceased firing, both the Admiralty and the War Office joined forces in a determined bid to abolish the Royal Air Force—the service in which technical advance was most apparent—as a separate organization. Both regarded the RAF as little more than a wartime expedient, although in fairness it should be said that the Army treated its own child, the Royal Tank Corps, in exactly the same way—with results that were to be all too apparent twenty years later.

One man—the Chief of the Air Staff, Sir Hugh Trenchard—was utterly opposed to the line taken by the Admiralty and War Office, and was equally as determined that the RAF should retain its separate identity. The subsequent squabble often reached a petty level; in 1919, for example, the Army and Navy refused to allow the RAF to use their officer ranks, and so Trenchard invented new ones. The new RAF rank titles—Pilot Officer, Flying Officer and so on, up to Marshal of the Royal Air Force—officially came into being after much controversy on 4 August 1919.

The main opposition to the RAF's continued existence as a separate Service came from the Admiralty, which at one stroke had lost all its officers and ratings who were experienced in aviation techniques. It must be admitted that the Admiralty had a strong point. Even seaborne aircraft were now flown by RAF aircrew and serviced by RAF mechanics, although the vessels from which they operated were still under Naval command. Known as Air Force Contingents, these seaborne RAF units were poorly trained, inexperienced in carrier operations and flew aircraft that were either obsolescent or totally unsuited to carrier work. Late in 1918, the Admiralty suggested a compromise; it proposed that all personnel connected with naval air operations afloat should be naval officers and ratings, although the RAF would still be responsible for their training. The proposal was rejected by the Air Ministry, and the battle of words was on.

While the bickering continued, the Admiralty went ahead with the formation of a 'flying squadron' consisting of six aircraft carriers, two of them new vessels, and RAF squadrons equipped with Sopwith Cuckoo torpedo-bombers were assigned to them. Then, in July 1921, the Admiralty informed the Air Ministry that it intended to form a branch of specialist naval observers for flying duties. The Air Ministry, after stalling for several months, eventually gave its reluctant agreement, although it insisted that the observers must be trained at establishments within the Coastal Area of the Royal Air Force. Coastal Area, the forerunner of RAF Coastal Command, was responsible for maritime air operations around the British Isles.

Meanwhile, in March 1921, Sir Hugh Trenchard had laid a proposal before the Committee for Imperial Defence in which he recommended that, in addition to providing the main defence against a possible invasion of Britain, the RAF should also exercise control over naval and military operations in the same way as it already controlled air units attached to the Army and Navy. There followed two months of heated discussion between the three Services until the Committee's conclusions were outlined in a report by Mr Balfour, Chairman of the Defence Sub-Committee. The first conclusion was that the RAF must play the leading part in defence against air attack; secondly, when acting in support of military or naval operations, the RAF units involved should come under the control of the senior Army or Navy officer in command; and thirdly, that in offensive operations against enemy territory, co-operation rather than subordination should be the keyword.

A Bristol Fighter which crashed at Cranwell in 1928.

Shortly afterwards, in August 1921, the Cabinet appointed a 'Committee on National Expenditure' under Sir Eric Geddes to study ways and means of effecting cuts in government expenditure, and in this the armed forces were a primary target. After a detailed examination of the estimates for 1922–23, the Committee recommended drastic cuts in the budgets of all three Services. The Navy and Army estimates were to be reduced by about £20 million each, while the RAF was to suffer a reduction of £5.5 million, bringing its estimate down to £11 million. For the RAF particularly, with by far the smallest estimate of the three Services, it was a serious blow. The strength of the RAF was now at a very low ebb; apart from training establishments, there were only four army co-

A Bristol Bulldog used for advanced training at the RAF College, Cranwell, in 1932.

operation squadrons and one fighter squadron (No. 25, equipped with Sopwith Snipes and based at Hawkinge) in the United Kingdom, five squadrons in Egypt, four in Iraq, four in India and one in the Far East, not counting the handful of floatplane or flying-boat squadrons for maritime reconnaissance and coastal patrol.

The Geddes Committee's recommendations were violently opposed by every Service department, and a new committee under Winston Churchill, who was then Secretary of State for the Colonies, was at once set up to analyze them. Churchill, it will be remembered, had presided over the Cairo Conference of 1921, at which the RAF's overseas role in peacetime had been clearly defined. Now, as a result of his committee's re-

commendations, the Imperial Defence Committee decided to embark on a full review of the requirements involved in the air defence of Great Britain. In April 1922, a defence sub-committee recommended that the strength of the RAF be greatly increased, and the Cabinet gave its approval to the formation of twenty new squadrons totalling some 500 aircraft for home defence. The following October, another committee, under Lord Salisbury, began a further study of the situation; in 1923, this led to a recommendation for the creation of a home defence force with 600 aircraft. However, the concrete decision to form a new RAF Command, the Air Defence of Great Britain, was not taken until 1925.

Trenchard had fought to save the RAF from extinction and to forge the embryo Service into a formidable weapon. It now seemed that he was well on the way to achieving his aim, but the task ahead of the Air Staff was daunting. In the spring of 1923, there was only one fighter squadron—No. 56, equipped with Snipes, which had re-formed at Hawkinge in November 1922—in the whole of the United Kingdom. The other, No. 25, was absent on detachment to Turkey and did not return until October. The re-equipment programme had to start from scratch and, to fulfil the air defence role, it was decided to standardize on the Sopwith Snipe, the fighter designed during the closing months of the 1914–18 War to replace the Camel.

The first squadron to re-equip fully with Snipes was No. 29, which re-formed at Duxford on 1 April 1923. No. 19 Squadron also re-formed at Duxford on the same date with a single flight of Snipes for training purposes, but was not brought up to full strength until June. At Kenley, No. 32 Squadron re-formed with a single flight of Snipes on 1 April; a second was added in December, and the Squadron was brought up to full strength in June 1924. Another unit that operated as a single flight from April 1923 was No. 41 Squadron, which was still one-third below normal squadron strength in May 1924. No. 43 Squadron re-formed with Snipes at Henlow on 1 July 1923, and was followed by No. 111 Squadron in October. The latter, in fact, started off with one flight of Gloster Grebes, to which a flight of Snipes was added in April 1924. Other squadrons which re-formed in that month were No. 17 at Hawkinge and No. 3 at Manston, both with Snipes. The last Snipe squadron to be re-formed was No. 23, at Manston in July 1925; it established itself at Upavon in Wiltshire at the end of the month. With the return of No. 25 Squadron from

A sight to make the Station Warrant Officer's hair curl: members of 'B' Flight, No. 99 (Bomber) Squadron in various states of mixed dress at the close of an apparently successful cricket season, at RAF Upper Heyford *circa* 1930.

Right
A rare shot of Fairey Fox J7957 of No. 12 Squadron during the late 1920s. No. 12 was the only squadron to operate the Fox, which was replaced by Hawker Harts in January 1931.

The Bristol Bulldog, one of the best-known RAF fighters of the early 1930s, eventually equipped ten RAF squadrons, beginning in 1929.

overseas detachment in October 1923, the fighter strength available to the Air Defence of Great Britain stood at eleven squadrons, equipped predominantly with Snipes. It was still a long way from the 52 squadrons, with 600 aircraft, recommended by the Salisbury Committee.

It was also clear that the Snipe, although invaluable as an interim aircraft, was quickly approaching obsolescence, and steps were taken to re-equip the fighter squadrons with post-war designs at an early date. The first such design to enter RAF service was the Gloster Grebe, which, as mentioned above, was delivered to a flight of No. 111 Squadron in October 1923; the type subsequently served with Nos 19, 25, 29, 32 and 56 Squadrons, replacing their Snipes. The true successor to the Snipe, however, was the Hawker Woodcock, designed by the firm that had replaced the famous Sopwith Company in November 1920. The Woodcock, however, only served with two squadrons, Nos 3 and 17, the first deliveries being made to No. 3 in May 1925.

The Woodcock was followed into squadron service by the Gloster Gamecock, which was delivered initially to No. 23 Squadron in May 1926. The type also equipped Nos. 3, 17, 32 and 43 Squadrons, but its service life was short-lived. This was partly because of an abnormally high accident rate; of 90 Gamecock Is built, 22 were lost in spinning or landing accidents.

The Snipe, Grebe, Woodcock and Gamecock were for the most part replaced in service by the Armstrong Whitworth Siskin IIIA. The first Siskin IIIs, in fact, were delivered to No. 41 Squadron at Northolt in May 1924, and a month later to No. 111 Squadron at Duxford. These were the only two units to use the early mark, but the Siskin IIIA, with a more powerful engine and a number of aerodynamic refinements, began to replace the Snipes of No. 1 Squadron and the Grebes of No. 56 from mid-1927, and subsequently equipped Nos 17, 19, 25, 29, 32, 41, 43, 54 and 111 Squadrons, all in the United Kingdom.

The RAF's fighter aircraft of the 1920s, resplendent in their silver finishes and with their squadron markings emblazoned on wings and fuselages, enthralled and captivated the British people with their appearances at air shows all over the country. The most famous venue of all was Hendon, with its annual air pageant, and it was here that the aerobatic teams of the Royal Air Force established for themselves a reputation which they were never to lose. The first such team was organized in 1921, and consisted of five Snipes of the Central Flying

A Hawker Osprey, the naval version of the Hart, being rigged for a practice catapult launch at RAF Leuchars, Scotland, in the 1930s.

School; for the next two years it was composed of SE.5As from the Royal Aircraft Establishment, then in 1924 it was once again the Snipes of CFS that thrilled the crowds.

Life in a bomber squadron during the 1920s was considerably less carefree, and certainly more arduous, than that of a fighter unit. Aircrews had to train in all kinds of weather conditions, while servicing and handling bomber aircraft and their equipment generally demanded much hard work on the part of the ground crews. In 1925, the Bombing Area of the Air Defence of Great Britain was divided into three Groups: No. 1 at Kidbrooke, No.3 at Spitalgate and No. 7 at Andover.

The sweeping disarmament measures of 1919, and the disbandment of the Independent Force, had left the RAF without a single home-based bomber squadron. It was not until early February 1920, when No. 207 Squadron was re-formed at Bircham Newton as a day-bomber unit and equipped with DH.9As, that the first step was taken to rectify the situation. However, it was another year before No. 207 Squadron was joined by another bomber unit, No. 39 Squadron, which re-formed at Spitalgate in February 1921, and was also equipped with DH.9As. Another year went by, and then, in February 1922, No. 100 Squadron moved to Spitalgate with DH.9As. Up to this time, it had been operating as a fighter unit with Bristol F.2Bs for two years against IRA guerrillas, flying from Baldonnel near Dublin.

The next bomber unit to re-form in the United Kingdom was No. 11 Squadron, which came back into existence as a day-

bomber squadron at Andover in January 1923 and was also equipped with DH.9As. The tempo of re-forming bomber squadrons now accelerated greatly; in April 1923 No. 12 Squadron re-formed at Northolt with DH.9As, No. 7 re-formed at Bircham Newton with Vickers Vimys in June, and in July No. 22 received a new lease of life at Martlesham Heath. However, although it was nominally a bomber squadron, No. 22 was engaged in experimental flying for the next eleven years, testing new combat aircraft of all kinds. Finally, three more squadrons re-formed in April 1924; these were No. 9 at Manston, No. 58 at Worthy Down and No. 99 at Netheravon, all three with Vimys.

Another nominal bomber unit re-formed in the spring of 1924 was No. 15 Squadron, although, like No. 22, it became part of the Aeroplane and Armament Experimental Es-

De Havilland Queen Bee K8642 being rigged for a catapult launch, location unknown, in 1938. The Queen Bee radio-controlled target drone, of similar configuration to the Tiger Moth, entered service in 1937, and large numbers were produced.

tablishment at Martlesham Heath, and until 1934 was engaged on experimental work and ballistics trials. On 15 May 1925, No. 502 Squadron was also formed at Aldergrove, Northern Ireland, as a cadre unit of the Special Reserve with Vimys in the night-bombing role, and in October 1925, the first four Auxiliary Air Force light bomber squadrons were formed, all with DH.9As. These were No. 600 (City of London) and No. 601 (County of London) Squadrons, both at Northolt; No. 602 (City of Glasgow) Squadron at Renfrew; and No. 603 (City of Edinburgh) Squadron at Turnhouse. A fifth Auxiliary AF squadron, No. 605 (County of Warwick), was formed at Castle Bromwich on 15 October 1926, and it too was equipped with DH.9As.

Another bomber squadron that came into being in 1926 was No. 503 (County of Lincoln), which was formed as a cadre unit of the Special Reserve at Waddington on 5 October and equipped with Fairey Fawn light bombers. Designed as a replacement for the DH.9A, the Fawn was not a success; it had a lower performance than the DH.9A and an inferior bomb-carrying capacity. Nevertheless, it also served with Nos 11, 12, 100 and 602 Squadrons for a period of about two years until it was replaced by more modern types. One of these was the Fairey Fox, a very clean aerodynamic design which had a low-drag Curtiss D–12 engine; it was a

A Boulton Paul Sidestrand bomber of No. 101 Squadron—the only unit to operate the type—at RAF Andover in 1929.

good 50 mph faster than the Fawn, and indeed was faster than any RAF fighter then in service. When the Fox was demonstrated before Sir Hugh Trenchard in October 1925, he was so impressed that he ordered a complete squadron. Because of financial restrictions, however, only one squadron was ever equipped with the type; this was No. 12, which received the Fox in August 1926, and the Squadron later adopted a fox's head as its emblem.

Three more squadrons joined the Bomber Arm's Order of Battle in 1928. The first of these was No. 10, which re-formed on 3 January at Upper Heyford and was equipped with Handley Page Hyderabad heavy bombers. This type had already been in service with No. 99 Squadron since the end of 1925, and had been evolved from the Handley Page W.8b commercial airliner to meet an Air Staff requirement for a four-seat heavy night bomber. It was replaced in squadron service from 1929 by the Hinaidi, and in addition to Nos 10 and 99 Squadrons served only with two Auxiliary units, Nos 502 and 503.

The other two squadrons re-formed in 1928 were Nos. 101 and 504. No. 101, which re-formed at Bircham Newton on 21 March, was initially equipped with DH.9As, but a year later it began to re-equip with Boulton Paul Sidestrands. This aircraft was the RAF's first twin-engined medium day bomber since the DH.10; it was powered by two Bristol Jupiter VI radials, was very easy to handle and had a good single-engined performance. Despite its promise, only twenty machines were built and only No. 101

Squadron operated them. The other new squadron of 1928, No. 504 (County of Nottingham), was formed at Hucknall on 26 March and equipped with the Hawker Horsley, an aircraft that filled the dual role of day bomber and torpedo bomber. It was already in service with Nos 11 and 100 Squadrons, and in the torpedo-bomber role, it equipped No. 36 Squadron, which was formed out of the Coastal Defence Torpedo Flight at Donibristle in October 1928.

No. 33 Squadron, which was re-formed in the day bomber role at Netheravon on 1 March 1929, also received the Horsley, but No. 35, which was re-formed in the same month at Bircham Newton, had to be content with an initial complement of DH.9As until the end of the year, when it began to receive Horsleys. By this time, two of the squadrons that had formed the original complement of the Air Defence of Great Britain's bomber force, Nos 11 and 39, had left for the North-West Frontier, and the formation of new units filled the gap created by their departure. The last bomber unit to be formed in the 1920s was No. 501 (County of Gloucester), which was formed on 14 June 1929 at Filton, Bristol. A Special Reserve unit, it remained a squadron on paper only until it received DH.9As in March 1930, later exchanging these for Wapitis.

By the end of the 1920s, six RAF squadrons were operational in the army co-operation role. The first of these, No. 2 Squadron, had spent the early years of the decade in Ireland, then returned to England to carry out its task until 1927, when it was

deployed to China for several months. During all this time it was equipped with Bristol F.2Bs, which it eventually exchanged for Armstrong Whitworth Atlas aircraft in January 1930. Also with Bristol F.2Bs was No. 4 Squadron, which like No. 2 co-operated with the army in Ireland until September 1922, when it was deployed to Turkey until September 1923. It, too, received Atlases in October 1929.

Two more army co-operation squadrons, Nos 13 and 16, re-formed on 1 April 1924, the former at Kenley and the latter at Old Sarum. Both were equipped with Bristol F.2Bs and, later, Atlases. No. 13 Squadron played a considerable part in developing close co-operation techniques between air and ground forces during the inter-war years, while No. 16 became the Service's specialist artillery-spotting unit. The fifth army co-operation squadron, No. 26, re-formed at Catterick on 11 October 1927, initially with a single flight of Atlas aircraft; and the sixth squadron, although designated an army co-operation unit, was in reality nothing of the sort. This was No. 24 Squadron, which had been re-formed at Kenley on 1 April 1920 as a communications and training squadron. Initially equipped with Bristol F.2Bs, it subsequently operated a wide variety of aircraft. As well as providing transport for Government, Air Ministry and RAF personnel, No. 24 maintained a flight of training aircraft to enable pilots 'flying desks' at the Air Ministry to keep their hands in. In 1927, the Squadron moved to Northolt.

As far as maritime air affairs were concerned, a Fleet Air Arm had been formally established in April 1924, administered by the Coastal Area of the RAF but under the operational control of the Royal Navy when embarked. Its observers were drawn wholly from the Royal Navy and the pilots from both Services. In the middle of 1925, the Royal Navy had at its disposal six Fleet Fighter Flights equipped with Fairey Fly-catchers, two Fleet Spotter Flights with Westland Walrus, one with Blackburn Blackburn and one with Avro Bison aircraft, four Fleet Reconnaissance Flights with Fairey IIIDs and one with Parnall Panthers, and three Fleet Torpedo Flights with Blackburn Darts. All flying at sea was controlled by a Royal Air Force officer, usually a squadron leader, and all servicing personnel were RAF except for W/T specialists and some deck hands. Life was strict, the airmen having to take part in naval activities and being subject to naval discipline, but the work was interesting and there were compensations, of which one was the daily rum ration.

In the United Kingdom, the nerve centre

of the RAF's maritime operations was Calshot, on the Solent, which in 1922 was made up of No. 480 (Coastal Reconnaissance) Flight, the Seaplane Training Squadron, the Air Pilotage Flight and the Marine Craft Training Section, which in 1927 became the centre for teaching boat building, marine engine fitting, and motor-boat crew training in the RAF. In August 1923, the first wooden-hulled Supermarine Southampton flying boats arrived at Calshot to replace the well-worn Felixstowe F.3 and F.5 flying boats, and three years later the Seaplane Training Course was replaced by the Coastal Reconnaissance Pilots' Course. From 1927, Calshot was famous for its association with the RAF High Speed Flight, which trained there in preparation for the Schneider Trophy races.

On 6 December 1928, Squadron Leader D.G. Donald took over command of No. 480 Flight from Squadron Leader I.T. Lloyd, and on 1 January 1929, the Flight was renamed No. 201 Squadron, still equipped with Southamptons. It was the start of a considerable shake-up in the RAF's mar-

itime patrol organization; at the same time, No. 482 (Coastal Reconnaissance) Flight at Mount Batten, also with Southamptons, was renamed No. 203 Squadron prior to its departure for Basra, Iraq, and at Kalafrana, Malta, No. 481 Flight—with Fairey IIIDs—was re-designated No. 202 Squadron. On 1 February, No. 204 Squadron formed at Mount Batten with five Southamptons, completing the re-organization.

In planning the peacetime RAF, Sir Hugh Trenchard had laid much emphasis on spirit. Such a spirit, he stated, had existed in a high degree during the war and it was of the utmost importance that it should continue to be fostered by every available means in peacetime. It had been at his suggestion that distinguished squadron numbers were retained in the post-war years, and he had also suggested the creation of an Air Force Col-

Part of the daily routine: a PT class at RAF Uxbridge in 1926.

Royal Air Force Order of Battle—1 August 1934

Sqn	Base	Aircraft	Sqn	Base	Aircraft	Sqn	Base	Aircraft
1	Tangmere	Fury Mk I	33	Bicester	Hart	202	Kalafrana	Fairey IIIF floatplane
2	Farnborough	Audax	35	Bircham Newton	Gordon	203	Basra	Rangoon
3	Kenley	Bulldog Mk IIA	36	Seletar	Horsley Vildebeest	204	Mount Batten	Southampton Mk II
4	Farnborough	Audax	39	Risalpur	Hart (Mk I)	205	Seletar	Southampton
5	Quetta	Wapiti Mk IIA	40	Abingdon	Gordon	207	Bircham Newton	Gordon
6	Ismailia	Gordon Mk I	41	Northolt	Demon			
7	Worthy Down	Virginia Mk X	43	Tangmere	Fury Mk I	208	Heliopolis	Audax
8	Khormaksar	Fairey IIIF	45	Helwan	Fairey IIIF	209	Mount Batten	Southampton Mk II
9	Manston	Virginia Mk X	47	Khartoum	Fairey IIIF			
10	Upper Heyford	Virginia Mk X	54	Hornchurch	Bulldog Mk IIA	210	Pembroke Dock	Southampton Mk II
11	Risalpur	Hart (Mk I)	55	Hinaidi	Wapiti Mk IIA			
12	Bicester	Hart	56	North Weald	Bulldog Mk IIA	216	Heliopolis	Victoria Mk V
13	Netheravon	Audax	57	Netheravon	Hart	500	Manston	Virginia Mk X
14	Amman	Gordon Mk I	58	Worthy Down	Virginia Mk X	501	Filton	Wallace Mk I
15	Abingdon	Hart	60	Kohat	Wapiti Mk IIA	502	Aldergrove	Wapiti Mk IIA
16	Old Sarum	Audax	70	Hinaidi	Victoria Mks V, VI	503	Waddington	Virginia Mk X
17	Kenley	Bulldog Mk IIA	84	Shaibah	Wapiti Mk IIA	504	Hucknall	Horsley
18	Upper Heyford	Hart	99	Upper Heyford	Heyford	600	Hendon	Hart
19	Duxford	Bulldog Mk IIA	100	Seletar	Vildebeest Mk II	601	Hendon	Wapiti Mk IIA
20	Peshawar	Wapiti Mk IIA	101	Andover	Sidestrand	602	Renfrew	Wapiti Mk IIA
23	Biggin Hill	Demon	111	Hornchurch (moved to Northolt 15/07/34)	Bulldog Mk IIA	603	Turnhouse	Wapiti Mk IIA Hart
25	Hawkinge	Fury Mk I				604	Hendon	Wapiti Mk IIA
26	Catterick	Audax	142	Netheravon	Hart	605	Castle Bromwich	Wapiti Mk IIA
27	Kohat	Wapiti Mk IIA	201	Calshot	Southampton Mk II			
28	Ambala	Wapiti Mk IIA				607	Usworth	Wapiti Mk IIA
29	North Weald	Bulldog Mk IIA				608	Thornaby	Wapiti Mk IIA
30	Mosul	Wapiti Mk IIA						
31	Quetta	Wapiti Mk IIA						
32	Biggin Hill	Bulldog Mk IIA						

lege, an Air Staff College, and a scheme whereby the bulk of the RAF's skilled tradesmen would be enlisted as boys and educated, as well as trained, within the Service. His scheme provided for the reduction of service squadrons to the minimum, every available resource after the provision of overseas garrisons being concentrated on the training of officers and men.

In 1919, Trenchard envisaged that the normal training of regular RAF officers would be carried out at a cadet college. The course would be of two years duration and would include practical flying. After passing out, cadets were to be commissioned and then undergo a short course in 'air pilotage and practical cross-country flying', after which they would be posted to an operational squadron. After five years service, officers would be required to specialize in some technical subject. Short Service officers were to be taught to fly at training wings, which effectively became Flying Training Schools, after which they would have similar courses in air pilotage.

Such was the pattern of officer training when the Royal Air Force Cadet College was opened at Cranwell, Lincolnshire, in February 1920, with Air Commodore C.A.H. Longcroft as the first Commandant. The first course was attended by 52 cadets, of whom seventeen were midshipmen transferred from the Royal Navy. Conditions then were primitive; the College facilities consisted of little more than a cluster of barrack huts and a few makeshift buildings scattered along one side of a large field that served as an aerodrome. Yet, as a University of the Air, Cranwell established a reputation second to none, and provided the RAF with a skilled and experienced nucleus of officers who were to become its operational commanders in the dark times of the future.

In 1919, demobilization had removed most of the best tradesmen from the RAF, and the efficiency of the peacetime squadrons which were on the point of being formed depended on the most thorough instruction and skill of those who were to take their place. To implement the second part of Trenchard's personnel training scheme, Wendover Camp, Halton, was selected as the site of No. 1 School of Technical Training. The choice was one of economics; there were already technical workshops at Halton, which had been a Royal Flying Corps recruit

training centre during the war. Some of the accommodation had been disposed of by 1920, when the school was opened; the initial intake was for 3,000, but pending the completion of new accommodation a third of the boys were given instruction at Cranwell. The first mechanic apprentices reported to Cranwell in February 1920, some two years before the apprenticeship scheme was fully established at Halton. Despite the somewhat derogatory nickname of 'Trenchard Brats', bestowed upon them by airmen who had not been apprentices, the Halton-trained boys— by then senior NCOs—served their country well during World War Two, when a flood of new entrants had in turn to be trained at very short notice.

Such, broadly, was the state of the Royal Air Force in the 1920s. It was a Service where discipline was still severe, reflecting its military origins, and where life could be hard for the ordinary airman, particularly if he were married. But it was a Service instilled with pride, an overall sense of belonging to an elite organization and, above all, determination to succeed. All three were qualities which, over the years, were to help it surmount innumerable difficulties.

5

Re-armament and the Approach of War

The expansion of the Royal Air Force towards the planned target of 52 squadrons was dictated, apart from economic considerations, by the activities of the French. In the late 1920s, an emasculated Germany was not regarded as a serious threat, but the idea of France, a mere 21 miles away across the Channel, possessing a larger and more effective air force than Britain's was unthinkable. The speed of formation of new RAF squadrons was therefore dictated by the need to match the French in air matters, and when the expansion of the French Air Force slowed down, so did that of the RAF. The original target date for the 52-squadron force was 1930, but by 1927 this had been put back to 1936, and two years later it was again postponed to 1938. Consequently, in April 1932 the Air Defence of Great Britain comprised 42 squadrons, of which thirteen were Auxiliary or Special Reserve units, while overseas there were eight squadrons in India, five in Iraq, six in Egypt, three in the Far East and one on Malta.

The events of 1933, and the rise to power of the Nazi Party under the leadership of Adolf Hitler, changed the picture dramatically. Hitler's policy was one of re-armament and expansion, and as far as the *Luftwaffe* was concerned that meant a planned strength of 48 squadrons by 1938. Although this was alarming enough, the Air Staff were confident that Germany would be in no position to offer a serious challenge to Britain until at least the end of 1936—assuming that the rate of German aircraft production did not increase much beyond its 1933 level. However, Air Chief Marshal Sir Edward Ellington, who took over the post of Chief of the Air Staff, was under no illusion; he knew full well that the Germans, if they so desired, had the capability to build up a combat force of 2,000 aircraft, with reserves, in a relatively short time, and he said so very plainly at a meeting of the Chiefs of Staff in June 1934.

Ellington's sense of urgency did not appear to affect Parliament. It was absent even in November 1934, when—since it was by then apparent that the Germans had no intention of limiting their arms production— Prime Minister Stanley Baldwin told the House that although further increases would be necessary in the strength of the RAF's home defence force, it would not be difficult for Britain to maintain the necessary degree of air superiority.

By that time, Expansion Scheme A had already been adopted by the Government in July 1934. This called for a home defence force of 43 bomber squadrons (eight heavy, eight medium, 25 light and two torpedo), 28 fighter squadrons, four general reconnaissance squadrons, four flying-boat squadrons and five army co-operation squadrons. The scheme, however, envisaged little in the way of reserves.

Then, in March 1935, the British Government received a profound shock. Two emi-

A fine study of Hawker Hart K3894 over Egypt in March 1936. No. 142 Squadron was deployed to the Middle East in 1935 during the Abyssinian Crisis.

ssaries, Sir John Simon and Anthony Eden, returned from a visit to Berlin with the news that, during a meeting with Hitler, they had been informed that Germany already had a first-line air strength equal to the RAF's home defence force. In numerical terms, that meant about 2,000 aircraft—the figure predicted by Sir Edward Ellington nine months earlier.

In fact, Hitler's claim was false. In March 1935, the *Luftwaffe* had 22 squadrons with about 500 aircraft, only about 200 of which were operational first-line types. The British Cabinet, however, was not aware of this, and appointed a special committee under the chairmanship of Sir Philip Cunliffe-Lister to carry out a full investigation into the growth of German air power. Its findings were that the position, although not as alarming as the Cabinet had been led to believe, was nevertheless serious enough.

The Air Staff, for their part, now realised that the provisions of Expansion Scheme A were inadequate. They were not, however, in favour of a crash expansion programme, as the equipment available was for the most part obsolescent. The feeling was that it was better to aim for a gradual expansion based on the new range of combat aircraft then on the drawing-board or flying in prototype form, with a strength of about 1,500 first-line machines by 1937 as the target.

The new plan, Scheme C, which was laid before the Government in May 1935, envisaged a home-based force of 68 bomber and 35 fighter squadrons, to be ready by March 1937. One-third of the bomber force was to be equipped with aircraft capable of reaching targets in the Ruhr from British bases. The emphasis on a strong bomber force, reflecting the Air Staff's policy that attack was the best form of defence, was also shown in Scheme F, which supplanted Scheme C in February 1936. This called for a front-line force of 1,736 aircraft by 1939, to be made up of twenty heavy bomber squadrons, 48 medium bomber, two torpedo bomber, 30 fighter and 24 reconnaissance, with an additional 37 squadrons based overseas. For the first time, Scheme F laid emphasis on the provision of reserves; first-line squadrons were to have a minimum of 75 per cent reserves available for immediate use, and there was to be a further reserve of 150 per cent available to maintain the RAF at full combat strength in the event of war.

Until the new light and medium bomber monoplanes became available in quantity, the mainstay of the RAF's light bomber force was the Hawker Hind biplane. Designed as a replacement for the Hawker Hart, the Hind first flew in September 1934 and entered

The standard RAF light bomber of the late 1930s, the Hawker Hind. This No. 83 Squadron example was photographed at RAF Scampton in 1938.

service with Nos 18, 21 and 34 Squadrons at Bircham Newton towards the end of 1935. Hinds subsequently equipped 25 home-based bomber squadrons up to 1938, and were used by eleven Auxiliary Air Force units for some time after that.

The Hind was in reality an interim aircraft, filling the gap between the Hart and the first of the monoplane light bombers—the Fairey Battle. The prototype Battle flew on 10 March 1936, powered by a Rolls-Royce Merlin engine, and production of an initial batch of 155 machines began in May of that year. In May 1937, the first Battles were delivered to No. 63 Squadron at Upwood, and aircrew were enthusiastic about the aircraft's clean lines and its ability to carry a 1,000-pound bomb load. Nevertheless, the Battle was underpowered and sadly lacking in defensive armament, two serious drawbacks that were to remain with it throughout its operational career.

The twin-engined Bristol Blenheim medium bomber was a far more promising design. It had its origin in the Bristol 142 *Britain First*, ordered as a personal transport by Lord Rothermere and later presented to the Air Ministry (yet another example of private enterprise coming to the RAF's rescue!). An order for 150 Blenheim Mk Is was placed in August 1935 and the prototype flew ten months later, on 25 June 1936. The first production machines were completed at Bristol's Filton factory towards the end of that year and went into service with No. 114 Squadron at Wyton early in 1937.

When it first appeared, the Blenheim was a good 40 mph faster than the biplane fighters that equipped Europe's air forces. Its maximum speed of 285 mph, coupled with its

ability to carry a 1,000-pound bomb load as far as German targets, represented a sensational advance in the design of bomber aircraft and, in 1936, the Air Ministry placed a follow-on order for 1,130 more. Production of the Blenheim Mk I went ahead very rapidly and by 1938 the type was available in sufficient numbers to permit the re-equipment of RAF bomber squadrons in India, Iraq and Egypt.

Two more interim designs that formed part of the mid-1930s expansion scheme were the Vickers Wellesley and Handley Page Harrow. The Wellesley, it will be recalled was the aircraft that made the record-breaking flight from Ismailia to Darwin in 1938. It could carry 2,000 pounds of bombs in two containers under the wings, and defensive armament consisted of one Vickers machine-gun in the port wing and a second mounted in the rear cockpit. A total of 158 Wellesleys was built before production ended in 1938, and it equipped six medium bomber squadrons (Nos 7, 35, 76, 77, 148 and 207) in the United Kingdom and four (Nos 14, 45, 47 and 223) abroad.

The Handley Page Harrow was a very different aircraft. Originally developed as a night bomber, it was eventually selected by the Air Ministry to meet a requirement for a bomber-transport and 100 machines were ordered in August 1935. Delivery of production Harrows began in April 1937 and the type equipped Nos 37, 75, 115, 214, and 215 Squadrons until it was finally replaced by more modern equipment in 1939. Powered by two Pegasus engines, the Harrow had a top speed of 200 mph, a range of 1,250 miles and could carry a 3,000-pound bomb load.

Another Handley Page design, the Heyford, was the backbone of the RAF's heavy bomber force during the expansion period. Designed in 1927 to replace the Hinaidi and the Vickers Virginia, the first Heyford flew in June 1930 and production machines entered service with No. 99 Squadron at Upper Heyford in December 1933. The aircraft could carry up to 3,500 pounds of bombs and was armed with three Lewis machine-guns. Heyfords served with eleven bomber squadrons until 1937, when they began to be phased out in favour of new monoplane bomber types.

The other aircraft designed to the same specification as the Heyford was the Fairey Hendon, which was selected in 1934 to be the main RAF heavy bomber type. An ugly, low-wing monoplane with twin fins, the Hendon prototype flew in November 1931, but much trouble was experienced with its Bristol Jupiter VIII engines and these were later replaced by Rolls-Royce Kestrels. The Hendon entered service with No. 38 Squadron at Mildenhall in November 1936, but by this time the prototypes of more advanced bombers were flying and only fourteen production Hendons were built. In June 1938, No. 38 Squadron detached one of its Hendon flights to Marham; this formed the nucleus of

No. 115 Squadron, which re-equipped with Harrows shortly afterwards.

By the mid-1930s, the Air Ministry was giving priority to the design and production of light bombers at the expense of heavy bombers and even medium types; the requirement now was for maximum range and maximum bomb load. The first of the new heavy bombers was the Armstrong Whitworth Whitley, designed to Specification B.3/34. The Whitley prototype flew on 17 March 1936, and the first production aircraft entered service with No. 10 Squadron at Dishforth a year later. In July 1937, the Whitley also went into service with No. 78 Squadron at the same station. Thirty-four Mk Is were built, and these were followed by 46 Mk IIs which entered service with Nos 51, 58 and 97 Squadrons from January 1938. A further contract, placed in 1936, led to the production of 80 Whitley Mk IIIs, and delivery of these aircraft to operational squadrons began in August 1938. The last Whitley version to go into service before the outbreak of war was the Mk V, which became operational with No. 77 Squadron at Driffield, Yorkshire, in August 1939. The Whitley Mk V had a maximum speed of 230 mph at 16,400 feet, a range of 2,400 miles and a bomb load of 7,000 pounds; defensive armament consisted of one Vickers gun in the nose turret and four Brownings in the tail turret.

The other two heavy bomber types which, together with the Whitley, were to form the backbone of the RAF's strategic bombing force on the outbreak of World War Two—

the Handley Page Hampden and the Vickers Wellington—were both designed to Air Ministry Specification B.9/32. Only a matter of days separated the first flights of the respective prototypes, the first Wellington flying on 15 June 1936 and the Hampden on 21 June.

An order was placed for 180 Wellington Mk Is, powered by two Bristol Pegasus XVIII engines, and the first of these were delivered to No. 99 Squadron at Mildenhall on 10 October 1938. By August the following year, eight squadrons of Wellingtons were operational with No. 3 Group in East Anglia. Like the earlier Wellesley, the Wellington was of geodetic construction, which enabled it to withstand fearful punishment when it was put to the test in combat. The aircraft's maximum speed was 255 mph at 12,500 feet, and its range was 2,200 miles with a 1,500-pound bomb load.

The Wellington's contemporary, the Hampden, showed outstanding promise during its early flight trials. Air Ministry experts liked the machine's radical design: the deep, narrow fuselage with its high single-seat pilot's cockpit, the slender tail boom supporting twin fins and rudders, the long, tapering wings with their twin Pegasus radial engines. The view from the pilot's seat was exceptionally good, and the Hampden possessed almost fighter-like manoeuvrability—an important factor and one which, the experts believed, would give it a fighting chance of survival during daylight operations in a hostile environment, taking into account

A Westland Wapiti of No. 39 Squadron over Risalpur in the 1930s.

the aircraft's top speed of 265 mph at 15,500 feet. The Hampden's main disadvantage, in fact, was that the crew stations in the three-foot-wide fuselage were far too cramped to permit any real degree of comfort, and this resulted in excessive crew fatigue. The defensive armament of four hand-operated guns was also inadequate, as Hampden crews learnt to their cost later on.

Turning from RAF bomber to fighter development and re-equipment during the expansion period, as far as the home defence fighter squadrons were concerned, the principal type during the first three years of the 1930s was the Bristol Bulldog, which equipped ten squadrons and, with a top speed of 180 mph, was much faster than the fighters it replaced. Its contemporary was the Hawker Fury, the epitome of British fighter biplane design and probably the most beautiful aircraft of its day. The first of 118 Fury Mk Is entered service with No. 43 Squadron at Tangmere in May 1931, and the type also equipped Nos 1 and 25 Squadrons. Further development of a version known as the High Speed Fury led to a production order for 23 Fury Mk IIs, followed by another 75, and

these went into service with No. 25 Squadron in December 1936, also serving with Nos 41, 43, 73 and 87 Squadrons. Other fighter units in the early 1930s were equipped with the Hawker Demon, a fighter variant of the Hart; 244 Demons were built for the RAF in the United Kingdom, serving with Nos 23, 25, 29, 41, 64 and 65 Squadrons and Nos 600, 601, 604, 607 and 608 Squadrons Aux AF.

The Bulldog was replaced in RAF service by the Gloster Gauntlet, the last of the RAF's open-cockpit fighter biplanes; it was an ironic state of affairs, because the prototype Gauntlet, which had first flown in 1928, had shown an inferior performance to both the Bulldog and another contender, the Hawker Hawfinch, and the Bulldog had been chosen in preference. Glosters, however, had proceeded with development of the Gauntlet as a private venture, re-fitting it with a 640 hp Bristol Mercury engine, and this gave it a top speed of 230 mph—well in excess of the Bulldog's. Production orders were placed, and the Gauntlet Mk I entered service with No. 19 Squadron in May 1935. The Gauntlet Mk II, with an uprated Mercury engine, began to enter service from May 1936, and at

the peak of its service in the spring of the following year it equipped fourteen home-based fighter squadrons.

Meanwhile, Glosters had been pursuing the development of a refined private successor to the Gauntlet, developed to Air Ministry Specification F.7/30. Designated SS.37, the prototype was flown in September 1937 and evaluated by the Air Ministry in the following year, the trials resulting in a production order for 23 machines. These were powered by 840 hp Mercury IXS engines and armed with four Vickers machine-guns. They were given the RAF name Gladiator. First deliveries were made to No. 27 Squadron at Tangmere in February 1937, and the type went on to equip eight home fighter squadrons of the RAF. The last of the RAF's biplane fighters, the Gladiator, although outclassed by German and Italian monoplane fighters, was to give gallant service during the early months of the war in both Europe and the Middle East.

The most radical changes in fighter design, however, came as a result of the development of new monoplane types, powered by the new Rolls-Royce Merlin engine and given the unprecedented armament of eight .303 machine-guns. The first such design, the Hawker Hurricane, evolved under the leadership of Sydney Camm to meet Air Ministry Specification F.36/34; the prototype flew on 6 November 1935, powered by a Merlin 'C' engine of 990 hp, and began Service trials at Martlesham Heath in March 1936. Hawkers, confident of the success of their design, began preparations for the production of 1,000 examples before the first Air Ministry order was forthcoming. An order for 600 machines eventually materialized in June 1936, and the first of these—after some delay caused by the decision to install the Merlin II engine—flew on 12 October 1937,

The Gloster Gladiator was the last of the RAF's biplane fighters. The aircraft shown belonged to No. 72 Squadron, RAF Church Fenton, in 1937.

an initial batch being delivered to No. 111 Squadron at Northolt in November.

The other eight-gun monoplane type, the Supermarine Spitfire, was designed by a team under the direction of Reginald Mitchell, and traced its ancestry to the S.6 series of Schneider Trophy racing seaplanes. The prototype made its first flight on 5 March 1936 and, like the Hurricane, was powered by a Rolls-Royce Merlin 'C' engine. A contract for the production of 310 Spitfires was issued by the Air Ministry in June 1936, at the same time as the Hurricane contract, and the first examples were delivered to No. 19 Squadron at Duxford in August 1938. Eight other squadrons had re-equipped with Spitfires by September 1939, and two Auxiliary units (Nos 603 and 609) were undergoing operational training.

In the mid-1930s, the Royal Air Force in the United Kingdom possessed six squadrons of maritime reconnaissance aircraft, equipped in the main with elderly Southampton flying-boats, and two squadrons of torpedo-bombers, equipped with Vickers Vildebeests. In March 1935, however, the first examples of an improved flying-boat, the Short Singapore Mk III, were delivered to No. 230 Squadron at Pembroke Dock, while No. 204 Squadron at Mount Batten re-equipped with Supermarine Scapas. Also at Pembroke Dock, No.210 Squadron was equipped with Short Rangoons, while in 1936 No. 204 Squadron at Mount Batten received a mixture of Blackburn Perth and Saro London flying-boats. The biggest leap forward in military flying-boat design, however, was marked by the Short Sunderland, which was based on the successful 'C' Class flying-boats used by Imperial Airways. The initial production version, the Sunderland Mk 1, was powered by four 1,010 hp Bristol Pegasus XXII engines and had a heavy defensive armament of four .303 Browning guns in a tail turret, one Vickers K or Lewis gun in the nose and two Vickers Ks amidships. It could carry an offensive load of up to 2,000 pounds. Production began in 1938, the first deliveries being made in June that year to No. 230 Squadron in Singapore, and 40 Sunderlands were in service with four RAF squadrons by September 1939.

Apart from new flying-boat types, the most important development in the maritime reconnaissance field during the expansion period was the service debut of the Avro Anson general reconnaissance aircraft. Developed from the six-seat Avro 652 commercial aircraft, the prototype Anson flew on 24 March 1935, powered by two Armstrong Siddeley Cheetah VI engines. The Air Ministry ordered 174 examples, and the first of

these equipped No. 48 Squadron at Manston in March 1936. In all, eleven squadrons were equipped with Ansons by September 1939. However, the Anson's range and offensive payload were insufficient for anything other than short-range coastal operations, and a replacement was found in the shape of a militarized version of the Lockheed 14 airliner. A batch of these aircraft was originally ordered for use as navigational trainers and the first examples reached England in February 1939. With the addition of a dorsal gun turret, and named the Hudson, the new general reconnaissance machine went into service with No. 224 Squadron at Leuchars in August 1939.

In 1934, all but one of the RAF's army co-operation squadrons at home were equipped with the Hawker Audax, a variant of the Hart, while overseas squadrons continued to use the Wapiti in this role. In February 1937, the home-based army co-operation squadrons began to equip with the Hawker Hector, and seven squadrons used the type by the middle of 1938. Overseas, army co-operation squadrons began to replace their Wapitis with the Hawker Hardy, another Hart variant. At home and abroad, the Hector and Hardy remained the standard army co-operation types until the advent of the Westland Lysander, the first examples of which were delivered to No. 16 Squadron at Old Sarum in July 1938. Before the outbreak of war, two squadrons of Blenheim Mk IVs were also allocated to army co-operation duties.

Another vital aspect of the 1930s expansion schemes was the increase in the number of Service Flying Training Schools from six to eleven, with the provision of additional schools at Montrose, Thornaby, Ternhill, Peterborough and Wittering. Ab initio training was carried out by civilian flying schools, but in the spring of 1937, under the new RAF Volunteer Reserve Training Scheme, Elementary and Reserve Flying Training Schools were established at a number of civil aerodromes. Throughout the 1920s, the most important RAF trainer had been the Avro 504, but from 1932 this venerable machine was progressively replaced by the Avro Tutor. Also in 1932, the Service received the first examples of the de Havilland Tiger Moth, which was to become the backbone of the RAF's initial training force both before and during the war. In October 1937, the RAF acquired its first monoplane basic trainer, the Miles Magister, and an advanced trainer, the Miles Master, was on order; this was delivered initially to No. 5 SFTS in September 1939, somewhat later than planned, and to meet the requirement for an

aircraft that would enable a pilot to bridge the gap from low to high-speed flying, 200 North American Harvards were ordered in the interim period. In the closing months of peace, the navigational training role was shared by the Avro Anson and Airspeed Oxford.

While the expansion schemes were in progress, the Royal Air Force at home underwent major organizational changes. On 14 July 1936, Home Defence was organized into four commands: Bomber (Air Marshal Sir John Steel—HQ Uxbridge); Fighter (Air Marshal Sir Hugh Dowding—HQ Stanmore); Coastal (Air Marshal Sir Arthur Longmore—Lee-on-Solent); and Training (Air Marshal Sir Charles Burnett—Ternhill). The four new commands immediately embarked on a series of air exercises to give collective defence training to the Metropolitan Air Force squadrons; for the first time in such an exercise, it was assumed that attacking forces would come in over the seaboard of south-east England. This, too, was the first real test for the Observer Corps, which had been formed under War Office control in October 1925 and transferred to the RAF in January 1929. Two more commands were formed in 1938: Maintenance Command (Air Vice-Marshal J.S.T. Bradley—HQ Andover) on 1 April, and Balloon Command (Air Vice-Marshal O.T. Boyd) on 1 November.

Meanwhile, early in 1937, the Air Ministry had realised that, if the *Luftwaffe* continued to expand at its present rate, the provisions of Scheme F would not be sufficient to maintain first-line parity in 1939, as had been planned. Accordingly, a revised plan—Scheme H—was submitted to the Cabinet. This called for an increase in the RAF's metropolitan first-line force to nearly 2,500 aircraft at the earliest possible date after April 1939, and the total figure was to include 1,659 bombers. The increase was to be made possible by drastically cutting down the number of machines in reserve and allocating them to first-line units. The revised scheme was rejected for two main reasons: first, it would have meant that obsolescent aircraft would have been committed to battle in unacceptable numbers in the event of war, and secondly, the Government had received assurances from Germany that the limit of the *Luftwaffe*'s expansion would be much lower than the British feared—And this at a time when, in Spain, German and Italian air units were already training for the next war!

It was nevertheless clear to the Cabinet during the spring of 1937 that, with the threat to European peace posed by the activities of Germany and Italy, and the poten-

The de Havilland Tiger Moth was the RAF's most widely-used primary trainer of the war years. Over 7,000 were built throughout the Empire.

tial threat to peace in the Far East created by the expansionist aims of Japan, the whole question of Britain's defence policy was in need of review. Defence thinking so far had been dictated by the prospect that Britain would have to cope with a single enemy—first France, then Germany—and now it looked as though she might find herself faced with three at the same time.

Two more expansion schemes, J and K, were proposed by the Air Ministry in 1937; Scheme K was accepted, but with the proviso that planned fighter strength would be retained at the expense of first-line bomber squadrons and reserves. Progressive re-equipment of Bomber Command with new types of heavy bomber would go ahead, but much more slowly than planned.

The overall picture was a gloomy one. At an Air Staff meeting held in January 1938, the Chief of the Air Staff pointed out that the changes recommended in Scheme K meant that the RAF would have only nine weeks' reserves, and if war came the full potential of

the aircraft industry would not have time to develop. He advocated a possible solution by making cuts in non-operational areas, such as training establishments.

However, it was the Germans themselves who provided the ultimate solution by marching into Austria in March 1938. The Cabinet, hitherto slow to react and still unable to agree on Britain's air defence needs, at last galvanized into action. Scheme K was quietly forgotten and replaced by Scheme L, which was drawn up in conditions of near panic in that same month. This envisaged the rapid expansion of the RAF's strength to 12,000 aircraft over a period of two years, should war make it necessary, but the emphasis was still on fighter production and there was still no provision to increase the strength and efficiency of Bomber Command to the point where it could launch an effective counter-attack on Germany.

It was in September 1938, at the height of the Munich crisis, that the critically weak position of the RAF was made manifest. At that time, only 100 Hurricanes and a mere six Spitfires had as yet reached Fighter Command's operational squadrons, and although 42 Bomber Command squadrons

were mobilized, 30 of them were equipped with light and medium bombers of insufficient range to reach German targets from British bases. Worse still, a critical shortage of spares meant that less than half this force was ready for combat; reserves amounted to only ten per cent, and there was a reserve of only 200 pilots.

It is a matter of history that, if war had come in 1938, the *Luftwaffe*—through lack of suitable aircraft—would not have been in a position to launch a large-scale air offensive against the British Isles. The RAF, on the other hand, would certainly have been able to strike at German targets, and the priorities that would govern a Bomber Command offensive had already been set down, in the autumn of 1937, in thirteen directives, known as Western Air Plans. At the head of the list was WA.1, which envisaged a major strike against the *Luftwaffe*'s airfields; WA.2 and WA.3 involved co-operation between Bomber and Coastal Commands and the Royal Navy in an action against the German fleet; WA.4 called for a bombing offensive against German lines of communication in the event of an enemy advance into France and the Low Countries; WA.5 was the blue-

Sqn	Base	Aircraft	Sqn	Base	Aircraft	Sqn	Base	Aircraft
1	Tangmere	Fury Mk I	53	Farnborough	Hector	149	Mildenhall	Heyford Mk II
2	Hawkinge	Hector	54	Hornchurch	Gauntlet	151	North Weald	Gauntlet
3	Kenley	Gladiator	55	Habbaniya	Vincent	166	Leconfield	Heyford
4	Odiham	Hector	56	North Weald	Gladiator			Mks IA, II, III
5	Risalpur	Wapiti	57	Upper Heyford	Hind	201	Calshot	London Mk I
6	Heliopolis	Hart	58	Driffield	Virginia	202	Kalafrana	Scapa
7	Finningley	Wellesley			Anson			London
8	Aden	Vincent	59	Old Sarum	Hector	203	Basra	Singapore Mk III
9	Scampton	Heyford Mk II	60	Kohat	Hart	204	Mount Batten	London
10	Dishforth	Whitley Mk I	61	Hemswell	Anson	205	Seletar	Singapore Mk III
11	Risalpur	Hart	62	Cranfield	Hind	206	Bircham Newton	Anson
12	Andover	Hind	63	Upwood	Battle	207	Worthy Down	Wellesley
13	Odiham	Hector	64	Martlesham	Demon	208	Heliopolis	Audax
14	Amman	Gordon	65	Hornchurch	Gauntlet	209	Felixstowe	Singapore Mk III
15	Abingdon	Hind	66	Duxford	Gauntlet	210	Gibraltar	Singapore Mk III
16	Old Sarum	Hector	70	Heliopolis	Valentia	211	Grantham	Hind
17	Kenley	Gauntlet	72	Church Fenton	Gladiator Mk I	213	Wittering	Gauntlet
18	Upper Heyford	Hind	73	Debden	Fury Mk I	214	Feltwell	Harrow
19	Duxford	Gauntlet Mk II	74	Hornchurch	Gauntlet	215	Driffield	Harrow
20	Peshawar	Audax	75	Driffield	Anson	216	Heliopolis	Valentia
		Hardy			Virginia	217	Boscombe Down	Anson
21	Lympne	Hind	76	Finningley	Wellesley	218	Upper Heyford	Hind
22	Thorney Island	Vildebeest Mk III	77	Finningley	Audax	220	Bircham Newton	Anson
23	Malta	Demon	78	Dishforth	Heyford	223	Nairobi	Vincent
24	Hendon	(mixed)			Mks II, III	224	Manston	Anson
25	Hawkinge	Fury Mk II	79	Biggin Hill	Gauntlet	226	Usworth	Battle
26	Catterick	Hector	80	Debden	Gauntlet	228	Pembroke Dock	Stranraer
27	Kohat	Wapiti			Gladiator	230	Seletar	Singapore Mk III
28	Ambala	Vincent	82	Cranfield	Hind	233	Leuchars	Anson
		Audax	83	Turnhouse	Hind	240	Calshot	Scapa
29	North Weald	Demon	84	Shaibah	Vincent	269	Bircham Newton	Anson
30	Mosul	Hardy	87	Debden	Gladiator	500	Manston	Hind
31	Karachi	Vincent	88	Waddington	Hind	501	Filton	Wallace
32	Biggin Hill	Gauntlet Mk II	90	Bicester	Hind	502	Aldergrove	Hind
33	Ismailia	Hart	97	Aldergrove	Heyford Mk IA, II	503	Waddington	Hind
34	Bircham Newton	Hind	98	Hucknall	Hind	504	Hucknall	Wallace
35	Worthy Down	Wellesley	99	Mildenhall	Heyford Mk II	600	Hendon	Demon
36	Seletar	Vildebeest Mk III	100	Seletar	Vildebeest Mk III	601	Hendon	Demon
37	Feltwell	Harrow	101	Bicester	Overstrand	602	Abbotsinch	Hind
38	Marham	Hendon Mk II	102	Honington	Heyford Mk III	603	Turnhouse	Hart
39	Risalpur	Hart	103	Usworth	Hind	604	Hendon	Demon
40	Abingdon	Hind	104	Upwood	Hind	605	Castle Bromwich	Hart
41	Catterick	Demon	105	Harwell	Hind	607	Usworth	Hart
42	Thorney Island	Vildebeest	107	Harwell	Hind			Demon
		Mks III, IV	108	Cranfield	Hind	608	Thornaby	Demon
43	Tangmere	Fury	110	Waddington	Hind	609	Yeadon	Hind
44	Waddington	Hind	111	Northolt	Gauntlet	610	Hooton Park	Hart
45	Helwan	Vincent	113	Grantham	Hind			Wallace
46	Digby	Gauntlet Mk I	114	Wyton	Blenheim Mk I	611	Speke	Hind
47	Khartoum	Vincent	115	Marham	Hendon			Tutor
48	Manston	Anson			Harrow	612	Dyce	Hind
49	Scampton	Hind	139	Wyton	Hind	614	Cardiff	Hind
50	Waddington	Hind	142	Andover	Hind			Tutor
51	Driffield	Anson	144	Hemswell	Blenheim Mk I	615	Kenley	Tutor
52	Upwood	Hind	148	Scampton	Heyford Mks II, III			

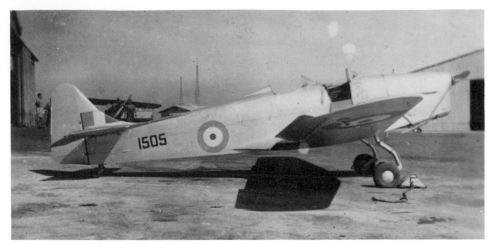

print for an attack on Germany's war industry in the Ruhr, Rhineland and Saar, with particular emphasis on oil installations; WA.6 was a plan for attacking Italian industrial targets; WA.7 was another plan for co-operation with the Navy, the big German base at Wilhelmshaven being the primary target; WA.8 was a scheme for attacking supply depots; WA.9 envisaged an attack on the Kiel Canal; WA.10 was yet another co-operative scheme with the Navy, this time for action against shipping in the Baltic; WA.11 was a plan to drop incendiaries on the big German forests; WA.12 called for attacks on the enemy fleet at sea; and finally, WA.13 was a plan for the precision bombing of enemy administrative centres.

In fact, only WA.5—the scheme to bomb Germany's industries in the Ruhr and elsewhere—was really feasible for a variety of reasons, and even then there was an obstacle in its path. On 21 June 1938, the Prime Minister announced in the House of Commons that only military targets would be attacked by the RAF, and that every possible care would be taken to avoid civilian casualties. Accordingly, Bomber Command switched its target priority to attacks on the

German fleet, an activity that was to be its main preoccupation in the early months of the war, in addition to dropping millions of leaflets.

By March 1939, with Germany busily dismembering Czechoslovakia, it was clear to both the British and French Governments that their policy of appeasement no longer held water. Somewhat belatedly, the British and French General Staffs met to work out a common defensive policy against the Axis powers. The German absorption of Czechoslovakia had been followed rapidly by the Italian invasion of Albania in April 1939, and the probability that Britain and France would be drawn into war if Hitler turned his armed might on Poland now loomed large. It was decided that a British Expeditionary Force (BEF), together with an Air Component and an Advanced Air Striking Force (AASF) of Bomber Command squadrons, should be sent to France; the British squadrons would be given full facilities on French airfields provided that their aircraft would not be used for unrestricted bombing of German targets from these bases. There followed months of disagreement between the British and French on how the RAF

squadrons were to be best employed, and the problems had still not been sorted out when, on 1 September 1939, the German *Wehrmacht* struck into Poland.

On 24 August, the British Government had issued a partial mobilization order. One of the formations most immediately affected by this was No. 1(Bomber) Group, RAF, which—in accordance with the pre-arranged plan—was earmarked to go to France as the first echelon of the AASF. The Group consisted of ten squadrons, all equipped with Fairey Battles and located in pairs at Abingdon, Harwell, Benson, Boscombe Down and Bicester. On receipt of the order to move to France, HQ No. 1 Group would become HQ AASF, while the five station headquarters with their paired squadrons would become Nos 71, 72, 74 75 and 76 Wings. It was proposed that a second echelon of the AASF, comprising the squadrons of No. 2 Group, would follow No. 1 Group's Battles to France; this Group was also organized into five wings—Nos 70, 79, 81, 82 and 83, equipped with Bristol Blenheims—and in August 1939, its squadrons were based on Upper Heyford, Watton, West Raynham, Wyton and Wattisham. No. 70 Wing, comprising Nos 18 and 57 Squadrons—then in the process of re-equipping with Blenheim Mk IVs—was to be assigned to the BEF Air Component in the army co-operation role. Other army co-operation squadrons, with Lysanders, were to follow, as were fighter units with Hurricanes and Gladiators.

On the morning of 2 September 1939, the sky over England's south coast near Shoreham was filled with the roar of engines as 160 Battles of the AASF, led by No. 226 Squadron, headed for their new bases in Champagne. Not many of them would be coming back.

6

Before the Storm

The German invasion of Poland in the early hours of 1 September 1939 by no means caught the Royal Air Force unprepared. General mobilization of the RAF had been ordered on 24 August, and on that day Coastal Command—perhaps the most combat-ready of the three operational commands—had begun regular armed patrols over the North Sea area. These were carried out mainly by Avro Ansons, for the first Hudson squadrons were not yet fully operational and the relatively small number of Sunderlands in service were engaged in fleet co-operation work and longer-range patrols over the Western Approaches. Coastal Command's primary task in the early days of the war was reconnaissance, both visual and photographic, of all shipping in the North Sea; attacking U-boats and positively-identified surface craft was a matter of opportunity, which presented itself infrequently. On 5 September, one such chance was seized by the eager crew of a No. 500 Squadron Anson, who bombed a U-boat in the North Sea and reported it possibly destroyed; however, no enemy submarines were lost on that day. Two more submarines were attacked by other Ansons, also without success, which was just as well: the submarines were British.

Despite inevitable errors of this sort, Coastal Command, under the leadership of Air Marshal Sir Frederick Bowhill, performed its task well during those early weeks of war, its crews operating under what were often extremely hazardous conditions. Yet, for the first year of hostilities, the Command was to suffer from an acute shortage of the right kind of aircraft and effective weaponry. It was to be well into 1941 before both became available on a considerable scale.

Bomber Command's war began with orders to implement Air Plan WA.14, which involved dropping leaflets over enemy territory. In the early hours of 1 September,

Whitleys of No. 51 Squadron at Leconfield and No. 58 Squadron at Linton-on-Ouse were each loaded with over half a million propaganda leaflets and their crews ordered to stand by. The order to take off on the operation, code-named 'Nickel', finally came through from No. 4 Group HQ at 17.00 hours on 3 September, six hours after Britain had declared war on Germany. The flight over enemy territory, which involved a leaflet-drop by three aircraft of No. 51 Squadron over Hamburg and seven of No. 58 Squadron over Bremen and the Ruhr, was quite uneventful, without as much as a searchlight being seen. On the way back, however, three of No. 58 Squadron's aircraft had to make forced landings in French territory because of engine trouble.

Further 'Nickel' operations were carried out during the first two weeks of September, but all were plagued by a mixture of technical problems and bad weather. Nevertheless, although these operations had not the slightest effect on the morale of the German people, they had an undoubted training value as far as Bomber Command was concerned in that they made possible not only a refinement of existing navigational techniques, but also revealed serious shortcomings in the quality of the navigational equipment available to Bomber Command, permitting at least some of these to be rectified before the RAF's strategic offensive began to develop in earnest. The leaflet raids continued on and off until late January 1940, when a spell of exceptionally bad weather brought them to a halt until the third week in February. They were finally abandoned alto-

In the crucial months before the outbreak of World War Two, several home-based fighter squadrons were still equipped with the Gloster Gladiator. The photograph shows an aircraft of No. 72 Squadron in flight; the Squadron began re-equipping with Spitfires in April 1940.

gether, except by aircraft of the Advanced Air Striking Force, on 6 April 1940, by which time Bomber Command had dropped over 65 million leaflets on targets as far afield as Vienna, Prague and Warsaw. It was during these operations, on the night of 1/2 October 1939, that three Whitleys of No. 10 Squadron became the first British aircraft to fly over Berlin during World War Two.

Bomber Command's first operational sorties of the war, however, were carried out by the aircraft of Nos 3 and 5 Groups. In the early afternoon of 3 September, Wellingtons of Nos 37 and 149 Squadrons (No. 3 Group) and Hampdens of 44, 49 and 83 Squadrons (No. 5 Group) flew armed reconnaissances over the North Sea as far as the Heligoland Bight, and shortly afterwards a lone Blenheim of No. 139 Squadron (No. 2 Group) took off from RAF Wyton to carry out a photographic reconnaissance of German naval units in the Schillig Roads, off Wilhelmshaven. The crew of this aircraft (N6215) were Flying Officer A. McPherson, Commander Thompson, RN, and Corporal V. Arrowsmith.

This Blenheim was the first British aircraft to cross the German frontier in World War Two. The photographs it brought back revealed the pocket battleship *Admiral Scheer* at anchor in the Roads, surrounded by several light cruisers and destroyers, and the battle cruisers *Scharnhorst* and *Gneisenau* moored in the Elbe. As a result of this intelligence, two Wattisham-based Blenheim squadrons of No. 2 Group, Nos 107 and 110, were briefed to attack the warships, and five aircraft from each squadron took off in the late afternoon of 4 September. The attack was to be carried out at low level, with the ammunition depot at Marienhof as the secondary target. Under no circumstances were civilian lives to be endangered. Five Blenheims of No. 139 Squadron also took off from Wyton, followed by twelve Hampdens of Nos 49 and 83 Squadrons, but bad weather prevented the latter aircraft from finding the target and they eventually returned to their bases.

The Blenheims, led by Flight Lieutenant K.C. Doran of No. 110 Squadron, attacked in two waves from different directions. The five aircraft of No. 110 Squadron were first in; three of the aircraft bombed the *Admiral Scheer*, but with no result. One Blenheim was shot down. Then the five aircraft of No. 107 Squadron made their attack; four were shot down as they ran-in across the anchorage, and the fifth escaped into the clouds after dropping its bombs on the *Scheer*. One bomb hit the battleship, but failed to explode. The only German sailors killed in the attack died when one of the stricken Blenheims crashed on the stern of the cruiser *Emden*. For his leadership of the raid, Ken Doran was awarded the DFC; but there was no escaping the fact that five out of ten Blenheims had failed to return, and that no damage had been inflicted on the German warships. The tragedy was that several hits had been registered, but in each case the 500-pound bombs had failed to explode.

Later that day, in greatly improved weather conditions, fourteen Wellingtons of Nos 9 and 149 Squadrons set out to attack warships lying off Brunsbüttel in the river Elbe. Three of the No. 9 Squadron aircraft bombed an unidentified warship with no apparent result and one jettisoned its bombs over the harbour, hitting a merchantman; of the No. 149 Squadron aircraft, one claimed to have bombed the target area and the others jettisoned their bombs into the sea. Two of No. 9 Squadron's aircraft failed to return; one was destroyed by anti-aircraft fire and the other was shot down by a Messerschmitt Bf 109 of II/JG77, operating out of Nordholz and flown by Unteroffizier Alfred Held. It was the *Luftwaffe*'s first victory against the RAF.

During the remainder of September, Bomber Command confined its activities to armed reconnaissance flights over the North Sea, much of the squadrons' time being occupied by operational training. Crews spent long, monotonous hours searching for elusive enemy warships that were seldom seen, and only occasionally did they have a chance to drop their bombs in anger. This work was not without its risks: on 29 September, eleven Hampdens of No. 144 Squadron, carrying out an armed reconnaissance of the Heligoland Bight, were surprised by Messerschmitt Bf 110s and five of them were shot down. The Bf 110s formated off the Hampdens' wingtips, boxing the bombers in from a position outside the arc of fire of the Hampdens' defensive weapons, and shot them into the sea one after the other. The deficiencies of Bomber Command's equipment were becoming apparent in a brutal fashion.

Reconnaissance sorties over north Germany were also carried out during this period, mainly by aircraft of the Advanced Air Striking Force but also by the Blenheims of No. 2 Group. Late in November, air reconnaissance revealed a large concentration of enemy warships in the Heligoland Bight, and the Admiralty brought pressure to bear on Bomber Command to attack them before they broke out in strength. On 3 December, 24 Wellingtons of Nos 38, 115 and 149 Squadrons, flying in tight formation through heavy flak, attacked the warships without success. The bombers were intercepted by Messerschmitt Bf 109s and 110s, one of which was damaged, but all the Wellingtons returned safely to base.

This operation seemed to vindicate the theory that a tight bomber formation was sufficient defence against fighter attacks in daylight, and on 14 December twelve Wellingtons of No. 99 Squadron, led by Wing Commander J.F. Griffiths, took off from Newmarket to attack the cruisers *Nürnberg* and *Leipzig*, which had been torpedoed by a British submarine and were limping back damaged to the Jade Estuary. The attack ended in disaster; the bombers were intercepted by the Bf 109s of II/JG77 and five of them were shot down in a matter of minutes, a sixth crashing on landing at Newmarket.

Despite this reverse, another daylight attack on the German Fleet was planned for 18 December. This time, 24 Wellingtons of Nos 9, 37 and 149 Squadrons, led by Wing Commander R. Kellet—veteran of the 3 December raid—set out with orders to patrol the Schillig Roads, Wilhelmshaven and the Jade Estuary and to attack any warships sighted. The bombers were detected by two experimental German 'Freya' radars on Heligoland and Wangerooge, which raised the alarm after some delay. The Wellingtons, now reduced to 22 in number—two having returned to base with engine trouble—detoured round Heligoland and turned in towards Heligoland from the south. Soon afterwards, they were attacked by the Bf 109s of 10/JG26 and JG77, followed by the Bf 110s of ZG76, and in the running fight that ensued twelve of the bombers were shot down. At the subsequent postmortem, it was established that some of the bombers had caught fire very quickly after being hit, and as a result priority was given to the fitting of self-sealing fuel tanks to No. 3 Group's Wellington force. In the meantime, there were to be no further armed reconnaissances of the Heligoland Bight area. There was one other consequence: in the light of the 18 December disaster, Bomber Command's policy underwent a complete revision. From now on, the emphasis would be on the development of night bombing techniques, and both Nos 3 and 5 Groups were ordered to take part in 'Nickel' operations to give their crews night flying experience.

Meanwhile, the Germans had also learned that daylight operations over enemy territory could not be carried out with impunity. On the morning of 16 October, the Junkers 88s of I/KG30 set out from Westerland to attack units of the Royal Navy in the Firth of Forth. The Germans believed that the RAF had only a handful of obsolescent Gloster Gladiators in the area, but they were wrong: the Spitfires of Nos 602 and 603 Squadrons were at Drem and Turnhouse, while the Hurricanes of No. 607 were at Usworth, near Sunderland, also in a position to cover the Firth. Two Ju 88s were shot down, one by Squadron Leader E.E. Stevens of No. 603 Squadron and the other by Flight Lieutenant G. Pinkerton of No. 602. It was Fighter Command's first action of World War Two; although there had been plenty of false alarms in the first weeks of the war—one of which had ended in tragedy when two Spitfires of No. 74 Squadron had shot down a pair of No. 56 Squadron Hurricanes in error—the anticipated German bombing onslaught had not materialized. The Auxiliary Air Force squadrons in the north had several more encounters with the *Luftwaffe* during the weeks that followed the action of 16 October, but it was not until 9 February 1940 that they scored their next success when a Heinkel 111 was brought down near North Berwick by Squadron Leader A.D. Farquhar of No. 602 Squadron, an action that earned him the DFC.

Understandably, it was the squadrons of the Advanced Air Striking Force and the BEF Air Component in France that saw the most action during this long period of relative inactivity. From 9 September, tactical reconnaissance sorties were flown over German territory by the Battles of the AASF, and when the HQ of the Air Component was established on 15 September the French-based Blenheims of Nos 18 and 57 Squadrons made a series of penetration flights into Germany. During their early operations, the Battles experienced only sporadic flak by way of opposition, but it was a different story on 20 September, when three aircraft of No. 88 Squadron set out to patrol the border. They were attacked by Bf 109s over Aachen and two Battles were destroyed; one 109 was shot down by Sergeant F. Letchford, the gunner of Battle K9243, who was officially credited with the first enemy aircraft to be destroyed by the RAF in World War Two. On 30 September, five Battles of No. 150 Squadron were also intercepted by 109s while making a reconnaissance of the Saarbrücken area; four of the Battles were quickly shot down. After that, the AASF's Battles were withdrawn from daylight operations.

craft. The next day, No. 1 Squadron's pilots also caught and destroyed a Heinkel 111.

The pilots of No. 73 Squadron were also active on 3 March, when a Bf 109 was shot down by Flying Officer Kain after a hectic fight between two Hurricanes and six German fighters. Kain's own aircraft was hit repeatedly, and he only just managed to regain French territory before making a forced landing. His 109 was No. 73 Squadron's eleventh victory; the unit had seen more action than No.1, mainly because its base at Rouvres lay on one of the principal routes followed by the German reconnaissance aircraft on their way into France. On 9 March, however, a pilot of No. 1 Squadron, Flying Officer Paul Richey, shot down a Bf 109, and later in the day three of the Squadron's Hurricanes trapped and destroyed a Bf 110 north of Metz. The Squadron had another brush with 109s on 29 March, when three Hurricanes were attacked over Bouzonville by a mixed formation of 109s and 110s. The Hurricanes shot down a 109 and a 110, but one Hurricane pilot was killed while attempting a forced landing.

Meanwhile, operations from the UK had also been hampered by bad weather, although Fighter Command succeeded in accounting for the occasional reconnaissance aircraft that ventured over the North Sea in the early weeks of 1940. Bomber Command was once more carrying out armed reconnaissances over the North Sea area and there were a few attacks on enemy ships and submarines, although only one of these produced a tangible result: on 30 January, a U-boat, already damaged by naval gunfire, was scuttled when a Sunderland of No. 228 Squadron arrived to finish her off. In February, Hudsons of Coastal Command located the German prison ship *Altmark* off Norway and led the Royal Navy's Fourth Destroyer Flotilla to her, culminating in the classic naval action that ended with the release of 299 British merchant seamen whose vessels had been sunk by the pocket battleship *Graf Spee*, herself trapped by British cruisers and scuttled off Montevideo in December 1939.

Apart from reconnaissance, the principal German activity in the winter of 1939–40 involved minelaying off the British coast, carried out by Heinkel 115 floatplanes based on Sylt, Borkum and Norderney. On 12 December 1939, at the request of the Admiralty, Bomber Command began a series of nightly patrols over the enemy bases in an attempt to prevent the minelaying aircraft from taking off. Forty-two sorties were made on Sylt and forty on Borkum before the end of the year, the aircraft occasionally bombing lights seen on the water.

Early in March 1940 there was a sharp increase in air activity on both sides. On the 11th, Bomber Command's armed reconnaissance missions over the German Bight at last met with a real success when a Blenheim of No. 82 Squadron, piloted by Squadron Leader M.V. Dunlap, attacked and sank the submarine U-31, which was surprised on the surface in the Schillig Roads. Five days later, a small force of *Luftwaffe* bombers attacked Scapa Flow; some bombs fell on the island of Hoy and killed a civilian. By way of retaliation, Bomber Command was authorized to carry out its first bombing attack against a land target: the seaplane base of Hörnum on the island of Sylt. The raid, which took place on the night of 19/20 March, was carried out by 30 Whitleys of Nos 10, 51, 77 and 102 Squadrons and twenty Hampdens of Nos 44, 50, 60 and 144 Squadrons. The aircraft flew singly to the target and bombed from levels varying between 1,000 and 10,000 feet, dropping 40 500-pounders, 84 250-pounders and some 1,200 incendiaries. Most of the bombs in fact fell into the sea, and photographs brought back by a reconnaissance aircraft some days later revealed no damage whatsoever. One Whitley failed to return. It was obvious that Bomber Command's navigation and bombing techniques would have to be greatly improved if the Command was to attack targets at night with any hope of success.

The increase in enemy air activity in March 1940 should have been warning enough that a major operation was brewing, and there were plenty of indications that such an operation would involve Scandinavia. On 4 April, a reconnaissance Blenheim reported a large concentration of warships and merchant vessels in the Schillig Roads; six Blenheims of No. 2 Group went out to attack them, but without result. The next morning, another sortie went out, only to return with the news that the ships had gone. Then, on 6 April, further air reconnaissance revealed major units of the German Fleet, including the battle cruisers *Scharnhorst* and *Gneisenau*, assembling in Wilhelmshaven, while bombers returning from 'Nickel' operations over north-west Germany reported sighting convoys of vehicles, headlights full on, heading towards the north German ports.

On 7 April, a squadron of Blenheims on armed reconnaissance over the North Sea sighted an enemy cruiser and four destroyers; the warships were shadowed, and a few minutes later the main body of the German Fleet was located about seventy-six miles NNW of Horns Reef. The Blenheims attacked a cruiser, believed to be either the *Scharnhorst* or the *Gneisenau*, but with no result. A squadron of Wellingtons sent out that afternoon failed to locate the warships, and another attempt the next day was frustrated by bad weather. Aircraft of Coastal Command, however, had more luck: on 8 April, a Sunderland of No. 204 Squadron located and reported the cruiser *Hipper* and four destroyers heading for Trondheim, and the following morning another Sunderland confirmed that the German naval force had entered Trondheimsfjord. At the same time, a third No. 204 Squadron Sunderland, despatched to check on enemy naval activity off Oslo, failed to return. There was no longer any doubt that the invasion of Norway had begun.

7

Flames over Norway

For the first two weeks of the Norwegian campaign, following the rapid destruction of the tiny Norwegian Air Arm, air operations—mainly in support of the Royal Navy—were sustained by aircraft of RAF Bomber and Coastal Commands and also by the Fleet Air Arm. During the first day of the invasion, the Royal Navy suffered heavily from continual air attack, and at dusk Bomber Command was ordered to strike at a concentration of enemy warships off Bergen. The attack was carried out by a squadron of Wellingtons and one of Hampdens. The bomber crews reported two hits on a cruiser; she was the *Königsberg*, and the following day she was sunk by Blackburn Skua dive-bombers of the Fleet Air Arm.

Meanwhile, the *Luftwaffe* had been concentrating its forces on the newly-captured airfields of Stavanger, Vaernes and Oslo/Fornebu. Stavanger, commanding the approaches to the vital ports of Bergen, Trondheim and Narvik, was the most important of the three, and the RAF was authorized to try to put it out of action. Two Bomber Command squadrons, Nos 9 and 115, had already been deployed to Kinloss and Lossiemouth in northern Scotland on 2 April, where they were placed under the operational control of No. 18 Group Coastal Command, and on 11 April six Wellington crews of No. 115 Squadron were briefed to attack Stavanger/Sola airfield. Two Blenheims of No. 254 Squadron, Coastal Command, were detailed to act as fighter cover: these went ahead of the bombers and strafed the airfield as dusk was falling. Three of the Wellingtons attacked the target and reported that a large fire had been started; the other three failed to attack and one of them was shot down. In addition to this, other sorties were flown by the Wellingtons of No. 3 Group against enemy surface forces in Norwegian waters, and the Hampdens of No. 5 Group—also deployed to Scottish bases—stood by all day to attack a concentration of shipping in Kristiansand. The operation was postponed through lack of cloud cover, but, on the night of 11/12 April, 40 Hampdens and Wellingtons attacked enemy shipping en route from Kiel to Oslo. Most of the aircraft failed to find the target, but others claimed a direct hit on an ammunition ship.

The next day, No. 3 Group Wellingtons and No. 5 Group Hampdens flew 92 sorties in search of major German naval units, including the *Scharnhorst, Gneisenau* and *Leipzig*, which were reported to be heading south across the entrance to the Skagerrak, but failed to find them. The Hampdens suffered severely during the day's operations; eight out of a formation of twelve were shot down by enemy fighters. After that, the Hampdens were restricted to night operations, their primary task being minelaying; the first operation of this kind was carried out on the night of 13/14 April, when fifteen Hampdens drawn from various No. 5 Group squadrons laid mines off the Danish coast. Twelve aircraft completed the operation, two aborted and one failed to return.

Stavanger airfield came in for continual attention, and aircraft of Coastal Command—mainly Hudsons—now joined in attacks on this objective. Sunderland flying-boats, with their long range and ability to land on water, were used to ferry key personnel to and from Norway in addition to carrying out their task of general reconnaissance; they were often attacked by enemy fighters, and their crews developed a very successful defensive 'corkscrew' manoeuvre which enabled them to bring all their guns to bear while presenting a fairly elusive target. Since the big flying-boats were vulnerable to attack from below, their pilots chose to fight as close to the sea as possible. On one occasion off Norway, a Sunderland shot down two out of six Ju 88s that attacked it and drove the others off.

On 15 April, Stavanger was attacked by Blenheims of No. 107 Squadron, No. 2 Group, which had been detached from Wattisham to Lossiemouth; six out of twelve aircraft managed to locate the target in heavy rain and snow. On the next night, it was the turn of the Whitleys of No. 4 Group; twelve aircraft of Nos 10 and 102 Squadrons, operating out of Kinloss, set out for Stavan-

ger and seven crews claimed to have attacked it. On the night of 17/18 April, Stavanger was again attacked by Coastal Command Hudsons and by the Wellingtons of Nos 37, 75 and 99 Squadrons; No. 75, the first Commonwealth (New Zealand) squadron in Bomber Command, had formed at RAF Feltwell a fortnight earlier.

Stavanger/Sola was attacked sixteen times by Bomber Command, as well as by aircraft of Coastal Command and the Fleet Air Arm, between 11 and 24 April. One of the best-executed raids was carried out on 17 April by twelve Blenheims of No. 107 Squadron; the bombers attacked in two formations, the first bombing from high level and the second from low level ten seconds later. Two Blenheims failed to return.

Attacking Oslo/Fornebu presented quite a different problem, for the Armstrong Whitworth Whitley was the only Bomber Command aircraft capable of reaching this objective. The first attempt was made on the night of 17/18 April by a lone Whitley of No. 58 Squadron, but the aircraft encountered bad weather and returned to base with its bombs still on board after a flight of nine and a half hours. The next night, however, Oslo/Fornebu was successfully attacked by two Whitleys of No. 58 Squadron; other airfield attacks were carried out against Aalborg, in Denmark, by the Hampdens of No. 83 Squadron.

By 19 April, a British brigade and three battalions of French Chasseurs had been landed at Namsos, and a second British brigade at Andalsnes, the idea being that these forces would advance jointly to capture Trondheim. At 18.00 hours on 24 April, in support of the operations on land, eighteen Gloster Gladiators of No. 263 Squadron began flying off the fleet carrier HMS *Glorious* and landed on the frozen surface of Lake Lesjaskog, about 40 miles from Andalsnes, a site that had been reconnoitred a few days earlier by Wing Commander R.L.R. Atcherley and an advance party airlifted to Norway in a No. 228 Squadron Sunderland. Conditions at Lesjaskog were appalling, and ground crews had to work all night in

During the battle for Norway, Blackburn Skuas of the Fleet Air Arm were used to navigate RAF Gladiators from aircraft carriers to their Norwegian bases. This rare shot shows a Skua on a frozen lake near Narvik, surrounded by French mountain troops.

sub-zero temperatures to refuel and arm the Gladiators; even then, when they checked the aircraft at daybreak they found that the carburettors and control surfaces were frozen solid. Two Gladiators were made airworthy by 05.00, and these took off to patrol the lake. They had not been airborne for long when they sighted a Heinkel 115 reconnaissance floatplane, which was attacked and shot down, but while the two fighters were thus engaged a lone Heinkel 111 flew across the lake and unloaded a stick of bombs, fortunately without causing damage.

The Gladiators flew in support of the ground forces throughout the morning of 26 April, often taking off from the lake while the latter was under air attack. The Squadron suffered its first aircraft loss at about 11.00, when a Gladiator was destroyed on the ground by a low-flying Heinkel; the pilot, Sergeant Forrest, had just stepped out of the aircraft. Nine more Gladiators were destroyed on the ground within the next hour, in exchange for one He 111 shot down by Flight Lieutenant Mills; a second He 111

was destroyed shortly after noon by a section of Gladiators led by Pilot Officer McNamara. There were further successes during the afternoon, when the surviving Gladiators destroyed two more He 111s and damaged a third, but by nightfall only four Gladiators were left, and these were evacuated to Andalsnes.

The small Gladiator force was further depleted on the morning of 27 April, when Pilot Officer Craig-Adams suffered an engine failure during a reconnaissance sortie and had to bale out, and later in the day 263's remaining fuel stocks ran out. On 28 April the ground crews were ordered to destroy the three surviving aircraft, and that evening all Squadron personnel embarked on the cargo vessel *Delius*, arriving at Scapa Flow on 1 May.

On 14 May No. 263 Squadron, now re-equipped with Gladiator Mk IIs, once more sailed for Norway on HMS *Glorious* and the aircraft flew from the carrier to a landing ground near Bardufoss, near Narvik, from where they were to provide air support for the Allied forces' second Norwegian Expedition. It was 21 May before the carrier reached her flying-off station, and the first two sections of Gladiators, each led by a Fleet Air Arm Swordfish, took off from her flight deck in sleet. With the weather deteriorating, one section returned to the car-

rier and landed-on safely; the other, lost in fog and snow, crashed headlong into a mountainside at Soreisa. The Swordfish crew was killed, as was one of the Gladiator pilots, Pilot Officer Richards; the other, Flight Lieutenant Mills, was badly injured.

An advance force of eight Gladiators finally reached Bardufoss on 22 May, and went into action immediately. On that day, No. 263 Squadron suffered its first aircrew loss when Pilot Officer Craig-Adams failed to return; his body was later found in the wreckage of his aircraft, which lay close to that of an He 111. The opinion was that the two had collided in the course of an air combat. The remaining Gladiators flew in the next day, making a total of fourteen airworthy fighters, and soon after their arrival Sergeant Whall shot down an He 111; however, his own aircraft ran out of fuel and he was forced to bale out.

On the morning of 24 May, Bardufoss was attacked by four Bf 110s. Pilot Officer Grant-Ede took off alone to intercept them, and succeeded in driving them off. Later in the day, Grant-Ede, Flying Officer Riley and Flight Lieutenant C.B. Hull shared in the destruction of an He 111, which they forced down near Salanger; the German crew was taken prisoner.

The next day, while on patrol, Grant-Ede encountered a big four-engined Junkers Ju

Preparing to bomb-up a Handley Page Hampden of No. 49 Squadron, RAF Scampton. The Hampden equipped the bulk of the bomber squadrons of No. 5 Group on the outbreak of war; fast and manoeuvrable, it lacked adequate defensive armament and suffered heavily at the hands of German fighters during daylight operations of the North Sea.

90 transport at 15,000 feet north of Harstadt. He closed in, firing two bursts at short range, and the aircraft went down into the sea off Dyroy Island. Grant-Ede caught a second Ju 90 on a subsequent sortie, killing its rear gunner and putting all four of the transports engines out of action with accurate bursts of fire; the aircraft crashed in flames on Finnoen Island, south of Narvik. A third Ju 90 was shot down that evening near Harstadt by Pilot Officer Purdy and Sergeant Kitchener.

Early on 26 May, Flight Lieutenant Williams and Sergeant Milligan destroyed a Ju 88 over Skaanland, and a little later in the day a section of three Gladiators, flown by Flight Lieutenant Hull, Lieutenant Lydekker, RN, and Pilot Officer Falkson was detached to the airstrip at Bødo, close to the front line. Soon after their arrival, Hull attacked an He 111 over Saltefjord and set one of its engines on fire, and immediately afterwards he sighted a Junkers Ju 52 transport flying in formation with another Heinkel. The latter turned away, and Hull shot the Junkers down in flames. Hull turned to intercept two more Heinkels, which eluded him, but then he spotted a pair of Ju 52s heading for the shelter of a cloud-bank. He attacked one of them, using the last of the ammunition in his wing guns and shot it down. Almost at once, he sighted another He 111 below him and dived to attack it; only one of his nose Brownings was working, but he succeeded in damaging the enemy bomber, which departed with smoke trailing from one engine. Hull had barely sufficient fuel to regain Bødo, where he landed at dusk.

At Bardufoss, the remainder of the Squadron had been involved in some heavy fighting, mainly over Harstadt. Pilot Officers Purdy and Bentley had engaged six Dornier 17s and claimed one each, while Pilot Officer Parnall and Flying Officer Riley had each accounted for an He 111, Riley being wounded in the neck and hands during the encounter.

On this day—26 May—the Gladiators were joined at Bardufoss by fifteen Hurricanes of No. 46 Squadron. These aircraft had, in fact, accompanied No. 263 Squadron on its first expedition to Norway aboard HMS Glorious, but had been unable to fly off because their intended landing ground at Skaanland had not been ready. Eighteen Hurricanes were actually flown off the carrier on 26 May, with Skaanland as their destination, but the first three to land nosed over in soft ground and so the rest were diverted to Bardufoss. The Hurricanes scored their first

success on 28 May, when Pilot Officer McGregor destroyed a Ju 88 over Tjelbotn, and later that day a section of Hurricanes surprised two Do 26 seaplanes on the water at Rombaksfjord, disembarking troops, and destroyed both of them.

Meanwhile, on 27 May, Bødo airstrip and the adjacent town had been heavily bombed and strafed by Ju 87 Stukas and Messerschmitt 110s. Hull and Lydekker took off to intercept, each shooting down a Ju 87, but Hull was attacked by a Bf 110 and forced down in the hills, wounded in the head and knee by cannon shell splinters. He was evacuated to England two days later. Lydekker was also wounded in the neck and shoulder, and—unable to land at Bødo because of the prowling Messerschmitts—he flew his aircraft 100 miles to Bardufoss, where he crash-landed.

On 28 May, Flight Lieutenant Williams intercepted an He 111 which was attacking shipping in Ofotfjord and drove it off with both engines streaming smoke. After that, there was a lull lasting about five days, during which time No. 263 Squadron flew about 30 sorties against ground targets, including the German Army HQ at Hundalen.

The end in Norway, however, was fast

Vickers Wellingtons of No. IX Squadron. A superb aircraft, able to withstand a tremendous amount of punishment, the Wellington was nevertheless incapable of surviving daylight operations in a hostile fighter environment. On 18 December 1939, Nos IX, 37 and 149 Squadrons suffered 50 per cent losses while attempting to attack units of the German Fleet at Wilhelmshaven.

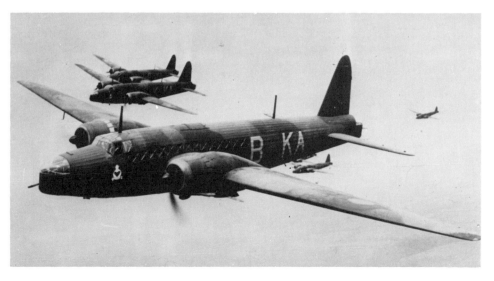

In the early months of the war, Bomber Command carried out numerous 'Nickel' operations, dropping leaflets over enemy territory. Here, a crew member of a No. 102 Squadron Whitley prepares to despatch a bundle through the flare chute.

approaching. On 2 June, General Auchinleck, commanding the Allied Expeditionary Force, gave orders for evacuation and, as soon as its reconnaissance aircraft detected what was happening, the *Luftwaffe* renewed its heavy air attacks on both shipping and ground forces in the area of Narvik, the principal port of embarkation. Narvik was to have been covered by the Hurricanes of No. 46 Squadron but, owing to the unserviceability of Skaanland, the pilots found themselves at a great disadvantage, for Bardufoss was a considerable distance away and the time that could be spent on patrol over Narvik was consequently short.

Nevertheless, the pilots of No. 46 Squadron did what they could, destroying or driving off several enemy aircraft as the evacuation got under way, and so did No. 263 Squadron. Between dawn and dusk on 2 June, the Gladiators flew 55 sorties, destroying four Heinkels and a Ju 87. One of the most magnificent air fights took place in the afternoon, when Pilot Officers Jacobsen and Wilkie encountered two Ju 88s near Narvik and attacked them. Wilkie was hit by accurate return fire from the Junkers—both of which escaped in cloud—and crashed near the Swedish border, but Jacobsen dived into a mixed formation of Junkers and Heinkels and shot down three He 111s in quick succession, despite the fact that his Gladiator had been badly damaged.

The two fighter squadrons flew their last patrols on 7 June, the Gladiators shooting down three more enemy aircraft and the Hurricanes two. Plans had been made to embark the Gladiators on HMS *Glorious*, and following their last patrol they duly set off for the carrier and landed-on safely; the Hurricane pilots, on the other hand, had been ordered to destroy their ten surviving fighters, since none of the aircrew had taken part in deck landing trials. Squadron Leader K.B.B. Cross, the CO of No. 46, immediately asked Group Captain M. Moore, commander of the RAF Component, for permission to fly his Hurricanes on to *Glorious*

so that the aircraft could be saved to fight again. Permission was granted, and, in the words of No. 46 Squadron's diary:

100% volunteered. Tests were carried out with extra weight in the tail of the Hurricanes. At 18.00 hours Flt Lt Jameson, Fg Off Knight and Sgt Taylor took off for HMS Glorious *and landed successfully. At 18.10 and 18.15 hrs Fg Off Mee and Plt Off Drummond returned from a patrol over Narvik during which they engaged four Heinkels. Each pilot claimed to have shot down an enemy aircraft, and Plt Off Drummond attacked and damaged the other two.*
8th June 1940. 00.45 hrs. Sqd Ldr Cross, Flt Lt Stewart, Fg Offs Cowles, Frost and Mee, Plt Off Bunker and Flt Sgt Shackley took off for HMS Glorious.

All the Hurricanes landed safely on the carrier, which then set course for Scapa Flow. But fate was to deal a cruel blow. A few hours later, HMS *Glorious* was trapped by the German battle cruisers *Scharnhorst* and *Gneisenau*, and after being shelled for 90 minutes, she turned over and sank. The ten Gladiator pilots of No. 263 Squadron all

perished in the Arctic waters, and of the Hurricane pilots only two, Squadron Leader Cross and Flight Lieutenant Jameson, survived on a Carley float to be picked up some time later and taken to the Faroe Islands.

So the Norwegian Campaign came to an end, and there was no doubt that the lack of adequate air support had contributed greatly to the failure of the Allied Expeditionary Forces to achieve their objectives. Gallant though the contribution of the two fighter squadrons had been, it had never gained the necessary air superiority, and direct air support from the United Kingdom—involving, as it did, a round trip of between 600 and 800 miles over the sea—had been out of the question. The raids mounted by Bomber and Coastal Commands had amounted to little more than pinpricks. Only a force of modern carrier-borne fighters and bombers might have redressed the situation, and in April 1940 the Fleet Air Arm's equipment was obsolescent and inadequate.

In any case, by mid-May 1940 the events in Norway had been overshadowed by what was taking place elsewhere. In France and the Low Countries, the German armies were at last on the move.

8

Blitzkrieg: The Battle in the West
May - June 1940

Between dawn and dusk on 10 May 1940, in support of German operations on land, *Luftwaffe* bombers struck at 72 Allied airfields in Holland, Belgium and France. Forty-two of these airfields were in northern, eastern and central France but, since the *Luftwaffe*'s main effort was directed against targets in Holland, these escaped with relatively light damage and the fighting strength of the British and French air forces remained relatively unimpaired.

Nevertheless, French GHQ was reluctant to release the Allied bombers against the German convoys that were cramming the roads leading to the Meuse and Sedan. It was not until 11.00 that the necessary orders were issued to Air HQ at Chauny, and even then the bombers were forbidden to attack the enemy in built-up areas—which was precisely where the biggest concentrations of troop-carrying vehicles and armour were to be found. General d'Astier de la Vigeric, commanding the Zone d'Operations Aeriennes Nord, signalled GHQ for further orders that might clarify the position, but Air Marshal Barratt, commanding the British Air Forces in France (BAFF) was not prepared to wait any longer. He telephoned General Georges, C-in-C of the North-Eastern Front, and informed him that he intended to send the Advanced Air Striking Force into action without further delay.

By this time it was noon, and most of the AASF's available squadrons had been at readiness for six hours, with half their aircraft ready for take-off at 30 minutes' notice and the rest at two hours' notice. One of the biggest problems confronting the squadron commanders was that they had no firm target information; the speed of the enemy advance was such that the situation was changing completely from one hour to the next, and reconnaissance aircraft sent out to locate the enemy were falling victim one after the other to the prowling Messerschmitts.

Shortly after mid-day, however, it was learned that strong enemy columns were advancing through Luxembourg, and 32 Battles—one flight each from Nos 12, 103, 105, 142, 150, 218 and 226 Squadrons—were despatched to attack them. The Battles approached the target area in four waves of eight, with five Hurricanes of No. 1 Squadron and three of No. 73 sweeping ahead of them. No enemy fighters were encountered during the attack, but the Battles suffered heavily from the mobile 20 mm Vierling anti-aircraft batteries that accompanied the German columns and thirteen of them were shot down. Almost all the remainder sustained varying degrees of battle damage.

At 15.30, 32 Battles were once again despatched to attack the columns of the German 16th Army in Luxembourg, this time without fighter escort. They were attacked by Messerschmitt 109s and ten Battles were shot down. The loss of 23 aircraft out of 64 was a rate of attrition that the AASF could not support, and no further attack sorties were flown that day.

So far, the AASF's two Blenheim squadrons had not been committed to the battle, but the four Blenheim squadrons of Air Vice-Marshal Blount's BEF Air Component went into action against the armoured spearheads of General von Bock's Army Group B, advancing into Belgium, and took heavy losses. The Air Component's two Gladiator squadrons, Nos 607 and 615, were in action right from the beginning; their primary task was to provide fighter escort for the tactical reconnaissance Lysanders, but the latters' airfields had come under heavy attack and the aircraft dispersed, undertaking only a few sorties on 10 May. Consequently, the Gladiators were free to tackle the enemy bomber formations that came into their sector at Virty-en-Artois, and by 08.00 their pilots had already claimed the destruction of seven aircraft.

Within hours of the German invasion, the Air Component's two Hurricane squadrons, Nos 85 and 87, were reinforced by three more: Nos 3, 79 and 504. A fourth Hurricane unit, No. 501, was also despatched to join Nos 1 and 73 Squadrons of the AASF, engaged in heavy fighting in the area of the Maginot Line. No. 501 scarcely had time to land and refuel at its new base, Bétheniville, when it was ordered to take off to intercept a formation of about 40 He 111s. It was not until the Squadron's first action in France was an hour old that its ground crews caught up with it, arriving from Tangmere in transport aircraft—one of which unfortunately crashed on landing, killing three replacement pilots and injuring six other personnel.

Meanwhile, the home-based squadrons of Bomber Command had gone into action against targets in Holland. In the afternoon of 10 May, nine Blenheims of No. 15 Squadron bombed Waalhaven airport and nine of No. 40 Squadron attacked Ypenburg, also strafing Ju 52 transport aircraft parked along the beaches between the Hague and Noordwijk. Four Blenheims failed to return from this operation. After dark, Waalhaven was attacked again by 36 Wellingtons of No. 3 Group, which caused some damage among the airport buildings; at the same time, in the RAF's first bombing attack on Germany, eight Whitleys of Nos 77 and 102 Squadrons bombed lines of communication on the enemy's route into southern Holland at Geldern, Goch, Aldekerk, Rees and Wesel at the request of Air Marshal Barratt—but no attacks east of the Rhine were as yet authorized, and it was to be another 24 hours before the UK-based squadrons once again flew in support of the Allied armies.

Air operations on 11 May once again emphasized the deficiencies of the Battle as a combat aircraft. During the morning, eight Battles—drawn from Nos 88 and 218 Squadrons—were sent out to make a low-level attack on enemy forces moving up to the Luxembourg border, but it is doubtful whether they ever got as far as the target area. Only one aircraft limped back to base, having been damaged by flak en route, and its crew reported having seen three Battles go down in heavy flak while still over the Ardennes.

The Battles flew no further operations that day, but the Blenheims of No. 114 Squadron received orders to attack the bridges over the Albert Canal, over which the German 16th Panzerkorps was thrusting towards Tongeren. The Blenheims, at Conde Vraux airfield on the north bank of the Aisne, not far from Soissons, were fuelled and bombed up for the operation and the crews briefed; then, without warning, Dornier 17s made a lightning low-level attack on the base and knocked out most of the aircraft in less than a minute. The few surviving Blenheims were pooled with those of No. 139 Squadron, but the attack had robbed the AASF of nearly half its medium-bomber strength.

The French and Belgian Air Forces both tried unsuccessfully to destroy the bridges, and a further attack was made before nightfall by the UK-based Blenheims of Nos 21 and 110 Squadrons. Six aircraft from each squadron attacked from different directions in the face of heavy flak, but as they were approaching the target area they were jumped by enemy fighters and four Blenheims were shot down. All the others suffered damage; none of the bombs hit the target.

Elsewhere, the Lysander squadrons of the Air Component were working hard to supply the BEF with desperately needed tactical reconnaissance, and were taking their first losses from enemy ground fire, although enemy fighters had yet to be encountered. After nightfall, again at the request of Air Marshal Barratt, Bomber Command made its first major attack on the German mainland; the target was road and rail communications around München-Gladbach, and the attack was made by Whitleys of Nos 51, 58, 77 and 102 Squadrons and Hampdens of Nos 44, 49, 50, 61 and 144 Squadrons. Thirty-six aircraft were despatched; five Hampdens came back early and about half the remaining aircraft bombed the target. One Whitley and two Hampdens failed to return, although both Hampden crews, less one pilot, survived and made their way to the Allied lines.

The destruction of the key bridges still remained a high priority task on the morning of 12 May, even though air reconnaissance had now revealed a major threat in the shape of four Panzer divisions, advancing towards Marche and Dinant. The first air attack of 12 May was carried out in the Maastricht-Tongeren axis by nine Blenheims of No. 139 Squadron, which took off from their base at Plivot to bomb a German column advancing towards Tongeren. Seven of the Blenheims were shot down by fighters and flak, and with that the AASF's medium bomber force ceased to exist.

Later on that Whit Sunday morning, five Fairey Battles of No. 12 Squadron, Amifontaine, set out to attack the bridges at Vroenhoven and Veldwezelt. The former was the target of 'A' Flight, led by Flying Officer Norman Thomas, and the latter was to be attacked by 'B' Flight, led by Flying Officer Donald Garland. The five Battles were flown by volunteer crews, for Air Marshal Barratt was aware that the operation was little short of suicidal. The bridges were by this time heavily defended by flak batteries, and the *Luftwaffe* was mounting continual fighter cover over them. To escort the vulnerable bombers, Barratt assigned all the fighters he could spare: the Hurricanes of Nos 1 and 73 Squadrons, AASF, and those of the Air Component's Nos 85 and 87 Squadrons.

No. 1 Squadron was the first to arrive over the bridges, and its eight Hurricanes at once engaged a mass of German fighters, with the Hurricanes of the other two squadrons joining in shortly afterwards. Under cover of the diversion—obtained at a cost of six Hurricanes destroyed—the five Battles slipped through to their objectives. What followed was a massacre. Four of the five Battles were

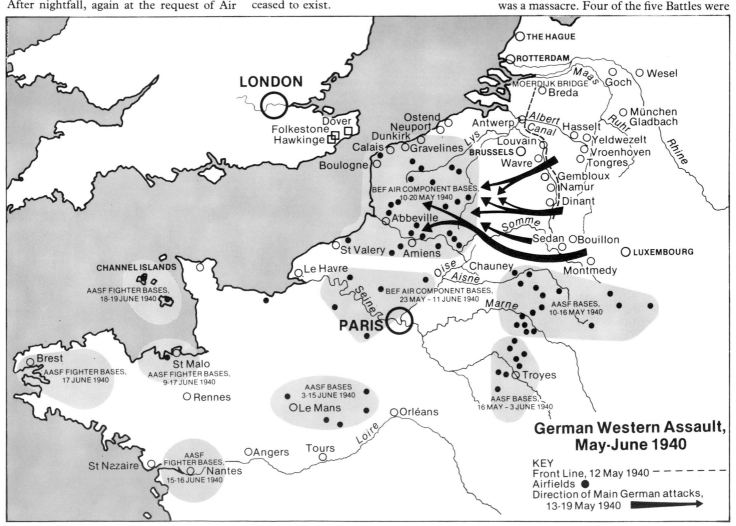

German Western Assault, May-June 1940

KEY
Front Line, 12 May 1940 - - - - -
Airfields ●
Direction of Main German attacks, 13-19 May 1940 ➡

HM King George VI inspecting units of a BEF Air Component in France during the winter of 1939–40. The photographs show Gladiators of No. 615 Squadron, Hurricanes of No. 85 Squadron and Blenheims of No. 57 Squadron.

shot down, and the bridges were undamaged except for the western end of the one at Vroenhoven, into which crashed Garland's stricken Battle. Garland and his observer, Sergeant Tom Gray, were both awarded posthumous Victoria Crosses—the first awarded to the RAF in World War Two—for their gallantry in pressing home the attack against hopeless odds, but it should be mentioned that the third member of Garland's crew, the gunner, LAC Reynolds, received no recognition at all. Not for the last time in the war, the meshes of 'red tape' had strangled what should have been the just reward for self-sacrifice.

Later in the day, 24 Blenheims of Nos 15 and 40 Squadrons mounted an attack on the Meuse bridges that lay within the perimeter of Maastricht. The *Luftwaffe* was waiting; No. 15 Squadron lost six Blenheims and No. 40 Squadron four. Six more Battles were also lost during the afternoon in the course of fifteen sorties against enemy concentrations in the Bouillon sector; this meant that 62 per cent of the Battles despatched on operations

throughout the day had failed to return. Attacks on the German columns in the Maastricht area were maintained after dark by 40 Blenheims of No. 2 Group, operating in twos and threes. In contrast to the day's operations, their losses were negligible.

For the RAF fighter squadrons, 12 May had been a day of hectic action. There were now eight Hurricane squadrons in France and Belgium: Nos 1, 73 and 501 with the AASF, and Nos 3, 79, 85, 87 and 504 with the Air Component. The pilots of No. 501 Squadron, who had destroyed two Bf 110s, two He 111s and two Do 17s on 11 May, now claimed a further seven He 111s, three Do 17s, a Bf 110 and a Ju 88 for the loss of two Hurricanes. Everywhere, the fighter squadrons had faced appalling odds, as the diary of No. 3 Squadron indicates:

Merville, 12 May 1940. Flying Officer Bowyer, Sergeants Ford and Simms (Blue Section) and Flight Lieutenant Carter, Pilot Officer Carey and Pilot Officer Stephens (Green Section) met between fifty and sixty Junkers Ju 87s, Dornier Do 17s and Heinkel He 111Ks between Diest and Louvain. Pilot Officer Carey destroyed one Ju 87 and one He 111; Pilot Officer Stephens destroyed two Ju 87s; Sergeant Simms destroyed two Ju 87s.

Between Diest and St Trond the Squadron also destroyed two Henschel Hs 126s.

The latter, German observation aircraft, were suffering just as badly as their RAF counterparts, the Lysanders; on 13 May, for example, two of No. 4 Squadron's Lysanders were shot down by Messerschmitts, followed by a third on the following day, and the other Lysander units fared little better. The Lysanders were used for bombing as well as Tac-R operations; on 15 May, sixteen Lysanders of No. 16 Squadron were brought up from reserve and sent out to attack an enemy convoy near Cambrai. The army co-operation squadrons, however, soon lost their cohesion in the face of the rapid enemy advance and, although they continued to carry out their task as best they could, their story soon became one of constant retreat, the aircraft pulling back from one airstrip to another. By 18 May, their losses had become unacceptable, and the Lysanders were ordered to begin a progressive withdrawal back to England.

Meanwhile, only one bombing sortie had been carried out by the AASF's depleted Fairey Battle force on 13 May: this was an attack by a small number of No. 226 Squadron aircraft on a factory near Breda in an

57

A Blenheim Mk IV of No. 139 Squadron over the characteristic landscape of northern France in the spring of 1940. No. 139 replaced No. 40 Squadron with the AASF in France, and together with No. 114 Squadron suffered appalling losses during the Blitzkrieg of May 1940.

Hurricanes of No. 87 Squadron, BEF Air Component, being subjected to a dummy gas attack at Merville in November 1939.

attempt to block the road and slow down the advance of the 9th Panzer Division, which was putting heavy pressure on the French 7th Army. By now, it was clear that the main German thrust was aimed at the Sedan sector and, in the early hours of 14 May, General Billotte, commanding the French Army Group One, telephoned Air Marshal Barratt and begged him to commit his remaining Battles—about 70 aircraft in all—against the pontoon bridges which had been thrown up by the Germans north of Sedan. Barratt accordingly authorized the AASF to attack

the pontoons, and the first two sorties, carried out by five Battles of No. 103 Squadron and five of No. 150, were encouraging; all the aircraft returned safely to base.

During the morning, the pontoons were attacked several times by bombers of the *Armée de l'Air*, but by noon the latter had completely exhausted its bomber reserves; from now on, it would be up to the AASF to try to stem the flood of men and material that was pouring across the Meuse. Air Vice-Marshal Playfair had been holding the AASF in reserve for as long as possible, giving his squadrons a few extra hours in which to scrape together their available resources, but, with the French bomber force out of action, he had no alternative but to send the battered remnants into action.

Between 15.00 and 16.00 on 14 May, the

AASF flung every aircraft that could still fly into the attacks on the Meuse bridgeheads. The result was a disaster. No. 12 Squadron lost four aircraft out of five; No. 142 four out of eight; No. 226 three out of six; No. 105 six out of eleven; No. 150 lost all four; No.88 one out of ten; No. 103 three out of eight and No. 218 ten out of eleven. Of eight Blenheims mustered by Nos 114 and 139 Squadrons, only three returned to base. It was the highest loss—56 per cent—in an operation of comparable size ever to be experienced by the RAF, and all that was achieved was the destruction of two pontoon bridges. During the days that followed, six Battle crews, all shot down behind enemy lines, came straggling back to their bases. All the others—102 young men—were either dead or prisoners.

At dusk, the bridges were again attacked by 28 Blenheims of No. 2 Group. Seven aircraft failed to return, including two which crash-landed in French territory.

The disasters of 14 May meant that the AASF had virtually ceased to exist as a fighting force. Moreover, they came at a time when the French General Staff were urgently requesting the transfer of ten more British fighter squadrons to France. Air Chief Marshal Sir Hugh Dowding, the C-in-C Metropolitan Fighter Command, appalled by the losses already suffered by the Hurricane squadrons in France, sought an interview with the Prime Minister, Winston Churchill, on 14 May, the day after he had been ordered to despatch a further 32 Hurricanes to the

continent. He pointed out that to deploy a further 120 fighters, as the French requested, would have no appreciable effect on the course of the battle, but would be little short of suicidal for Britain's own air defences. Dowding made an historic and impassioned plea to the War Cabinet not to fritter away any more of the precious 39 fighter squadrons earmarked for the defence of Britain, supporting his argument by pointing out that, if the present rate of attrition were allowed to continue, there would not be a single Hurricane left in either France or Britain within a fortnight. Dowding had his way and no more fighters were sent to France, a decision that was to have incalculable consequences in the months that lay ahead.

With the AASF shattered, the brunt of the RAF's bombing offensive against the Meuse bridgeheads on 15 May had to be borne by the home-based squadrons of Bomber Command. During the morning, the German forces broke through at Sedan, and at 11.00 twelve Blenheims of No. 2 Group attacked enemy columns in the Dinant area under an umbrella provided by 150 French fighters. Sixteen more Blenheims, escorted by 27 French fighters, made an attack at 15.00 on bridges in the Samoy region and on enemy armour at Monthermé and Mezières; four Blenheims failed to return. What was left of the Battles made only one operational sortie, a small-scale raid on enemy positions in the Sedan bridgehead after dark.

Other bomber command units, together with Coastal Command Hudsons, had been in action against targets in Holland; among these were the oil storage tanks at Rotterdam, which were set on fire before the Germans

could lay their hands on their contents. Rotterdam had surrendered on 14 May following a savage German bombing attack on the Old Town, and this was one of the factors that persuaded the British War Cabinet, early on 15 May, to release Bomber Command for attacks on targets east of the Rhine. That same night, 99 Wellingtons, Whitleys and Hampdens of Nos 3, 4 and 5 Groups were sent out to attack oil plants, steelworks and railway targets in the Ruhr and the area immediately west of the Rhine. Very few of the bombers located the industrial targets, but considerable damage was done to the railway junctions and marshalling yards at Aachen, Roermond, Bocholt, Wesel, München-Gladbach and Cologne. In all, Bomber Command went on to make 27 attacks at night on German targets up to 15 June, but the damage inflicted was insignificant. There was little attempt at co-ordination between squadrons; it was left to individual crews to plan their own methods of attack. Nevertheless, it was the start of what was to become a mighty strategic air offensive against Germany.

By nightfall on 15 May, the RAF in France had lost 86 Battles, 39 Blenheims, nine Lysanders and 71 Hurricanes and Gladiators. On the 16th, two of the Battle squadrons, Nos 105 and 218, with only four aircraft between them, were disbanded. The remainder were pulled back to the Troyes area to be reorganized, and for the next five days only limited operations were carried out, mainly at night. The Blenheims of No. 2 Group, attempting to sustain air support operations on the 17th, suffered terrible losses. On one occasion, No. 82 Squadron lost eleven air-

craft out of twelve while attempting to attack enemy tanks near Gembloux; the Blenheim formation became dislocated in heavy flak and the Messerschmitts pounced on individual aircraft, destroying them one after another.

By 17 May, the Air Component's Hurricane squadrons had destroyed some 65 enemy aircraft for the loss of 22 Hurricanes and fifteen pilots in air combat. The two Gladiator squadrons, which were now partly equipped with Hurricanes, claimed to have destroyed 72 enemy aircraft and damaged 56 since the fighting began, although this claim was clearly greatly exaggerated in the heat of battle. No accurate account of the operations of either squadron exists for this period, as all operations records were destroyed during the subsequent withdrawal and evacuation. After 15 May, at which date No. 615 is thought to have had about twelve serviceable Gladiators and No. 607 six, together with half a dozen Hurricanes each, both units pooled their resources to provide air cover for the retreating BEF. Their final victories in France were scored on the afternoon of 18 May during a battle with Bf 109s and 110s over Arras. Shortly after the Gladiators had returned to Vitry following this engagement, the airfield was heavily attacked and several

59

of the biplanes destroyed. Deprived of fuel, the surviving Gladiators were set on fire by the RAF personnel, who then made their way to Boulogne. From there, on 21 May, they sailed for Dover. On that same day, Air Vice-Marshal Blount ordered the evacuation of the surviving Hurricanes and their pilots to bases in southern England, from where they could continue to provide air cover for the BEF without the continual risk of their airfields being attacked. Two of the squadrons, Nos 32 and 79, were immediately sent to Yorkshire to rest and re-equip, their place being taken by Nos 213 and 242.

Beginning on 20 May, RAF fighter operations over the battlefield were carried out by the Hurricanes and Spitfires of No. 11 Group, flying from their bases in southern England. The task of these aircraft was to provide air cover over the principal northern evacuation ports of Boulogne, Calais and Dunkirk, but in this they were not alone: aircraft of every operational command were active over the French coast during the latter days of May 1940. For example, on 22 May, seven Lysanders of No. 16 Squadron dropped supplies to the besieged garrison at Calais and also bombed enemy positions on the coast, and on the following day, the Squadron attacked gun positions near Boulogne, while Lysanders of No. 2 Squadron dive-bombed enemy concentrations north of Calais. Further supply drops to both Calais and Boulogne were carried out by these two units and also by Nos 16, 26 and 613 Squadrons. By the time these operations came to an end in the first week of June, more than 30 Lysanders had been lost.

On 23 and 24 May, Spitfires and Messerschmitts met in combat for the first time over the French coast. One of the biggest successes was registered by the Spitfires of No. 92 Squadron from Hornchurch, which encountered six Bf 109s between Calais and Dunkirk and claimed the destruction of all of them for the loss of one Spitfire. During a second sortie on 24 May, the Squadron clashed with a formation of over 30 Messerschmitt 110s, and the RAF pilots claimed seventeen destroyed for the loss of three Spitfires. Although these claims—like all air combat claims—were greatly exaggerated, the *Luftwaffe* pilots were left in no doubt that the Spitfire was the most formidable opponent they had faced so far.

Boulogne fell on 25 May, followed by Calais the next day. This left Dunkirk as the only North Sea port still open for the evacuation of Allied troops and, from 26 May, it was the object of very heavy air attack. British fighter cover over Dunkirk was provided by a total of sixteen first-line squad-

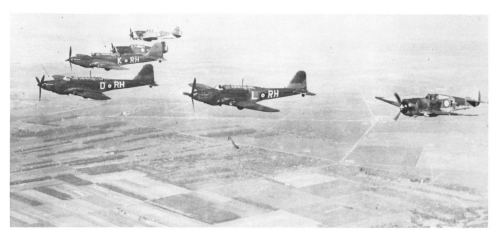

Fairey Battle light bombers of No. 88 Squadron, AASF, in formation with Curtiss Hawk fighters of the Armée de l'Air's *Groupe de Chasse I/5 over France. The Battles, underpowered and under-armed, subsequently suffered appalling casualties in action.*

rons drawn from Air Vice-Marshal Keith Park's No. 11 Fighter Group, spread out over the airfields of Biggin Hill, Manston, Hornchurch, Lympne, Hawkinge and Kenley, to name the principals. This standing cover of sixteen squadrons was frequently rotated, those which suffered a high rate of attrition being sent north for a rest and replaced by fresh units drawn from Nos 12 and 13 Groups, so that, in fact, 32 fighter squadrons in all participated in the nine days of Operation Dynamo, as the Dunkirk evacuation was code-named. No more than sixteen, however, were committed at any one time, for Sir Hugh Dowding was conscious that the real test would soon come in the skies over southern England, and was anxious to preserve what remained of his fighter strength to meet it.

On 27 May, AVM Park's sixteen fighter squadrons carried out 23 patrols over Dunkirk, using 287 available aircraft. During the course of the day, fourteen Spitfires and Hurricanes were lost, but the RAF claimed the destruction of 38 enemy aircraft—including two Bf 109s and three He 111s shot down by the Boulton Paul Defiants of No.

264 Squadron, newcomers to the battle. The Defiant was a single-engined fighter with an armament of four .303 machine-guns in a power-operated turret behind the pilot's cockpit; it bore some resemblance head-on to the Hurricane and was frequently mistaken as such by the *Luftwaffe* pilots during these early encounters, but they soon got the measure of it and the squadrons using it were decimated.

Although Fighter Command emerged from the battles of the 27th as the decided victors, some of the squadrons had suffered heavily. At Hornchurch, for example, No. 54 Squadron ended the day with only six serviceable aircraft; it had to be withdrawn to

A Fairey Battle on a French airfield with Morane 406 fighters. This Battle appears to be a Belgian Air Force machine; Belgium's small force of Battles was almost wiped out in a single attack on the Meuse bridges in May 1940.

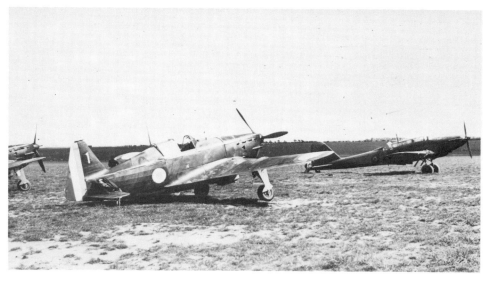

German reconnaissance aircraft suffered heavily during the winter of 1939–40. Photographs show a crashed Dornier Do 17 of Aufklärungsgruppe 123 and a Heinkel 111 of Fernaufklärungsgruppe (long-range recce group) 122.

Arm. By this time, the RAF airfields in southern England were crammed with a remarkable collection of aircraft, all engaged in air operations over Dunkirk; while the Spitfires and Hurricanes of Fighter Command took on the *Luftwaffe* high overhead, Coastal Command's Ansons and Hudsons flew what became known as the 'Sands Patrol', covering the beaches and the rescue craft. Often, these slow machines engaged vastly superior enemy formations, the pilots attacking with little regard for their own safety; on at least two occasions, two or three Hudsons tackled formations of up to 40 Stukas and shot several of the dive-bombers down, while three Ansons of No. 501 Squadron, fitted with machine-guns firing out of the side windows, destroyed two out of nine Bf 109s. That was on 1 June, a day in which Fighter Command carried out eight squadron-strength patrols and lost 31 aircraft. The Command claimed the destruction of 78 enemy machines, a figure that was later reduced to 43, but the actual score was probably much lower.

By 3 June, the RAF squadrons committed to the battle over the beaches and beyond had carried out 171 reconnaissance, 651 bombing and 2,739 fighter sorties. Combat losses for the RAF during the nine-day period were 177 aircraft destroyed or severely damaged, including 106 fighters. By 4 June, Fighter Command had suffered such attrition over Dunkirk that its first-line strength was reduced to 331 Spitfires and Hurricanes, with only 36 fighters in reserve.

On the other side of the coin, the pilots of Fighter Command claimed the destruction of 377 enemy aircraft, a figure that was later officially reduced to 262; the gunners of the Royal Navy claimed 35 more. German records for this period, however, admit a loss of 240 aircraft of all types along the whole Franco-Belgian front, of which 132 were lost in the Dunkirk sector, and this number corresponds roughly with the losses of Fighter Command.

The Dunkirk evacuation was over, but farther south the RAF squadrons of the AASF continued the fight as best they could from French soil. On 3 June, the surviving Battles were withdrawn to new bases in the Le Mans area; ten days later, they made their last major effort when ten aircraft attacked enemy columns along the Seine in the morning of 13 June and 38 more strafed troops on the Marne in the afternoon. Six Battles failed

Catterick in Yorkshire (in No. 13 Group's area) to rest and refit, and its place was taken by No. 41 Squadron. Poor weather hampered air operations during the next three days; on the 28th, No. 11 Group flew eleven squadron patrols in the Dunkirk sector, with 321 individual fighter sorties, and claimed the destruction of 23 enemy aircraft for the loss of thirteen of their own number, while on the following day the Group carried out nine patrols, with formations of between 25 and 44 fighters providing air cover for the BEF. They intercepted three out of five major attacks launched by the *Luftwaffe* that day, but all the German raids were heavily escorted by fighters and the RAF could not succeed in breaking them up. The score at

the end of the day was marginally in the *Luftwaffe*'s favour, with sixteen British fighters shot down against fourteen German aircraft.

Fog and rain persisted on the 30th, but Fighter Command nevertheless carried out nine squadron patrols without making contact with the enemy. On the 31st, however, in the course of eight fighter sweeps in the Dunkirk sector, No. 11 Group destroyed seventeen enemy aircraft. On this day, Wellingtons of No. 3 Group and Blenheims of No. 2 Group also joined in attacks on the enemy in support of the Allied forces in the Dunkirk perimeter, and were joined by the Hudsons and Ansons of RAF Coastal Command, as well as aircraft of the Fleet Air

to return, and on 15 June orders were issued for all serviceable aircraft to be evacuated to England.

Meanwhile, on 10 June, Italy had declared war on Britain and France, and Bomber Command had been authorized to create a special bombing force—known as Haddock Force—to attack targets in Italy from bases near Marseille. Its initial efforts were frustrated by French non-co-operation, but on the night of 11/12 June, 36 Whitleys of No. 4 Group, drawn from Nos 10, 51, 58, 77 and 102 Squadrons, were despatched to bomb Italian targets, having refuelled in the Channel Islands. Twenty-three aircraft aborted because of bad weather; ten claimed attacks on the primary target, the Fiat works in Turin, two more bombed Genoa and one failed to return. On 15/16 June, eight Wellingtons of Nos 99 and 149 Squadrons were despatched from Salon, near Marseille, to bomb the Ansaldo factory in Genoa, but only one aircraft claimed to have made a successful attack; the same two squadrons attacked industrial targets in Genoa and Milan on the following night. It was the last raid by aircraft of Haddock Force; the Wellingtons were flown back to the UK the following day.

On 15 June, the remnants of the AASF's Hurricane squadrons were ordered to cover the final evacuation of British forces from the ports still held by the Allies, and for this purpose two more units—Nos 17 and 242—were deployed to France. Nos 1, 73 and 242 Squadrons were given the task of defending Nantes, Brest and St Nazaire, while Nos 17 and 501—operating from Dinard and later from the Channel Islands—were assigned to St Malo and Cherbourg. Finally, on 18 June, the squadrons were ordered back to the UK, although all but a few of their aircraft had to be left behind because of a shortage of fuel and spares. The last two to leave were Nos 1 and 73, which had been the first to arrive in France in 1939. One of the last RAF victories of the campaign was scored by the pilots of No. 1, who shot down the German bomber responsible for the sinking of the troopship *Lancastria* in the Channel with heavy loss of life. This brought the Squadron's total of 'kills' during the operations in France to 155, the highest score of any RAF unit.

On the day the last Hurricanes left France, the great voice of Winston Churchill rang out to the free world. The Battle of France, he said, was over; the Battle of Britain was about to begin.

The crew of a Hudson of No. 206 Squadron had just landed at Bircham Newton and were walking back to the crew room, depressed and dispirited after the events in France, when they came upon a group of WAAFs, sitting on the grass and listening to Churchill's speech on the radio. They paused to listen too, and one of them, Sergeant Jack Holywell, described the effect it had on them:

Our morale was at rock bottom. Then we listened to those incredible, inspired words—'Let us therefore brace ourselves to our duties, and so bear ourselves that, if the British Empire and its Commonwealth last for a thousand years, men will still say, This was their finest hour'—and our spirits soared. Things suddenly didn't seem so bad. The Germans were not going to set foot on our soil. We were going to win through.

9

The Battle of Britain

Following the collapse in France, while Fighter Command strove to make good the losses it had sustained, Bomber and Coastal Commands both stepped up their offensive operations against enemy targets. In Coastal Command's case, this involved intensifying attacks on enemy shipping, with particular reference to convoys, off the Dutch coast; night attacks were also made by Hudsons on Dutch oil targets and harbour installations.

Meanwhile, on 18 June, Bomber Command had begun phase two of its air offensive against Germany, extending its attacks to aircraft factories and aluminium and oil plants. On the night of 1/2 July, Hampden L4070 of No. 83 Squadron dropped Bomber Command's first operational 2,000-pound semi-armour-piercing bomb over Kiel; after six attempts to bomb warships in the harbour, the bomb finally fell in the town itself because of a defect in the release mechanism. The pilot was Flying Officer G.P. Gibson, who was to win the VC in the historic raid on the Ruhr Dams three years later.

Also in the first week of July, Bomber Command attacked the marshalling yards at Hamm, the Focke-Wulf factory at Bremen and oil refineries at Emmerich. These attacks were generally unsuccessful, for the Command's navigation and bombing techniques still left much to be desired. At the same time, an Air Staff directive ordered that in no circumstances '. . . should night bombing be allowed to degenerate into mere indiscriminate action, which is contrary to the policy of His Majesty's Government.' The gloves were not yet off.

In June, while the Battle of France was still being fought, the *Luftwaffe* had begun to turn its attention to targets in the United Kingdom. From 5 June, small numbers of bombers attacked 'fringe' targets on the east and south-east coasts of England. These attacks lasted for about eight weeks and caused little significant damage; their main purpose was to provide the *Luftwaffe*'s bomber units with operational and navigational experience. On 30 June, Reichsmarschall Hermann Göring, C-in-C *Luftwaffe*, issued a general directive setting out the aims of the planned air assault on Britain. The *Luftwaffe*'s main target was to be the Royal Air Force, with particular reference to its fighter airfields and aircraft factories; as long as Fighter Command remained unbeaten, the *Luftwaffe*'s first priority must be to attack it by day and night at every opportunity, in the air and on the ground, until it was destroyed. Only then would the *Luftwaffe* be free to turn its attention to other targets, such as the Royal Navy's dockyards and operational harbours, as a preliminary to invasion.

Early in July, as a first step towards meeting this objective, Göring authorized his bombers to begin attacks on British convoys in the Channel, the twofold object being to inflict serious losses on British shipping and to bring Fighter Command to combat. The first such attack on a large scale took place on 10 July, when a large formation of enemy bombers and fighters assembled over the Pas de Calais to attack a convoy off Dover. They were detected by radar stations on the south coast, and a plot of their movements built up rapidly on the operations tables of Fighter Command HQ at Stanmore, No. 11 Group at Uxbridge and the Group's various sector stations.

The reaction of Air Vice-Marshal Keith Park, AOC 11 Group, was cautious. Two hundred Spitfires and Hurricanes, about one-third of the RAF's first-line fighter force, were under his command in nineteen squadrons—six of Spitfires and thirteen of Hurricanes—and he had no intention of allowing them to fall into an enemy trap. Six Hurricanes of No. 32 Squadron were already on patrol near the convoy, and to support them Park ordered twenty more fighters—drawn from Nos 11, 56, 64 and 74 Squadrons—into the air. By the time the latter arrived over the convoy No. 32 Squadron's Hurricanes were already in action against over 70 Dorniers and Messerschmitts; in the ensuing battle the Germans lost four aircraft, the RAF three, and one small coaster was sunk. The next day, another convoy was attacked, this time by ten Ju 87s of Fliegerkorps VIII, escorted by twenty Bf 109s. They were intercepted by three Hurricanes of No. 501 Squadron and six Spitfires of No. 609 but, although the convoy escaped unharmed, the Germans shot down two Spitfires and a Hurricane for the loss of one Stuka.

The convoy attacks continued during July and the first week of August. Although there were several big air battles during this phase, usually in the Dover area, the enemy form-

An early casualty of the Battle of Britain, this Heinkel He 111, fitted with balloon cable-cutting gear, was brought down over the south coast in July 1940.

The enemy: Dornier Do 17s in tight defensive formation over Biggin Hill in September 1940.

ations were usually intercepted by only small numbers of British fighters. Nevertheless, during this period the RAF claimed the destruction of 186 enemy aircraft (again, a much exaggerated figure) for the loss of 46 Hurricanes and 32 Spitfires. Six Boulton Paul Defiants of No. 141 Squadron were destroyed in a single encounter with Bf 109s on 19 July, and after that the Defiant played no further part in the daylight phase of the battle. In four weeks of operations, the Germans sent 40,000 tons of shipping to the bottom, and at the end of July the bombers inflicted a severe blow on the Royal Navy when they sank three destroyers off Dover and damaged a fourth in the space of 48 hours.

On 21 July, Göring summoned the commanders of his *Luftflotten* (Air Fleets) and ordered them to work out the final details of how the forthcoming air offensive was to be implemented. However, the plan had still not been finalized when, on 30 July, Hitler personally intervened and ordered Göring to put the *Luftwaffe* in a state of immediate readiness to carry out the attack. The primary aim was to destroy the flying units, ground organization and supply installations of the RAF, as well as the British air armaments industry. The code-name for the offensive was *Adler Angriff*—Eagle Attack.

To meet the expected German air offensive, Fighter Command possessed a tightly-knit defensive network where control and standardization were the keywords—a far cry from the cumbersome organization that

had prevailed at the time of the Munich crisis, two years earlier. The modernization was attributable in no small measure to the energetic leadership of one man: 54-year-old Air Chief Marshal Sir Hugh Dowding. There was no room for compromise in Dowding's character, and his approach to the requirements of Fighter Command was essentially a scientific one. He believed that Britain's air defences should have the benefit of the latest technological developments, and this was reflected in Fighter Command's network of operations rooms, linked with one another by an elaborate system of telephone and teleprinter lines to provide an integrated system of control. This enabled fighter aircraft to be passed rapidly from sector to sector and from Group to Group, wherever they were most needed.

Nowhere was technology more apparent in Britain's air defences than in the use of radar—or radio direction-finding, as it was then known. Developed by Robert Watson-Watt from earlier experiments in thunderstorm detection by the use of radio waves, the use of radar as an integral part of the British air defence system was largely the fruit of Dowding's initiative; he had worked with Watson-Watt during the 1930s and had not been slow to recognize the potential of the new invention. The Germans had made several determined efforts to ferret out Britain's radar secrets before the war with the help of special radio equipment installed in commercial airliners and the airship *Graf Zeppelin*, but reconnaissance of this kind had come to a virtual standstill after the outbreak of war, and the erection of the radar chain

along the south and south-east coasts of England had gone ahead without interference.

Nevertheless, the destruction of the radar stations was recognized as a vital preliminary to the main air offensive against England, the planning for which was completed by 2 August. Luftflotten 2 and 3 were to attack simultaneously, their main task being to bring the British fighters to combat, to destroy the airfields and the coastal radar stations, and to disrupt the RAF's ground organization, principally within the area of No. 11 Group. On the second day, the attacks would be extended to airfields around London, and would continue at maximum effort throughout the third day. In this way, the *Luftwaffe* High Command hoped to weaken the RAF by a few decisive blows, so establishing the air superiority necessary for further operations.

To fulfil this task, Göring had three Luftflotten at his disposal. Luftflotte 2, under General Albert Kesselring, was based in Holland, Belgium and north-east France; Luftflotte 3, under General Hugo Sperrle, in north and north-west France; and Luftflotte 5, under General Hans-Jürgen Stumpff, in Norway and Denmark. Together, their resources amounted to some 3,500 aircraft, of which 2,250 were serviceable. To counter this force, Dowding had 704 serviceable fighters, including 620 Spitfires and Hurricanes.

After some delay caused by unfavourable weather, 'Eagle Day', *Adlertag*, was scheduled for 13 August. On the day before that, however, bomb-carrying Messerschmitt Bf 109s and 110s of Erprobungsgruppe 210, together with Ju 88s of Kampfgeschwader 51 and 54, attacked several radar stations on the south coast, putting the one at Ventnor on the Isle of Wight out of action and damaging three others. While these attacks were in progress, Do 17s of KG2 raided the airfield at Lympne with 100-pound bombs, causing some damage to the hangars, buildings and tarmac; a convoy in the Thames estuary was also bombed by Stukas. In the afternoon, twenty Messerschmitts of Erprobungsgruppe 210 attacked Manston just as the Spitfires of No. 65 Squadron were taking off, their bombs temporarily putting the airfield out of action. Later that afternoon, the German bombers struck at Hawkinge and again at Lympne, causing heavy damage to both airfields. By nightfall on 12 August, Luftflotten 2 and 3 had sent 300 bombers against British targets; the *Luftwaffe* had lost 36 aircraft, the RAF 22, and the main offensive had yet to develop.

At 07.30 on the morning of 13 August the

Air Defences of England and Wales, August 1940

KEY
Group Headquarters ◯
Fighter Command Headquarters △
Sector Airfields △
Group Boundaries
AA Guns ◯

Grangemouth △
Drem △
Turnhouse △

Acklington △

No. 13 GROUP, FIGHTER COMMAND

NEWCASTLE
Usworth △

Catterick △

Leconfield △
Church Fenton △

Kirton-in-Lindsey △

Ringway △
Digby △

WATNALL
Tern Hill △
Wittering △
Coltishall △

No. 12 GROUP, FIGHTER COMMAND

Duxford △
Debden △
Martlesham △

Hornchurch
Hendon
Stanmore
North Weald
Stapleford
Rochford

UXBRIDGE
Northolt
Gravesend
Eastchurch (CCD)
Manston
Detling (CCD)
Hawkinge
Lympne
West Malling
Biggin Hill

No. 11 GROUP, FIGHTER COMMAND

Pembrey △

Filton
Colerne △
Northolt

BOX

Middle Wallop
Boscombe Down
Croydon
Kenley
Westhampnett

No. 10 GROUP, FIGHTER COMMAND

Warmwell

Roborough

Ford (N)
Tangmere
Thorney Island (CCD)
Gosport (CCD)
Lee-on-Solent (N)

Donaldson and the Hurricanes of No. 111 led by Squadron Leader J.M. Thompson, and a fierce air battle developed over the Thames estuary, the Germans losing four bombers. Later that morning, three squadrons of Hurricanes and Spitfires took off to intercept a radar plot off the south coast; the enemy aircraft turned out to be Bf 110s, acting as a diversion to draw off the fighter squadrons while a raid slipped through, but the plot failed to work. The bombers did not attack for another three hours, by which time the RAF fighters were ready for them, and the diversionary Messerschmitts lost five of their number.

At 15.00, 52 Ju 87s of Stuka-Geschwader 77, escorted by the Bf 109s of JG 27, set out to attack RAF airfields near Portland. As they circled over the coast, searching for a gap in the cloud, they were attacked by the Spitfires of No. 609 Squadron while Hurricanes from Exeter and Middle Wallop took on the fighter escort. Five Stukas were shot down. A few minutes later, a force of Ju 88s attacked Southampton harbour and the No. 10 Group sector station of Middle Wallop; their bombs caused only light damage, but severe damage was inflicted by another Ju 88 formation on Andover, a few miles away.

Meanwhile, over Kent, the fighters of No. 11 Group had been heavily engaged against the Stukas of Fliegerkorps VIII, which had carried out heavy attacks on several airfields. The heaviest of all fell on Detling, near Maidstone, which was hit by 86 Ju 87s. The hangars and operations room were wrecked, the station commander killed and twenty British aircraft destroyed. But there were no RAF fighters at Detling; it was a Coastal Command station.

At the close of 'Eagle Day', the *Luftwaffe* bombers had flown 485 sorties, mostly against RAF airfields, and intelligence reports claimed that five of these objectives had been attacked with such success that they could now be regarded as unserviceable. In reality, three airfields had been badly damaged, but not one of them was a fighter base. The *Luftwaffe* had lost 34 bombers and eleven fighters; the RAF's loss was thirteen aircraft and seven pilots.

Luftwaffe squadrons stood ready to launch the onslaught, but H-Hour was postponed because of bad weather. One unit, KG2, failed to receive the signal in time, and its Dorniers set out over the Channel without fighter escort. The 55 Do 17s were tracked by radar and Air Vice-Marshal Park immediately 'scrambled' two squadrons of Hurricanes and a squadron of Spitfires, dividing them between the damaged airfields of Hawkinge and Manston and a convoy in the Thames estuary. He also ordered most of a squadron of Hurricanes to patrol between Arundel and Petworth, leaving behind one section to cover their home base of Tangmere, near Chichester. Lastly, a squadron

of Hurricanes orbiting over Canterbury could be called upon to support any of the other units engaging the enemy. Farther west, the AOC No. 10 Group, Air Vice-Marshal Sir Quintin Brand, scrambled a squadron of Hurricanes to patrol the Dorset coast. Another squadron and a half of Hurricanes were held on immediate readiness at Exeter.

KG2's Dorniers were attacked by the Spitfires of No. 74 Squadron from Hornchurch, led by Squadron Leader A. G. Malan, as they were in the act of bombing Eastchurch airfield. Soon afterwards, the Spitfires were joined by the Hurricanes of No. 151 Squadron under Squadron Leader E. M.

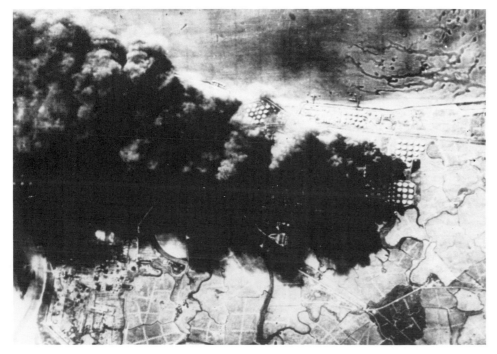

The battle was not Fighter Command's alone. With the opening of the initial phase of the air offensive, Bomber and Coastal Commands had intensified their attacks on barges and other seaborne traffic in enemy-held ports; these operations, which had begun on a small scale on 15 July, were to comprise Bomber Command's main effort until the end of October. However, other attacks continued against enemy aircraft production and oil targets, as well as against communications, and during one of the latter, carried out against the Dortmund-Ems Canal on the night of 12/13 August by five Hampdens of No. 49 Squadron, Flight Lieutenant R.A.B. Learoyd was awarded the Victoria Cross. His was the only aircraft to reach the objective through heavy flak and, although his Hampden was badly damaged, he pressed home his attack at low level and put the canal out of action.

On 14 August, *Luftwaffe* air operations were frustrated by bad weather; only one major raid was carried out by sixteen Bf 110s of Erprobungsgruppe 210, which attacked Manston. On 15 August, however, the weather cleared in mid-morning, and 40 Stukas of Fliegerkorps II, escorted by a similar number of Bf 109s, were despatched to attack the airfields of Lympne and Hawkinge. The raid was intercepted over the coast by the Spitfires of Nos 54 and 501 Squadrons but, while they took on the fighter escort, the Stukas broke through to hit Lympne, putting the airfield out of action for two days. The damage was less severe at Hawkinge, where German bombs destroyed a hangar and a barrack-block.

At the same time, aircraft of Luftflotte 5 from Norway and Denmark launched their first major attack on the north of England. The two units involved, KG 26 and KG 30, had to fly between 400 and 450 miles from their bases at Stavanger and Aalborg to reach their targets on the north-east coast between Tyne and Humber. The first to approach over the North Sea were the 63 Heinkels of KG 26, escorted by 21 Bf 110s of ZG 76, and they were intercepted off the Farne Islands by the twelve Spitfires of No. 72 Squadron from Acklington, in Northumberland. As it turned out, the size of the enemy formation had been greatly underestimated by the radar plot which in fact had been picking up a formation of twenty He 115 seaplanes, sent towards the Firth of Forth as a diversion.

The German plan had been to cross the north-east coast south of the Tyne and then fly south to their objectives, the bomber airfields of Dishforth and Linton-on-Ouse, in Yorkshire. But the enemy had made a

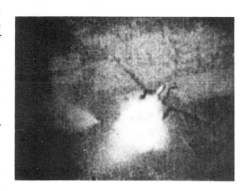

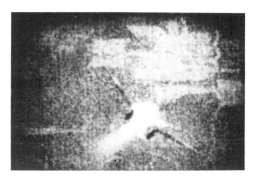

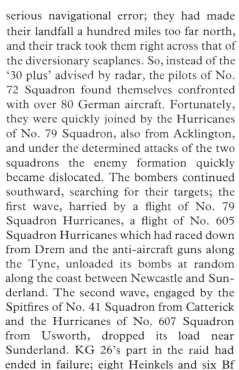

serious navigational error; they had made their landfall a hundred miles too far north, and their track took them right across that of the diversionary seaplanes. So, instead of the '30 plus' advised by radar, the pilots of No. 72 Squadron found themselves confronted with over 80 German aircraft. Fortunately, they were quickly joined by the Hurricanes of No. 79 Squadron, also from Acklington, and under the determined attacks of the two squadrons the enemy formation quickly became dislocated. The bombers continued southward, searching for their targets; the first wave, harried by a flight of No. 79 Squadron Hurricanes, a flight of No. 605 Squadron Hurricanes which had raced down from Drem and the anti-aircraft guns along the Tyne, unloaded its bombs at random along the coast between Newcastle and Sunderland. The second wave, engaged by the Spitfires of No. 41 Squadron from Catterick and the Hurricanes of No. 607 Squadron from Usworth, dropped its load near Sunderland. KG 26's part in the raid had ended in failure; eight Heinkels and six Bf

Death of a Stuka. The Junkers Ju 87, although highly successful in an environment not strongly defended by enemy fighters, suffered very severe losses in the Battle of Britain and was withdrawn.

110s had been shot down for the loss of one RAF fighter.

Meanwhile, the 40 Ju 88s of KG 30 were approaching the Yorkshire coast near Flamborough Head. Radar detected them while they were still a long way out to sea, and Air Vice-Marshal Trafford Leigh-Mallory, commanding No. 12 Group, ordered eighteen Spitfires and Hurricanes of Nos 616 and 73 Squadrons up from Church Fenton to intercept them. Six Ju 88s were shot down, but the majority got through to their target, the No. 4 Group airfield of Driffield, and destroyed four hangars as well as several Whitley bombers.

While the fighters of Nos 12 and 13 Groups were engaging Luftflotte 5 in the north-east, the battle flared up again in the south. At 15.00, a big radar plot began to build up as the Do 17s of KG3 assembled

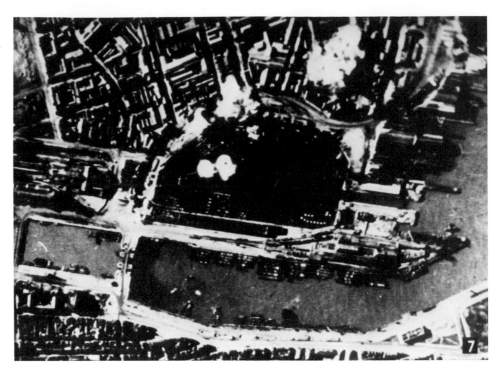

While Fighter Command beat off the *Luftwaffe* in the skies of England, Bomber Command kept up its night offensive against enemy communications, airfields and harbours. Here, bombs burst among invasion barges assembled in Cherbourg Harbour.

over their Belgian airfields and set course over the Channel with a massive fighter escort of Bf 109s. Eleven fighter squadrons—about 130 Spitfires and Hurricanes—were scrambled to intercept, but such was the diversity of the incoming raid plots that the fighters were shuttled backwards and forwards by the sector controllers with no real co-ordination. KG3 got through to bomb the airfields of Eastchurch and Rochester; at the latter field their bombs caused severe damage to the Short aircraft factory, setting back production of the Stirling four-engined heavy bomber—which had entered service with No. 7 Squadron at Leeming on 2 August—by several months. Also, the fighter airfield of Martlesham Heath was heavily damaged by the bomb-carrying Messerschmitts of Erprobungsgruppe 210 and put out of action for 36 hours.

Two hours later, a mixed formation of Ju 87s and 88s of Luftflotte 2, again under heavy escort, took off from their airfields in the Cherbourg area. It took them a long time to assemble, and it was not until 18.00 that the armada of 200 aircraft set course towards the English coast. By that time, the Germans had thrown away their tactical advantage; the time that had elapsed between the major raids enabled Air Vice-Marshals Park and Brand to take adequate counter-measures, and they were able to put up fourteen fighter squadrons to meet the enemy assault. The Spitfires and Hurricanes engaged the bombers over the coast and concentrated on the Stukas, which were soon fighting for their lives; other Spitfires pounced on the Ju 88s of Lehrgeschwader 1, which were trying to slip through to their targets, and inflicted heavy losses on them. Out of fifteen aircraft, II/LG 1, for example, only three managed to reach their objective, the Fleet Air Arm base at Worthy Down; the others jettisoned their bombs and turned for home. The worst hit was IV/LG 1, one of whose flights lost five aircraft out of seven.

The day's fighting was by no means over. At 19.35, fifteen Bf 110s and eight Bf 109s of Erprobungsgruppe 210 set out to attack Kenley, south of London, but they made a navigational error and bombed Croydon by mistake, destroying 40 training aircraft. The Messerschmitts were engaged by the Hurricanes of Nos 32 and 111 Squadrons, and four Bf 110s were shot down. As the rest ran for the Channel, they were intercepted by the

Spitfires of No. 66 Squadron, which destroyed two more Bf 110s and a 109. This brought the day's loss for the *Luftwaffe* to 75 aircraft, mostly bombers and Bf 110s. The RAF's loss was 34.

On 16 August, the *Luftwaffe* struck hard at eight RAF airfields in the south, but half of these were training or Fleet Air Arm establishments. Forty-six training aircraft were destroyed in an attack on the airfield at Harwell, and the radar station at Ventnor on the Isle of Wight was attacked again. On this day, Flight Lieutenant J.B. Nicolson of No. 249 Squadron was patrolling near Southampton when he was attacked by a Bf 110; its cannon shells set his Hurricane on fire and wounded him in the leg and eye, but he remained in the burning cockpit and managed to shoot down his attacker before baling out. Nicolson was awarded the Victoria Cross, the only one to be won by a Fighter Command pilot during World War Two.

In the afternoon of 16 August, bad weather frustrated the *Luftwaffe*'s attempts to make further attacks on RAF airfields. Nevertheless, air combats that day, mostly in the morning, cost the *Luftwaffe* 45 aircraft and the RAF 22. Poor weather once again prevailed on 17 August, bringing a brief respite for the hard-pressed RAF fighter squadrons, but on the 18th, the *Luftwaffe* launched a series of heavy attacks on the important sector stations of Kenley and Biggin Hill. Kenley was badly hit, and its operations room put out of action. In the afternoon, a strong force of enemy bombers attacked the airfields at Ford, Gosport and Thorney

Island; the aircraft involved were the Stukas of Fliegerkorps VIII, and they ventured over the coast with inadequate fighter escort. They were engaged by the Hurricanes of No. 43 and the Spitfires of No. 152 Squadrons, which destroyed 30 of their number. The dive-bomber casualties accounted for nearly half the *Luftwaffe*'s loss of 71 aircraft that day, and it was the last time that the Stuka was used in operations over England. The RAF lost 27 fighters.

The weather improved steadily during the last week of August, and the *Luftwaffe* stepped up its airfield attacks, striking hard at the fighter bases that formed a defensive shield around London. By mid-week, every squadron in No. 11 Group was suffering seriously from exhaustion; the strength of some units was halved, and they had to be withdrawn from the battle and sent north into No. 13 Group's area for a rest. On 30 August, Biggin Hill was completely wrecked, and it was attacked again the following afternoon, together with Hornchurch. On this day, the *Luftwaffe* lost 39 aircraft against the RAF's 32.

The situation for Fighter Command was now very serious indeed. In the space of a fortnight, between 24 August and 6 September, the RAF lost 103 pilots killed and 128 badly wounded; this represented almost a quarter of the available trained fighter pilots, and replacements were not arriving fast enough to make good the losses. Also, the Germans were increasing the strength of their fighter escorts; on occasions, the ratio was four fighters to every bomber. By 3

The fighter aircraft that won the Battle: the Spitfire and Hurricane. These aircraft in fact belong to the Battle of Britain Memorial Flight and are a Spitfire Mk VB repainted to represent an aircraft of No. 92 Squadron flown by Wing Commander Robert Stanford Tuck, and a Hurricane Mk II repainted as a No. 242 Squadron aircraft flown by Squadron Leader Douglas Bader.

The weapon that won the battle against the night bomber: early AI (Airborne Interception) radar equipment installed in a Beaufighter. From November 1940, the Beaufighter gradually took over the night defence role from the Blenheim and Defiant and as a result *Luftwaffe* night bomber losses began to mount.

September, for the first time in the battle, *Luftwaffe* crews were returning to base and reporting that they had encountered no opposition; it was beginning to look as though the final collapse of Fighter Command was imminent.

However, circumstances were on the point of bringing about a dramatic and unexpected change in enemy policy. On the night of 24 August, a few bombers of KG1 had made a navigational error and dropped some bombs on London, and on the following night Bomber Command had retaliated by attacking industrial targets in Berlin. Eighty-one aircraft of Nos 3, 4 and 5 Groups had been despatched, and 29 crews claimed to have carried out successful attacks; five aircraft had failed to return. Now, early in September, Hitler pressed Göring to switch the main *Lüftwaffe* bombing offensive to London, away from the airfields. This plan was bitterly opposed by Sperrle, who believed—quite rightly—that if the airfield attacks continued for another few days the *Lufwaffe* would have air superiority over south-east England. Kesselring, on the other hand, thought that the RAF was about to evacuate its fighters from the hard-hit No. 11 Group airfields and withdraw them to safer bases to the north and west of London, out of range of the German fighter escorts; his belief was that an all-out assault on London would force the RAF to throw its last fighter reserves into the defence of the capital. Göring was persuaded by Kesselring's argument, and attacks on London were authorized. The first took place on 5 September, when 70 bombers attacked the London docks; then, beginning at 15.00 on 7 September and lasting until dawn the next day, 625 bombers pounded the docks area almost non-stop.

By this time, Dowding's 'first reserve'—the squadrons of No. 12 Group, normally based on airfields to the north of London—had been committed to the battle, and the *Luftwaffe* crews once more found themselves engaged in bitter air combat as Fighter Command showed that it was still very much in evidence. For the RAF, the sternest test came on 15 September, when the *Luftwaffe* threw 200 bombers against London in two waves; when the first wave attacked, the RAF had no more fighter squadrons in reserve and, if the second wave had come immediately, its bombers would have caught the Spitfires and Hurricanes on the ground. But it was two hours before the second wave attacked, and by that time the fighter squadrons were once more ready for it. A total of 148 bombers got through to bomb London, but 56 were shot down and many more staggered back to their bases with severe damage. To the *Luftwaffe* crews, 15 September 1940 was remembered as 'Black Sunday'.

Towards the end of September, dense cloud cover stretched over much of the British Isles, and the *Luftwaffe's* tactics underwent a complete change. The large daylight formations were gone; instead, the *Luftwaffe* began to send over small groups of aircraft, including bomb-carrying Messerschmitts. The *Luftwaffe* had clearly failed to achieve its objective during daylight, but from the beginning of November it began to step up its night attacks on London and other targets. The Battle of Britain had ended in victory for Fighter Command, but the ordeal of Britain's cities was only just beginning.

On the night of 14/15 November, 450 German bombers wiped out the heart of Coventry, the main bomber stream following a pathfinder unit, KG100, that navigated its way to the target along a radio beam. Night after night, during the winter of 1940–41, the pattern was to be repeated as the night bombers pounded London, the Midlands, Lancashire, Merseyside, South Wales, Tyneside, Plymouth, Exeter, Southampton, Bristol and many other targets. The RAF was virtually powerless to stem the onslaught; Fighter Command's night-fighter defences were primitive, and the majority of the early successes were achieved by pilots flying Spitfires and Hurricanes, which were day fighters. One pilot, Flight Lieutenant R. P. Stevens of No. 253 Squadron, flying a Hurricane, destroyed fourteen enemy bombers at night during 1941.

The mainstay of the RAF's embryo night-fighter force in the summer of 1940 was the Blenheim Mk IF, which was completely unsuited to night operations and which was slower than some of the bombers it was supposed to catch. Then, in August, two squadrons of Boulton Paul Defiants—Nos 141 and 264—which had just been withdrawn from the day battle following severe losses, were assigned to the night-fighter role. Both squadrons saw their first real night actions during the second week of September, when the *Luftwaffe* stepped up its night attacks on London; on the night of the 15/16 two Heinkels were shot down by Defiants of No. 141 Squadron's 'B' Flight, operating from Biggin Hill. Early in November, No. 141 moved to Gravesend to guard the approaches to London, while No. 264 operated north of the Thames. Other Defiant squadrons joined the night-fighter force in the weeks that followed; the first was No. 307 (Polish) Squadron, which was formed at Jurby in the Isle of Man and later moved to Squires Gate to defend Merseyside early in 1941. By the spring of that year, five more Defiant squadrons had been formed: Nos 85, 96, 151, 255 and 256. All were active during the *Luftwaffe's* night offensive against the major British cities in the early months of 1941, but claims were few.

The RAF's night-fighter force began to score its first real successes with the operational debut, in September 1940, of the Bristol Beaufighter. Fast and heavy, this twin-engined aircraft had a formidable armament of four cannon and six machine-guns; moreover, it was big enough to carry the early, bulky Mk IV airborne interception radar without sacrificing other weight in fuel and fire-power. The first squadrons to receive Beaufighters were No. 25 at North Weald, No. 29 at Digby, No. 219 at Catterick and No. 604 at Middle Wallop, and a fifth squadron, No. 600 at Hornchurch, also began to re-equip on 8 September. No. 219 Squadron scored the first confirmed Beaufighter 'kill' on the night of 25 October, when Sergeant Hodgkinson and Sergeant Benn (observer) destroyed a Do 17. The first kill following a radar interception was scored on 19/20 November by a No. 604 Squadron crew, Flight Lieutenant John Cunningham and Sergeant J. Phillipson, who shot down a Ju 88.

January 1941 saw the establishment of a network of GCI—Ground Controlled Interception—stations along the south and east coasts of England. From these stations, controllers were able to steer the night-fighters to within a mile or so of their target, at which point the airborne radar took over to complete the interception. On 15/16 April, 1941, Cunningham destroyed three enemy bombers in a single night with the aid of GCI.

On the night of 19/20 April, the *Luftwaffe* launched a massive attack on London. Over 700 bombers were despatched, of which 24 were shot down by night-fighters. This raid marked the end of the almost non-stop air offensive against Britain. When that offensive had begun, 44 *Luftwaffe* bomber groups had occupied bases stretching from Cherbourg to Norway; by 21 May 1941, only four were left. The rest had been withdrawn to the east, in readiness for Hitler's assault on Russia. A month later, Britain no longer stood alone.

10

The Middle East
1940~41

The task that confronted Air Chief Marshal Sir Arthur Longmore, the AOC-in-C RAF Middle East, on Italy's declaration of war in June 1940 was a formidable one. His responsibility encompassed all Royal Air Force units in Egypt, the Sudan, Palestine, Trans-Jordan, East Africa, Aden and Somaliland, Iraq and its adjacent territories, Cyprus, Turkey, the Balkans, the Mediterranean, the Red Sea and the Persian Gulf—an area of some four and a half million square miles. To defend that area, he had at his disposal just 29 squadrons, totalling about 300 first-line aircraft, about half of which were based in Egypt. Compounding his problems was the fact that although he had substantial numbers of reserves, reinforcements would not be readily forthcoming to make good future combat attrition.

Of the fourteen bomber squadrons, nine were equipped with Bristol Blenheims, which compared favourably with anything the Italians possessed but which were severely limited in range; four more were equipped with Vickers Wellesleys, which had a superlative range performance but which were obsolescent in every other respect. The seven fighter squadrons were equipped with Gloster Gladiators, with the exception of No. 203 at Khormaksar, which had Blenheim Mk IVFs; the army co-operation units used a miscellany of machines, ranging from elderly Hawker Hardys, Harts and Audaxes to Westland Lysanders; and there was a solitary Sunderland squadron, No. 203 at Alexandria, to keep a watch over the eastern Mediterranean.

Against this, the Italians had about 480 combat aircraft in Libya, Italian East Africa and the Dodecanese, and they could easily call upon reinforcements from the home-based squadrons of the *Regia Aeronautica*. The bulk of the Italian squadrons was concentrated in Libya, and it was from this direction that the first threat began to develop when the Italian armies under Marshal Graziani began to build up in eastern Cyrenaica for an offensive into Egypt.

The air defences in the Western Desert were the responsibility of No. 202 Group,

under the command of Air Commodore Raymond Collishaw (who, it will be recalled, commanded No. 47 Squadron in south Russia in 1919). On 10 June, immediately on the Italian declaration of war, Collishaw moved his squadrons up to forward bases and ordered them into action at dawn the next day, their main objectives being the enemy air base at El Adem and the harbour of Tobruk.

During this early phase, bombing operations were carried out mainly by the Blenheims of No. 55 Squadron, with the Blenheims of No. 113 Squadron ranging farther afield on reconnaissance tasks; however, the Vickers Valentia and Bristol Bombay transports of No. 216 Squadron from Heliopolis also played their part, attacking Tobruk with small bomb loads on several occasions by night.

Fighter cover over the British and Commonwealth ground forces that advanced to the Libyan frontier to meet the expected Italian offensive was undertaken by the Gladiators of No. 33 Squadron, operating from Mersa Matruh and a variety of forward strips, the other two Gladiator squadrons in Egypt—Nos 80 and 112—being held back for the defence of Cairo. The first recorded

air combat took place on 14 June, when seven Gladiators of No. 33 Squadron attacked a Caproni Ca 310 escorted by three Fiat CR.32s; the Caproni and one of the Fiats was shot down. Shortly afterwards, the Squadron was joined at Mersa Matruh by a solitary Hurricane, the only one in the Middle East, and this destroyed its first Italian aircraft, a G.50 Falco, on 19 June.

No. 33 Squadron continued to register successes during the remainder of the month, its own losses being extremely light. On 4 July, No. 112 Squadron was also moved up to Mersa Matruh and, at the end of that month, No. 33 was pulled back to Helwan, where it later handed over its Gladiators to No. 3 Squadron, Royal Australian Air Force. In six weeks of combat, No. 33 had shot down 38 enemy aircraft and destroyed twenty more on the ground.

No. 80 Squadron now moved up to join No. 112 at the front, where one of its primary duties was to escort the Tac-R Lysanders of No. 208 Squadron, recently arrived from

The Gloster Gladiator equipped most RAF fighter units in the Middle East until well after the start of World War Two. The example shown here is a No. 33 Squadron aircraft at Helwan, Egypt, *circa* June 1940.

The Fiat CR.42 was the RAF's principal early opponent in the Middle East War. This example was destroyed during the British offensive in Cyrenaica at the end of 1940.

Palestine. Until September, when detachments of No. 6 and No. 3 (RAAF) Squadrons were also sent forward, No. 208 was the only army co-operation unit in the Western Desert, and as a result its work-load was high. Losses were heavy, and due as much to accidents as to enemy action.

During these early weeks, Collishaw, on Sir Arthur Longmore's orders, had been carefully husbanding his resources; bombing and reconnaissance sorties were undertaken only when absolutely necessary, at the request of the army or navy, and offensive operations were restricted to fighter patrols, attacks on airfields and lines of communication. Then, on 9 September, reconnaissance revealed that the Italian offensive was about to begin, and No. 202 Group's Blenheims once again mounted a series of attacks on Tobruk harbour and selected enemy airfields. As the enemy columns advanced along the coast road, they were subjected to increasingly heavy air attack and, as the Italian lines of communication lengthened, the effects of this became apparent. A few miles east of Sidi Barrani, long before they were within sight of the main British defences at Mersa Matruh, the enemy columns had ground to a standstill.

Until he had built up his supplies in the forward area, Marshal Graziani could not hope to mount a successful assault into Egypt, and the British land forces commander, General O'Connor, used the delay to good effect by laying plans to strike first. He now had an armoured brigade at his disposal, and although five of Longmore's air squadrons had been sent to Greece, three fresh units had arrived from England, to redress the balance. They were Nos 37 and 38, with Wellingtons, and No. 73 with Hurricanes.

The arrival of the first pair brought the number of Wellington squadrons in Egypt up to three; No. 70 Squadron had begun operations in the area from Kabrit in mid-September, having exchanged its Valentias for Wellington Mk ICs. Longmore also ordered three more Blenheim squadrons—Nos 11 and 39 from Aden and No. 45 from the Sudan—to move to bases in Egypt, while the newly-formed No. 274 Squadron brought its Hurricanes up from the Cairo area to Sidi Haneish, nearer the front. By 8 December, therefore, Longmore had sixteen squadrons in Egypt, many of them equipped with aircraft of far better performance than those of the *Regia Aeronautica*, to support General O'Connor's counter-offensive.

In late November and early December, Longmore's Blenheims and Wellingtons stepped up their attacks on targets deep behind the enemy lines; Blenheims and Lysanders, under heavy fighter escort, also provided complete coverage of the Italian positions south of Sidi Barrani. These sorties were often flown in the teeth of fierce opposition, mainly from Fiat CR.42s, but the RAF Gladiators and Hurricanes established a definite measure of air superiority; on 20 November, for example, nine Hurricanes and six Gladiators fought an hour-long battle with 60 CR.42s and destroyed seven of them for no loss.

The counter-offensive was launched on 9 December, and the squadrons of No. 202 Group now switched their attacks to troop concentrations and transport columns. Relentless pressure was maintained, and by 16 December the last of the Italian forces had been driven over the Egyptian border. With the enemy in full flight, chased by the tanks of 7th Armoured Division, Longmore's

bombers once again pounded Italian airfields and supply dumps, while his fighters provided constant air cover for the ground forces and also for warships of the Royal Navy that were shelling troop concentrations north of the Bardia-Tobruk road.

By this time, events were happening which would soon change the whole spectrum of operations in the Middle East; the first *Luftwaffe* squadrons had arrived in Sicily and were in action against Malta and fleet units in the Mediterranean, and it was clear that the Germans were on the verge of intervening in both the Balkans and North Africa. All this would mean an extra drain on Longmore's resources, and it was vital that Generals Wavell and O'Connor achieved their main target, the capture of Tobruk, with the minimum delay. The attack began on 21 January, and was accompanied by the biggest air effort so far; for example, No. 45 Squadron, with eight serviceable Blenheims, carried out 32 sorties on that day alone. Tobruk fell within 48 hours and the pursuit rolled on; there seemed to be no stopping O'Connor's 13th Corps. In front of the Commonwealth forces now lay the Jebel Akhdar, the fertile crescent of hills rolling down to the coastline of Cyrenaica, and, beyond it, the city of Benghazi. Along the coast road, which wound between the Jebel Akhdar and the sea to the Gulf of Sirte, the broken remnants of Graziani's Tenth Army, harrassed all the while by No. 202 Group, were struggling to escape into Tripolitania.

It was now that O'Connor took his greatest

There was no room for luxury in the desert. The photograph depicts aircrew kitting themselves out at an improvised clothing rack; note the 'Baghdad Bowlers' adorning the operations board on the right.

Wear and tear to engine components, caused by ingestion of sand particles, was a continual problem in the desert—and one well illustrated by this shot of a P–40 Kittyhawk of No. 112 Squadron taxying out for take-off.

gamble. Although his tanks and trucks were almost falling apart, he hurled them across the appalling, uncharted desert tracks south of Jebel Akhdar in a bid to reach the coast road ahead of the enemy and bar their retreat. On 5 February, the British spearhead made it with half an hour to spare. For the next two days, a fierce battle raged around Beda Fomm as the Italians tried desperately to break through. They failed, and when the two days were ended O'Connor had achieved complete victory. The Italian Tenth Army had been utterly destroyed, and in ten weeks the British had taken 130,000 prisoners, 400 tanks, 1,290 guns and 1,000 trucks. It had been a campaign of classic brilliance; the tragedy was that the overwhelming successes gained by O'Connor were soon to be thrown away.

Graziani's attempted invasion of Egypt had by no means represented the only serious threat to British control of the Suez Canal and the Red Sea. In East Africa, 19,000 troops in the Sudan, Kenya and British Somaliland had been faced by 200,000 enemy troops in Eritrea, Italian Somaliland and Abyssinia in the summer of 1940; the Italians also had a substantial numerical superiority in aircraft. The Dominion forces in British Somaliland, numbering only 1,500 men, had soon been forced to retreat to Berbera, from which port they were evacuated to Aden in August; the retreat and evacuation took place with the support of the RAF squadrons in Aden, the Blenheims and Wellesleys operating from forward bases in Somaliland and the Sudan as well as from their permanent homes across the Gulf. Here, the Wellesley's long-range performance proved invaluable; on 18 August 1940, while the evacuation from Berbera was under way, the Wellesleys of No. 223 Squadron struck at Addis Ababa airfield, bringing back valuable reconnaissance photographs as well as bombing their objective. The evacuation itself was covered by the Blenheim Mk IVF fighters of No. 203 Squadron from Khormaksar.

Italian attacks on the frontiers of Kenya

Tobruk was heavily defended by anti-aircraft guns during the siege, making it a hazardous target for the *Luftwaffe*. On the order 'Tobruk Engage', every anti-aircraft gun would open up to provide a curtain of fire over the harbour and its environs.

and the Sudan were opposed by three and a half RAF squadrons that comprised No. 203 Group under Air Commodore L.H. Slatter; these operated a miscellany of aircraft, including Wellesleys, Blenheims, Vincents and Gladiators, and, in addition to providing close support for Dominion forces, they struck incessantly at enemy airfields, supply dumps and lines of communication. Between June and the end of October, they lost 33 aircraft, including eight Wellesleys and two Vincents of No. 47 Squadron which were destroyed in an air attack on Gedaref on 16 October.

Much of the RAF's bombing effort was concentrated on attacks on the Eritrean ports of Assab and Massawa; the latter was hit hard on the first day of the war, when the Wellesleys of No. 14 Squadron from Port Sudan sent 780 tons of fuel up in smoke. Actions such as this, together with effective patrolling over convoys using the Red Sea, completely thwarted Italian plans to close that waterway; between June and the end of December, only one ship was sunk by enemy air attack and one damaged, out of 54 convoys that passed through the Red Sea. By the end of the year, it was plain that Italian aspirations in East Africa had met with total failure.

On 28 October 1940, while Graziani was still preparing to invade Egypt, Italian forces attacked Greece. Under his terms of responsibility, Sir Arthur Longmore was obliged to contribute to the defence of the Balkan countries in the event of such an invasion and, although the Greek Government declined an offer of British ground forces for fear of provoking a German reaction, the British offer of air support was eagerly accepted. The first squadron to be despatched was No. 30, with a mixture of Blenheim bombers and fighters; this was given the task of defending Athens, and by the end of November 1940, it had been joined by two more Blenheim squadrons, Nos 84 and 211, and a squadron of Gladiators, No. 80. In December, No. 112 Squadron's Gladiators also arrived in Greece and were deployed at Larissa in the central region; No.80 Squadron went to Paramythia in the north-west to support the Greek army on the Albanian frontier, while the Blenheim squadrons were deployed at Eleusis and Menidi, close to Athens. From time to time, during the moon periods, the bomber force was assisted by small numbers of Wellingtons, detached from squadrons in the Canal Zone.

Air operations over Greece were severely hampered by bad weather; nevertheless, by the end of the year the Gladiator pilots of No. 80 Squadron had claimed the destruction of 40 enemy aircraft for the loss of six of their own, and although the claim was probably exaggerated there is no doubt that the Gladiators succeeded in establishing a measure of air superiority during those winter months. On 9 February 1941, fourteen Gladiators of No. 80 Squadron, led by Flight Lieutenant M.T. St J. Pattle, encountered a formation of 40 Fiat G. 50 fighters and shot down four of them without loss. Pattle, a South African, was credited with the destruction of 30 enemy aircraft—and possibly more—during operations in Egypt and Greece; he was shot down and killed on 20 April 1941 while commanding No. 33 Squadron.

By the end of February 1941, all three

RAF operations against Vichy French Syria were opposed by a variety of modern fighter types. Pictured here are Morane MS 406s at Rayak, Lebanon, en route to a Syrian base.

A Blenheim Mk IVF of No. 203 Squadron, Khormaksar, in August 1940. These aircraft covered the evacuation of Dominion forces from British Somaliland.

The Martin Maryland performed invaluable service with the Desert Air Force, carrying out both bombing and long-range reconnaissance.

fighter squadrons in Greece were re-equipping with Hurricanes, and these operated side by side with the remaining Gladiators. On 28 February, sixteen Hurricanes and twelve Gladiators were patrolling at 14,000 feet when they sighted a formation of 50 Italian fighters and bombers. While the Gladiators circled round the enemy formation to cut off its escape, the Hurricanes attacked it furiously. In the ensuing air battle the RAF fighters claimed no fewer than 27 enemy aircraft destroyed—all of which were confirmed by observers on the ground—and a further eleven probably destroyed.

Early in 1941, the RAF air commitment in Greece was reinforced by the arrival of Nos 11 and 113 Squadrons with Blenheims, and No. 33 with Hurricanes. The Lysanders of No. 208 Squadron were also ordered to move across, and while their move was under way

the Germans entered the battle for Greece. By 19 April, concentrated attacks by the *Luftwaffe* on the Greek airfields had reduced the strength of the RAF fighter squadrons to only 22 serviceable aircraft, and a few days later all but seven of the Hurricanes were destroyed in low-level strafing attacks by Messerschmitts. With this blow, Allied air resistance over Greece virtually ceased to exist.

On 1 May, the last Commonwealth forces were evacuated from the Greek mainland, and 30,000 Allied troops worked desperately to prepare the island of Crete to meet an enemy invasion. The island's entire air defence force consisted of fourteen fighters—a few Hurricanes and some Fleet Air Arm machines—against which were ranged 430 enemy bombers, 180 fighters, 700 transport aircraft and 80 assault gliders. During the

first two weeks of May, German dive-bombers carried out a furious air bombardment of Crete, with the island's three air-fields as their main objectives, and by the 19th only four Hurricanes and three Sea Gladiators were still airworthy. The next day this pitiful remnant was withdrawn to Egypt, and the Germans were now free to launch their airborne invasion. In a desperate, last-ditch attempt to re-establish a fighter defence, the RAF sent six Hurricanes back to Crete, but two were shot down by friendly naval forces as they approached the island and the others were destroyed in bombing attacks soon after their arrival. By the end of May, the battle of Crete was over, with about half the island's defenders killed or captured. The Sunderlands of Nos 228 and 230 Squadrons played a tremendous part during the final phase of the battle, carrying out maritime reconnaissance by day and evacuation by night, often under the most hazardous conditions.

In March 1941, with the Allies committed to the Greek campaign, the German Afrika Korps arrived in Libya under the command of General Erwin Rommel, and the Commonwealth forces were soon in retreat along the road they had taken in their victorious advance against the Italians a few months earlier. The Germans were supported by about 110 aircraft in the early stages, mainly Ju 87s and Bf 110s, but before long these were reinforced by 50 or so Bf 109Fs of JG27, which proved more than a match for the ageing Hurricane Mk Is that equipped the RAF fighter squadrons. Admittedly, Hurricane Mk IIs were beginning to arrive via the trans-Africa route that had been set up in the autumn of 1940, but they were slow to reach the squadrons. In April 1941, the Afrika Korps surrounded Tobruk and, to provide fighter cover, the Hurricanes of Nos 6 and 73 Squadrons were flown in. With their airstrip under continual shellfire and air attack, operational conditions were grim, and by 23 April No. 73 Squadron was so depleted that it had to be withdrawn, leaving the Hurricanes of No. 6 as the only operational aircraft within the Tobruk perimeter. They, too, had to be pulled out on 10 May. No. 6 Squadron still operated a few Lysanders in addition to its Hurricanes, but these had been withdrawn from the campaign by the end of May, together with those operating with other army co-operation units. The

The opposition: a Junkers Ju 87 Stuka, captured during the Eighth Army's early offensive in the Western Desert, in RAF markings at an Egyptian base.

Lysanders could not hope to survive in an environment where the Messerschmitts had mastery of the air, as the Battle of France had proved a year earlier.

The requirements of the Greek campaign had left the RAF in Cyrenaica, now under the command of Group Captain L.O. Brown, with only four squadrons—Nos 3 (RAAF), 6 and 73, with Hurricanes, and No. 55 with Blenheims—supported by three Wellington squadrons from the Canal Zone and one from Malta. By the middle of May, all the original four, seriously under strength, had been pulled back into Egypt. It came as a great relief when, on 12 May, a convoy bringing 50 more Hurricanes docked at Alexandria after a hard-fought passage through the Mediterranean; nevertheless, there was no escaping the fact that the desert squadrons could do little to provide air cover for the beleaguered Tobruk garrison, for their nearest bases were at Sidi Barrani, 120 miles away.

Tobruk's capture was now the Germans' main objective, and for the moment the threat of a thrust into Egypt by the Afrika Korps had been lifted. The enemy decision provided a welcome breathing-space, and new Allied squadrons were hurriedly formed to challenge the *Luftwaffe*, the RAF being joined by more Commonwealth units from Australia and South Africa. The build-up of what was to become known as the Desert Air Force was to continue unchecked throughout the summer months, and would eventually provide the Allies with the massive air superiority they needed to bring about Rommel's defeat. In the middle of 1941, however, that was still a long way off.

There were, however, bright spots in other areas. In East Africa, Dominion forces launched a counter-offensive into Eritrea from the Sudan and Kenya, supported now by six and a half squadrons; three Italian destroyers were sunk by the RAF off Massawa, and two more ran aground under fierce air attack. By April 6, the offensive had reached Addis Ababa and operations in East Africa were practically complete, permitting the release of four squadrons for service in the Western Desert.

Meanwhile, early in April, the British had found themselves with a crisis in Iraq, where an unscrupulous politician named Rashid Ali, encouraged by Germany, had seized power. On 30 April, his forces laid siege to Habbaniya, the big RAF training establishment 50 miles west of Baghdad; this was the home of No. 4 Flying Training School, which operated a variety of aircraft that included Hawker Audaxes and twin-engined Airspeed Oxfords, as well as three Gladiators for advanced training. On the orders of Air Vice-Marshal H.G. Smart, the AOC Iraq, these aircraft were adapted to carry bombs on underwing racks; in addition, five more Gladiators were flown over from Egypt, while Wellingtons of Nos 70 and 37 Squadrons were detached from the Canal Zone to Shaibah. At dawn on 2 May, preceded by an attack by the Wellingtons, the converted trainers—flown not only by instructors, but also by the more promising student pilots—went into action against Rashid Ali's forces on the plateau overlooking Habbaniya. In the course of the day they flew 193 bombing and strafing sorties, losing two aircraft in the air and two on the ground. Pressure was maintained on 3 and 4 May, during which period Blenheims of No. 203 Squadron

Prime Minister Winston Churchill disembarking from a Lockheed Lodestar VIP transport at Abu Sueir, Egypt, during a visit in 1942. This was one of the celebrated occasions when Churchill was represented by a 'double' back at home for security reasons.

thwarted attempts by the Iraqi air force to intervene, and by 5 May the Iraqis had had enough; reconnaissance the following morning found the plateau deserted. The Habbaniya aircraft immediately sought and found the retreating enemy columns, wreaking terrible havoc on some of them.

The prompt British action against Rashid Ali was fully justified for, on 13 May, a Blenheim of No. 84 Squadron was intercepted by a Bf 110 over Mosul. The German fighter was fitted with long-range tanks, and had been flown in via Crete and Syria. Three days later, a Gladiator of No. 94 Squadron, newly arrived from Egypt, interecepted three He 111s near Habbaniya; one of the bombers was destroyed, but the Gladiator was also shot down by return fire and its pilot, Flying Officer Herrtage, killed. However, the next day two more pilots of No. 94 Squadron, Sergeants Smith and Dunwoodie, each destroyed a Bf 110. By this time Hurri-

canes had begun to arrive in Iraq, and these went into action immediately over Baghdad, occasionally sighting enemy aircraft and driving them away. Several more He 111s and Bf 110s were destroyed before the revolt finally fizzled out at the end of May and Iraq's ruler was restored.

The *Luftwaffe*'s presence in Iraq would not have been possible without the help of the Vichy French in Syria, and it was reluctantly decided to eliminate pro-German elements there by launching an invasion. This began on 8 June 1941 and was supported by four and a half squadrons of fighters and bombers, as well as a Lysander flight of No. 208 Squadron. The Vichy forces fought back vigorously and their air strength in fact outnumbered the RAF's, with 100 machines against about 60, and some of the French aircraft, such as the Dewoitine 520, were very good indeed. The French pressed home attacks on the Allied columns until 28 June, when six Martin Maryland bombers were shot dcwn by the Curtiss Tomahawks of No. 3 Squadron, SAAF; after that, the tempo of the attacks slowed down markedly. In addition, constant attacks by RAF aircraft on enemy airfields severely hampered French

air operations. A ceasefire was eventually concluded on 14 July, and the potential threat to Britain's Middle East oil supplies and Egypt's 'back door' effectively removed.

The key to British control of the Mediterranean, and therefore the Middle East, was the island of Malta. On 10 June 1940, although the island possessed three serviceable airfields, its aircraft inventory comprised only five Fairey Swordfish of the Fleet Air Arm, used mainly for AA co-operation, four Gloster Sea Gladiators and a Queen Bee target drone. On 11 June, the day following Italy's entry into the war, the airfields were attacked by 25 S.79s of the *Regia Aeronautica*, escorted by Macchi C.200 fighters; two of the Sea Gladiators took off to intercept, and one of them slightly damaged an S.79. More air raids in the days that followed revealed the Gladiators' main deficiency: they were slower than the bombers they were supposed to catch, and the fighter pilots were forced to adopt new tactics. These involved climbing above the enemy formations before the latter reached the island of Gozo, north of Malta, and then diving through them, using the speed of their dive to make one quick firing pass and upset the Italians' bombing runs.

The Italians carried out seven major raids on Malta during the first ten days of the war, and the Gladiators failed to shoot down any enemy aircraft. (Three of the Gladiators, incidentally, were later immortalized by the names *Faith*, *Hope* and *Charity*, but there is no evidence that they were known as such during their spirited defence of the island). Their first victory came on 22 June, when a lone S. 79 reconnaissance aircraft was intercepted by Squadron Leader G. Burges; the Italian aircraft went down into the sea and the crew was taken prisoner. The Gladiators shot down two more enemy aircraft that week, and, on 28 June, by which time only two of the biplane fighters were airworthy, four Hawker Hurricanes were flown in from North Africa. More Hurricanes arrived on the aircraft carrier HMS *Argus* early in August, and a complete Hurricane squadron—No. 261—was soon fully operational on the island. In addition, a small strike force gradually built up on the Maltese airfields; this consisted of the Swordfish of No. 830 Squadron, FAA, detachments of Wellingtons from the Canal Zone squadrons and detachments of two Sunderland squadrons, Nos 228 and 230.

The Italians launched a new series of attacks in November 1940. Several enemy aircraft were shot down by No. 261's Hurricanes and the enemy changed their tactics, sending small numbers of fighter-bombers over the island on hit-and-run raids. No. 261 countered these by mounting standing patrols over Malta, with a flight of Hurricanes patrolling at high level and the two surviving Gladiators lower down.

Towards the end of 1940, the Wellingtons on the island were formed into a single squadron, No. 148, and these—in conjunction with aircraft of the Fleet Air Arm—carried out attacks on targets in Italy and North Africa at every opportunity. They were supported in these activities by the photo-recce Marylands of No. 431 Flight, which was later to be re-designated No. 69 Squadron.

By the end of 1940 Malta was developing into a vital offensive base, its strike aircraft preying on Italian convoys passing over the Mediterranean. Then, in December, came a new development: the *Luftwaffe* entered the battle, with the Stukas, Ju 88s and Messerschmitts of Fliegerkorps X occupying Sicilian airfields in strength.

On 11 January 1941, the *Luftwaffe* began a massive air onslaught against Malta. It continued almost without pause through the first three months of the year, during which period the Hurricanes of No. 261 Squadron and half a dozen Fleet Air Arm fighters remained the island's sole defence. The fury of the attacks abated a little after March 1941, although they never ceased entirely. Meanwhile, the build-up of RAF aircraft on the island continued, and by October, three fighter squadrons—Nos 126, 185 and 261, all with Hurricanes—were based there, in addition to the recently-arrived Beaufighters of No. 252 Squadron for night defence.

Throughout the summer months of 1941 the Malta-based bomber squadrons had been striking hard at German and Italian shipping in the Mediterranean, and the losses they inflicted were so severe that the *Luftwaffe* High Command decided to make a final all-out attempt to destroy the island's air capability. For this purpose the Germans assembled 250 bombers and 200 fighters on airfields in Sicily and southern Italy; against this armada the RAF could muster only 60 Hurricanes. As 1941 drew to a close, the sternest test for Malta was still to come.

11

The Atlantic and Western Europe
1941~42

At the end of 1940, Fighter Command had fought its great defensive battle of the war and had emerged narrowly victorious; its increasing role, from now on, would be to carry the war to the enemy in concert with the medium bombers of Bomber Command.

It was Coastal Command, however, that had to cope with the biggest immediate increase in operational commitments. Between the beginning of June and the end of December 1940, over three million tons of British, Allied and neutral merchant shipping was sunk by enemy action, and U-Boats accounted for some 59 per cent of this total. The priority of Coastal Command under Air Chief Marshal Sir Frederick Bowhill, therefore, was to come to grips with the undersea threat, while still carrying out its other tasks of maritime reconnaissance and attacks on enemy surface forces.

Technical improvements were beginning to help in the fight against the submarine; at the beginning of 1941, for example, about a sixth of Coastal Command's aircraft were equipped with ASV radar, although this was still in a primitive stage of development and as yet was only effective against U-boats that were fully surfaced and within three miles of the search aircraft. Coastal Command's maritime patrol squadrons were still equipped with either Hudsons or Sunderlands, and the anti-shipping units with Bristol Beauforts; new aircraft, however, were on the horizon, such as the Consolidated Catalina, an aircraft of exceptional endurance which had been evaluated by the RAF in July 1939. One hundred Catalinas had been ordered in 1940, and these began to reach the squadrons in the spring of 1941. In May of that year, the Command also acquired a squadron of Beaufighters, No. 252; its task was to intercept the enemy's Focke-Wulf Fw 200 reconnaissance aircraft, which co-ordinated U-boat attacks, as they headed out from their bases at Brest and Lorient to search for Allied Atlantic convoys. Based in Northern Ireland, No. 252's aircraft formed an effective barrier between the Focke-Wulfs and the convoys in the Western Approaches.

Farther north, Coastal Command squadrons in Scotland and Iceland patrolled the dangerous gap between the Shetland Islands and the Arctic Circle. Since August 1940, patrol work from Iceland had been carried out by the Battles of No. 98 Squadron, which were completely unsuited to this type of work, but in January 1941, they were joined by a squadron of Sunderlands and one of Hudsons. Also based in Iceland were the Northrop N-3PB floatplanes of No. 330

Avro Anson Mk 1 of No. 224 Squadron, RAF Coastal Command, on patrol over a convoy in the early months of the war. No. 224 Squadron began to re-equip with Lockheed Hudsons in August 1939, but continued to use Ansons for some time after that.

As the war progressed, the development of ASV (air to surface vessel) radar became of paramount importance. Here, a trial installation of a later mark ASV is seen under the nose of a Wellington at the Telecommunications Research Establishment, Defford.

(Norwegian) Squadron; these remained in service until December 1942, by which time the Squadron had received Catalinas.

In the early months of 1941, one of the biggest threats to the Atlantic convoy routes was the battleship *Bismarck*, which the enemy intended to send into the Atlantic as the central unit of a formidable battle group that also included the battle-cruisers *Scharnhorst*, *Gneisenau* and *Prinz Eugen*. Of the other major enemy surface units, one, the *Graf Spee*, had been effectively dealt with in December 1939, and another, the *Lützow*, was bottled up in Norwegian waters, but the *Bismarck*'s battle group, when operating at full strength, could almost certainly outgun anything the Royal Navy could pit against it, with the possible exception of the new 'King George V' class battleships.

In readiness for the warships' breakout into the Atlantic, the Germans deployed the *Scharnhorst* and *Gneisenau* to the French Atlantic ports, where their presence was detected by air reconnaissance in March

1941. The ports were repeatedly attacked by Bomber Command, but no damage was inflicted on the warships; however, on 5 April, a reconnaissance Spitfire revealed that the *Gneisenau* had been moved from dry dock to the outer harbour at Brest, and a Coastal Command strike was arranged. The sortie was flown at dawn on 6 April by four Beauforts of No. 22 Squadron, but only one aircraft succeeded in locating the target in poor visibility. Its pilot, Flying Officer Kenneth Campbell, made his torpedo run at mast height through intense flak put up by more than 250 guns around the anchorage, as well as by three flak ships and the *Gneisenau*'s main armament; the Beaufort was shot down with the loss of all its crew, but not before Campbell had released his torpedo at a range of 500 yards. The torpedo exploded on the *Gneisenau*'s stern below the water-line, putting the cruiser out of action for months. For his gallant action, Campbell was posthumously awarded the VC; the other members of his crew were Sergeants J.P. Scott, W. Mullis and R.W. Hillman.

The *Gneisenau* was further damaged by Bomber Command on the night of 10/11 April, and bomb damage to the harbour facilities delayed the refitting of her companion, the *Scharnhorst*. The German Naval High Command therefore decided to send out the *Bismarck* accompanied only by one escort, the *Prinz Eugen*. It was a decision that was to have fatal consequences.

The story of the chase and destruction of the *Bismarck* is well known. On 20 May, the two warships were sighted as they passed through the Kattegat, and the following day they were located near Bergen by a Spitfire of the Photographic Reconnaissance Unit, flown by Flying Officer Mike Suckling. On 22 May, a Maryland reconnaissance aircraft of No. 771 Squadron, Fleet Air Arm, confirmed that the warships had departed, and the hunt was on. On 24 May, the *Bismarck* and *Prinz Eugen* were sighted in the Denmark Strait, and in the ensuing surface action the *Bismarck* sank the battle cruiser HMS *Hood* and damaged the *Prince of Wales*; the latter's shells, however, hit the German warship and damaged her fuel tanks, making her foray

Hunting down the underwater menace: an aircraft of Coastal Command makes a successful attack on a U-boat in the Western Approaches. The U-boat surfaces and, as its wake shows, vainly tries to take violent evasive action.

Air-Sea Rescue was one of Coastal Command's vital tasks. Here, an airborne lifeboat is being fitted to a Wellington.

into the North Atlantic impracticable. The German commander, Admiral Lutjens, detached the *Prinz Eugen* and set course for Brest.

After weathering an attack by Fleet Air Arm Swordfish from the carrier HMS *Victorious*, the *Bismarck* was sighted again on 26 May by a Catalina of No. 209 Squadron, piloted by Flying Officer Denis Briggs. Although subjected to fierce anti-aircraft fire, Briggs continued to shadow the *Bismarck* until he was relieved by another Catalina. He nursed his damaged aircraft back to Northern Ireland and was later awarded the DFC. The second Catalina, of No. 240 Squadron, retained contact with the *Bismarck* and passed on her position to the Royal Navy; later, her steering gear was crippled in a torpedo attack by Swordfish from the *Ark Royal*, leaving her at the mercy of the pursuing surface forces. She was sent to the bottom on 27 May, fighting gallantly to the end.

On Friday, 13 June 1941, Coastal Command scored another success when a Beaufort of No. 42 Squadron, operating out of Wick in northern Scotland and flown by Flight Sergeant Raymond Loveitt, tor-

Pilots of No. 72 Squadron indulge in some horseplay before a sweep from Manston in 1941. The Hurricanes visible in the photograph belong to No. 601 Squadron, which re-equipped with Airacobras in August. These were not successful, and were replaced by Spitfires in 1942.

pedoed the battleship *Lützow* off Norway in the early hours of the morning, causing severe damage that compelled her to return to base and effectively removed her as a threat to the Atlantic convoys for the remainder of the war. It was a fitting farewell present for Sir Frederick Bowhill, who was posted the following day to form Ferry Command; his place as AOC Coastal Command was taken by Air Marshal Sir Philip Joubert de la Ferté, an energetic officer who had already completed a tour with the Command in the late 1930s. When he assumed his post, the strength of Coastal Command had risen to 40 squadrons, and under his direction the weapon forged by Sir Frederick

Bowhill would register increasing successes in the bitter conflict that was to become known as the Battle of the Atlantic.

By this time, much of the Command's effort had been concentrated in the Western Approaches, where operations were directed by No. 15 Group, but increasing shipping losses off West Africa led to the establishment of a Sunderland squadron, No. 95, at Bathurst and Freetown. Six Hudsons, later to form the nucleus of No. 200 Squadron, were also sent to West Africa in June, and they were followed by the Sunderlands of No. 204 in September. As a result, U-boat successes tailed off dramatically, and after September 1941 the enemy withdrew their submarines from the West African area altogether.

With the German invasion of Russia in June 1941, and the need to protect convoys taking supplies to the Soviet Union from Britain, Coastal Command's task virtually doubled, and the need to inflict the maximum damage on the enemy's naval bases assumed paramount importance. The latter was a requirement that was to occupy much of Bomber Command's resources during the year.

In December 1940, Bomber Command had adopted new tactics in its night offensive against Germany's industry. Hitherto, the Command had concentrated on making precision attacks on selected targets, but the accuracy achieved was low, and this fact—together with the German attack on Coventry—brought about a major policy change. Bomber crews, from now on, were given clear instructions to find and bomb targets in large industrial areas where, even if their bombs missed the primary target, they

Spitfire Mk IIs of No. 72 Squadron in formation over the Northumberland coast 1941. The V-type formation was for the benefit of the camera; most Fighter Command Squadrons ceased to use combat formations of this kind after the lessons of the Battle of Britain.

might nevertheless still inflict considerable damage on other worthwhile objectives in the vicinity.

The first of these so-called 'area' attacks, code-named Operation Abigail, was mounted against Mannheim on the night of 16/17 December 1940. A total of 134 Wellingtons, Whitleys, Hampdens and Blenheims—the largest number of aircraft so far detailed to attack one target—were despatched, and 102 aircraft claimed to have made successful attacks. Post-raid analysis, however, showed that most of the bombs had fallen outside the target area; it was clear that the standard of target marking left much to

A cannon-armed Hurricane Mk IIC of No. 87 Squadron, 1941. This unit specialised in night intruder operations and later moved to Gibraltar to cover the Operation Torch landings in North Africa in November 1942. Hurricanes served in every theatre of war, including North Russia; in the summer of 1941, Nos 134 and 144 Squadrons formed No. 151 Wing at Murmansk to provide fighter cover for Russian bombers and defensive patrols over the North Russian ports. The Hurricanes were handed over to the Soviet Navy in October 1941.

be desired, and equally clear that this would only improve with better aids to long-range navigation.

By this time, Bomber Command had begun to receive new types of heavy bomber. The first of these was the Short Stirling, which entered service with No. 7 Squadron at Leeming in August 1940; however, the rest of the year was spent in converting crews to the new type, and it was not until January 1941 that the Squadron moved to Oakington

in readiness for its first operational mission. This was flown on the night of 10/11 February, and involved an attack on the oil storage depot at Rotterdam.

The second of the new four-engined heavy bombers, the Handley Page Halifax, entered service with No. 35 Squadron at Leeming in November 1940. The Squadron was up to full strength by 5 December, and moved to its operational base at Linton-on-Ouse. The first Halifax operation was carried out on

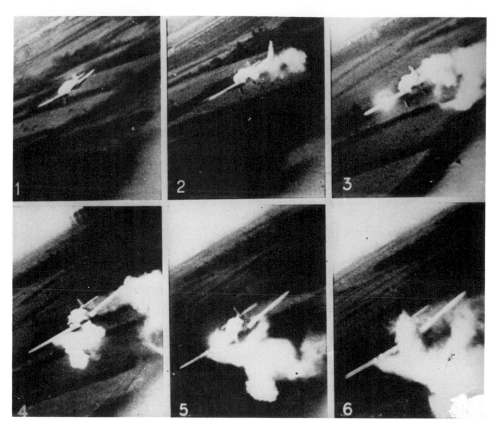

The end of a Messerschmitt Bf 109F over France, shot down by a Spitfire during a Fighter Command sweep.

Blenheims of No. 114 Squadron, No. 2 Group, attacking one of two power stations near Cologne on 12 August 1941. This was Bomber Command's deepest daylight penetration up to that time; 54 bombers took part and were escorted by Westland Whirlwind long-range fighters.

engines instead of four Rolls-Royce Merlins, with unfortunate results. Serious trouble with the Vultures dogged the bomber throughout its operational career, which began on 24/25 February 1941 when aircraft of No. 207 Squadron attacked warships in Brest harbour. The engines were unreliable in their behaviour; often, they would carry the aircraft on long-distance raids without the slightest hint of trouble, only to burst into flames for no apparent reason when the Manchester arrived back over its base. To solve the problem, Avro experimented with a converted Manchester, known as the Mk III, fitted with four Merlins. This aircraft made its first flight on 9 January 1941, and a few weeks later it received a new name: the Lancaster.

Bomber Command's offensive against the German naval bases began on the night of 30/31 March 1941 with an attack on Brest, and was to last more than ten months. However, the large number of sorties flown by the Command against the French Atlantic ports in the spring of 1941 produced little result, and the AOC Bomber Command, Air Chief Marshal Sir Richard Pierse, felt that the tonnage of bombs would have been used to better effect in attacks on Germany's industrial complexes. Area attacks therefore continued, and for the first time Bomber Command began to inflict damage on a large scale. On the night of 12/13 March, the RAF's new heavy bombers flew over German territory for the first time when Manchesters and Halifaxes raided Hamburg, and on the last night of the month the town of Emden received a foretaste of things to come when Wellingtons of Nos 9 and 49 Squadrons dropped two of the new 4,000 pound bombs on that target. The offensive reached a new level of intensity on the night of 8/9 May, when 360 aircraft were sent out to attack Hamburg and Bremen.

The German invasion of Russia in June 1941, accompanied by the withdrawal of several *Luftwaffe* fighter wings from the Western Front, gave rise to hopes that Bomber Command might be in a position to renew daylight attacks on enemy targets without fear of crippling losses. The idea was to launch strong and co-ordinated fighter and bomber attacks on objectives in the area immediately across the Channel; it had already been given a trial run on 10 January 1941, when six Blenheims of No. 114 Squadron, escorted by six squadrons of fighters, attacked ammunition and supply dumps in the Forêt de Guines.

By March 1941, fighter sweeps over the continent—known as 'Circus' operations—

10/11 March, when six aircraft were despatched to attack Le Havre dockyard; four bombed the primary, one bombed Dieppe and one aborted. One of the Halifaxes was shot down by an RAF night-fighter on the return flight.

The third new heavy bomber to enter service, the Avro Manchester, was a bitter disappointment to Bomber Command. It was designed to the same specification as the original Halifax, but retained two Vulture

were becoming organized affairs, with the Spitfire and Hurricane squadrons of Nos 11 and 12 Groups operating in wing strength. A Fighter Command Wing consisted of three squadrons, each with twelve aircraft. There were Spitfire wings at Biggin Hill, Hornchurch and Tangmere, mixed Spitfire and Hurricane wings at Duxford, Middle Wallop and Wittering, and Hurricane wings at Kenley, Northolt and North Weald, all commanded by highly experienced officers who had been squadron commanders in the Battle of Britain—men such as Douglas Bader, A.G. 'Sailor' Malan and 'Al' Deere. Together, they and their successors developed the fighter tactics that soon gave the Allies complete mastery of the sky over Western Europe.

By May 1941, 56 squadrons of fighters and fighter-bombers were regularly taking part in offensive sweeps over occupied Europe. Of these, 29 still flew Hurricanes. In June, the Spitfire Mk II began to be replaced by the Mk V, armed with two 20 mm cannon and four .303 machine-guns in place of the original eight .303s; it entered service just in time to counter the Messerschmitt Bf 109F, but—with its clipped wings—proved to be inferior to the German fighter at high altitude, where many air combats took place, and several squadrons equipped with the Spitfire Mk V took a severe mauling that summer.

By no stretch of the imagination could the Circus operations be called a success. Handling the large formations of fighters that were being pushed over the Channel presented enormous problems, and it was soon apparent that the Spitfire was quite unsuited to escort duties. It was only when they were escorting bombers attacking targets near the coast that the Spitfire pilots enjoyed some freedom of action in seeking out enemy fighters; when escorting raids that penetrated deeper inland they were forced to stay close to the bombers in order to conserve fuel, and there was very little margin left for actual combat. The German tactics were to stay high above the RAF formations until the latter turned for home, short of fuel, when the 109s would dive down on selected victims and then climb hard for altitude again. A classic case was Circus 62, one of the biggest mounted in 1941; on 7 August eighteen squadrons of Spitfires and two of Hurricanes accompanied six Blenheims in an attack on a power station near Lille, and at the end of the

day the RAF had lost six fighters against a claim of only three 109s destroyed.

Matters became even worse in September, when pilots reported encountering a new radial-engined enemy fighter. It was the Focke-Wulf Fw 190, and within weeks it had established air superiority for the Germans. Not until the advent of the Spitfire Mk IX, resulting from the marriage of a Merlin 61 engine to a Mark V airframe, was the balance restored—but the first Mark IXs did not enter service with No. 64 Squadron until June 1942, and in the meantime Fighter Command had a hard time of it. In the end, on Winston Churchill's orders, large-scale sweeps over the Continent were discontinued in November 1941, to enable Fighter Command to gather its strength for a renewed offensive in the following spring.

Groundcrew working as the port Hercules of a Short Stirling at an RAF base. The Stirling was the earlier of the RAF's four-engined bombers, carrying out its first operation on 10 February 1941, an attack on an oil storage depot at Rotterdam, and in 1942 opened the heavy bombing continued by Halifaxes and Lancasters.

The bombing station in a Wellington. This photograph demonstrates the bomb-aimer's exposed position during the run over the target; a successful bombing run needed plenty of nerve and concentration.

at La Pallice; a similar attack had been carried out by Stirlings the day before. These raids were carried out in conjunction with diversionary attacks made by escorted Blenheims on targets in the Cherbourg area. The warships were also attacked from high level by the Boeing Fortress Mk Is of No. 90 Squadron on 24 July, together with over 70 Hampdens and Wellingtons; eleven bombers

Architect of airborne victory: Air Chief Marshal Sir Arthur Harris, C-in-C Bomber Command 1942–45.

Nevertheless, in the summer of 1941 Bomber Command had attempted a number of deep-penetration missions into enemy territory in daylight, in the belief that Fighter Command could keep the Messerschmitts at bay. On 30 June, Halifaxes of No. 35 Squadron made a daylight attack on Kiel without loss, and this was followed by a dramatic daylight raid on Bremen by the Blenheims of Nos 105 and 107 Squadrons on 4 July. To reach the target the Blenheims had to fly at very low level across 50 miles of enemy territory from the sea and negotiate the formidable Bremen anti-aircraft defences on the final run-in. All the Blenheims were hit and four out of fifteen shot down, but the target—a factory—was destroyed. The leader of the raid, Wing Commander H.I. Edwards, was awarded the Victoria Cross.

On 12 August, the medium bombers of No. 2 Group made their deepest penetration so far when 54 Blenheims bombed two power stations near Cologne. They were escorted by Westland Whirlwind fighters of No. 263 Squadron, the only fighter aircraft with sufficient range to carry out this task. The Whirlwind was highly manoeuvrable, faster than a Spitfire at low altitude, and its armament of four closely-grouped 20 mm cannon made it a match for any *Luftwaffe* fighter of the day. As it was, the Whirlwind experienced a spate of troubles with its Rolls-Royce Peregrine engines and, since all Merlins were earmarked for Spitfires, only two squadrons were ever equipped with the type. Eventually, it was used in the fighter-bomber role with considerable success.

Bomber Command also switched to daylight attacks on the elusive German warships; one of the biggest raids of this period was mounted on 24 July, when fifteen Halifaxes were sent out to attack the *Scharnhorst*

An Avro Lancaster of No. 622 Squadron. No. 622 was one of the main force heavy bomber squadrons formed in 1943 and had a short career, disbanding in August 1945.

failed to return. The Fortress was Bomber Command's most recent acquisition, and turned out to be a disappointment. Attempts were made to use the type in precision attacks on targets such as Kiel, Wilhelmshaven and Berlin, but most were thwarted by icing and engine troubles. In October 1941, after a number of abortive raids and several losses, the Fortresses were sent to the Middle East, where they operated at night. As a high-altitude day bomber, the Fortress Mk I had fallen far short of expectations; but its successor, the Fortress Mk II, would carry out that role with distinction.

The shortcomings of Bomber Command's equipment were highlighted under tragic circumstances on the night of 7/8 November 1941. when 400 aircraft were despatched to the Ruhr, Berlin, Mannheim, Ostend, Boulogne and Cologne. Of the 37 aircraft that failed to return, 25 ran out of fuel when they encountered unexpectedly strong head-winds during the return flight. Winston Churchill demanded a full report, but it was not until 4 January 1942 that the facts were laid before him. As a result, an amount of unfair blame for the disaster was laid at the door of the AOC, Sir Richard Pierse, whose policies had been strongly criticized in some quarters during 1941.

Pierse had presided over the fortunes of Bomber Command when they were at their lowest ebb, when bomber crews had paid with their lives for the short-sighted policies and reduced standards of training brought about by decisions taken in previous years. He had been blamed for policy decisions that were none of his doing, such as the drain of vital aircraft and crews from Bomber Command to reinforce squadrons in the Middle East. He had undoubtedly made errors of judgement, but then so had others in higher authority. Yet, in the final reckoning, it was he who had to bear the burden of failure; early in the new year he was appointed C-in-C of the Allied air forces in the Far East.

The man who stepped into his place as AOC-in-C Bomber Command was a man who had sworn to make the enemy 'scream for mercy'. His name was Air Marshal Arthur Harris.

12

North African Victory

In the summer of 1941, the Allied forces in North Africa, now under the command of General Sir Claud Auchinleck, were building up their resources for a major offensive. In preparation for this, the AOC-in-C, Air Chief Marshal Sir Arthur Tedder, undertook a complete reorganization of the forces at his disposal. No. 257 Wing, which had directed bombing operations from the Canal Zone bases, now became No. 205 Group; No. 201 Group at Alexandria was tasked exclusively with naval co-operation; No. 202 Group became Air Headquarters Egypt and assumed all responsibility for air defence; and No. 204 Group was designated Air Headquarters, Western Desert. It was this Group, No. 204 that was to go down in history as the near-legendary Desert Air Force. Its task was to carry out offensive operations deep into enemy territory—an important change of role, which hitherto had been to provide air cover over the army. A further Group, No. 206, was set up by Air Vice-Marshal Graham Dawson of the Ministry of Aircraft production to recover and repair aircraft damaged in action; the fact that it employed 23,000 civilians by the end of 1941 is indicative of the vital nature of its work.

The Allied offensive, Operation Crusader, was aimed at destroying the bulk of the enemy's armour, relieving Tobruk and retaking Cyrenaica as a preliminary to invading Tripolitania. To meet the air task, Tedder had at his disposal 29 squadrons in the Western Desert, under Air Vice-Marshal Arthur Coningham, and eleven in the Canal Zone—not counting the offensive squadrons on Malta. This amounted, in all, to some 700 first-line aircraft against about 280 German and Italian, although the enemy had reserves of 1,500 more in Tripolitania and on bases across the Mediterranean.

Preceded by a series of fighter sweeps by the Desert Air Force's Hurricane and Tomahawk squadrons, which quickly established air superiority deep inside Libya, Operation Crusader began on 18 November, with the British 8th Army thrusting towards Tobruk. In addition to attacks on the Axis armour and transport by the Allied fighter and fighter-bomber squadrons, the offensive was supported by bombing attacks on enemy shipping, oil and supply storage facilities and the ports used by Rommel's forces in North Africa and Italy. By 21 November, the Tobruk garrison, besieged since April, succeeded in breaking out and set out to join up with the 8th Army's forward units; this, however, was forestalled by a brilliant move by Rommel, who sent an armoured column through the desert to the south of the main battle area in a bold thrust towards the Egyptian border. The raid placed several of the Desert Air Force's forward airfields under serious threat and caused enormous confusion; nevertheless, the columns were repeatedly hammered from the air, particularly by Hurricane fighter-bombers and Tomahawks, and with the Axis situation worsening around Tobruk, Rommel abandoned his foray and hastened north to help isolate the garrison again. However, strong pressure on the enemy was maintained on the new enemy defensive line based on Gazala; this was subjected to air attacks by day and night using all available aircraft, and the line was broken in December. The 8th Army pushed on towards Benghazi, but was halted at El Agheila.

At this juncture, the Allied commanders confidently anticipated that the Axis forces would stay put to rest and regroup; however, they reckoned without the dash and initiative of Erwin Rommel. Fortified by two supply convoys that reached Tripoli in January, he launched a counter-offensive almost immediately and on 22 January almost succeeded in destroying the Kittyhawks and Hurricanes of No. 258 Wing at Antelat. The airfield was badly flooded, and this had prevented the RAF fighters from interfering with the *Luftwaffe* squadrons that supported Rommel's drive eastwards; nevertheless, most of them managed to escape just before the airfield was overrun by Rommel's tanks. The ground crews also got away, covered by Nos 1 and 2 RAF Armoured Car Companies. Before long, despite the efforts of the Desert Air Force, the British forces in Cyrenaica were once more in full retreat; only intense air attack stopped Rommel's armour break-

One of Malta's early defenders: a Hurricane Mk I of No. 261 Squadron at Hal Far in May 1941.

Martin Baltimore at Luqa in 1942. Baltimores and other bombers were frequently deployed to Malta from North Africa to assist the 'resident' bomber squadrons in attacks on enemy targets in Sicily and southern Italy.

Martin Maryland of No. 69 Squadron, Malta, early 1942. The Squadron's Marylands ranged far and wide on reconnaissance over Sicily, Italy and Libya until March 1942, when Spitfires began to take over the reconnaissance task.

ing through into Egypt and, in February, the Afrika Korps was halted on a line stretching from Gazala to Bir Hakim.

Bitter though the loss of most of Cyrenaica undoubtedly was, it was by no means a crushing defeat. The 8th Army still held territory in eastern Cyrenaica, and the defensive line was a long way west of the Egyptian border. Moreover, the Desert Air Force retained some forward bases in Cyrenaica from which its aircraft could strike deep into the enemy's rear areas.

Rommel's success, achieved with fairly limited forces, would not have been possible without the drastic reduction of Malta's offensive capability caused by the renewed air onslaught that opened in December 1941. By the first week in January 1942, only the principal Maltese airfield of Luqa was still serviceable; as a direct result of these attacks, the volume of supply traffic crossing the Mediterranean to replenish the enemy forces in North Africa showed a marked increase and, with German bombers inflicting substantial losses on Allied supply convoys to Malta, the island's own position was fast becoming critical.

In March 1942, Malta's air defences were reinforced by the arrival of fifteen Spitfires, ferried in at enormous risk by the aircraft carrier HMS *Eagle*; they arrived at a time when only 30 serviceable Hurricanes were left. In April, while these aircraft continued the fight, the courage and fortitude of the Maltese people was recognized by the award to the island of the George Cross.

On 20 April, 47 more Spitfires arrived on Malta after flying from the aircraft carrier USS *Wasp*; their arrival, however, had been detected by enemy monitoring stations and within hours their airfields came under heavy attack. By the end of the next day, after further heavy raids, only eighteen of the original 47 Spitfires were still in an airworthy condition. On 9 May, the USS *Wasp* returned, together with HMS *Eagle*, and between them the carriers flew off 64 more Spitfires, which were thrown into action almost immediately. The following day saw a major air battle over the island when the *Luftwaffe* made a determined effort to sink the minelayer HMS *Welshman*, which had docked in Valletta harbour laden with supplies and ammunition. Between them, the island's Spitfires and Hurricanes flew 124 sorties that day, destroying fifteen enemy

aircraft. Three Spitfires were lost, but two pilots were picked up by the air-sea rescue service.

Seventeen more Spitfires arrived later in May and deliveries of fighter aircraft continued throughout the summer months of 1942; HMS *Eagle* alone delivered 182 Spitfires before she was sunk by a U-Boat on 11 July. Most of the ferry work was subsequently undertaken by HMS *Furious*, which flew off 37 Spitfires on the day HMS *Eagle* went down, followed by 27 more on 7 August. Several RAF pilots distinguished themselves during the bitter air fighting over Malta in the summer months of 1942; one of them was the Canadian Pilot Officer George F. Buerling, who scored 27 victories while flying Spitfires over the island. He survived the war only to be killed while ferrying an aircraft to Israel in 1948.

The enemy air raids continued throughout the autumn and reached their climax in November 1942, when the Germans and Italians subjected Malta to a savage round-the-clock bombardment that lasted ten days. The defenders remained unbroken, and the offensive against the supply convoys ferrying reinforcements to the Axis forces in North

Liberator Mk II, squadron unknown, in a blast pen at Luqa.

gomery assumed command of the 8th Army in place of General Alexander. At this time the Allied forces were holding a short defensive line in western Egypt between El Alamein and the Qattara Depression; this line was attacked in strength by the *Afrika Korps* on 31 August, but the 8th Army held on and inflicted heavy losses on the enemy.

Meanwhile, the Desert Air Force continued to increase its overall superiority. By this time, the Spitfires and Hurricanes that

Wellington Mk VIII, the torpedo-bomber and general reconnaissance variant, at Luqa in 1942. The Wellington may have been a No. 179 aircraft detached from Gibraltar.

Africa went on almost unchecked. The Wellingtons, which for a time had been driven away by the intensity of the air attacks, had now returned in the shape of No. 104 Squadron, replaced before the autumn of 1942 by the torpedo-carrying Wellingtons of Nos 38 and 221 Squadrons; the Beauforts of No. 217 Squadron also arrived and joined the Wellingtons in their attacks on enemy shipping, alongside Swordfish and Albacores of the Fleet Air Arm. The island's air defences also had a new commander: Air Vice-Marshal Sir Keith Park, who replaced Air Vice-Marshal Sir Hugh P. Lloyd—the man who had endured the fearful pressure of the early part of 1942.

Meanwhile, in May 1942, the *Afrika Korps* had launched a fierce assault on the Gazala Line, three German divisions outflanking Bir Hakim and isolating the 1st Free French Brigade. The French gallantly resisted every enemy assault for ten days and the Desert Air Force threw every aircraft it could spare into the battle. The Hurricanes and Kittyhawks wrought great execution among the formations of Ju 87 Stukas which were hammering the French Brigade Box; one of the Hurricane squadrons, No. 6, was now equipped with anti-tank Hurricane Mk IIDs armed with 40-mm cannon, and this struck hard at the encircling enemy armour and artillery. By 10 June, however, the position of the French Brigade was hopeless, and the survivors were ordered to fight their way out. However, by pinning down the German divisions the French had bought valuable time, enabling the 8th Army to regroup and withdraw into Egypt.

In August 1942, General Bernard Mont-

The fury of the *Luftwaffe*'s attacks on Malta is well illustrated by these shots of a Wellington of No. 40 Squadron hurled out of its blast pen during a bombing raid in 1942.

had borne the brunt of Allied fighter operations for so long were being replaced by more modern combat types, including Spitfires and Beaufighters. The first squadron to receive Spitfires in the desert, in June 1942, was No. 145; it was joined later by Nos 92 and 601 Squadrons. Some of the first Spitfires to arrive were used to good effect against the high-flying Junkers Ju 86P-2 reconnaissance aircraft that made daily flights over the Canal Zone bases; one was attacked at 42,000 feet at the end of May by Flying Officer G.W.H. Reynolds, flying a stripped-down Spitfire, and forced down in the desert, and a second was attacked at 45,000 feet a few days later by Pilot Officer G.E. Genders. He forced it down to lower altitude after hitting it several times, and it was finished off by a second Spitfire. Genders himself ran out of fuel and came down in the Mediterranean; after a marathon swim lasting 22 hours, with only his Mae West for support, he crawled ashore more dead than alive and thumbed a lift back to Aboukir. A third Ju 86 was shot down later by Reynolds at 50,000 feet—a record height for 1942—and after that enemy reconnaissance flights over the Canal Zone ceased abruptly.

By 5 September 1942, it was clear that Rommel's offensive—hampered by continual air attack on his overstretched supply lines—had failed, and the 8th Army prepared a massive counter-attack at El

A lonely desert grave for a Luftwaffe pilot: Sgt Hans Fraütag of JG53, shot down in his Messerschmitt Bf 109 by Desert Air Force fighters two months short of his 22nd birthday. The grave was at Fuka, November 1942.

Scene at El Daba after the airfield was overrun during the Eighth Army's advance. Much of the Luftwaffe's strength was destroyed in devastating attacks on airfields in the Daba area by Desert Air Force fighter-bombers on 9 October 1942.

Alamein. As a preliminary, the Desert Air Force redoubled its efforts to achieve complete air superiority; on 9 October 1942, for example, two weeks before the start of the 8th Army's offensive, three squadrons of Kittyhawks—Nos 3, 112 and 450 (RAAF)—carried out a devastating low-level attack on enemy airfields in the vicinity of Daba, some ten minutes' flying time away from the Alamein defensive positions, where reconnaissance had revealed large numbers of German fighters bogged down in mud. Thirty-two Kittyhawks swept down on Daba in the wake of a medium-level bombing attack by Martin Baltimores, and in the space of a few minutes they knocked out 30 enemy aircraft. The *Luftwaffe* loss, which could not readily be made good, contributed in no small measure to the subsequent Commonwealth fighter superiority over the El Alamein front.

The 8th Army's counter-offensive began on 23 October 1942, and the entire stength of the Desert Air Force's fighter-bomber squadrons were turned on the reeling enemy, who finally broke on 4 November. The coast road leading to the west was jammed with enemy convoys, which were harried mercilessly by the fighter-bombers during the pursuit into Cyrenaica. Meanwhile, farther west, events were about to unfold which, ultimately, would render the German and Italian position utterly hopeless.

On 8 November, Anglo-American forces carried out a series of simultaneous landings in Morocco and western Algeria: Operation Torch. Apart from the tragic and abortive Dieppe operation of August 1942, Operation Torch was the first large-scale amphibious operation undertaken by the Allies, and was

supported by seven British and four American aircraft carriers. Air cover during the preliminary phase of the landings and the subsequent consolidation was therefore undertaken by naval fighters, with the exception of the Hurricanes of No. 43 Squadron which were flown into Maison Blanche, Algiers, less than an hour after the field had been captured by an American combat team. They were quickly followed by the Hurricanes of No. 225 Squadron, the Spitfires of Nos 72, 81, 93, 111, 152 and 242 Squadrons and the Beaufighters of No. 255. An RAF bomber wing was also established, comprising the Bisleys (Canadian-built Blenheim Mk Vs) of Nos 13, 18, 114 and 614 Squadrons.

As the Allies began their advance, the lack of suitable forward airstrips became a serious problem. Existing airfields became overcrowded, and their ever-increasing distance from the front line meant that the fighters could spend only ten minutes, or even less, in the combat area. Early in December, in an attempt to remedy the situation, the Spitfires of No. 93 Squadron were sent forward to a muddy strip at Medjez el Bab, but they had barely arrived when Bf 109s swept down on them and shot them up.

There was still plenty of fight left in the *Luftwaffe*, and daylight bombing attacks had to be carried out under heavy escort. When this was not possible, the result could be disastrous; on 4 December, for example, nine Bisleys of No. 18 Squadron set out unescorted to bomb the enemy airstrip at Chouigui, and all nine were shot down. For his determination in pressing home the attack, and in trying to shepherd his aircraft to safety afterwards, the raid leader, Wing Commander H.G. Malcolm, was awarded a posthumous Victoria Cross.

A new challenge to Allied air superiority now arrived in North Africa in the shape of the Focke-Wulf 190, which operated as fighter-bombers under the direction of Fliegerführer Tunis, and which for a time enabled the *Luftwaffe* in Tunisia to hold its own against numerically superior forces. The Focke-Wulfs flew a prodigious number of sorties and became a real thorn in the Allies' flesh, carrying out numerous low-level bombing attacks against Allied ports and supply dumps as well as providing close support in the defence of the last Axis strong-

Spitfire Mk VCs on patrol over the Tunisian coast, 1943. The Desert Air Force's Spitfire squadrons did much to establish Allied air superiority during the Tunisian Campaign.

hold. To counter them, some Spitfire Mk IXs under Squadron Leader Stanislaw Skalski were sent out to North Africa early in 1943 and were attached to No. 145 Squadron. Known as the Polish Fighting Team, Skalski's pilots destroyed more enemy aircraft in a two-month period than any other Polish unit in the RAF managed to do in the whole of 1943, and the pilots achieved such reputations that they were subsequently offered posts as commanding officers of other RAF fighter squadrons. Skalski himself became CO of No. 601 Squadron, and later led No. 2 (Polish) Wing. He ended the war with a score of nineteen enemy aircraft destroyed and afterwards returned to his homeland, only to be imprisoned by the Russians for the 'crime' of having fought for the British. His fate was typical of that of so many gallant Poles who served with such distinction in foreign air forces against the common enemy.

On 7 April 1943, following desperate fighting, the US II Corps linked up with the British 8th Army and the drive northwards into Tunisia began. At the same time, the Allied air forces began an all-out campaign to destroy the remnants of the *Luftwaffe* in North Africa; they also launched a series of heavy attacks on enemy airfields in Sicily and Southern Italy, where the enemy was assembling fleets of transport aircraft—Junkers Ju 52s and massive, six-engined Messerschmitt Me 323s—in a frantic attempt to get supplies and reinforcements through to the *Afrika Korps*.

Some enemy transports managed to slip across the Mediterranean under cover of darkness. When they came by day, however, they were shot down like flies by the Allied fighters. On 18 April, for example, 47 P-40 Warhawks of the US 9th Air Force, together with twelve Spitfires of No. 92 Squadron, RAF, intercepted a formation of 90 Ju 52s escorted by 50 German and Italian fighters and destroyed 77 enemy aircraft for the loss of six Warhawks and a Spitfire. This great air battle, which went down in history as the 'Palm Sunday Massacre', resulted in the destruction of more enemy aircraft than the RAF shot down at the height of the Battle of Britain. On 22 April, RAF Spitfires and SAAF Kittyhawks followed up this success by shooting down fourteen Me 323s, all laden with fuel, and seven of their escorting fighters. When night fell, the coastal waters off Cape Bon were still ablaze with burning petrol, and of the 140 aircrew of Transport-Geschwader 5 who took part in the operation, only nineteen survived.

For the *Afrika Korps*, it was the end. Yet, right up to the last, the Germans persisted in their reckless attempts to fling reinforcements into the cauldron of Tunisia. The few who did get through were sacrificed on the battlefield or were captured when the final offensive rolled over them in May 1943.

13

Air operations in the West
January 1942 - May 1944

Nineteen forty-two, a year of crisis in the Mediterranean and the Far East, was marked by a series of profound changes in the quality of the equipment available to the home-based RAF commands. This was particularly true of Bomber Command, which had struggled on for so long with inadequate aircraft and navigation aids; at the end of 1941, No. 44 (Rhodesia) Squadron at Waddington became the first unit in No. 5 Group to exchange its weary Hampdens for the newest of the RAF's four-engined heavy bombers, the Avro Lancaster, and in January 1942, Lancasters also began to replace the

Manchesters of No. 207 Squadron at Coningsby. In all, 59 squadrons of Bomber Command were to be equipped with this superlative aircraft before the end of the war. The spring of 1942 also saw the introduction of the first of Bomber Command's long-awaited radar aids: the TR1335, better known as 'Gee'. The basis of Gee was that pulses transmitted by three separate stations were displayed on a cathode-ray tube in the aircraft, enabling the navigator to fix the position of his aircraft from the place where the Gee co-ordinates intersected on his chart. Gee could also be used as a blind bombing aid; no longer would bomber crews be frustrated by ten-tenths cloud cover over their targets. The first large-scale use of Gee was on the night of 8/9 March 1942, when 74 Wellingtons equipped with the device formed the leading wave of a force of 211 aircraft despatched to bomb Essen.

In the early weeks of 1942, part of Bomber Command's effort was still directed against the German battle cruisers sheltering in Brest harbour. The fear now was that they would attempt to break out and join up with the latest addition to the German fleet, the powerful battleship *Tirpitz*, which had put to sea and taken temporary refuge in a Norwegian fjord. In January, air reconnaissance revealed that a breakout by the battle cruisers appeared to be imminent, and on 4 February every available aircraft of Bomber Command was bombed-up and placed on two hours' readiness. At the same time, Nos 10, 11 and 12 Groups of Fighter Command stood ready to provide air cover, while Coastal Command stepped up its reconnaissance sorties over the Channel area. After a week, however, the state of readiness was downgraded and squadrons released for other operations, with the proviso that they could immediately be switched to attacks on the warships if need be.

Meanwhile, Coastal Command was trying to assemble its available torpedo-carrying aircraft; a far from easy task, for the three squadrons of Beauforts operational in the UK were scattered all over the country. No. 42 was at Leuchars, ready to go into action against the *Tirpitz* if it got the chance; half of No. 217 was at Thorney Island and the other half at St Eval; and also at St Eval was No. 86 Squadron, whose crews had only recently converted to the torpedo strike role. Between them, they could muster only 35 aircraft, to which were added six Swordfish of the Fleet Air Arm.

The main hope of inflicting damage on the warships therefore rested with Bomber Command. When the German warships finally broke out on 12 February, however, it was in bad weather, with a cloud base of only 600 feet—which meant that the armour-piercing bombs with which many of the aircraft were loaded were useless, as they had to be dropped from at least 6,000 feet for maximum effect. By the time the bomb loads were changed and the first wave of bombers got airborne, the warships had already been subjected to a gallant and suicidal attack by

Cologne, target of Operation Millennium, the RAF's first thousand-bomber raid. The devastation of Cologne began on the night of 30/31 May 1942; these target shots, taken towards the end of the war, show the destruction wrought upon the city over a three-year period. The cathedral stands in isolation amid the ruins.

Bremen, target of the third thousand-bomber raid on 25/26 June 1942. The Focke-Wulf aircraft factory here was a primary target.

the Swordfish of No. 825 Squadron, Fleet Air Arm (which earned a posthumous VC for their leader, Lieutenant-Commander Eugene Esmonde) and a torpedo strike by a handful of Coastal Command Beauforts.

A total of 242 Bomber Command aircraft set out in three waves but, although most of them reached the target area, only one in six managed to attack the warships. Most failed to sight the enemy vessels at all; others were unable to bomb because of the low cloud base. Fifteen bombers were shot down, in addition to the six FAA Swordfish and three Beauforts. Overhead, RAF fighters fought savage battles with the *Luftwaffe*, which was up in strength to provide cover for the vessels.

The passage of the warships through the English Channel in broad daylight, apart from constituting a serious blow to British pride, revealed the seriously depleted state of Coastal Command's in terms of torpedo strike capability. Soon afterwards, No. 144 Squadron was transferred to Coastal from Bomber Command and its Hampdens converted to carry torpedoes; three other squadrons, Nos 51, 58 and 77, were also withdrawn from the Bomber Command order of battle and assigned to maritime patrol duties. All three used Whitleys in this role until the end of 1942, when they re-equipped with Halifaxes.

The operations against the enemy warships saw the first operational use in the RAF of the first of the new light bomber types destined to replace the ageing Blenheims of No. 2 Group: the Douglas Boston. It entered service with No. 88 Squadron at RAF Swanton Morley in October 1941, and a second squadron, No. 226, received Bostons in November. The Boston, which eventually equipped ten tactical bombing squadrons, carried out its first sortie against a land target on 8 March, when aircraft of No. 2 Group attacked the Matford works at Poissy under cover of diversionary Circus operations, the latter having been resumed after a five-month break.

By the end of March, the use of Gee by aircraft of Bomber Command, together with the development of new target-marking

The Krupps armament factory at Essen and its environs. The Krupps factory was attacked many times by Bomber Command; after one heavy raid in July 1943, Dr Gustav Krupp von Bohlen und Halbach took a look at the devastation and fell down with a heart attack, from which he did not recover until 1947. Ironically, this meant that he had the RAF to thank for the fact that he was not put on trial for war crimes.

techniques, was beginning to have an effect. On 28/29 March, for example, 191 bombers out of 234 despatched carried out a massive incendiary attack on Lübeck, leaving 200 acres of the town devastated. The experiment was repeated a month later, when Rostock was the target for incendiary attacks on four consecutive nights; when they ended, some 60 per cent of the old town lay in ruins, and for the first time the expression 'Terror Raid' became part of the German people's vocabulary.

Meanwhile, Bomber Command had once again learned the hard way the folly of mounting deep-penetration daylight attacks without escort into an environment heavily defended by enemy fighters. On 17 April twelve Lancasters of Nos 44 and 97 Squadrons flew at low level across occupied Europe to attack the M.A.N. factory at Augsburg, which manufactured diesel engines for U-boats. Four Lancasters were shot down by fighters en route, and three more by flak over the target. Considerable damage was inflicted on the factory by the remaining five, and the raid leader, Squadron Leader J.D. Nettleton of No. 44 Squadron, was awarded the Victoria Cross.

On the night of 30/31 May 1942, Bomber Command, encouraged by the increasingly favourable results of night bombing operations in March and April, mounted Operation Millennium, a thousand-bomber raid on Cologne. By using aircraft provided by Nos 91 and 92 Operational Training Groups, amounting to 367 aircraft, Sir Arthur Harris managed to assemble a force of 1,042 bombers. Navigated to the target by Gee-

Ground crews await the return of 'their' bomber at an airfield somewhere in East Anglia. All too often they waited in vain; World War Two cost the RAF over 70,000 killed in action.

equipped aircraft, 898 crews claimed to have made successful attacks, dropping 1,445 tons of bombs. Over 600 acres of Cologne's built-up area were destroyed, and the raid caused severe psychological repercussions throughout Germany. Forty bombers failed to return. Early the following morning, as the Germans were just beginning to assess the damage, the sirens wailed again. High above the pall of smoke that towered up to 15,000 feet over the shattered city, four fast, twin-engined aircraft raced over Cologne and dropped several 500-pound bombs into the heart of the inferno. They were the latest addition to the growing striking power of No. 2 Group: the de Havilland Mosquitos of No. 105 Squadron, carrying out their first bombing operation of the war.

Two more thousand-bomber attacks were

carried out, both of them in June. The first took place on the first night of the month, when 956 bombers were despatched to Essen; 767 crews claimed to have bombed the target area, but subsequent reconnaissance showed little damage. Many crews had, in fact, bombed Oberhausen, Mulheim and Duisburg by mistake. Thirty-one aircraft failed to return.

In the third raid, on 25/26 June, 1,006 aircraft were despatched to Bremen, including 102 Hudsons and Wellingtons of Coastal Command. Despite heavy cloud over the target, the bombers caused considerable damage, particularly to the Focke-Wulf aircraft factory. Forty-four aircraft of Bomber Command and five of Coastal Command failed to return. The raid marked the last operational use of the Avro Manchester, which had been plagued by engine troubles since its service debut; the squadrons involved—Nos 49, 50, 61 and 106—subsequently converted to Lancasters.

Air Chief Marshal Harris had originally hoped to mount thousand-bomber raids at the rate of five a month. However, the strength of Bomber Command was not increasing in proportion to its losses, and nineteen squadrons had been transferred to other Commands in the first half of 1942. This left Harris with only 30 operational squadrons, backed up by the OTUs, with which to carry on the air offensive. It was therefore agreed that the thousand-bomber attacks should be halted until there had been

An H2S radar display. H2S, first used in January 1943, gave Bomber Command the means to obtain accurate target fixes and to bomb through cloud.

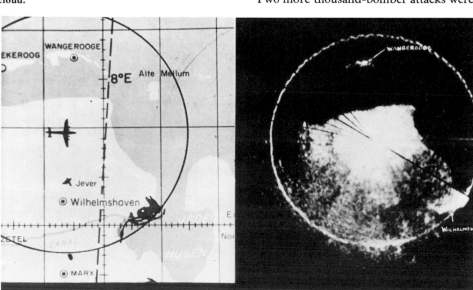

a substantial increase in the strength of Bomber Command, and the opportunity for launching another raid of this size was not to occur again until two more years had passed. In the meantime, the biggest attack launched by Bomber Command during the remainder of 1942 involved a raid by 630 aircraft on the night of 31 July/1 August, and this was not surpassed in strength until a raid on Dortmund carried out on 23/24 May 1943.

An important step forward in the efficiency of Bomber Command was taken on 15 August 1942, when orders were issued for the creation of a Pathfinder Force to be responsible for target marking ahead of the main bomber stream. With its headquarters at Wyton, in Huntingdonshire, the new Force consisted originally of five squadrons, one drawn from each operational Group. From No. 1 Group came No. 156 Squadron, with Wellingtons, and from No. 2 Group No. 109 Squadron with Wellingtons and Mosquitos. No. 3 Group provided No. 7 Squadron, with Stirlings, No. 4 Group transferred the Halifaxes of No. 35 Squadron, and No. 5 Group contributed the Lancasters of No. 83 Squadron. All five squadrons were based on adjacent airfields within the area of No. 3 Group: No. 7 at Oakington, No. 35 at Graveley, Nos 83 and 109 at Wyton and No. 156 at Warboys. The Pathfinder Force was expanded into a new Group—No. 8—in January 1943, and its squadrons eventually re-equipped with Lancasters or Mosquitos. By the end of the European war, it had become the largest Group in Bomber

Command, with nineteen squadrons, a fact that indicated its vital role. The commander of the PFF on its formation was an Australian, Group Captain D.C.T. Bennett, who had helped to pioneer long-range flying before the war; he was to remain with the Pathfinders for the duration of hostilities.

There was, admittedly, no dramatic breakthrough in bombing techniques as a result of the creation of PFF; it was only with the introduction of two new aids, Oboe and H_2S, that the accuracy curve began to climb sharply. Oboe was a radio aid to bombing in which two ground stations transmitted pulses to an aircraft, which received them and re-transmitted them. By measuring the time taken for each pulse to go out and return, the distance of the aircraft from the ground stations could be accurately measured. If the distance of the target from Station A was known, the aircraft could be guided along the arc of a circle whose radius equalled that distance. The bomb release point was calculated and determined by Station B, which 'instructed' the aircraft to release its bomb load when the objective was reached. The first operational use of Oboe was on the night of 20/21 December 1942, when six Mosquitos were despatched by No. 109 Squadron to bomb a power station at Lutterade; three aircraft bombed the primary, but the remainder developed faults in their Oboe equipment and bombed alternates.

H_2S, a completely self-contained unit which was independent of such factors as range from base, was a radio aid to navigation, target location and bombing; it transmitted pulse signals to earth and received back the echoes, which then formed a display on a cathode-ray tube. The display consisted of a series of light spots of varying brilliance, which formed a picture of the terrain over which the aircraft was flying. H_2S was first used on 30/31 January 1943 by the Stirlings and Halifaxes of Nos 7 and 35 Squadrons, PFF, leading the main force in an attack on Hamburg.

Towards the end of 1942, part of Bomber Command's effort was once again directed against targets in Italy. In October and November, Lancasters and Halifaxes flew a

Hamburg. The city was devastated in a series of attacks in July 1943, code-named Operation Gomorrah; the raids marked the first use of 'Window' by the RAF.

A Halifax over Hamburg, silhouetted in the glare of the fires below. Pilots of *Luftwaffe* day fighters used the glare to advantage, patrolling high above the target and then diving to attack bombers silhouetted in this manner.

total of 1,336 sorties against Italian targets. Meanwhile, the light bombers of No. 2 Group had been striking hard at enemy communications, power stations and electronics factories on the continent; one of the most spectacular attacks took place on 6 December, when 93 Bostons, Mosquitos and Lockheed Venturas—the latter having become operational in November—were despatched to make a low-level daylight attack on the Philips factory at Eindhoven. Thirteen aircraft failed to return and two more were lost on the way home; of the remainder, 53 were damaged to some extent. This was the first operational mission by Nos 464 RAAF and 487 RNZAF Squadrons, part of the growing Commonwealth commitment to air operations in the European theatre.

On 21 January 1943, the Combined Chiefs of Staff issued what was known as the Casablanca Directive, which was to lead to the massive, non-stop RAF night offensive that was to become known as the Battle of the Ruhr and to round-the-clock bombing by

the RAF and USAAF. Its main theme was simple: to achieve the progressive destruction and dislocation of the German military, industrial and economic system, and the undermining of the morale of the German people to a point where their capacity for armed resistance was fatally weakened.

Bomber Command's Battle of the Ruhr began on the night of 5/6 March 1943 with an attack by 345 aircraft on Essen, a raid in which Oboe was used on a large scale for the first time. It was as part of this offensive that the newly-formed No. 617 Squadron carried out its celebrated attack on the Ruhr Dams on 16/17 May, its Lancasters breaching the Möhne and Eder Dams and damaging the Sorpe. The cost to the Squadron was high; of seventeen aircraft that attacked their objectives, eight failed to return. The squadron commander, Wing Commander G.P. Gibson, was subsequently awarded the VC.

By mid-1943, increasing successes against the night bombers by the *Luftwaffe*'s night-fighter arm led to the introduction of countermeasures. The first of these was 'Window', strips of tinfoil cut to the wavelength of enemy warning radar and dropped in bundles from attacking aircraft to

confuse the defences. It was first used on the night of 24/25 July 1943, when Bomber Command carried out the first of four large-scale attacks on Hamburg (Operation Gomorrah). Later in the year, No. 100 (Bomber Support) Group was formed under the command of Air Commodore E.B. Addison with the task of operating airborne and ground radio countermeasures and carrying out a long-range fighter offensive against the German air defences.

By this time, the war in the air had become a grim and bloody affair, and Allied intelligence had received indications that the enemy were about to make use of new and devastating secret weapons. On 18 August, Bomber Command despatched 597 heavy bombers in the first attack on the German rocket research centre at Peenemünde, on the Baltic coast; 40 aircraft failed to return, but development of the V-2 rocket was set back by several vital months. Bomber Command was now beginning to receive devastating new weapons too, albeit of a conventional nature; the first of them was the 12,000-pound Tallboy deep-penetration bomb, which was first used on 15/16 September by Lancasters of No. 617 Squadron in a low-level attack on the Dortmund-Ems Canal. The mission cost five aircraft out of eight.

In November 1943, in conjunction with the day bombers of the USAAF, Bomber Command launched the Battle of Berlin. It was to last until the end of March 1944, during which time the Command carried out sixteen major attacks involving the despatch of 9,111 sorties and sixteen minor attacks involving 208 sorties, the latter by Mosquitos. During this period 492 aircraft failed to return and 954 were damaged, of which 95 crashed on return to base. Bomber losses continued to mount, and the success rate of

The German rocket research centre at Peenemünde before and after the first heavy RAF attack on 18 August 1943 that set back V–2 production by several months and killed key enemy scientists. The arrows point to V–2s in covered trailers.

the German fighter force reached an unprecedented peak in the spring of 1944. In the course of three big air battles over darkened Germany, Bomber Command suffered crippling losses. On the night of 19/20 February, 78 out of a force of 823 heavy bombers despatched to attack Leipzig failed to return; 72 more were destroyed during the final big assault on Berlin on 24/25 March; and then, five nights later, came the most catastrophic loss of all when, out of 795 heavy bombers that set out to attack Nuremberg, 95 failed to return and 71 were damaged. It was the worst loss ever sustained by the main force of Bomber Command.

For Fighter Command, the years 1942–43 saw rapid expansion. Most of the day-fighter squadrons were now equipped with Spitfire Mk IXs, although some units had begun to re-equip with a fast and powerful new fighter, the Hawker Typhoon. Unfortunately, this aircraft, rushed into service to combat Focke-Wulf Fw 190 hit-and-run attacks on the south coast of England, was plagued by technical problems well into 1943; nevertheless, it showed outstanding strength and agility at low altitude, and it was later to find its true métier as one of the most superlative ground-attack aircraft of all time with the squadrons of the Tactical Air Force, formed on 1 June 1943 on the dissolution of Army Co-operation Command and led by Air Marshal J.H. d'Albiac.

The sternest test for Fighter Command during this period was the Dieppe operation of 19 August 1942, one object of which was to bring to battle the whole forces of the *Luftwaffe* in northern France and the Low Countries. Control of RAF operations was given to Air Vice-Marshal Trafford Leigh-Mallory of No. 11 Group, and 56 fighter squadrons of Hurricanes, Spitfires and Typhoons were placed at his disposal, as well as five Blenheim and Boston squadrons of No. 2 Group and four Mustang squadrons of Army Co-operation Command. The North Amer-

Avro Lancaster B Mk II of No. 426 (Thunderbird) Squadron, No. 6 Group RCAF, at Linton-on-Ouse early in 1944. The B Mk II, powered by Bristol Hercules engines, was built as an insurance against supplies of Rolls-Royce Merlins running out, but in the event there were plenty of Merlins to go around and only 300 B Mk IIs were built. In addition to No. 426 Squadron, they also equipped Nos 61, 115 and 514 Squadrons of the RAF.

The Hawker Typhoon. Plagued by technical troubles at the outset of its career, the Typhoon nevertheless went on to be an outstanding fighter-bomber with the 2nd Tactical Air Force and inflicted terrible casualties on enemy armour.

'Lichtenstein' radar array on a Ju 88. By early 1944, enemy AI radar was as effective as Allied equipment and required a major jamming effort. For this purpose, No. 100 (Countermeasures) Group came into being.

ican Mustang was a recent addition to the RAF, having become operational in July.

Dieppe, in the event, was a disaster for the RAF as well as for the troops who went ashore on the great combined raid. In the day's operations, the RAF lost 106 aircraft against the *Luftwaffe*'s 48. Apart from that, the RAF had shown itself to be seriously lacking in adequate ground support techniques, and it was this fact that was later to lead to the establishment of the Tactical Air Force that would soon blast a path through northern Europe to the Baltic shores.

In 1942, Fighter Command carried out 43,000 offensive cross-Channel sorties, as well as 73,000 sorties involving such tasks as air defence and shipping protection. The night-fighter squadrons, equipped with a mixture of Beaufighters and Mosquitos, were registering growing successes against enemy bombers, and intruder operations were being carried out on an increasing scale against enemy airfields.

The activities of the night-fighter squadrons during the 1942–43 period can best be illustrated by the following combat report, submitted by Wing Commander J.R.D. Braham of No. 141 Squadron. It involves an action off Ameland on the night of 17/18 August 1943. Braham was flying a Beaufighter Mk VI, and his navigator was Flight Lieutenant H. Jacobs.

We took off from Coltishall at 22.00 hours on intruder patrol to Stade. We flew to a point north of Schiermonnikoog and then turned NE at 22.54. We continued on course for about five minutes when we sighted one Me 110 flying east and jinking. We turned and followed him towards the coast, closing in on the aircraft until we were at 300 yards range, 20 degrees starboard astern and a little below. Fire was opened with a two-second burst from all guns and strikes were seen all over the enemy aircraft. Smoke came from the port engine and the Me 110 dived to port. We gave him another two-second burst from 250 yards and he caught fire and dived into the sea, burning on the water. Immediately afterwards we saw a second Me 110 (which had been chasing us) a little above and turning gently to starboard on an easterly course. We gave a one-second burst of cannon and machine-gun at 50 yards in a gentle turn. The enemy aircraft appeared to blow up and we had to pull up and turn to port to avoid ramming it. At that point we saw one man bale out and his parachute open, and the enemy aircraft dived vertically to the sea in flames . . . we landed at Wittering at 01.45.

Equally as illustrative, this time of a day-fighter squadron's activities, is an extract from the war diary of No. 118 (Spitfire) Squadron, 29 January 1943:

Misery [the Squadron Intelligence Officer] went on a 48 and of course things happened: there were four flights by 27 aircraft in fine weather. In the morning there was drogue towing, air-to-air and air-to-sea firing, camera gun practice, camera tests and in the afternoon a sweep over Ijmuiden . . . In the afternoon the Squadron made rendezvous with 167 and twelve Venturas over Mundesley and flew at sea level to within a few miles of the Dutch coast, then climbed to 9,000 feet over Ijmuiden.

As we crossed the coast four Fw 190s were seen breaking cloud below at 2,000 feet. Our allotted task was to give top cover to the bombers which, instead of bombing immediately, went inland for ten minutes then turned round and bombed from east to west on an outward heading. Squadron Leader Wooton decided not to go down for the 190s until the bombers had carried out their task, or while they were still in danger of being attacked. While the bombers and escorts were making their incursion the 190s climbed up and were joined by others, but before they could attack the bombers they were engaged by 118 Squadron. In the resultant dogfight, of which no-one seemed to have a very clear picture, Sgt Lack destroyed a Fw 190 which he followed down to sea level and set on fire; it was eventually seen to crash into the sea by Hallingworth.

Hallingworth was attacked and his aircraft hit, and he in turn claimed a 190 damaged. The CO, who engaged the leading Fw 190, also claimed one damaged, the enemy aircraft breaking away after being hit by cannon fire and going down followed by Sgt Buglass, who lost sight of it. Shepherd went to Hailingworth's rescue when he was being attacked, and was himself fired at head-on by two Fw 190s. Flight Sergeant Cross is missing from this engagement; no-one saw what happened to him, but as he was flying number two to Shepherd it is believed that he must have been hit during the double attack on his section leader. The Squadron got split up during the engagement, seven aircraft coming back together and the other four in two pairs. No-one saw Cross crash. He was a very nice, quiet Canadian and will be very much missed . . .

14

From Sicily to the Balkans
1943~45

In the early summer of 1943, the bomb-battered island of Malta underwent a complete transformation. It was now that the gallant resistance of the island's people and garrison bore fruit, for in June Malta swarmed with aircraft and personnel, all standing ready for the next phase of the Allied plan in the Mediterranean: the invasion of Sicily. The whole of the Desert Air Force flew in, together with much of the 1st Tactical Air Force from Tunisia; to accommodate the influx, another airstrip was bulldozed on Gozo and the overspill went to the newly-captured islands of Pantelleria and Lampedusa.

At the beginning of July, 40 Allied squadrons were in position on the Mediterranean islands, and bombers were hammering enemy communications in southern Italy around the clock. During the first week of July the bombers switched their main effort to airfields and gun emplacements on Sicily itself; these attacks effectively paralyzed the *Luftwaffe* presence on the island, forcing the remnants of Luftflotte 2's squadrons to re-establish themselves at bases on the Italian mainland.

The seaborne invasion of Sicily was to be preceded by airborne landings carried out by glider-borne troops of the British 1st Airborne Division and parachute troops of the US 82nd Airborne Division. Assembling the necessary gliders—Waco Hadrians and Airspeed Horsas—for the operation had been no easy task, for they had had to be air-towed from England by the Albemarles and Halifaxes of No. 38 Wing, flying in broad daylight within 100 miles of enemy-held south-western France. Despite all the hazards, 27 out of 30 Horsas reached North Africa by 7 July.

The plan called for the 1st Air Landing Brigade of the 1st Airborne Division to put down its gliders near Syracuse and capture the Ponte Grande, the strategic bridge south of the town, while the US 82nd Airborne dropped farther west in the Gela/Licata area. The operation, code-named Husky, got under way on the night of 9/10 July, with 1,200 men of the Air Landing Brigade towed

to the battlefield in 137 gliders. The tugs were Dakotas of the US Troop Carrier Command and 28 Albemarle and seven Halifax aircraft belonging to Nos 296 and 297 Squadrons, No. 38 Wing, all flying from airfields in the vicinity of Kairouan. Ahead of the glider force, Hurricanes of No. 73 Squadron patrolled the drop zones, ready to knock out any searchlights. At the same time, Wellingtons of No. 205 Group attacked Syracuse, Catania and several other targets; these aircraft also dropped dummy parachutists to confuse the defences.

The glider operation was not a success. Twelve gliders, all towed by the RAF, reached the landing zone; of the remainder, mostly towed by the Americans, 69 came down in the sea with heavy loss of life and 56 were scattered all over the south-east coast of Sicily. The problem was that the American Dakota crews were not experienced in night flying, and even less experienced in glider towing and release techniques. Nevertheless, the Ponte Grande was captured by eight officers and 65 other ranks, who held on until the middle of the following afternoon. Reduced to fifteen in number, they were finally overwhelmed—but the bridge was retaken almost immediately by units of the 8th Army, who had landed by sea, before the enemy had a chance to destroy it.

The seaborne landings took place under a massive fighter umbrella of Spitfires and Warhawks, which flew 1,092 sorties on that first day of the invasion. The *Luftwaffe* made no attempt to interfere with the landings, but small numbers of Ju 88s appeared during the course of the day and twelve ships were sunk. In one attack, the aircraft carrier HMS *Indomitable* was torpedoed by a lone Ju 88 and put out of action for almost a year. After dark, the beaches were patrolled by the Beaufighters of No. 108 Squadron, operating out of Malta, and intruder Mosquitos of No. 23 Squadron.

The first RAF aircraft to land in Sicily was a Spitfire of No. 72 Squadron (Flying Officer D.N. Keith) which ran out of fuel after shooting down two enemy aircraft and landed on the airfield at Pachino, which was

being repaired by Royal Engineers and men of No. 3201 RAF Servicing Commando Unit on the morning of 11 July. The airfield's surface was still unsuitable for take-off, so after being refuelled Keith's Spitfire was dragged to a nearby road, from which he took off successfully. The first Spitfire squadrons of No. 244 Wing arrived from Malta on 13 July, and six more Spitfire squadrons, together with six USAAF fighter units, flew in on the 16th. From then on, the build-up of the 1st Tactical Air Force in Sicily proceeded at a rapid rate.

If the air operations over Sicily proved anything, it was that there was an urgent need for tighter co-operation between air and ground or naval forces. This was illustrated on the night of 13/14 July, when men of the 1st Parachute Brigade set out to capture an important bridge at Primo Sole in 107 US Dakotas and seventeen gliders, the latter towed by RAF Albemarles and Halifaxes. As the aircraft crossed the invasion fleet—which they should never have done in the first place—they came under heavy anti-aircraft fire, as the warships were being attacked by Ju 88s and were scattered all over the sky. Ten Dakotas, three Albemarles and a Halifax were shot down, and only a quarter of the airborne force reached the objective at the right time. Despite this, the operation succeeded.

As the days went on, the *Luftwaffe*'s attacks on the Sicilian beach-heads became fewer; the Allied fighters were taking their toll of Luftflotte 2's bombers by day and night. On the night of 15/16 July, for example, the Mosquito crews of No. 256 Squadron encountered six enemy aircraft and shot down five of them. Meanwhile, bombers of No. 205 Group, RAF, and the USAAF were striking hard at enemy airfields in Italy, in addition to their continuing onslaught against communications, ports and supply depots. At sea, aircraft of the Northwest African Coastal Air Force—mainly Wellingtons—harried enemy shipping in the Mediterranean.

As they had done in Tunisia, the Germans made determined attempts to keep their

Spitfire Mk IXs of No. 241 Squadron fly past Mount Vesuvius. No. 241 Squadron moved to Italy in December 1943 and carried out tactical and shipping recce, escort and ground attack duties for the remainder of the war.

A Spitfire Mk Vc of a Desert Air Force unit on an Italian airfield in 1944.

forces supplied and reinforced by flying in personnel and equipment—and, as in Tunisia, these operations often met with disaster. On 25 July, for example, 33 Spitfires of the RAF's No. 322 Wing intercepted a formation of Ju 52s attempting to land on a coastal strip near Milazzo, in the north of the island. Twenty-one Ju 52s and four escorting Bf 109s were shot down within ten minutes.

Despite the overwhelming Allied air superiority, the Germans succeeded in withdrawing the bulk of their forces from Sicily in an orderly manner, using tanks and any other means to bulldoze a path through demoralized Italian columns that were streaming back towards the Straits of Messina. It was hardly surprising that when the battle for Sicily ended in mid-August, the bulk of the 162,000 prisoners taken were Italians. In the air, the Allies had lost less than 400 aircraft; on the credit side, they had destroyed or captured 1,850 Axis machines.

On 3 September, British forces landed at Reggio in Calabria, and on the 9th—the day after the Italian government surrendered unconditionally, a move that resulted in the Germans seizing full control of all defensive measures—a second Allied landing was made at Salerno, with the object of capturing the port of Naples and cutting off the German forces retreating before the British advance from Reggio. But things went badly from the start; the Germans, under Field Marshal Kesselring, counter-attacked ferociously and for a time it looked as though the Anglo-American forces would be hurled back into the sea. This time, because of the distance of Salerno from the recently-captured airfields in Sicily—which meant that the RAF's Spitfires and Kittyhawks

The Focke-Wulf Fw 190 became operational in North Africa during the Battle for Tunisia and was superior to most Allied fighter types. This propaganda photograph, issued in Portugal, shows an Fw 190 purporting to be attacking a British tank near the Via Balbia, but the smoke appears to be faked.

could only patrol the invasion area for less than 30 minutes at a time, and then only in small numbers—much of the air cover was provided by the USAAF's longer-range Mustangs and Lightnings and by Seafires of the Fleet Air Arm, the latter operating from escort and fleet carriers. This reduced fighter cover enabled the *Luftwaffe* bombers to score a number of successes against the Allied naval forces; the battleship HMS *Warspite*, for example, was hit by glider bombs and put out of action for six months, while the Italian battleship *Roma*, en route for Malta to surrender, was sunk by similar weapons.

The air cover situation improved considerably after 12 September, when US Lightnings, FAA Seafires and three squadrons of Spitfires of No. 324 Wing were flown to a hastily-prepared airstrip at Paestum, but for some days the situation remained critical. The crisis of the battle came on 14 September, a day that saw 700 sorties flown by the fighters and fighter-bombers of the 1st Tactical Air Force; meanwhile, heavy and medium bombers of the USAAF and No. 205 Group RAF attacked road and rail targets to prevent enemy reinforcements reaching the battle area.

By 16 September, the Salerno beachhead was secure, and on 1 October the 7th Armoured Division entered Naples. The 5th and 8th Armies now began a steady advance; by 6 October the former was on the line of the Volturno river and the 8th was facing

Termoli, so completing the second phase of the campaign. The third phase envisaged the capture of Rome, to be followed by a rapid advance on Leghorn, Florence and Arezzo.

October and November 1943 saw the Allies across the Volturno, Trigno and Sangro rivers, all of which involved bitter fighting against a determined enemy. This, in essence, was to be the continuing story of the Italian campaign: one swift-flowing river after another, each one more heavily defended than the one before. There were to be no brilliantly-executed armoured dashes here, as there would be later in north-west Europe. Italy was a hard slog from beginning to end, and in many instances an advance of a few miles was only accomplished with an overwhelming weight of tactical air power.

It was amid the mountains and rivers of Italy that tactical air support was brought to a fine art by the Desert Air Force, in co-operation with the 8th Army. In the desert, a request for air support had been passed through a mobile operations room, which allotted the target to a particular Wing. This had worked quite well in an area where there was a good deal of room for manoeuvre, and where considerable time often elapsed between enemy forces being sighted and engaged. In Italy, however, it was a different story; army units fighting in close country usually needed air support very quickly indeed. A system known as Rover David was therefore instituted, under which fighter-bombers maintained standing patrols over the battle area. When a call for assistance was received, aircraft were detached from the overhead 'Cab Rank' to attack whatever

target was designated. The system worked in conjuction with an RAF Forward Air Controller, but the fact that it worked at all was due entirely to the absence of *Luftwaffe* fighters over the front line.

On 10 December 1943, all Allied air units in the Mediterranean came under the aegis of a new organization, the Mediterranean Allied Air Forces. One of the first major operations under the control of the new Command was mounted in support of the Allied landings at Anzio and Nettuno on the west coast of Italy, a move designed to outflank the formidable enemy defences at Monte Cassino, which commanded the coastal road approach to Rome. As a preliminary to the landings, which took place on 22 January 1944, the Allied air forces struck hard at enemy airfields in central Italy, and it was not until several hours after the troops went ashore that *Luftwaffe* reconnaissance aircraft were able to give Kesselring a clear picture of what was happening.

Unfortunately, the invasion forces failed to exploit their initial success for a variety of reasons, and although the Allied air forces dropped 12,500 tons of bombs on enemy airfields and communications between 22 January and 15 February 1944, they could not prevent the Germans launching a fierce counter-attack. With the help of strong air support, including the dropping of more than 10,000 fragmentation bombs on enemy troop concentrations, the counter-attack was

A Martin Baltimore of a Desert Air Force squadron attacking an enemy target over northern Italy in 1944.

contained. It had, however, come perilously close to succeeding, and the forces at Anzio were as yet in no state to break out.

The spotlight now fell on Monte Cassino, where the ancient monastery was reduced to rubble by USAAF bombers on 15 February. It is not within the scope of this book to discuss the necessity for, or the implications of that action; but later that day the town of Cassino itself was also destroyed, and this time RAF aircraft played an active part. The main attacks were carried out by eleven groups of the Strategic Air Force and five groups of the Tactical Air Force, while Kittyhawks of the Desert Air Force attacked gun positions in the neighbourhood and RAF Spitfires provided part of the overhead air cover. The bombing attacks created exactly the opposite effect to that required, the tumbled blocks of masonry and piles of rubble forming excellent defensive positions where none had previously existed. Not until two months later, after one of the most bitter and prolonged close-quarter battles of the war, did Cassino fall.

In the meantime, during March 1944, the Mediterranean Allied Air Forces made a determined effort to paralyze the enemy communications network in Italy by mounting Operation Strangle, in which 19,460 tons of bombs were dropped on the road and railway system. A further 51,500 tons were dropped in a subsequent operation, code-named Diadem, but although severe damage was inflicted on the Italian railway system the attacks lacked concentration; with hindsight, it would have been more profitable to select a limited number of very important targets, such as repair and maintenance facilities, and subject them to continual heavy attacks. As it was, the enemy managed to carry out the majority of repairs quickly and efficiently. Although the supply of material to troops at the front was undoubtedly slowed down, the flow never ceased.

A new Allied offensive opened on 11 May 1944, and on 4 June the Allies at last entered Rome, which had been declared an open city. Within two weeks, the Allied invasion of Normandy had brought about a profound change in the situation in Italy, at least insofar as air operations were concerned; *Luftwaffe* units were hurriedly transferred to north-west Europe from northern Italy, leaving Luftflotte 2's commander, General Ritter von Pohl, with only three Staffeln of Bf 109s (about 30 aircraft) for tactical reconnaissance, about 100 fighters of all types, including Italian, a long-range reconnaissance group and three Staffeln of night bombers. It was a far cry from the formidable striking power that Luftflotte 2 had hurled across

the English Channel in the summer of 1940.

In support of the Allied advance into northern Italy, the Tactical Air Force flew an average of 1,000 sorties daily, with roads, railways and supply dumps still the primary objectives. Despite this, there was little prospect of any rapid Allied victory; Field Marshal Alexander, the Allied commander, had lost seven divisions which had been withdrawn to take part in the invasion of Normandy, while his opponent, Kesselring, had been reinforced by eight. Moreover, in August 1944 a large part of the Allied effort in the Mediterranean was diverted to Operation Dragoon, the invasion of the French Riviera, which began on the night of the 14/15. Much of the tactical support and the airborne operations was undertaken by the USAAF, although the transport aircraft were escorted by RAF Spitfires and Beaufighters and the Coastal Air Forces covered the approach of the seaborne convoys. With the capture of Toulon and Marseille later in August, the Germans no longer had any U-boat bases in the Mediterranean and the task of the Coastal Air Forces consequently became much lighter.

While US and Free French forces were pushing inland from the Riviera late in August, Halifaxes, Wellingtons and Liberators of No. 205 Group, RAF, launched a series of heavy night attacks on targets in the Ravenna area in preparation for the 8th Army's assault on the Gothic Line, the major enemy defensive position following the line of the Po Valley. The pressure was maintained during daylight by aircraft of the Desert Air Force, which hit enemy communications, gun positions and strongpoints. By the end of September, after hard fighting, enemy resistance had been broken and the Allies were through the main defences. For six months thereafter, however, the onset of the northern Italian winter brought an effective halt to further major advances for six months, and the tempo of air operations declined dramatically.

The early spring of 1944 had seen a major effort by the nine squadrons of No. 205 Group against railway targets in south-east Europe, the aim being to assist the Soviet advance into Romania. Oil targets were also attacked, often in the teeth of strong flak and night-fighter opposition. The bulk of the oil from the Romanian fields was transported to Germany via the River Danube, and in the summer of 1944 this vital waterway was heavily mined by Wellingtons and Liberators of No. 205 Group. By 5 October, after eighteen major attacks over a period of six months, the Group's aircraft had laid 1,382 mines; at the same time, Beaufighters of the

Mediterranean Allied Coastal Air Force flew many intruder operations against enemy river craft, destroying eight large oil barges and 102 other vessels amounting to some 100,000 tons of shipping.

When the Allied tactical air offensive resumed in northern Italy in 1945, priority was given to the disruption of rail communications between Italy and Austria, the only supply route that was now open to the enemy. In January, 1,725 tons of bombs were dropped on the road and rail approaches to the Brenner Pass, which were completely dislocated, and marshalling yards in both Austria and northern Italy were also hard hit. By the middle of March, the German forces in Italy were virtually isolated.

The last great air offensive of the Italian campaign was launched on 9 April 1945 against sixteen German and one Italian divisions on the Appenine-Senio line, when more than 1,700 heavy, medium and fighter-bombers dropped 2,000 tons of bombs on the enemy positions. This massive air attack was followed up by an equally devastating artillery barrage, which was lifted for four-minute intervals to allow fighter-bombers to attack strongpoints. After dark, Liberators of No. 205 Group unloaded their bombs on objectives which the Allied artillery had designated with red smoke markers. On the following day, when the 8th Army launched its assault, the line began to crumble, and by 21 April, after the 5th Army had also attacked in the centre, it was completely broken. There was no stopping the relentless advance of the Allied armies now; the remaining objectives fell in rapid succession, and on 24 April German representatives signed the instrument of unconditional surrender at Field Marshal Alexander's Headquarters. The ceasefire would not officially take effect until 2 May, but to all intents and purposes the war in the Mediterranean Theatre, started by Benito Mussolini in the Western Desert five years earlier, was over.

Meanwhile the RAF's support of the various resistance movements in the Balkans had started as early as October 1941, when two Whitleys of No. 138 (Special Duties) Squadron were deployed to Malta to carry out a special operation involving the dropping of agents and supply containers into Yugoslavia. In the event, the operation was only a partial success; one of the Whitleys, flown by Pilot Officer Austin, found the Yugoslav DZ in daylight and dropped containers, but for a variety of reasons (one of which was that the agents arrived in Malta without parachutes, and no spares were available) no personnel were dropped.

A Beaufighter of the Balkan Air Force attacking a target in Greece with rocket fire during the winter of 1944–45.

The next mission to Yugoslavia was flown in May 1942, when four Liberators of No. 108 Squadron from Egypt dropped supplies to partisan forces; a limited number of similar operations were subsequently carried out by an Egypt-based unit known as X Flight, and in March 1943 this formed the nucleus of No. 148 Squadron, re-formed after its disbandment as a Wellington unit the previous December. In April 1943, the Squadron moved to Derna with ten Halifaxes and the four Liberators of the former X Flight; for the remainder of the year it shared special operations with No. 624 Squadron, which formed at Blida in September from No. 1575 Flight, the latter having arrived in North Africa from the UK in June with a mixture of Halifaxes and Venturas.

In September 1943, following the surrender of Italy, the Allies made an ill-starred attempt to regain a foothold in the Aegean. The primary objective was to seize the island of Rhodes as a preliminary to an invasion of Greece. Eight Dakotas of No. 216 Squadron were detailed to drop paratroops on the islands of Kos, Leros and Samos as a first step; the operation was also to be supported by four Beaufighter squadrons, one squadron of Wellingtons, three of Baltimores, one of Hudsons, three of Spitfires and two of Hurricanes. Two heavy bomber squadrons of No. 240 Wing, which formed part of the US IX Bomber Command, were also assigned.

On 13 September, a British Commando force landed on Kos and occupied the port and airfield. At dawn the next day two Beaufighters flew in, followed by the Spitfires of No. 7 Squadron, SAAF, and the ground forces were further strengthened by the arrival of 120 paratroops. The islands of Leros and Samos were also occupied by 16 September. However, the Germans had strengthened their defences in the Aegean following Italy's collapse, and they now launched a furious air onslaught on the three islands. Nine Spitfires of No. 74 Squadron were flown in to assist the air defences, but the Germans soon achieved complete air superiority and on 3 October they landed on Kos, which was defended by 880 soldiers and 235 men of the RAF Regiment. Within 24 hours Kos had been retaken, the remnants of its garrison taking to the hills to carry on a guerrilla war, and Leros and Samos were also recaptured in November, despite heavy air action against enemy shipping by Beaufighters, Liberators and Mitchells.

In January 1944, Nos 148 and 624 Squadrons moved to Brindisi, where both units operated alongside a Polish SD Flight, No. 1586. All SD units in the Mediterranean now came under the control of No. 334 Wing, which had been formed the previous November and which had established its HQ at the Italian airfield. No. 148 now had a flight of Westland Lysanders, and these were used for pick-up operations from various locations in Greece; in May 1944 they were detached to Calvi, in Corsica, for similar operations in southern France as a preliminary to the Allied landings on the Riviera.

From April 1944, Dakotas of No. 267 Squadron, based on Bari, were attached to No. 334 Wing from time to time for special operations. The first of these was carried out on the night of 15/16 April, when a Dakota piloted by Flight Lieutenant E.J. Harrod made a ten-hour, 1,600-mile round trip to Poland to pick up vital intelligence documents and five passengers, including a senior officer of the Polish Home Army. A second Dakota mission to Poland was flown on 29 May and a third on 25 July. The latter, made by Flight Lieutenant S.G. Culliford, a New Zealander, was a hazardous venture, because it had to be flown partly in daylight, but Culliford returned safely with 1,000 pounds of equipment—the fragments of a V-2 rocket which had exploded over Poland on a test flight.

The Dakotas of No. 267 Squadron, together with their American counterparts, were to carry out many more pickup operations on behalf of No. 334 Wing before the end of hostilities. Meanwhile, in June 1944, the special duties squadrons at Brindisi had been hard at work over Yugoslavia, northern Italy and Greece, flying a combined total of 169 sorties, and on 7 June a new RAF Group was formed at Bari with the object of co-ordinating operations on behalf of the partisan forces in the Balkans. This Group, under the command of Air Vice-Marshal William Elliott, contained units of no fewer than eight nationalities. No. 334 Wing was absorbed into it, and for a time it also had two Soviet air force squadrons under its operational control.

The sternest test for the special duties units came in August 1944, when they flew intensively in support of the Polish uprising in Warsaw. In addition to the SD squadrons, supplies were also dropped by the Liberators of No. 178 Squadron from Amendola and Nos 31 and 34 Squadrons, SAAF, from Foggia. In four nights, between 13 and 16

A Junkers Ju 52/3m under attack over the Mediterranean. The Ju 52 is a mine countermeasures aircraft and is equipped with a degaussing ring to detonate magnetic mines.

August, seventeen Polish and 62 British and South African Halifaxes and Liberators attempted to reach Warsaw. Thirty-four of them succeeded, but of this total only twenty were able to make their drops, fifteen of which reached the Home Army. These four nights cost the Poles three aircraft, the South Africans seven and the British five—in other words, nearly 50 per cent of those which got through to the Polish capital. Another three aircraft were destroyed when they crashed on landing, and almost all the others had battle damage. Fourteen more aircraft were lost during the last two weeks of August and, with the prospect of further serious losses during the September moon period, operations to Warsaw were halted. It made no difference; Warsaw's death warrant had already been signed by the Russians, who refused to advance in support of the insurgents.

Air Vice-Marshal Elliott's Group was now known as the Balkan Air Force, and early in October the SD units at Brindisi were engaged in air supply operations in support of Operation Manna, the Allied invasion and occupation of southern Greece, a venture made possible by planned German withdrawals northwards. During the Greek operations, Allied aircraft dropped or landed some 2,700 tons of supplies to the partisans and the British forces, the RAF delivering about two-thirds of the total.

The Allied invasion was followed by a bitter civil war, with left wing partisans (ELAS) taking advantage of the confusion and attempting to seize control of Athens. Rocket and cannon attacks were carried out by Beaufighters and Spitfires in support of the troops fighting ELAS, and on one occasion rocket-firing Beaufighters of No. 39 Squadron blasted holes in the walls of the Averoff prison, which was being used as an ELAS stronghold, allowing an assault by men of the 2nd Parachute Brigade. The ELAS terrorists were gradually driven from the city, their transport harrassed all the way by the RAF, and a cease-fire was eventually agreed on 12 January 1945.

The Balkan Air Force now turned its attention to Yugoslavia, where the German forces were in full retreat. As they fell back towards Sarajevo, the enemy were hotly engaged by partisan forces, and the latter were constantly supported by Spitfires and rocket-firing Hurricanes. Meanwhile, Beaufighters struck at the last enemy shipping in the Adriatic, while squadrons of the Desert Air Force—their Kittyhawks now replaced by Mustangs—destroyed road and rail bridges in the path of the German retreat. The climax came in April 1945, when the Balkan Air Force, in the course of some 3,000 sorties, destroyed or damaged 800 vehicles, 60 locomotives and 40 naval craft. In the closing weeks of these operations, the heavy bombers of No. 205 Group joined transport aircraft in dropping supplies to both Allied forces and to the starving Yugoslav population, who had laboured for so long under the German yoke but who had never admitted defeat.

One RAF unit, which had seen air operations in the Middle East and the Mediterranean through from the very beginning, was not there to see their conclusion in the mountains of Yugoslavia. In February 1945, No. 267 Squadron took its Dakotas to Burma in support of the 14th Army's coming offensive. The war in Europe might be drawing to a close, but in the Far East there was still a long road to travel.

15

Air operations in the West
1944-45

By the beginning of 1944, the squadrons of the 2nd Tactical Air Force—formed in the previous June—were giving frequent demonstrations of their capabilities in action against targets on the Continent. While the medium bombers of No. 2 Group continued their attacks on the enemy power industry and communications, the tactical fighter-bombers of Nos 83 and 84 Groups—Spitfires, Typhoons, Mustangs and Mosquitos—stepped up their operations against the transport system in France and the Low Countries, carrying out low-level attacks on rolling stock and other targets of opportunity.

By this time, the Mosquito squadrons of No. 2 Group had brought low-level precision attacks to a fine art. This was ably demonstrated on 18 February 1944 when three Mosquito squadrons of No. 140 Wing—Nos 21 RAF, 487 RNZAF and 464 RAAF—carried out a daring low-level operation to breach the walls of Amiens Prison, where several hundred French Resistance workers were threatened with execution. The raid was successful, but the leader, Group Captain P.C. Pickard, and his navigator, Flight Lieutenant Alan Broadley, were killed when their Mosquito was shot down by a Fw 190.

Attacks on enemy shipping reached a new level of importance in 1944 as the invasion date approached. Here, Beaufighters of Coastal Command carry out rocket attacks on enemy minesweepers off the Dutch coast. By mid-1944, Coastal Command had a powerful force of strike wings equipped with either Beaufighters or Mosquitos.

Two months later, in what an Air Ministry bulletin described as 'probably the most brilliant feat of low-level precision bombing of the war', the Mosquitos struck again. On 11 April, six Mosquitos of No. 613 Squadron led by Wing Commander Bob Bateson hit the Gestapo Headquarters at the Hague, the nerve-centre of German operations against the Resistance in the Low Countries. The raid was a complete success; the Gestapo building was completely destroyed, but the buildings that surrounded it suffered only slight damage. All six Mosquitos returned safely to base.

As the spring of 1944 approached, and with it the date when the long-awaited invasion of Europe could be finalized, the importance of attacks on enemy shipping within range of the British Isles reached a new level. This was the responsibility of Coastal Command. Low-level shipping attack techniques had been pioneered in 1941–42 by Nos 206 and 220 Squadrons RAF, No. 320 (Dutch) Squadron and No. 407 Squadron RCAF, all with Hudsons. The Command's three UK-based squadrons of torpedo-carrying Beauforts had also registered notable successes, as we have seen in a previous chapter, but they suffered from a slow reaction time; what Coastal Command needed was a force of aircraft fast enough to intercept enemy shipping whenever and wherever it was reported in the North Sea and Channel areas, and powerful enough to inflict crippling damage upon it.

The answer lay in the formation of strike wings equipped with Beaufighters. The first was formed at RAF North Coates in November 1942 and consisted of No. 143 Squadron, with Beaufighter Mk IIs, No 236 with Beaufighter Mk Is and No. 254 Squadron with torpedo-carrying Beaufighter Mk VIs. The strike wing flew its first operation on 20 November against a convoy off Rotterdam, and results were discouraging; one large merchant vessel and two escorts were hit, but the attacking aircraft became split up in bad weather and arrived over the target in ones and twos, falling victim to escorting Fw 190s. Three Beaufighters were shot down, and four more were so badly damaged that they had to be written off. After this episode the strike wing was withdrawn from operations for further training; it returned to action the following spring, and this time produced excellent results. On 18 April, nine Torbeaus of No 254 Squadron, together with six Beaufighters each from Nos 143 and 236 Squadrons, escorted by Spitfires and Mustangs, virtually destroyed an enemy convoy in Dutch waters and all the attacking aircraft returned safely to base. The idea was therefore proven to be basically sound, and in the summer of 1943 a second Coastal Command Strike Wing was formed. This comprised No. 455 Squadron RAAF and No. 489 Squadron RNZAF, both operating Torbeaus from RAF Leuchars.

Meanwhile, the long-range squadrons of Coastal Command—equipped now with Sunderlands, Catalinas, Wellingtons, Liberators and Fortresses—were at last helping to turn the tide of war in the Atlantic. By January 1943, the first production ASV Mk III anti-submarine radars were being evaluated at the Coastal Command Development Unit, RAF Chivenor; these could detect a surfaced submarine at a range of twenty nautical miles. At the same time, American-designed ASV Mk V equipment was also coming into service in RAF Liberator aircraft. As a result, the number of U-boat sightings and successful attacks increased dramatically; in 1943, Coastal Command destroyed 72 enemy submarines in Atlantic, Arctic and home waters, com-

contact was lost to a low attack height, in some cases only 40 feet. At night, the use of the Leigh Light—an airborne searchlight developed by Squadron Leader Leigh with the assistance of the Coastal Command Development Unit—solved the problem if the aircraft could be homed to within searchlight range, but the real answer was a low-altitude radar bombsight and this was developed in 1943. By the beginning of 1944, the air war over the ocean had become a matter of measure and countermeasure, and it was a war in which the U-boat was always one jump ahead of the aircraft that sought to destroy it. Also, as the war progressed and the German navy received more powerful U-boats with heavy defensive armament, their crews became more inclined to remain on the surface and shoot it out. Actions of this kind resulted in the award of three Victoria Crosses to Coastal Command pilots. The first went to Flying Officer L.A. Trigg,

pared with sixteen in 1942. At the end of 1943, however, the Germans introduced countermeasures in the form of S-band Naxos receivers, which could detect an approaching aircraft at ranges of up to ten nautical miles, and U-boat sightings once again fell away.

Even when a U-boat was caught on the surface, a successful interception was far from simple. The conversion from a radar contact to a visual acquisition for an attack was complicated by the need for the aircraft to descend at the critical time at which the

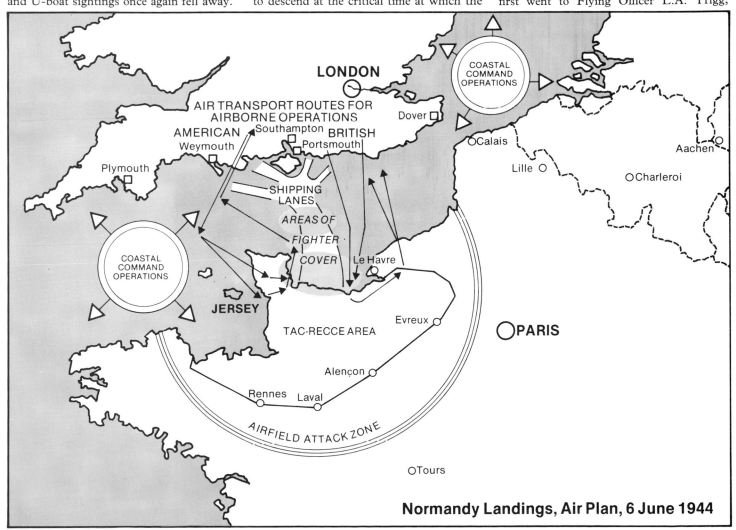

Normandy Landings, Air Plan, 6 June 1944

RNZAF, of No. 200 Squadron, who had already won a DFC for a certain submarine kill and other probables. On 11 August 1943, his Liberator was brought down over the Atlantic by accurate and heavy return fire after sinking another U-boat. Trigg, who could have broken off the attack, died in his aircraft, and the award of the VC was made on the evidence of submarine survivors.

The second VC was Flight Lieutenant D.E. Hornell of No. 162 (RCAF) Squadron who, while commanding a Catalina on Atlantic patrol on 24 June 1944, sank a surfaced U-boat in the face of concentrated enemy fire. One of the Catalina's two engines then fell from the burning wing, but Hornell ditched successfully. However, only one dinghy was available, so Hornell stayed in the sea. He died after being picked up hours later. Three weeks later, on 17 July, Flying Officer J.A. Cruickshank, flying a Catalina of No. 210 Squadron, attacked a heavily-armed U-boat but could not release his depth charges. He consequently made a second approach, by which time the submarine crew were fully alerted and put up intense fire in the attacking aircraft's path and inflicted enormous damage on the Catalina. Despite being wounded in no fewer than 72 places, Cruickshank insisted on helping to fly the Catalina from its attack position inside the Arctic Circle to its base at Sullom Voe, in the Shetlands. Cruickshank survived, the only one of the Coastal Command VCs to do so.

Two other Coastal Command activities reached their peak in 1943–44: long-range photographic reconnaissance and air-sea rescue. Spitfires and Mosquitos of No. 106 Wing—the Spitfires sometimes flying at altitudes of over 40,000 feet—ranged far and wide over enemy territory, providing target intelligence of every kind. Their pilots, flying on the edge of the stratosphere, were literally operating at the boundary of human knowledge; they were the first to encounter the phenomenon of the Jet Streams, the 200-mph corridors of air that whirl around the globe in the upper reaches of the atmosphere. In the early days, they flew in unpressurized cockpits, relying only on a pressure waistcoat to force oxygen into their lungs. They were truly among the RAF's unsung heroes, for without the information they brought home the operational Commands would have been blind.

The Air-Sea Rescue Service, whose activities had been co-ordinated since February 1941, possessed 32 marine craft units by the beginning of 1944, supported by search squadrons equipped with a variety of aircraft of which the best-known was probably the Supermarine Walrus. Between February 1941 and the end of 1943, the Service had rescued 3,306 Allied airmen, 1,684 of them in 1943 alone—a figure indicative of the volume of air operations proceeding between the United Kingdom and the Continent since the arrival of the USAAF in Britain. In addition, Coastal Command was responsible for long-range meteorological flights, which in 1943 were carried out by Halifaxes and Fortresses. Without accurate foreknowledge of the Atlantic weather systems, the sustained air offensives of 1943–44—not to mention the great amphibious operations of 1944—would have been impossible to plan.

The year 1943 saw a considerable expansion of two other branches of the Royal Air Force, both of which merit far more space than the length of this book permits. The first was the Royal Air Force Regiment, formed in February 1942 by Royal Warrant as a Corps within the RAF, a unique status. The origins of the RAF Regiment dated back to the early days of World War Two, when the Battle of France showed that air bases were particularly vulnerable to enemy ground and low-level air action. Because the Army was hard-pressed, it could not spare troops to protect RAF bases; a new, specialist force was needed for this purpose, and so the RAF Regiment came into existence.

Formed into wings, squadrons and independent flights operating as field (infantry) or light anti-aircraft units, the Regiment expanded rapidly during the war. By the end of hostilities, it had reached a strength of

85,000 officers and men and a front line of 240 squadrons. Although its primary role was the defence of RAF airfields and installations, it was clear from the start that the Regiment must develop an aggressive fighting spirit and be capable of meeting the immediate tactical needs for offensive action. This stood it in good stead as the war progressed and, as the initiative passed from the enemy to the Allies in the various theatres of war, so the Regiment participated in an increasingly offensive capacity, often spearheading the Allied advance to seize forward air installations. As an example of this, Regiment units were the first Allied forces to enter Tunis and Bizerta; later, towards the

After D-Day, increasing use was made of 12,000–pound Tallboy bombs against 'hard' targets. Here, a Tallboy impacts on a German U-boat pen.

end of hostilities, small Regiment detachments which had moved ahead of the Army to secure enemy airfields in North-West Germany accepted the surrender of some 55,000 enemy troops.

The other branch of the Service was the Women's Auxiliary Air Force, formed in June 1939 from 48 RAF Companies of the Auxiliary Territorial Service (ATS). There had previously been a Women's Royal Air Force in 1918, but this had been disbanded two years later. On its inception, the new WAAF numbered not more than 2,000 women; by mid–1943, its strength had risen to 182,000, serving in 22 officer branches and 75 trades ranging from Fighter Control to stores clerks. These women were an integral part of the Royal Air Force, and they served both at home and overseas. Many were decorated for gallantry and outstanding ser-

vice, and hundreds were mentioned in despatches.

In November 1943, a large number of RAF squadrons were transferred from other Commands to the 2nd Tactical Air Force, created to provide the necessary air striking power in support of the coming Allied invasion of Europe. It consisted of four Groups: Nos 83 and 84 Groups were to provide tactical support for the 1st Canadian and 2nd British Armies, No. 85 Group was to defend the Allied bridgehead across the Channel once it had been established, and the medium bombers of No 2 Group—Marauders, Mitchells, Mosquitos and Bostons—were to strike at communications and supplies behind the enemy lines. There was also a Reconnaissance Wing and an Air Spotting Pool, and the massive task of furnishing air transport and supply fell to Nos 38 and 46 Groups. All these units, together with the mighty power of the United States 9th Air Force, formed the framework of the Allied Expeditionary Air Force, commanded by Air Chief Marshal Sir Trafford Leigh-Mallory. Its total strength was 5,667 aircraft, of which 3,011 were fighters, medium bombers, light bombers and fighter-bombers.

In the spring of 1944, Air Chief Marshal Sir Arthur Tedder, the Allied Deputy Supreme Commander, pushed through a policy of sustained air attacks on enemy railways, rolling stock, marshalling yards, repair and maintenance facilities, roads and bridges—in other words, anything that would impede the transfer of German reinforcements to the battlefield. This plan was bitterly opposed by General Carl Spaatz, commanding the US Strategic Air Force, who wanted the main air offensive to be concentrated against oil targets. Nevertheless, Tedder had his way, and in the two months prior to 6 June 1944 Allied bombers dropped 66,517 tons of bombs on 80 selected targets, mostly involving railways. It was not until the Allied forces set foot on the Continent and began to push deeper inland that the full extent of the havoc wrought by the air attacks on enemy communications was appreciated. By D-Day, the enemy transport system in western Europe was on the verge of collapse, a state of affairs brought about mainly by heavy attacks on marshalling yards and repair centres.

As D-Day approached, a proportion of the Allied air striking force was earmarked to carry out heavy attacks on enemy coastal batteries and radar installations, and by the

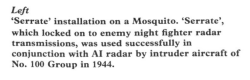

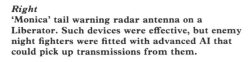

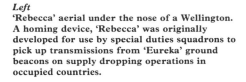

first week in June air attacks had knocked out some 80 per cent of the enemy's coastal radar capability. To confuse what remained, in the early hours of 6 June 1944, as the invasion fleet of over 3,000 Allied vessels turned in towards their objectives on the Normandy coast, eight Lancasters of No. 617 Squadron carried out Operation Taxable, dropping bundles of Window at precise intervals over the Channel north of Le Havre. Immediately afterwards, six Stirlings of No 218 Squadron carried out Operation Glimmer, a similar mission over the Straits of Dover off Boulogne. Both these missions were so successful that German coastal batteries opened up a furious barrage on a large expanse of empty sea, and when the first Allied troops hit the Normandy beaches the Germans at first believed that these landings were a feint, and that the main assault was about to fall farther north.

Before dawn on June, Allied bombers dropped 5,000 tons of bombs on the defences of the 'Atlantic Wall', and as the troops fought their way towards their initial objectives in the dawn of D-Day, waves of tactical bombers and fighter-bombers continued to batter the German defences ahead of them, while high overhead squadrons of Spitfires, Thunderbolts and Mustangs effectively dealt with the small number of *Luftwaffe* formations that tried to interfere with the landings. In all, the Allied air forces flew 14,674

sorties during the 24 hours of D-Day for the loss of 113 aircraft—some of which, sad to relate, were shot down by friendly naval forces. The contribution to the day's operations by Nos 38 and 46 (Transport) Groups was the despatch of 264 aircraft and 98 glider combinations; among the first sorties were those flown by the Albemarles of Nos 295 and 570 Squadrons, which dropped the advance party of the 3rd Parachute Brigade over the River Orne. The remainder of the Brigade was dropped by 108 Dakotas of Nos 48, 233, 271, 512 and 575 Squadrons. Coastal Command also played its part in the day's activity, carrying out a series of attacks on submarines and surface vessels that had been sighted putting to sea from ports on the Bay of Biscay.

With the Allied forces safely ashore, the priority now was to construct forward airstrips in Normandy. In the meantime, operating from the UK, eighteen squadrons of Typhoons of Nos 83 and 84 Groups, supported by a number of Mustang Mk III units, carried out non-stop tactical reconnaissance operations, and in the early morning of 7 June they delivered a savage attack on the Panzer Lehr Division that was hurrying to the battle area from Alençon. With rockets and cannon fire, the Typhoons and Mustangs destroyed 90 lorries, 40 fuel trucks and 84 half-tracks. For the Germans, it was a bitter foretaste of what was to come.

By the morning of 8 June, a temporary airstrip had been set up at Ste Croix-sur-Mer, the construction crews working under constant shellfire. Eventually, 31 similar strips were set up in the British zone and 50 in the American, enabling the fighter-bombers to take off and attack targets on demand. Among the first units to operate from French soil was No. 144 Wing, RCAF, which was in action from a forward strip by 10 June.

In the days after the landings the Allied bombers continued to pound enemy lines of communication, and in one of these attacks—against the Saumur railway tunnel, a vital point on the main line running from the south-west to the Normandy front—Lancasters of No 617 Squadron dropped 12,000-pound Tallboy bombs for the first time on the night of 8/9 June. Bomber Command also turned its attention to the concentrations of enemy light naval forces at Le Havre and Boulogne, and once again enormous damage was done by 12,000-pound bombs. On 12 June, during night operations over Cambrai, Pilot Officer A.C. Mynarski of No. 419 (RCAF) Squadron, a mid-upper gunner in a Lancaster, committed an act of bravery that later brought the posthumous award of the Victoria Cross. Over the target, a night fighter set fire to both the Lancaster's port engines and the wing fuel tanks; Mynarski stayed aboard, surrounded by flames, and attempted to release the trapped rear gunner. When he eventually jumped, he was too low for his parachute to open properly, and he died from his injuries soon afterwards. Miraculously, the rear gunner, Flying Officer G.P. Brophy, survived the subsequent crash of the Lancaster and was able to tell of Mynarski's heroism.

On the night of 12/13 June, while bombing operations in support of the Allied offensive in Normandy were still in full stride, the first V-1 flying bomb was launched against London from a site in the Pas de Calais. The launch sites, code-named 'No-Balls', had been frequently attacked by the RAF since their existence was first discovered late in 1943, but they were extremely well camouflaged and well defended, and although the attacks had slowed down the construction programme they had not succeeded in halting it. In June 1944, when the V-1 offensive started, Bomber Command sent 4,661 sorties against the sites, dropping 16,000 tons of bombs on them for the loss of 38 aircraft. A further 44,335 tons of bombs were dropped in the course of 11,939 more sorties between the end of June and 3 September, when the launch sites were overrun by the Allied advance.

The small, fast V-1s presented enormous problems for the British air defences. Of the 144 that crossed the coast on 15 and 16 June, fourteen were shot down by anti-aircraft fire and seven by fighters. In an attempt to come to grips with the problem, the fighters of No. 11 Group instituted 'Diver Patrols'. These involved fighters patrolling along three clearly-defined lines, the first between Beachy Head and Dover, the second over the coast between Newhaven and Dover, and the third between Haywards Heath and Ashford. At the same time, nearly 400 anti-aircraft guns and 480 barrage balloons were deployed over the V-1s' approach route to London.

The eleven fighter squadrons that carried out the Diver Patrols were equipped with Spitfires Mks IX, XII and XIV, Typhoons, Mustangs, Mosquitos and the latest type to enter service with the Air Defence of Great Britain: the Hawker Tempest. Sydney Camm, chief designer of Hawker Aircraft, had designed a brilliant fighting machine in the Tempest Mk V. Taking as his basis the Hawker Typhoon, he had created an aircraft that was the fastest, most potent piston-engined fighter in service anywhere in the world. From the outset, the Tempest had been designed to achieve air superiority at low and medium levels—in other words, to counter the threat posed by fast enemy fighter-bombers. It had a combat radius of 500 miles, and its 2,400 hp Napier Sabre engine gave it an impressive acceleration and a top speed, straight and level, of 440 mph. Armament was four 20-mm cannon, whose magazines held 800 shells—enough for twenty seconds of firing time.

When the V-1 offensive started there were two squadrons of Tempest Mk Vs, Nos 3 and 486 (RNZAF) in No. 11 Group; No 56 Squadron also re-equipped with the new fighters late in June. In the battle against the flying bombs, No. 3 Squadron was to score the most kills, with 258 bombs destroyed; No. 486 Squadron came second with a score of 223. These operations, however, revealed some snags with the Tempests' Sabre engines, and the fighters were withdrawn from front-line service for some weeks while the troubles were rectified. The Tempest squadrons subsequently moved to the Continent with 2nd TAF and became a potent addition to the Allies' air striking power during the closing months of the war.

Another new fighter type that joined in the battle against the flying bombs late in July was the Gloster Meteor F Mk I jet, the prototype of which had flown in January 1944. The first operational Meteors were delivered to No. 616 Squadron, which moved to Manston and flew its first Diver Patrol on 27 July. On 4 August, Flying Officer Dean became the first RAF jet pilot to destroy an enemy aircraft when he knocked down a V-1 near Ashford; the technique he used was to insert his Meteor's wingtip under that of the flying bomb so that the airflow upset the missile's equilibrium, turn-

The Bielefeld Viaduct, destroyed on 14 March 1945 by a 22,000–pound 'Grand Slam' bomb dropped by a Lancaster of No. 617 Squadron.

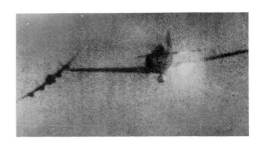

The *Luftwaffe* did what it could to stem the tide of Allied day bombers. Here, an Fw 190, attacking a Lancaster, is itself attacked and hit by a Mosquito.

ing it over on its back so that it dived into the ground. These tactics were used frequently by pilots on Diver Patrols, and were a good deal safer than attempting to shoot the missiles down; several pilots had very narrow escapes when the V-1s they were attacking exploded, filling the sky ahead with debris.

On 7 July 1944, 457 bombers of Bomber Command dropped 2,363 tons of bombs on targets north of the City of Caen in support of the Anglo-Canadian drive to capture that objective. The Allied advance became bogged down—partly because of the bombing, which had filled the area with craters and rubble—and on 18 July, 1,570 heavy and 349 medium bombers of Bomber Command, the US 8th Air Force and the Allied Expeditionary Air Force unloaded 7,700 tons on Caen itself. Four more major bombing attacks took place up to mid-August, but not all were successful; in some cases, bombs fell wide of the mark and caused heavy casualties among our Allied troops. The fight for Caen was long and bitter before what was left of the city fell into Allied hands.

On 7 August, a German armoured counter-attack in the Mortain sector was

The island of Walcheren, where Canadian troops encountered bitter German resistance, was heavily attacked by Bomber Command.

Above left
Wesel, one of the Rhine crossing points, was repeatedly hit by Allied bombers and turned into a lunar landscape.

The island of Flushing after it had been deliberately flooded by the Germans. Relief for the Dutch population was Bomber Command's first postwar task; 10,000 tons of provisions were air-dropped into Holland by the RAF.

smashed by Allied fighter-bombers, notably Typhoons. Ten days later, the remnants of sixteen German divisions, including nine Panzer divisions, were trapped in a 25-mile-wide corridor near Falaise and systematically destroyed by concentrated air attacks. On average, the pilots of 2nd TAF flew 1,200 sorties a day; the *Luftwaffe*'s available fighter squadrons, desperately trying to stem the slaughter, were decimated.

After Falaise, the Allied breakout was rapid. While the Americans and Fighting French pushed on to liberate Paris and its environs, the British 2nd Army swept over the Seine and crossed the Belgian frontier; on 3 September, to an ecstatic reception, the 1st Battalion the Welsh Guards entered Brussels. The difficulty for the squadrons of 2nd TAF now was in keeping up with the speed of the advance; the repair of captured airfields assumed top priority, for there was no longer time to construct even temporary strips.

On 17 September, 1944, there unfolded the first act in one of the most gallant and tragic dramas in the history of British arms: the attempt to capture the Rhine crossings at Arnhem. The operation, code-named Market Garden, was designed to facilitate a thrust into Germany by the 2nd Army and also to remove the threat of the enemy's V-2 rockets, against which there was no defence and which had been bombarding London from sites in Holland since the beginning of the month.

Operation Market, the RAF's side of the venture, was carried out by the Dakota squadrons of No 46 Group, together with No 38 Group's six Stirling, two Halifax and two Albemarle squadrons. It is perhaps fitting to let the terse words of No 38 Group's Intelligence Summary tell the story.

On 17 Sep 44 began the second and largest airborne operation ever attempted. Operation object the conveyance and landing of 1st Airborne Corps in Holland at strategical points such as railway crossings and bridges over railways and the Rhine in furthering progress of Allied forces, and quick passage of the forces under General Dempsey who is already driving forward into Holland with massed armour.

38 Group provided 240 A/C, 12 acting as PFF. Total loads carried were made up of troops, jeeps, cars, trailers, 17 lb and 75 mm guns, Bren carriers, containers, panniers, bicycles, stretchers and carts. Enemy failed to provide Luftwaffe opposition and flak reported negligible. No A/C losses sustained by Group. When one realises the vulnerability of airborne operations, their length of formation, duration over enemy territory and inability to take evasive action, freedom from loss is astonishing. Credit due to cover provided by fighter escort and bombing of airfields and flak positions.

D + 1. 38 GP operated 210 A/C comprising Halifax/Hamilcar, Stirling/Horsa and Albemarle/Horsa and Waco combinations. Object strengthening and resupply of areas captured. 88 A/C successful dropped loads comprising troops, jeeps, cars, Bren carriers, 17 lb

The fearful devastation of war: Hamm, *top left*; Duisburg, *top right*; Hannover, *above left*; Cologne; from a Lancaster at the war's end.

guns, howitzers, M/C, cycles, panniers, stretchers, compressors, W/T set, charging set, mine detectors, hoses, ammunition and RMLS.

19 A/C unsuccessful. 9 tow-ropes breaking, 4 mech failure, 1 missing, 1 hit by flak, 1 bad loading and three slipstream difficulties falling into sea. Reports of A/C in distress, Stirling with smoke coming from it, second hit by flak seen to crash and explode. Third burning on ground, fourth crash-landed. Fifth hit by flak and one member of A/C seen to bale out, sixth

(No. 2) ST/BD tank leaking and Dakota seen going down and four chutes seen to open. Large silver rocket towing silver coloured kite, speed est 200 mph travelling due west. Gratifying to note operation has gone so smoothly and that Gen Dempsey's 2nd British Army has already contacted forces we dropped on D-Day.

D + 2. *Object resupply and strengthening and capture of another DZ NW of Arnhem. 144 A/C engaged, 120 successful. 10 A/C reported missing, some may have delivered gliders before becoming casualties. Operations no longer having element of surprise, produced considerably stiffer opposition from enemy. Again most noticeable feature was non-interference by Luftwaffe who were taken care of by our fighter cover. Crews report flak opposition extremely active along route to DZ ranging from small arms fire to 40 mm. Waterborne flak encountered along River Waal.*

Stirling seen to crash and explode on DZ. N-NAN 299 Squadron seen by X9Y/299 to fall in flames, three of crew baled out but chutes failed to open. Stirling letters FFT seen to force land, crew seen to be safe. Dakota burning on ground S of Eindhoven. Some Horsas burning on DZ.X. Dinghy sighted 5122N/0143E crew picked up by ASR Walrus.

Captains of A/C report successful trips but observe fighters not on hand to deal with flak positions. They also report loads being dropped from as high as 4,000 ft and over wide area because of stiff flak opposition.

D + 3. *38 GP operated 101 A/C. 34 Stirlings 190 and 620 Sqns Fairford, 34 Stirlings 295 and 570 Sqns Harwell, 33 Stirlings 196 and 299 Sqns Keevil and 1 A/C from 1665 HCU (Heavy Conversion Unit) Tilstock. 87 A/C successful dropping 2063 containers, 325 panniers, 3 packages, 2 kitbags and 1 sack. 11 A/C missing. While reports of interception by enemy fighters nil, ground defences have stiffened considerably. In addition to A/C lost, a large number of hits on other A/C are reported.*

Reports of rocket projectiles being fired from two different positions. Returning A/C report seeing a number of A/C in difficulty. ASR launch seen to pick up crew E of Ramsgate.

Captains generally describe their experience as good trip. Weather hazy and DZ not too clear, added danger of going in low because of containers being dropped from high levels and often short of DZ. Considerable bunching by the stream of A/C when converging on DZ tended to squeeze A/C out over a wide dropping area.

D + 4. *38 GP operated 64 A/C on resupply to airborne force NW Arnhem. 3 reported abortive due to (I) RG sick (II) engine failure (III) take-off too late unable to contact stream. 14 A/C missing. One station reports 10 Fw 190 at Oosterbeek. Fw 190 attacked and*

followed one A/C to ground level for 8 mins. RG returned fire and claims one probable. While enemy fighters seem to have been in evidence, reports of flak indicate that it was on a lower scale. Most A/C seem to have found very heavy light flak opposition from actual DZ area.

Reports indicate that loads were still being dropped from as high as 2,000 ft and congestion of A/C in DZ area. Apparently flak positions are not being eliminated before and during our mission. Suggested that a light bombing raid on the L/F nests be made prior to our sorties.

D + 5. *38 GP did not resupply on 22 Sep.*

D + 6. *38 GP operated 73 A/C, 64 reaching DZ and dropping 1,540 containers, 235 panniers and 50 jeep tyres. Results of two A/C unknown but phone report from one landed at Manston with engine U/S claims to have dropped on D/Z.*

Increasing number of aircrew finding their way back from Holland, to date ten complete or almost complete crews.

Number of A/C seen in distress in areas where flak was encountered. Captains state having seen: Stirling (intact) on ground 3 miles S of Grove. Stirling seen to make good crash landing 3 mls W of Valkenswaard with S/1 on fire, SB wing fell off. DZ area 4 Stirlings seen to crash in flames, 2 seen to bale out of one A/C. Stirling seen on ground W of Nijmegen with crew standing round. SW of Arnhem E7W [author: No. 570 Sqn] seen on fire and crashing. Stirling with engine on fire seen to go into wood then flames seen from wood. Stirling seen to belly-land W of DZ. A/C V8G [author: No. 570 Sqn] crashed south of river and burst into flames. Dakota in river before DZ, only tail showing above water. Stirling on ground W of Nijmegen, crew seen waving. Dakota burning in woods S. of Eindhoven.

Most crews describe trip as satisfactory despite very hot reception at DZ. Fighter cover received praise varying from OK to excellent. A/C are reported dropping at 2000—2500 ft causing others considerable inconvenience, endangering low flying A/C and restricting movement to avoid flak.

The Battle of Arnhem was over: transport crews were risking their lives to deliver supplies to dropping zones that were already in enemy hands. Operation Market had cost Nos 38 and 46 Groups 55 aircraft lost, with a further 320 damaged by flak and seven by fighters. One Dakota pilot, Flight Lieutenant D.S.A. Lord of No 271 Squadron, was awarded a posthumous Victoria Cross for his bravery in pressing through intense flak to drop his load of supplies, his aircraft hit repeatedly and in flames. It was the first and only VC to be awarded to a pilot of Trans-

port Command, which had been formed out of Ferry Command in March 1943.

While the squadrons of 2nd TAF continued to support the 2nd Army's drive through north-west Europe, and the strike wings of Coastal Command intensified their attacks on enemy shipping everywhere from the Dutch coast to Norway's North Cape, Bomber Command, after operating in support of the Normandy breakout, had resumed its offensive against enemy oil targets. The absence of the *Luftwaffe* in the west during June and July, at least in any strength, had encouraged the Air Staff to believe that bombers might once again carry out strong daylight attacks deep inside enemy territory with relative impunity, provided targets were not too heavily defended and the attacking forces were carefully routed. The theory was put to the test in June 1944, when a total of 2,716 daylight sorties were sent out to targets in Occupied Europe. The majority of these were flown by Lancasters and Halifaxes, and the loss rate was only 0.4 per cent —an extremely low casualty figure attributable in the main to the lack of day fighter opposition. In July, the number of sorties despatched was 6,847, and once again the loss rate was only 0.4 per cent. All these sorties, however, had been relatively short-range operations against poorly-defended targets, and full fighter cover had been provided by the Spitfires of No. 11 Group.

It was not until the end of August 1944 that RAF heavy bombers penetrated into Germany with fighter escort. On the 27th, 216 Halifaxes of No. 4 Group, together with 27 Mosquitos and Lancasters of the Pathfinder Force, were despatched to attack the oil plant at Homburg, in the Ruhr. The bombers were accompanied on the outward trip by nine squadrons of Spitfires from Nos. 10, 11 and 12 Groups, which made rendezvous with them near Overflakkee at 17,000 feet. Seven more Spitfire squadrons arrived over the target at the same time as the bombers, providing a strengthened escort on the homeward run. Only one enemy fighter —a Bf 110 —was sighted during the entire round trip, and this prudently made no attempt to attack. Despite very heavy anti-fire over Hamburg, all the attacking force returned to base. The target itself was severely damaged.

Bomber Command's next major daylight operation against Germany was carried out in the early evening of 6 September, when 181 Lancasters and Halifaxes from No. 6 Group and the Pathfinder Force — accompanied by six squadrons of Spitfires and four of Mustangs —were despatched to Emden. The bombing, which began at 18.30,

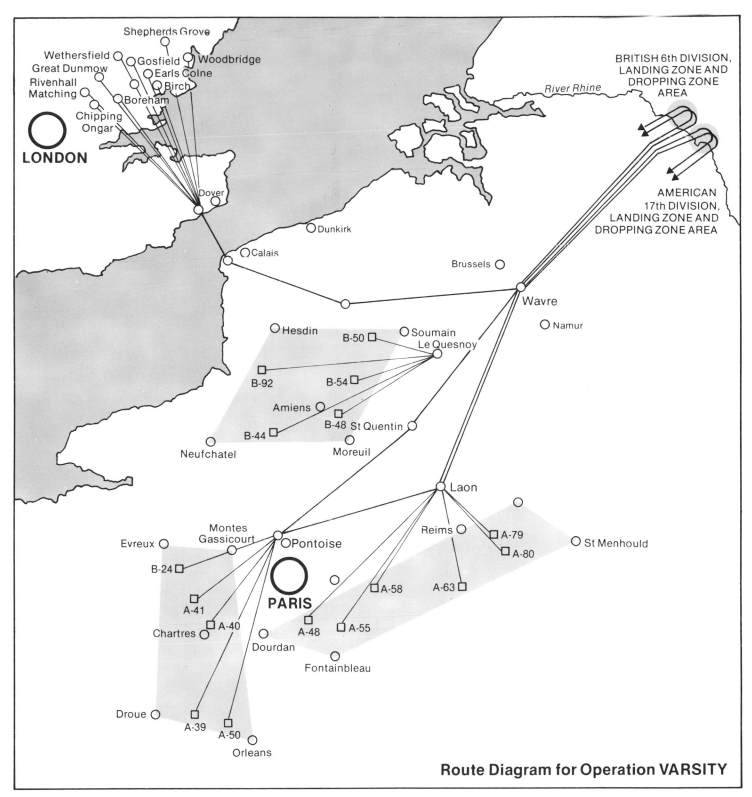

Route Diagram for Operation VARSITY

was highly accurate and concentrated around the city centre. Only one aircraft, a PFF Lancaster, failed to return. Five days later, encouraged by these successes, Bomber Command launched three separate attacks in one day against oil targets in the Ruhr. The Nordstern plant at Gelsenkirchen was attacked by 129 Lancasters, Halifaxes and Mosquitos of No. 4 Group and the PFF; 116 Lancasters of Nos 3 and 5 Groups and the PFF were despatched to Kamen; while 134 Halifaxes, Lancasters and Mosquitos of Nos 6 Group and the PFF hit Castrop Rauxel. Fighter cover for the three assaults was provided by twenty squadrons of Spitfires, three of Tempests and three of Mustangs. No enemy fighters were encountered, and the nine bombers that failed to return were all victims of the flak. All three attacks, particularly those on Kamen and Castrop Rauxel, caused widespread damage.

On 6 October, there came a new development in the RAF's daylight offensive, when Bomber Command authorised the use of the blind bombing system known as G-H on daylight raids. G-H, which was first used on the night of 3/4 November 1943 in an attack on the Mannesmann Steel Works near Düsseldorf, was a highly accurate blind bombing device similar to Oboe but working in the opposite sense. Using G-H, an aircraft transmitted pulse signals to two ground stations, which received them and transmitted them back; the aircraft could therefore continuously measure its distance from two known points and track itself over any target within range of the system, determining its bomb release point with great precision. The range of G-H was about 350 miles at 30,000 feet, much the same as Oboe; its great advantage, however, was that up to 80 aircraft could operate simultaneously from one pair of ground stations.

The first objective selected for a daylight G-H attack was Bonn, on 18 October 1944. The force despatched consisted of 128 Lancasters of No. 3 Group, escorted by a large number of Spitfires and Mustangs. Only one enemy fighter was seen, and this was quickly driven off. The bombers approached the target in flights of three, each one led by a G-H aircraft, and the subsequent attack—carried out through broken cloud—caused heavy damage to the centre of Bonn. One Lancaster failed to return.

Meanwhile, night attacks on German oil targets continued. In the last two weeks of July Bomber Command struck at Wesseling, Scholven-Buer, Homberg, Bottrop and Wanne-Eickel, and also carried out area attacks on Hamburg, Kiel and Stuttgart. A total of 3,419 sorties were despatched to these targets, and 132 Lancasters and Halifaxes failed to return. Most of the losses were due to enemy night-fighter action. Although the enemy air defences were being thrown into considerable confusion by radio countermeasures, the night-fighters still remained a force to be reckoned with; on the night of 28 July, for example, they accounted for most of the 62 missing bombers out of a force of 803 which attacked Hamburg and Stuttgart.

In August, the Command carried out twelve major night attacks on German targets, involving the despatch of 3,764 sorties. The loss was 141 bombers, all of them Lancasters and Halifaxes. During the following month, 3,188 sorties were despatched in the course of twelve strategic attacks, but this time the total loss was 69 Lancasters and Halifaxes and three Mosquitos—a significant drop indicating that the effectiveness of the German night-fighter force was on the decline.

In terms of striking power, Bomber Command—together with the United States Strategic Air Forces—was now approaching its operational climax. During the last three months of 1944, the Ruhr was subjected to its final and most devastating onslaught, with Bomber Command dropping over 163,000 tons of bombs—four times the weight it had dropped during the same period in 1943. Over half the Command's effort was directed at large industrial cities, the remainder being shared in roughly equal proportions between oil targets, communications and support of the land offensive. In the area bombing offensive sixteen towns were repeatedly attacked, with Duisburg receiving the greatest tonnage of bombs. Duisburg was heavily attacked on four occasions; 13,000 tons of bombs were dropped on it in the course of 3,119 sorties. Nine thousand tons fell on Duisburg in one 24-hour period alone; this was on 14 August, the day that saw Bomber Command despatch its largest number of sorties, and drop the greatest tonnage of bombs of the entire war. Essen was also attacked four times, receiving 11,500 tons of bombs; Cologne was hit three times with 9,500 tons; one massive attack on Düsseldorf involved the despatch of 992 sorties and the dropping of 4,400 tons of bombs; and a total of 22,000 tons were dropped in the course of other attacks on Bochum, Gelsenkirchen, Dortmund, Hagen, Witten, Oberhausen, Nauss, Solingen, Munster, Hamm, Duisburg and Leverkusen. During this three-month campaign against the Ruhr, 136 bombers failed to return, representing a loss rate of less than one per cent. Other area attacks were carried out during the same period in sixteen major towns in northern, southern and south-western Germany; the biggest such attack took place on the night of 19/20 October, when 583 bombers were sent out to drop 2,500 tons of bombs on Stuttgart.

In November 1944, RAF attacks on oil targets, which had been somewhat neglected during October, were once again stepped up. Between the beginning of November and the end of the year, Bomber Command carried out 27 heavy attacks on 15 oil plants, involving the despatch of 5,194 sorties and the dropping of 23,000 tons of bombs. The loss to the Command was 57 bombers. Nineteen of these missions were flown in daylight. Although the flak was usually intense, there was little opposition from the enemy night-fighters. Several of the targets were bombed with a high degree of accuracy through complete cloud cover with the aid of G-H.

Bomber Command also made several notable precision attacks on small strategic targets during the last four months of 1944. The first of these was carried out against the Dortmund-Ems Canal on the night of 23/24 September by 99 Lancasters of No. 5 Group. The crews achieved an impressive bombing concentration, and several direct hits were obtained on both branches of the canal. Subsequent reconnaissance showed that an 18-mile stretch of the canal had been almost completely drained, with strings of barges stranded in the mud on the bottom. Nevertheless, repairs were quickly effected, and by the end of October the canal was fully operational again. On the night of 4/5 November, No. 5 Group made a second attack, this time with 170 heavy bombers, and once again serious breaches were torn in the embankments. The eastern branch of the canal—the narrower of the two waterways—was rendered completely irreparable and was sealed off by the Germans, but the western branch was in service again within three weeks. On 21/22 November, 128 Lancasters of No. 5 Group attacked yet again, aiming from 4,000 feet at the aqueduct carrying the western branch of the canal over the River Glane. Four direct hits were achieved on the aqueduct, and a 190-foot breach was torn in the embankment south of the aiming point, releasing large quantities of water into the surrounding countryside.

By the end of December, however, German forced labour gangs—working day and night—had once more repaired most of the damage, and the flow of canal traffic continued. On 1 January 1945, No. 5 Group sent out a fourth striking force, this time in daylight; hits were again achieved on the aqueduct, the embankment was breached and the safety gates were wrecked. On this occasion, delayed action bombs were dropped to hinder the work of repair.

The daylight raids on the Dortmund-Ems Canal, and other major daylight attacks mounted by Bomber Command during the last weeks of 1944, tended to be overshadowed by the more spectacular precision attacks carried out during this period by the Lancasters of No. 5 Group, and principally by No. 617 Squadron. On 7 October, for example, thirteen Lancasters of No. 617, led by Wing Commander J.B. Tait, set out to attack the Kembe dam, which lay on the upper Rhine north of Basle. The Germans intended to release the massive volume of water contained by the dam to block the Allied advance across the upper Rhine, but this plan was effectively forestalled by No. 617 Squadron. Attacking from as low as 600 feet in the face of intense light flak, the Lancasters' Tallboy bombs breached the structure and released the pent-up waters.

In December 1944, much of the Allied strategic bombing effort was diverted to tactical operations in support of the land

offensive in Belgium, temporarily reeling under the impact of the last German offensive on the Western Front, Field-Marshal von Rundstedt's armoured counter-attack in the Ardennes. Supported by the remnants of the *Luftwaffe*, which launched a highly effective surprise attack on Allied air bases in Belgium and Holland on New Year's Day 1945, the German push met with some initial success. Bomber Command and the US 8th Air Force carried out intensive daylight attacks on enemy armour and troop concentrations and against railheads, and by the middle of January 1945 the Germans' last gamble had ended in failure. The swift German collapse was due to three main factors: a critical shortage of tanks and aircraft to support such a large-scale operation, a shortage of fuel and oil reserves, and the disrupted condition of the German transport system. All three were the direct result of Allied strategic bombing over the preceding months.

The end for Germany came quickly now. The Allied Air Forces roved virtually unopposed by daylight over the length and breadth of the shattered Reich, striking at a steadily decreasing list of strategic and tactical targets. Between 1 January and 8 May 1945, RAF Bomber Command—with a daily average of 1,500 bombers available for operations—dropped more than 181,000 tons of bombs, one-fifth of the Command's total for the entire war. During this period the Command launched 67,483 sorties for the loss of 608 aircraft, devoting the main part of its effort to oil targets and industrial cities. Thirty of the latter were attacked in

January, February and March, twelve of them in daylight. The smallest of these raids was carried out on the night of 22 January, when 152 bombers were despatched to Gelsenkirchen, and the largest was made in daylight on 12 March when 1,079 Lancasters, Halifaxes and Mosquitos dropped 4,851 tons of bombs on Dortmund. The total number of bombers sent out against Dortmund on this occasion was actually, 1,107, the largest number ever despatched by Bomber Command in one raid against a single target.

In terms of destruction achieved, the most effective of all these area attacks was that carried out against Dresden on the night of 13/14 February, when 805 bombers struck at the town in two waves. The pretext for the assault on Dresden, in which large areas of the city were razed to the ground by firestorms and in which at least 80,000 people died, was that it was a key base and communications centre for the German armies facing the advancing Russians in the east. Although the attack was made primarily at the request of the Soviet Government, controversy still rages over the justification for it. Be that as it may, the fact remains that Dresden is to this day the symbol of the terrible power of conventional strategic air warfare.

The area attacks on Germany's cities by Bomber Command involved the despatch of 15,588 sorties for the loss of 240 aircraft. Ten per cent of this loss was sustained on the night of 16/17 March, when 277 Lancasters and 16 Mosquitos were despatched to Nuremberg. The enemy night-fighter force was unexpectedly active and 24 aircraft failed to return.

None of the RAF's heavy bomber raids were directed against Berlin in 1945; however, beginning on the night of 20/21 February, the Mosquitos of No. 2 Group began a series of 36 consecutive attacks on the German capital. In 3,900 sorties, the Mosquitos dropped over 4,400 tons of bombs, including 1,800 4,000-pounders. Fourteen Mosquitos failed to return.

Bomber Command also carried out a sustained offensive against the enemy's oil targets between January and April 1945, making 74 raids on 49 objectives. Thirty-eight of these missions were flown at night and 36 in daylight, many of the latter delivered through ten-tenths cloud with the aid of G-H. One of the most destructive attacks was carried out against Scholven-Buer in daylight on 10 March, when 153 Lancasters dropped 755 tons of bombs on the target through the overcast. The plant was completely devastated and all the bombers returned to base.

Precision attacks also continued. In February 1945, No. 617 Squadron received the first examples of a new and formidable weapon designed by Dr Barnes Wallis, a ten-ton bomb known as Grand Slam. This 22,000 pound monster was first used operationally on 14 March 1945, when one was dropped on the Bielefeld Viaduct by a No. 617 Squadron Lancaster piloted by Squadron Leader C.C. Calder. The objective was completely destroyed. Forty more Grand Slams were dropped before the end of hostilities, some of them against naval targets such as the U-boat pens at Farge, attacked by Nos 9 and 617 Squadrons with Tallboys and Grand Slams on 27 March. Tallboys were again used against the Kriegsmarine on 9 April, when Bomber Command capsized the German pocket battleship *Admiral Scheer* during an attack on Kiel. The Germans had planned to use the heavy armament of the *Scheer*—which had been the objective of the very first raid carried out by Bomber Command during World War Two, on 4 September 1939—in a defensive role against the Allied advance. Two more warships, the cruisers *Admiral Hipper* and *Emden*, were so severely damaged in the same attack that they were unfit for further use.

The destruction of the Bielefeld Viaduct was part of the Allied bombing offensive against enemy communications that preceded Operation Varsity, the crossing of the Rhine. On 21 and 22 March 1945, as the time approached, some 1,800 US bombers attacked enemy air bases while Bomber Command flew diversionary attacks and Coastal Command played an important part in diversionary operations along the Dutch coast. The operation, launched on 24 March, was carried out by the First Allied Airborne Army, commanded by Lieutenant General L.H. Brereton, and the British element consisted mainly of the 6th Airborne Division, airlifted to battle by Nos 38 and 46 Groups. The former comprised Nos 190, 196, 295, 570 and 620 Squadrons, with a total of 180 Stirlings, and Nos 296, 297, 298 and 644 Squadrons with 112 Halifaxes; the latter, Nos 48, 233, 271, 437, 512 and 575 Squadrons, all with Dakotas.

There was a shortage of crews, and the 320 available were obtained by using every crew in No 38 Group, including the retention of tour-expired aircrew. In No. 46 Group, available aircraft and crews were increased by drawing on an operational training unit. After Arnhem, only 48 officers and 666 other ranks remained in the Glider Pilot Regiment, so deficiencies were made up from the RAF reserve of aircrew who were given glider conversion courses.

A total of 440 crews and aircraft were available for the airlift, and 439 tug and glider combinations took off. Of these, 34 failed to carry out their missions; sixteen failures were due to slipstream accidents and nine to broken towropes. Two of the gliders ditched in the North Sea, but were reached by the ASR organization. Although nearly 300 gliders were damaged by ground fire, only ten were shot down.

The subsequent resupply operation was assisted by 239 Liberators of the US 8th Air Force, the first of which were taking off before the last glider had landed. To direct the resupply aircraft to the DZs, the RAF used three Halifaxes as Master Supply Aircraft; when within 50 miles of the target area, these aircraft contacted the Forward Visual Control Posts, which were special RAF units consisting of a squadron leader controller and two wireless operators with a jeep and trailer fitted out for transmissions. Some Stirlings were also fitted out as Master Supply Aircraft for R/T contact with the Independent Paratroop Brigade. Throughout the operations, responsibility for preventing interference from enemy air opposition was undertaken by 2nd TAF; less than twenty enemy aircraft were sighted, but flak caused heavy casualties and in all 75 aircraft were shot down.

With the Allies established across the Rhine, the defeat of Germany was inevitable. Nevertheless, the *Luftwaffe* continued to fight hard, and new combat aircraft appeared which, had they been available in sufficient numbers, would have presented a definite challenge to the Allies' air superiority. Potentially the most dangerous was the Messerschmitt Me 262 jet, which might have inflicted severe losses on the Allies if it had not been for Hitler's earlier insistence that it should be turned into a 'reprisal bomber'.

One of the first encounters between the Allies and the Me 262 occurred on 25 July 1944, when one of them intercepted a Mosquito of No. 544 on a photo-reconnaissance mission over Munich. Although damaged, the Mosquito shook off its pursuer and made an emergency landing in northern Italy.

During the 2nd Army's advance through Belgium and Holland the Me 262s were used extensively for photo-reconnaissance. For weeks, they roved at will over the entire battlefront; slipping over the front line at zero feet, they usually achieved complete surprise and completed their missions before the Allied defences had time to react. Their high speed made it impossible for anti-aircraft guns to track them successfully, and Allied piston-engined fighters could only hope to catch them by means of a dive from several thousand feet higher up. In an effort to combat the menace, the Allies maintained almost continual air patrols, with their latest fighter aircraft—such as the Tempest—operating in pairs over the front line and a second pair held at cockpit readiness on the ground in the hope of catching the 262s as they slipped across. More often than not, however, the expertly camouflaged 262s, which were extremely difficult to spot from a higher altitude, eluded this fighter screen and got clean away. Attacks on the jets' bases were prohibitively costly, for their airfields were heavily defended by all kinds of flak.

In the closing months of the war, Bomber Command had several encounters with German jet and rocket fighters. On 8 February 1945, for example, a Me 262 was shot down by two gunners in a Halifax of No. 427 (RCAF) Squadron engaged in a daylight raid on Goch, while the gunners of another Halifax of the same squadron claimed a Me 163 rocket fighter probably destroyed.

For the RAF, the most serious conflict with the jets came on the night of 30/31 March and the next day. One German night-fighter squadron, 10/NJG 11, was equipped with Me 262s, and on 30/31 March its CO, Oberleutnant Welter, shot down no fewer than four Mosquitos on the approaches to Berlin. The following morning, Halifaxes of No. 6 Group, operating without fighter cover because they arrived over the target ten minutes late, were bounced by 30 Me 262s and eight Halifaxes were shot down.

For the *Luftwaffe*, however, these were futile successes. Germany was plunging towards catastrophic defeat, its greatest cities devastated wildernesses, its industries in ruins, its communications system torn asunder by the weight of air attack. The *Luftwaffe*'s latest jets stood idle on their bomb-cratered airfields and among the trees alongside stretches of autobahn, crippled by the swarming Allied fighters and lack of fuel; the piston-engined Focke-Wulfs and Messerschmitts, flown for the most part by hopelessly inexperienced pilots, were massacred day after day.

Germany was defeated; but for the Allied air forces there remained two tasks to be carried out. On 26 April 1945, the British and Americans began an airlift of ex-PoWs from Germany to the UK. This task, code-named Operation Exodus, lasted until 1 June, during which time aircraft of Bomber Command alone flew more than 75,000 prisoners home.

On 29 April, the RAF and USAAF initiated Operation Manna, the dropping of food and medical supplies to the starving Dutch population. DZs were marked by aircraft of the Pathfinder Force, and up to 8 May, the date of Germany's unconditional surrender, the RAF delivered 10,000 tons of provisions to Holland by air.

So, on a note of humanity and mercy, the greatest fighting machine in history ended the conflict in Europe.

Royal Air Force Order of Battle (United Kingdom), 5 June 1944.

Sqn	Base	Aircraft	Command
1	Predannack	Spitfire Mk IXB	ADGB*
2	Gatwick	Mustang Mk II	2 TAF
3	Newchurch	Tempest Mk V	ADGB
4	Gatwick	Mosquito Mk XVI Spitfire Mk XI	2 TAF
7	Oakington	Lancaster Mks I, III	Bomber
9	Bardney	Lancaster Mks I, III	Bomber
12	Wickenby	Lancaster Mks I, III	Bomber
15	Mildenhall	Lancaster Mks I, III	Bomber
16	Northolt	Spitfire Mk XI	2 TAF
19	Funtington	Mustang Mks III, IV	2 TAF
21	Gravesend	Mosquito Mk VI	2 TAF
23	Little Snoring	Mosquito Mk VI	Bomber (No. 100 Group Bomber Support)
24	Hendon	York C Mk I	Transport
25	Coltishall	Mosquito Mks VI, XVII	ADGB
26	Lee-on-Solent	Spitfire Mks VA, VB, VC	2 TAF
29	West Malling	Mosquito Mk XIII	ADGB
33	Lympne	Spitfire Mk IXE	2 TAF
35	Graveley	Lancaster Mks I, III	Bomber
41	Bolt Head	Spitfire Mk XII	ADGB
44	Dunholme Lodge	Lancaster Mks I, III	Bomber
48	Down Ampney	Dakota Mks III, IV	Transport
49	Fiskerton	Lancaster Mks I, III	Bomber
50	Skellingthorpe	Lancaster Mks I, III	Bomber
51	Snaith	Halifax Mk III	Bomber
53	St Eval	Liberator Mks V, VA	Coastal
56	Newchurch	Spitfire Mk IX	ADGB
57	East Kirby	Lancaster Mks I, III	Bomber
58	St David's	Halifax Mk II	Coastal
59	Ballykelly	Liberator Mk VIII	Coastal
61	Skellingthorpe	Lancaster Mks I, III	Bomber
63	Lee-on-Solent	Spitfire Mk VC	2 TAF
64	Deanland	Spitfire Mks VB, VC	ADGB
65	Funtington	Mustang Mk III	2 TAF
66	Bognor	Spitfire Mk IX	2 TAF
68	Fairwood Common	Beaufighter Mk VI	ADGB
69	Northolt	Wellington Mk XIII	2 TAF
74	Lympne	Spitfire Mk IXE	2 TAF
75	Mepal	Lancaster Mks I, III	Bomber
76	Holme-in-Spalding Moor	Halifax Mk III	Bomber
77	Full Sutton	Halifax Mks III, IV	Bomber
80	Detling	Spitfire Mk IX	2 TAF
83	Coningsby	Lancaster Mks I, III	Bomber
85	Swannington	Mosquito Mk XII	Bomber (No. 100 Group Bomber Support)
88	Hartfordbridge	Boston Mks III, IIIA	Bomber
90	Tuddenham	Stirling Mk III Lancaster Mks I, III	Bomber
91	West Malling	Spitfire Mk XIV	2 TAF
96	West Malling	Mosquito Mk XIII	ADGB
97	Coningsby	Lancaster Mks I, III	Bomber
98	Dunsfold	Mitchell Mk II	2 TAF
100	Grimsby	Lancaster Mks I, III	Bomber
101	Ludford Magna	Lancaster Mks I, III	Bomber
102	Pocklington	Halifax Mks III, IIIA	Bomber
103	Elsham Wolds	Lancaster Mks I, III	Bomber
105	Bourn	Mosquito Mks IX, XVI	Bomber
106	Metheringham	Lancaster Mks I, III	Bomber
107	Lasham	Mosquito Mk VI	Bomber
109	Little Staughton	Mosquito Mks IV, IX, XVI	Bomber
115	Witchford	Lancaster Mks I, III	Bomber
116	Croydon	Hurricane Mk IIA Tiger Moth Oxford Mks I, II	AA calibration Unit
118	Skeabrae	Spitfire Mk VB	ADGB
120	Ballykelly	Liberator Mk V	Coastal
122	Funtington	Mustang Mk III	2 TAF
124	Bradwell Bay	Spitfire Mk VIII	ADGB
125	Hurn	Mosquito Mk XVII	ADGB
126	Culmhead	Spitfire Mk IX	2 TAF
127	Lympne	Spitfire Mk IX	2 TAF
129	Coolham	Mustang Mk III	2 TAF
130	Horne	Spitfire Mks VA, VB, VC	2 TAF
131	Culmhead	Spitfire Mk VII	ADGB
132	Ford	Spitfire Mk IXB	2 TAF
137	Manston	Typhoon Mk IB	2 TAF
138	Tempsford	Halifax Mk II	Bomber (Special Duties)
139	Upwood	Mosquito Mks IV, IX, XVI, XX	Bomber
140	Northolt	Mosquito Mks IX, XVI	2 TAF
141	West Raynham	Mosquito Mk II	Bomber (No. 100 Group Bomber Support)
143	Manston	Beaufighter Mk X	Coastal
144	Davidstowe Moor	Beaufighter Mk X	Coastal
149	Methwold	Stirling Mk III	Bomber
151	Predannack	Mosquito Mk XIII	ADGB
156	Upwood	Lancaster Mks I, III	Bomber
157	Swannington	Mosquito Mks II, XIX	Bomber (No. 100 Group Bomber Support)
158	Lissett	Halifax Mk III	Bomber
161	Tempsford	Halifax Mk V Hudson Mks III, V	Bomber (Special Duties)
164	Thorney Island	Typhoon Mk IB	2 TAF
165	Predannack	Spitfire Mk IX	ADGB
166	Kirmington	Lancaster Mks I, III	Bomber
168	Odiham	Mustang Mk I	2 TAF
169	Great Massingham	Mosquito Mk II	Bomber (No. 100 Group Bomber Support)
171	North Creake	Stirling Mk III	Bomber (No. 100 Group Bomber Support)
174	Holmsley South	Typhoon Mk IB	2 TAF
175	Holmsley South	Typhoon Mk IB	2 TAF
179	Predannack	Wellington Mk XIV	Coastal
180	Dunsfold	Mitchell Mk II	2 TAF
181	Hurn	Typhoon Mk IB	2 TAF
182	Hurn	Typhoon Mk IB	2 TAF
183	Thorney Island	Typhoon Mks IA, IB	2 TAF
184	West Hampnett	Typhoon Mk IB	2 TAF
190	Fairford	Stirling Mk IV	Bomber
192	Foulsham	Wellington Mk X Mosquito Mk IV	ADGB (Signals)

Sqn	Base	Aircraft	Command
193	Need's Oar Point	Typhoon Mk IB	2 TAF
196	Keevil	Stirling Mk IV	ADGB (No. 38 Group)
197	Need's Oar Point	Typhoon Mk IB	2 TAF
198	Thorney Island	Typhoon Mks IA, IB	2 TAF
199	North Creake	Stirling Mk III	Bomber (No. 100 Group Bomber Support)
201	Pembroke Dock	Sunderland Mk III	Coastal
206	St Eval	Liberator Mk VI	Coastal
207	Spilsby	Lancaster Mks I, III	Bomber
210	Sullom Voe	Catalina Mk IV	Coastal
214	Oulton	Fortress Mk II	Bomber (No. 100 Group Bomber Support)
218	Woolfox Lodge	Stirling Mk III	Bomber
219	Bradwell Bay	Mosquito Mk XVII	2 TAF
224	St Eval	Liberator Mks II, V	Coastal
226	Hartfordbridge	Mitchell Mk II	2 TAF
228	Pembroke Dock	Sunderland Mk III	Coastal
229	Detling	Spitfire Mk IX	ADGB
233	Blakehill Farm	Dakota Mk III	Transport
234	Deanland	Spitfire Mks VB, VC	ADGB
235	Portreath	Beaufighter Mk XI	Coastal
236	North Coates	Beaufighter Mk X	Coastal
239	West Raynham	Mosquito Mk II	2 TAF
245	Holmsley South	Typhoon Mk IB	2 TAF
247	Hurn	Typhoon Mk IB	2 TAF
248	Portreath	Mosquito Mks VI, XVIII	Coastal
254	North Coates	Beaufighter Mk X	Coastal
257	Need's Oar Point	Typhoon Mks IA, IB	2 TAF
263	Harrowbeer	Typhoon Mk IB	2 TAF
264	Hartfordbridge	Mosquito Mk XIII	ADGB
266	Need's Oar Point	Typhoon Mk IB	2 TAF
268	Gatwick	Mustang Mks I, IA, II	2 TAF
271	Blakehill Farm	Harrow Mks I, II Hudson Dakota Mks III, IV	Transport
274	Detling	Spitfire Mk IX	ADGB
275	Warmwell	Walrus Mks I, II Anson Mk I Spitfire Mk VB	Coastal
276	Portreath	Walrus Mks I, II Spitfire Mk VB Warwick Mk I	Coastal
277	Shoreham Hawkinge	Lysander Mk IIIA Walrus Mks I, II Spitfire Mk VB	Coastal
278	Martlesham Heath	Walrus Mks I, II Anson Mk I Spitfire Mk VB Warwick Mk I	Coastal
279	Bircham Newton	Hudson Mks III, V, VI	Coastal
280	Strubby	Warwick Mk I	Coastal
281	Tiree	Warwick Mk I Sea Otter Mk II	Coastal
282	Davidstowe Moor	Walrus Mks I, II Warwick Mk I	Coastal
285	Woodvale	Oxford Mk II Beaufighter Mk I Hurricane Mk IIC	ADGB
286	Colerne	Oxford Mk II Defiant Mks I, III Hurricane Mks IIC, IV Martinet Mk I	ADGB

Sqn	Base	Aircraft	Command
287	Croydon	Oxford Mk II Martinet Mk I	ADGB
288	Collyweston	Hurricane Mks I, IIC Oxford Mks I, II Beaufighter Mks VI, X Spitfire Mks IX, XVI	ADGB
289	Turnhouse	Hurricane Mks I, IIC, IV Oxford Mk II Martinet Mk I	ADGB
290	Long Kesh	Oxford Mk II Martinet Mk I Hurricane Mk IIC	ADGB
291	Hutton Cranswick	Martinet Mk I Hurricane Mk IIC	ADGB
295	Harwell	Albemarle Mks I, II	Transport
296	Brize Norton	Albemarle Mks I, II	Transport
297	Brize Norton	Albemarle Mks I, II, V, VI	Transport
298	Tarrant Rushton	Halifax Mk V	Transport
299	Keevil	Stirling Mk IV	Transport
300	Faldingworth	Lancaster Mks I, III	Bomber
302	Chailey	Spitfire Mks IXC, IXE	2 TAF
303	Horne	Spitfire Mk VB	2 TAF
304	Chivenor	Wellington Mk XIV	Coastal
305	Lasham	Mosquito Mk VI	2 TAF
306	Coolham	Mustang Mk III	2 TAF
307	Church Fenton	Mosquito Mks II, XII	ADGB
308	Chailey	Spitfire Mk IX	2 TAF
309	Drem	Hurricane Mk IIC	ADGB
310	Appledram	Spitfire Mks VB, VC, IX	2 TAF
311	Predannack	Liberator Mk V	Coastal
312	Appledram	Spitfire Mk IX	2 TAF
313	Appledram	Spitfire Mk IX	2 TAF
315	Coolham	Mustang Mk III	2 TAF
316	Coltishall	Mustang Mk III	2 TAF
317	Chailey	Spitfire Mk IX	2 TAF
320	Dunsfold	Mitchell Mk II	2 TAF
322	Hartfordbridge	Spitfire Mk XIV	2 TAF
329	Merston	Spitfire Mk IX	2 TAF
330	Sullom Voe	Sunderland Mks II, III	Coastal
331	Bognor	Spitfire Mk IX	2 TAF
332	Bognor	Spitfire Mk IX	2 TAF
333	Leuchars Woodhaven	Mosquito Mk VI Catalina Mks IB, IVA	Coastal
340	Merston	Spitfire Mk IXB	2 TAF
341	Merston	Spitfire Mk IXB	2 TAF
342	Hartfordbridge	Boston Mk IIIA	2 TAF
346	Elvington	Halifax Mk V	Bomber
349	Selsey	Spitfire Mk IX	2 TAF
350	Friston	Spitfire Mks VB, VC	2 TAF
501	Friston	Spitfire Mk IX	ADGB
502	St David's	Halifax Mk II	Coastal
504	Digby	Spitfire Mks VB, VC	ADGB
511	Lyneham	Liberator Mks I, II Dakota Mks I, III York C Mk I	Transport
512	Broadwell	Dakota Mks I, III	Transport
514	Waterbeach	Lancaster Mks I, III	Bomber
515	Little Snoring	Mosquito Mk VI	Bomber (No 100 Group Bomber Support)
516	Dundonald	Anson Mk I Blenheim Mk IV Hurricane Mks IIB, IIC	2 TAF
517	Brawdy	Halifax Mk V	Coastal

Sqn	Base	Aircraft	Command	Sqn	Base	Aircraft	Command
518	Tiree	Halifax Mk V	Coastal	598	Peterhead	Oxford Mks I, II	ADGB
519	Skitten	Spitfire Mk VI	Coastal			Lysander Mk IIIA	
		Ventura Mk V				Martinet Mk I	
521	Docking	Gladiator Mk II	Coastal			Hurricane Mks IIC, IV	
		Ventura Mk V		602	Ford	Spitfire Mk IX	2 TAF
524	Davidstowe Moor	Wellington Mk XIII	Coastal	604	Hurn	Mosquito Mks XII, XIII	2 TAF
				605	Manston	Mosquito Mk VI	2 TAF
525	Lyneham	Warwick Mk I	Coastal	609	Thorney Island	Typhoon Mks IA, IB	2 TAF
526	Inverness	Blenheim Mk IV	ADGB	610	Harrowbeer	Spitfire Mk XIV	ADGB
		Hornet Moth		611	Deanland	Spitfire Mks VB, VC	ADGB
		Oxford Mk I		612	Chivenor	Wellington Mk XIV	Coastal
		Dominie Mk I		613	Lasham	Mosquito Mk VI	2 TAF
527	Digby	Blenheim Mk IV	ADGB	616	Culmhead	Spitfire Mk VII	ADGB
		Hurricane Mk IIB		617	Woodhall Spa	Lancaster Mks I, III	Bomber
		Hornet Moth		618	Skitten	Mosquito Mk IV	Bomber
528	Digby	Blenheim Mk IV	ADGB	619	Dunholme Lodge	Lancaster Mks I, III	Bomber
		Hornet Moth		620	Fairford	Stirling Mk IV	ADGB (No. 38 Group)
529	Halton	Rota Mk I	ADGB				
		Hornet Moth		622	Mildenhall	Lancaster Mks I, III	Bomber
		Cierva C Mk 40		625	Kelstern	Lancaster Mks I, III	Bomber
540	Benson	Mosquito Mks IX, XVI	Coastal	626	Wickenby	Lancaster Mks I, III	Bomber
541	Benson	Spitfire Mks XI, XIX	Coastal (PR)	627	Woodhall Spa	Mosquito Mk IV	Bomber
542	Benson	Spitfire Mks IV, XI, XIX	Coastal (PR)	630	East Kirkby	Lancaster Mks I, III	Bomber
544	Benson	Mosquito Mks IX, XVI	Coastal (PR)	631	Towyn	Henley Mk III	ADGB
547	St. Eval	Liberator Mk V	Coastal			Hurricane Mk IIC	
550	North Killingholme	Lancaster Mks I, III	Bomber	635	Downham Market	Lancaster Mks I, III	Bomber
				639	Cleave	Henley Mk III	ADGB
567	Detling	Barracuda Mk II	ADGB	640	Leconfield	Halifax Mk III	Bomber
		Martinet Mk I		644	Tarrant Rushton	Halifax Mk V	ADGB
		Hurricane Mk IV		650	Bodorgan	Martinet Mk I	ADGB
		Oxford Mk I				Hurricane Mk IV	
570	Harwell	Albemarle Mks I, II, V	ADGB (No. 38 Group)	667	Gosport	Defiant Mks I, III	ADGB
						Hurricane Mk IIC	
571	Oakington	Mosquito Mk XVI	Bomber			Barracuda Mk II	
575	Broadwell	Dakota Mk III	Transport	679	Ipswich	Martinet Mk I	ADGB
576	Elsham Wolds	Lancaster Mks I, III	Bomber			Hurricane Mks IIC, IV	
577	Castle Bromwich	Oxford Mk I	ADGB			Barracuda Mk II	
		Hurricane Mks IIC, IV		691	Roborough	Hurricane Mk IIC	ADGB
578	Burn	Halifax Mk III	Bomber			Defiant Mks I, III	
582	Little Staughton	Lancaster Mks I, III	Bomber			Oxford Mk I	
587	Culmhead	Martinet Mk I	ADGB			Barracuda Mk II	
		Oxford Mks I, II		692	Graveley	Mosquito Mks IV, XVI	Bomber
		Hurricane Mks IIC, IV		695	Bircham Newton	Henley Mk III	ADGB
595	Aberporth	Henley Mk III	ADGB			Hurricane Mk IIC	
		Hurricane Mks IIC, IV				Martinet Mk I	
		Martinet Mk I					

ADGB: Air Defence of Great Britiain

16

The Far East
1941-45

For two days the monsoon rains had been sweeping across the Malay peninsula, the water falling in sheets from the clouds that rose in leaden banks from the roof of the jungle. The rain lashed the surface of Kota Bharu airfield, on Malaya's north-east coast, into stinking mud and danced in an explosive mist on the tarpaulins that shrouded the engines and cockpits of the thirteen Lockheed Hudsons of No. 1 Squadron, Royal Australian Air Force, standing squat and silent on the flight line.

It was 7 December 1941. Seven thousand miles away, in mid-Pacific, on the other side of the international date line, it was still 6 December, and a Japanese carrier task force was at that moment heading for the Hawaiian Islands. Its target: Pearl Harbor.

Both the Commander-in-Chief Far East, Air Chief Marshal Sir Robert Brooke-Popham, and his deputy, Air Vice-Marshal C. W. H. Pulford, had been aware for some time that Japanese action in south-east Asia was imminent. The signs could not be ignored; neither could the fact that the RAF in Malaya and Singapore had precious little in the way of modern equipment with which to counter the threat. Four squadrons, Nos 27, 34, 60 and 62, were equipped with Blenheim Mk Is (No. 27, in fact, had Blenheim Mk IFs, and was a fighter unit); Nos 1 and 8 Squadrons of the RAAF had Hudsons; but the remainder of the available strike force, Nos 36 and 100 torpedo-bomber squadrons, still used obsolete Vickers Vildebeests. The fighter defence of Malaya rested on the shoulders of No. 243 Squadron, RAF, No. 488 Squadron, RNZAF, and Nos 21 and 453 Squadrons, RAAF, all of which were equipped with Brewster Buffalo Mk Is, a heavy, underpowered fighter of American origin armed with a pair of .303-in machine-guns. Although comparatively manoeuvrable, the Buffalo had a top speed of only 270 mph at 10,000 feet and had little to commend it. It had, in fact, been rejected for European service. To complete the sorry line-up, there were three Catalina flying-boats of No. 205 Squadron at Seletar for long-range maritime reconnaissance.

Early in December, Brooke-Popham dispersed his squadrons to airfields on the Malay peninsula and ordered the stepping-up of reconnaissance flights following the receipt of intelligence that a Japanese invasion of Siam appeared imminent. For 30 hours after the order was issued, however, operations were severely hampered by bad weather, and it was not until the morning of 6 December that the pilot of a No. 1 Squadron Hudson, Flight Lieutenant Jack Ramshaw, sighted a Japanese battleshop, five cruisers, seven destroyers and 22 freighters, 265 miles due east of Kota Bharu and apparently heading straight for it. A Catalina of No. 205 Squadron was despatched to shadow the enemy convoy through the night, but failed to make contact; a second Catalina did make contact, and was shot down by Japanese fighters.

After that, there was no news of the Japanese force until 01.00 on 8 December, when Wing Commander Reg Davis, OC No. 1 Squadron, received an urgent call from the Indian troops who were defending the beaches at Kota Bharu; a break in the weather had revealed enemy ships lying offshore. Soon afterwards, coastal defence batteries opened fire on them, and Davis received orders from Singapore to send his bombers into the attack. The Hudsons attacked singly, the first bombing run being made by Flight Lieutenant Jimmy Lockwood, who set a freighter on fire. The first blow had been struck in the war against Japan—three hours before Japanese naval aircraft swept down on Pearl Harbor.

The Australians continued their bombing attacks throughout the morning, losing several crews, and by mid-day only five Hudsons were left out of the original thirteen. With the airfield under heavy fire, these were evacuated to Kuantan, 150 miles farther south. The Australians had no way of knowing that their determined raids had almost wrecked the Japanese landing; they had killed a staggering 15,000 troops, three times as many as were estimated at the time. The worst enemy casualties were on the 9,700-ton freighter *Awagisan Maru*, which

blew up. The Vildebeests of No. 36 Squadron from Gong Kedah also attacked the enemy warships in heavy rain, but without success.

Early on 8 December, Singapore received its first air raid, but for some reason the Buffalos of No. 453 Squadron were not authorized to take off. As the day wore on, Japanese bombers, under heavy fighter escort, carried out attacks on airfields at Sungei Patani, Penang, Alor Star and Butterworth; they used fragmentation bombs which caused much damage to parked aircraft and many human casualties, but left the airfields themselves intact. Alor Star was very badly hit, No. 62 Squadron losing all but two of its Blenheims; No. 27 Squadron and No. 21 Squadron, RAAF, were reduced to four serviceable aircraft each. By nightfall, only 50 of the original 110 Commonwealth aircraft in northern Malaya remained airworthy and, to make matters worse, the key airfields of Singora and Patani in Siam were in enemy hands.

On the morning of 9 December, the surviving Blenheims of Nos 34 and 62 Squadrons were ordered to attack these objectives. The first attack was successful, the densely-packed airfield at Singora being hard hit at a cost of five Blenheims, but before the second raid could be launched the Japanese bombed and strafed Butterworth and knocked out every Blenheim except one. This aircraft, flown by Flight Lieutenant A.S.K. Scarf of No. 62 Squadron, took off and flew to Singora alone, pressing home an attack through fierce fighter opposition. Scarf, although mortally wounded, shook off the fighters that pursued him and regained Malay territory, crash-landing near Alor Star. He later died in hospital, and five years later, when the full facts of his heroism were established, he was awarded a posthumous Victoria Cross.

RAF bomber losses were by now so severe that Air Vice-Marshal Pulford vetoed any further daylight attacks. Disaster followed disaster; on 10 December, the battle cruiser *Repulse* and the battleship *Prince of Wales* were sunk by Japanese air attack. Eleven Buffalos of No. 453 Squadron, led by Flight

RAF Unit Location in the Malay Peninsula, 8 December 1941

THAILAND

PERLIS

Haad Yai ●

Singora

Patani

KEDAH

Alor Star △ ○ Jabi
No. 62 Sqn

Kota Bharu △
No. 1 Sqn and
No. 243 Sqn detachment

Gong Kedam △
No. 36 Sqn detachment

△ Sungei Patani
Nos 21 and 27 Sqn

○ Ka Ketil

Machang ○

Butterworth △

PENANG △

George ○
Town

WELLESLEY

○ Sungei Bakap
○ Lubok Kiap
○ Malakoff

KELANTAN

PERAK

○ Taipang

TRENGGANU

○ Ipoh

○ Stiawan

PAHANG

Kuantan △
Nos 8 and 60 Sqns

SOUTH CHINA
SEA

STRAIT OF
MALACCA

SELANGOR

△ Kuala Lumpur
HQ NORGROUP and No. 153 MU

Port Swettenham ○

NEGRI SEMBILAN

○ Tebrau

MALACCA

○ Labis

Mersing ●

JOHORE

○ Kahang

Yong Peng ○

△ Kluang
No. 81 R&SU

Batu Pahat

Sembawang △
No. 453 Sqn

△ Seletar
Nos 36, 100 and 205 Sqns,
PR Flt and No. 151 MU

△ Tengah
No. 34 Sqn and No. 4 AACU

○ Sime Road
ANQFE

△ Kallang
Nos 243 and 488 Sqns

SINGAPORE

△△△ Bukit
Chunang

SINGAPORE

KEY
Operation airfields △
Other airfields ○

January 1942, 51 Hurricanes arrived in crates at Singapore. They were accompanied by 21 pilots, and their arrival prompted Air Vice-Marshal P.C. Maltby, in command of Singapore's air defences, to write in a despatch: 'The feeling spread that at last the Japanese were going to be held on the ground ... whilst it was confidently expected that the Hurricanes would sweep the Japanese from the sky.'

The faith seemed to be justified when, on 20 January, 27 enemy bombers attacked Singapore and the Hurricanes destroyed eight of them without loss. But the next day the bombers returned, this time escorted by Mitsubishi Zero fighters, and five Hurricanes went down. Although the Hurricane possessed slightly better climb, speed performance and manoeuvrability than the Zero at heights above 20,000 feet, the Japanese preferred to operate well below that level, where the British fighters were completely outclassed. Moreover, the Hurricanes shipped to Singapore had been intended for the Middle East and were fitted with tropical filters that reduced their speed by as much as 30 mph.

The Hurricane pilots did what they could, dividing their operations between intercepting enemy bomber formations and lending support to the army. On 26 January, the Japanese landed at Endau on the east coast of Malaya and moved rapidly to link up with their forces in the west, and the RAF made a desperate attempt to oppose the new landing. At 13.00, nine Vildebeests of No. 100 Squadron and three of No. 36, escorted by a small number of Hurricanes and Buffalos, attacked the enemy transports off Endau; five Vildebeests were shot down, mostly by Japanese fighters. At 15.00 nine Vildebeests of No. 36 Squadron, again with a small fighter escort, launched a second attack, and this time nine of the obsolete torpedo-bombers were destroyed.

By 28 January only twenty airworthy Hurricanes remained and of these, only ten were serviceable at any one time. The number of airworthy Buffalos had been reduced to six, while what was left of the bomber force and three replacement Catalinas were withdrawn to Sumatra. The Hurricanes and Buffalos fought on, and the decision was taken to concentrate any fighter reinforcements on Sumatra, where a new Fighter Group—No. 226—was formed at Palembang under Air Commodore S.F. Vincent. By 9 February, the Buffalos had been all but wiped out, but the Hurricanes continued to register successes; on that day, for example, six Japanese bombers were shot down over Singapore and fourteen damaged, for the loss

Lieutenant Tim Vigors, arrived in the area too late to intervene. Air Vice-Marshal Pulford had received no signal that the fleet units were returning to Singapore, and had therefore not been aware that they were within range of fighter cover.

By 11 December, the decimated air squadrons in Malaya were reduced to operating their aircraft in ones and twos, giving assistance to the hard-pressed ground forces whenever they could. Gradually, the squadrons fell back before the Japanese advance and were concentrated on Ipoh. The surviving Buffalos were used for ground attack and tactical reconnaissance, claiming some suc-

cesses against Japanese aircraft in the Ipoh area. Also active was the small Malayan Volunteer Air Force, which was equipped with a variety of light aircraft such as Tiger Moths and Avro Cadets; in addition to communications work, these little machines also carried out valuable reconnaissance, and in the process risked being shot at by friend and foe alike.

Japanese successes continued to mount; Hong Kong and Borneo, with no aircraft to defend them, fell on Christmas Day and Boxing Day. By that time, a trickle of air reinforcements—six Hudsons and seven Blenheims—had reached Malaya, but, on 3

of one RAF fighter. But it was the end; on 10 February, the last Hurricanes were also withdrawn, and five days later Singapore surrendered.

Conditions on Sumatra were appalling, with airfields severely congested and their surfaces in a fearful state as a result of the heavy rains. Nevertheless, the Hudsons and Blenheims of the newly-formed No. 225 (Bomber) Group under Air Commodore H.J.F. Hunter maintained pressure whenever possible on the airfields recently captured by the Japanese in Malaya. By this time, what was left of Nos 34 and 60 Squadrons had been evacuated to India; their places in Sumatra were filled by Nos 84 and 211 Squadrons, with Blenheims.

The task of the Commonwealth units in Sumatra became doubly difficult after 14 February, when the Japanese launched a heavy attack on Palembang airfield and then captured it using airborne forces. From then on, the Allied air units had to operate from a secret airfield designated P.II, and it was from here that reconnaissance aircraft detected a Japanese naval force en route to occupy Sumatra. The convoy was unsuccessfully attacked in bad weather by Blenheims on the night of 13/14 February, but the following morning it was attacked by every available bomber aircraft of Nos 1 and 8 Squadrons, RAAF, and Nos 27, 62, 84 and 211 Squadrons of the RAF. They enjoyed a conspicuous success by sinking six enemy transports for the loss of seven aircraft, and on 15 February, this time escorted by Hurricanes, they attacked the convoy again, inflicting enormous destruction on the landing ships in the Banka Strait and the mouth of the Palembang River. The enemy landing plan was completely dislocated, and thousands of troops killed. In addition, the Hurricanes destroyed a number of Zero fighters on the ground at Banka Island. Unfortunately, no Allied troops or naval forces were available to exploit this success, and the position in Sumatra quickly became untenable. With stocks of food and ammunition running dangerously low, the order was given for a move to Java.

The evacuation was completed on 18 February. By that time, 25 Hurricanes remained, of which eighteen were serviceable; these were divided between Nos 232 and 605 Squadrons and immediately thrown into the defence of Batavia. The bomber force had been reduced to twelve Hudsons and six Blenheims, operating from Semplak and Kalidjati; these struck hard at Japanese shipping on 19, 20 and 21 February, but on the 22nd the Japanese hit both their airfields,

destroying all twelve Hudsons and three Blenheims. A few replacement aircraft were scraped together and were thrown into action against Japanese convoys heading for the invasion of Java; together with some American B-17s, they sent seventeen enemy ships to the bottom. One of their finest actions involved an attack on enemy warships that had sunk the outgunned and outclassed Dutch fleet of Admiral Karel Doorman on 27 February; even the Vildebeests of No. 36 Squadron took part. Together, the Allies claimed the sinking of fifteen ships.

The pace could not last. By 2 March, the bomber force had virtually ceased to exist, leaving only the dwindling number of Hurricanes to fight on. Sadly, the two surviving Vildebeests of No. 36 Squadron, which had fought gallantly to the end, were both lost when they crashed en route to Burma. At the same time, the three remaining Hudsons of No. 1 Squadron, RAAF, were flown out to Australia.

After carrying out a series of strafing attacks on enemy invasion forces at Eretanwetan, 100 miles east of Batavia, the surviving Hurricanes—now concentrated in No. 605 Squadron—were flown to Badoeng, harassed all the way by enemy fighters. They covered the remaining ground forces as best they could until 7 March, when only two were left; they fought alongside the remnants of a Dutch squadron which had earlier received twenty Hurricanes and which had destroyed 30 enemy aircraft in a fortnight before it was wiped out. On 8 March all organized resistance ceased, and the Japanese were masters of the Dutch East Indies. Some of the RAF air and ground crews who had taken part in the spirited defence of the islands managed to escape; most were captured to face the horror and misery of Japanese prison camps, a three-and-a-half-year nightmare from which more than half did not return.

There remained Burma, whose seizure by the Japanese would mean an abrupt cessation of foreign aid to China and would also give Japan a base from which to launch an invasion of India. The original Allied plan had been to provide an air defence of some 280 aircraft, and for this purpose an RAF Group, No. 221, had been formed under the command of Group Captain E.R. Manning, RAAF. Under his direction, seven new airfields had been built between Mingaladon in the south and Lashio in the north; these were supported by a series of satellite landing grounds. In addition, there was another airfield at Akyab, on the west coast, and seaplane mooring sites in the Andaman and Nicobar Islands. By December 1941, there-

fore, the facilities for the defence of Burma were well established; unfortunately, the aircraft that were to form No. 221 Group's offensive and defensive power were not.

On 7 December 1941, the air defence of Burma comprised sixteen Buffalos of No. 67 Squadron, RAF, and 21 Curtiss P-40s of the 3rd Pursuit Squadron, American Volunteer Group, the remainder of which was based on Kunming in China. The Japanese were not aware that the Americans had joined the RAF fighters at Mingaladon, near Rangoon, and when they launched their first air attack on the Burmese capital on 23 December 1941, they were certain that an escort of twenty fighters—not Zeros this time, but earlier Nakajima Ki27s—would be more than enough to handle the dozen or so Buffalos they expected to encounter. In the fierce air battle fought over Rangoon that day, the Buffalos and P-40s destroyed six bombers and four fighters—but the RAF lost five Buffalos and the AVG four P-40s, a rate of attrition that could not long be supported.

There was a better score-sheet on Christmas Day, when the Japanese mounted a second major raid on Rangoon with 60 bombers escorted by twenty fighters. The enemy formation split up some distance away from the city, one half heading for Mingaladon airfield and the other for Rangoon's docks. This time, the Allied fighter pilots had received plenty of warning of the attack (early warning in Burma was always a problem; the mountainous terrain effectively masked the approach of enemy aircraft and there was only one radar unit in the whole of Burma) and, while the RAF's Buffalos provided top cover over Rangoon, the AVG's thirteen P-40s made contact with the enemy ten miles away. The Americans had the advantage of height, and while one P-40 flight attacked the fighter escort—composed of Zeros on this occasion—the rest tore into the bombers. As the latter scattered, the AVG pilots fell upon them, shooting one after another out of the sky. Eighteen bombers and six fighters fell burning into the Burmese countryside; over Rangoon, the jubilant pilots of No. 67 Squadron accounted for twelve more—the biggest success ever achieved by the Buffalos.

On 28 December, the Japanese despatched a small force of fifteen bombers towards Rangoon. Ten P-40s were sent off to intercept them, but as soon as the fighters were sighted, the enemy turned tail and fled. The P-40 pilots chased them across southern Burma until they were forced to land through lack of fuel at Moulmein. Then, while the bombers made their escape and the

P-40s refuelled, the Japanese put the second part of their plan into operation. Ten more bombers, escorted by twenty Zeros, swept down on Mingaladon. Four P-40s and ten Buffalos intercepted the enemy force 40 miles south-east of Rangoon, but they were beaten off by the fighter escort and the bombers caused considerable damage to hangars, fuel dumps and grounded aircraft. The Japanese came back the following day, and this time Rangoon was once again the target. Severe damage was inflicted on the railway station and the docks area, where large quantities of equipment destined for China went up in flames. It seemed that the dwindling Allied fighter force was growing powerless to stem the enemy's air onslaught.

The enemy attacks, however, tailed off dramatically during January and, in this period, the AOC-in-C Bengal Command, Air Vice-Marshal D.F. Stevenson, diverted 30 Hurricane Mk Is and the Blenheims of No. 113 Squadron, newly arrived from the Middle East, to the defence of Burma. The Hurricanes were immediately assigned to the defence of Rangoon, leaving the AVG and the Blenheims free to attack the enemy's bases in Thailand. This they did to good effect, and by the end of January they had destroyed nearly 60 enemy bombers and fighters on the ground, robbing the Japanese of their immediate goal of air supremacy and seriously upsetting their timetable for the conquest of Burma. By this time the Hurricanes—now formed into No. 135 Squadron—had also begun attacks on enemy airfields, for a few long-range fuel tanks had arrived to give them the necessary combat radius.

More Hurricanes, together with personnel of No. 17 Squadron, arrived early in February. With the remnants of No. 67 Squadron and the 3rd Pursuit Group, these formed the Mingaladon Wing under the command of Wing Commander Frank Carey.

The Japanese were now advancing rapidly into Burma and air activity had once more been stepped up; the enemy raids took place by both day and night, which presented problems for the defenders. Nevertheless, several successful night interceptions were carried out by aircraft that were completely ill-equipped for the task.

In the last week of January 1942, the Japanese made a determined effort to establish air superiority over Rangoon, employing some 200 aircraft in a series of raids that lasted six days. They failed, and lost 50 aircraft in the process. Three weeks later, reconnaissance aircraft began to appear over Rangoon, a sure sign that another major onslaught was in the offing; one of them was

destroyed by Frank Carey on 23 February, and three days later he shot down three Nakajima Ki 43 *Oscar* fighters, bringing his total score to 23. In the intervening two days the Japanese had sent 160 bombers and fighters over the capital, and the defenders claimed to have shot down 37 of them, with a further seven probably destroyed.

By now a third Hurricane squadron, No. 136, had also arrived in Burma, and No. 67 Squadron had at last exchanged its tired Buffalos for the more modern Hawker fighters—although, so desperate was the fighter situation, that the surviving Buffalos continued in use for some time longer. The main task of the Mingaladon Wing was now to cover the progressive withdrawal of the Allied forces, who were being pushed steadily back towards the Indian frontier, and for operational purposes the RAF squadrons, still working in close co-operation with the

AVG, were dispersed over a number of makeshift airstrips in the Rangoon area. This reduced the risk of losses during enemy air attacks but made it difficult to mount a sizeable force of fighters for either attack or defence at short notice. This was precisely the problem that faced Wing Commander Carey when, at the beginning of March, he received information that a large number of Japanese fighters and bombers were moving into the captured airfield of Moulmein. Carey mustered his eight serviceable Hurricanes and ordered them off for a strike, but the presence of enemy aircraft over the RAF airstrips made it impossible for them to rendezvous and in the end only Carey and one other pilot attacked the objective, causing considerable havoc among the densely-packed aircraft. Carey's companion was shot down, and his own Hurricane sustained much damage.

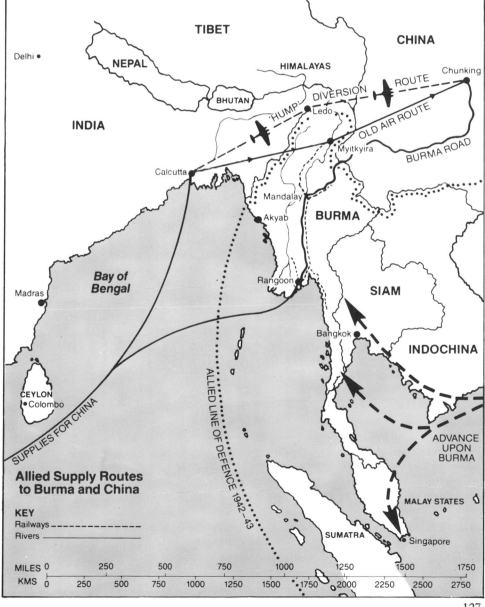

Allied Supply Routes to Burma and China

KEY
Railways ----------
Rivers ————

On 8 March, the Japanese entered Rangoon, and it was no longer possible for the Allies to carry out an organized defence of Burma. The army now began the long retreat northwards along the Irrawaddy and Sittang rivers, protected by the handful of fighters that remained. The remnants of No. 221 Group were moved north to the civil airport at Magwe and the island of Akyab, where they were formed into Burwing under Group Captain S. Broughall and Akwing under Group Captain N.C. Singer. Burwing comprised No. 17 Squadron, which had absorbed the remnants of Nos 135 and 136 Squadrons, together with the Blenheims of No. 45 Squadron; Akwing consisted of No. 67 Squadron and a flight of No. 139 Squadron, which—now equipped with Hudsons—had arrived in Burma some weeks earlier to carry out general reconnaissance duties.

On 20 March, ten Hurricanes and nine Blenheims from Magwe attacked Mingaladon, where they destroyed sixteen Japanese aircraft on the ground and eleven in the air. The enemy reprisal was swift: in a period of 24 hours more than 230 aircraft struck at Magwe, destroying all but six Blenheims and eleven Hurricanes. The survivors flew out to Akyab, while the AVG's three remaining P-40s were evacuated to Lashio. On 27 March, the enemy launched a three-day air assault on Akyab, destroying seven Hurricanes and some transport aircraft.

It was the end. These attacks had wiped out the last vestiges of Allied air resistance, and Burma's towns—together with the long columns of troops and refugees struggling towards India—were at the mercy of the Japanese air force. Yet the Royal Air Force still had a part to play; during this period, the Douglas Dakota transport aircraft of No. 31 Squadron, operating alongside the USAAF's 2nd Troop Carrier Squadron, airlifted over 8,600 men, women and children to safety under conditions of extreme hardship and often under air attack.

The Allied fighters in Burma had given a magnificent account of themselves, claiming the destruction of 233 enemy aircraft in the air and 58 on the ground, with a further 76 probably destroyed and 116 damaged, for the loss in air combat of 38 of their own number, of which 22 were Hurricanes. At least some of the success was probably due to the relatively low calibre of the Japanese Army pilots; elsewhere, when the Allies encountered the highly-trained squadrons of the Imperial Japanese Navy, it was a very different story.

On 4 April 1942, a reconnaissance Catalina reported that units of the Japanese fleet were approaching Ceylon and, at dawn the following day, a strong force of Japanese aircraft attacked Colombo harbour in the hope of surprising the Royal Navy's Eastern Fleet at anchor. The Aichi D3A *Vals* were hotly engaged by 36 Hurricanes of Nos 30 and 258 Squadrons and six Fairey Fulmars of the Fleet Air Arm; eighteen Japanese aircraft were shot down, but fifteen Hurricanes and four Fulmars were destroyed as well. Four days later, fifteen Hurricanes of No. 261 Squadron and six Fulmars intercepted a raid on Trincomalee; fifteen enemy aircraft were destroyed, but the defenders lost eight Hurricanes and three Fulmars.

Fortunately, Admiral Nagumo, the Japanese naval commander—after his torpedo-bombers had wrought havoc with the Eastern Fleet, sinking the aircraft carrier HMS *Hermes*, the cruisers *Dorsetshire* and *Cornwall*, the Australian destroyer *Vampire* and several smaller vessels—withdrew his task force in readiness for the next major Japanese adventure. The carriers of the Imperial Japanese Navy never again appeared in the Indian Ocean, and the next venture—the attempted invasion of Midway Island—was to mark the beginning of the end for Japan's Pacific conquests.

The successful campaign by the Japanese in Burma had brought their army to within striking distance of the Plain of Bengal and its teeming capital city of Calcutta, but the expected invasion failed to materialize in 1942—the enemy was not yet strong enough. It was not until December that a threat began to develop and, as a preliminary, the Japanese began to send small numbers of bombers over Calcutta in an attempt to panic the civilian population. Initially, the bombers were engaged by the Hurricanes of Nos 17 and 19 Squadrons, but in January 1943 the air defences received a boost in the shape of some Beaufighters. In less than a week, they destroyed five Japanese bombers at night and the air raids ceased.

The Allied forces in India were in the charge of two commanders of formidable reputation: Field Marshal Sir Archibald Wavell and Air Chief Marshal Sir Richard Peirse. Under the latter's direction the Air Command South-East Asia underwent a complete re-organization. The first step was to reform No. 221 Group at Calcutta for the purpose of undertaking bombing and reconnaissance missions over the Burma front and the Bay of Bengal; No. 222 (General Reconnaissance) Group stayed at Calcutta to patrol the Indian Ocean and the islands; No. 223 Group was responsible for training and administration; and No. 224 Group was responsible for fighter operations. By the end of 1942, Peirse had over 1,400 aircraft at his disposal, on paper at least; these included Blenheims, Hurricanes, Vengeances, Catalinas, Hudsons and Beauforts.

With the air defences of India growing stronger by the week, Wavell felt secure enough to launch a campaign in the Arakan, in north-west Burma, the object being to clear the Japanese from the Mayu Peninsula by thrusting towards Akyab Island. The offensive, which began on 9 December 1942, was supported by the Hurricanes of Nos 28, 261 and 615 Squadrons and enjoyed some initial success, the ground forces pushing 100 miles along the coast before they were halted. Large Japanese reinforcements eventually compelled a withdrawal in May. Meanwhile, in February, the first Chindit expeditions had set out from the Naga hills in northern Burma, their objective being to disrupt lines of communication and generally sow confusion deep behind the enemy lines; the Chindit columns were supplied by the Dakotas and Hudsons of Nos 31 and 194 Squadrons, mostly at night, and air drops continued to sustain them throughout the three-month duration of the First Chindit Expedition.

By June 1943, when the onset of the monsoon brought a halt to all but the most vital air operations, there were 53 squadrons in Air Command South-East Asia, 38 of them operational. Seventeen of these were fighter units, seven bomber, nine general reconnaissance, one photo-reconnaissance (with Spitfires—the first to arrive in the theatre) and one transport. There were also three Indian Air Force squadrons on the North-West Frontier for police duties. Importantly for the future of long-range operations, the Catalina GR squadrons of No. 222 Group were starting to be reinforced by Liberators; No. 160 Squadron arrived in India with these aircraft late in 1942 and began patrols over the Bay of Bengal in February 1943.

During 1943, the Blenheim squadrons received Vultee Vengeance dive-bombers or else re-equipped with Hurricanes, which were proving enormously successful in the ground support role. In October 1943, the first Spitfire fighters arrived in India and were allocated to Nos 136, 607 and 615 Squadrons, replacing their elderly Hurricanes. Two squadrons in India, Nos 5 and 155, were equipped with Curtiss Mohawks; No. 5 replaced these with Hurricane Mk IICs in June 1943, but No. 155 retained the obsolescent American fighters until January 1944, when the Squadron received Spitfire Mk VIIIs. The number of Beaufighter squadrons was also increased, and these aircraft became a valuable addition to the Command's medium-range strike force; the Japanese bestowed the nickname 'Whispering Death' upon them.

By May 1944, the number of squadrons under Sir Richard Peirse's command had risen to 64, together with 28 of the USAAF. Many of these were transport units, tasked with flying supplies over the Himalayas ('The Hump') to the Chinese-American forces under General Stilwell; RAF Dakotas also took part in these operations.

In the meantime, as a preparatory move to launching the Second Battle of the Arakan in February 1944, Sir Richard Peirse had set about achieving complete air superiority over western Burma with the aid of his squadrons of Spitfires. There were now five, for Nos 81 and 152 Squadrons had arrived with their Spitfire Mk VIIIs, which had a substantially better performance than the Spitfire Mk Vs which equipped the other fighter squadrons. The Spitfires wrought havoc among the Mitsubishi Ki.46 *Dinah* reconnaissance aircraft sent over the Arakan front, shooting four down inside a month and denying vital intelligence to the enemy as a result. On 31 December, the Spitfires of No. 136 Squadron destroyed twelve Japanese fighters and bombers that were attempting to attack shipping off the Arakan coast; before long, the 'kill' ratio was eight to one in favour of the RAF fighters.

In November 1943, all Allied forces in the China-Burma-India Theatre had come under the control of the newly-formed South East Asia Command (SEAC), under the leadership of Admiral the Lord Louis Mountbatten. Wavell had paved the way, just as he had done for ultimate victory in the desert; now his successor gave the signal for the start of the Second Arakan Campaign. The Japanese counter-attacked in great strength, expecting to split the British 14th Army in two, destroy each half in succession and then drive on into India, but their plan failed for two major reasons: first, because they committed their usual tactical blunder of relying upon the enemy doing what they, the Japanese, wished them to do, and secondly, because they had ignored the overwhelming Allied air superiority. Instead of falling back in disorder, as the Japanese had confidently anticipated, the 14th Army dug in and fought where it stood, relying on the Allied air forces for ground support and air supply.

A Catalina of No. 205 Squadron over Ceylon. Apart from carrying out general reconnaissance tasks, Catalinas were used extensively for special duties operations in support of Force 136 Commandos operating in enemy-occupied territory.

The transport squadrons did not fail them. As each 14th Army formation was cut off by the Japanese assault it was passed to the air supply list; soon, three divisions (5, 7 and 81) were all on the receiving end of air drops and getting exactly what they wanted. For instance, 81 Division received 95 transport bullocks, all specially flown in by Dakota (there were originally 96, but one died of heart failure) as well as badly-needed Bofors guns. Major General Messervy, commanding 7 Indian Division, had his HQ overrun with the consequent loss of all domestic items such as razors, soap and so on; all of it was replaced by air within 48 hours, and the replacement would have taken place earlier had not the first air drop gone to the Japanese. With the two forces only yards apart in

By the spring of 1944, the Allied air forces in Burma had established complete air superiority. Here, Beaufighters carry out a low-level attack on a Japanese airfield.

some places, and positions shifting continuously, such errors were unavoidable. Overhead, the Spitfire squadrons flew top cover, dealing effectively with the few Japanese aircraft that put in an appearance, and Vengeance dive-bombers struck at enemy positions with great accuracy.

Phase One of the Japanese plan to invade India ended in failure, but this by no means deterred the enemy from launching Phase Two. On 8 March 1944, three Japanese divisions, supported by armour, attacked across the Kabaw valley and reached Tiddim, cutting the important supply route to

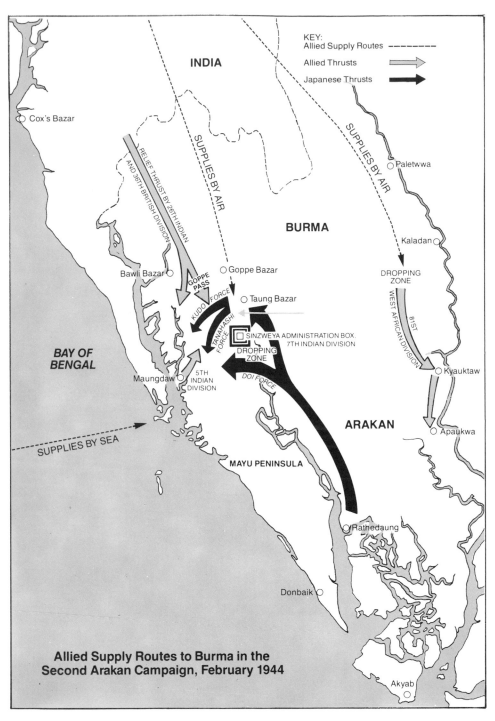

KEY:
Allied Supply Routes ----------
Allied Thrusts →
Japanese Thrusts →

INDIA

BURMA

Cox's Bazar

RELIEF THRUST BY 26TH INDIAN AND 36TH BRITISH DIVISION

SUPPLIES BY AIR

SUPPLIES BY AIR

Paletwwa

Bawli Bazar

Goppe Bazar

Goppe Pass

KUDO FORCE

Taung Bazar

Kaladan

DROPPING ZONE

WEST AFRICAN DIVISION

81ST

TANAHASHI FORCE

SINZWEYA ADMINISTRATION BOX, 7TH INDIAN DIVISION

BAY OF BENGAL

DROPPING ZONE

Maungdaw

5TH INDIAN DIVISION

DOI FORCE

Kyauktaw

ARAKAN

SUPPLIES BY SEA

Apaukwa

MAYU PENINSULA

Rathedaung

Allied Supply Routes to Burma in the Second Arakan Campaign, February 1944

Donbaik

Akyab

Imphal and Kohima, bases which lay 40 miles inside Indian territory and were of great defensive importance. The enemy breakthrough at Tiddim isolated the 17th Indian Division, and to help extricate it Mountbatten decided to commit all available reserves at Imphal. The latter were replaced by the 5th Indian Division, and to move it Mountbatten authorized the use of all available RAF and USAAF transport aircraft, temporarily withdrawing the latter from their operations over 'The Hump'. During the days that followed, although 5 Division's

heavy transport and guns went by road and rail, everything else—mules, jeeps and all—was flown in. The RAF unit involved in this airlift was No. 194 Squadron, with Dakotas.

On 4 April, the Japanese opened their attack on Kohima, and one of the bloodiest battles of the war ensued. Once again, the Hurricanes lent valuable support; in sixteen days, four Hurricane fighter-bomber squadrons flew 2,200 sorties against the Japanese 31st Division, attacking enemy positions, while four Vultee Vengeance squadrons struck at the enemy's supply dumps and base

camps. Later, the official report stated that the Hurricanes '... performed an indispensable service in the early period of the Japanese offensive by their persistent attacks upon the forward Japanese lines of communication at a time when the enemy was making every effort to bring up his stores and armament westwards. One squadron in particular came to specialise in what proved very remunerative attacks upon Japanese lorries on moonlight nights. At first the vehicles were easily detected by their headlights, but after two or three evenings they took to moving about without artificial illumination and the Hurricane pilots were thus compelled to seek their prey by selecting such well-known traffic lines as the Ye-U/Kelewa road and searching for lorries as they picked their way in the moonlight ...'

The Kohima garrison was completely supplied by air; even their water was dropped by parachute. The task required great precision on the part of the transport crews, for the DZ was confined to a very small area and the Dakotas, flying at low level, had to run through intense small arms fire. Although many were hit, however, not one was lost.

Kohima was relieved in mid-May by XXXIII Corps, which then swung south towards Imphal. The siege of Imphal, begun on 16 March when the Japanese 33rd Division advanced across the Manipur plain and cut the access routes to the garrison, lasted for three months. During that time, the Imphal garrison of 150,000 men, nearly 140 miles from the nearest railhead, had to rely entirely on air supply for their survival; it meant flying more than 400 tons of stores every day into a valley surrounded by enemy guns.

The air defence of Imphal was in the hands of No. 221 Group, commanded by Air Commodore S.F. Vincent. In the immediate vicinity of Imphal, as well as three squadrons of Spitfires for local air defence, Vincent had at his disposal six squadrons of Hurricane fighter-bombers positioned on six airfields, and, as Sir Richard Peirse later commented, 'The enemy's efforts to deploy in the Imphal Plain during May 1944 were decisively defeated by Hurricane attacks at short intervals on any concentrations reported by ground troops through our Army Air Support Control operating at a high standard of efficiency.'

In May and June 1944, with the enemy decisively defeated on the Imphal Plain and at Kohima, the Allies turned to the offensive and there now began a great pursuit which was virtually to end in Rangoon. The rout of the Japanese 15th Army was pursued right

In June 1945, No. 205 Squadron re-equipped with Sunderland Mk V aircraft, some of which are seen here at Koggala, Ceylon.

through the monsoon season, and as the Commonwealth forces pushed on through the terrible Kabaw Valley, Hurricane fighter-bombers sprayed the entire road ahead of the advance with DDT, reducing what would otherwise almost certainly have been fearful casualties from malaria.

The RAF fighter-bomber line-up in Burma was now quite formidable. Seven former Hurricane squadrons (Nos 79, 123, 134, 146, 258 and 261) were now progressively re-equipping with powerful Republic Thunderbolts, and the six Hurricane squadrons that had taken part in the defence of Imphal (Nos 11, 28, 34, 42, 113 and No. 1 Indian Air Force) were now joined by Nos 4, 6 and 9 IAF Squadrons and Nos 20 and 60 Squadrons RAF, the former equipped with rocket-firing Mark IVs for anti-tank work and the latter with bomb-carrying Mark IVs, popularly known as 'Hurribombers'.

Meanwhile, in the spring of 1944, General Orde Wingate and his Chindits had embarked on Operation Thursday, involving a massive airlift of 10,000 men behind the Japanese lines. On 5 March, 80 Hadrian gliders were towed by Dakotas from Lalaghat in Assam and cast off in the dark over two jungle clearings named Piccadilly and Broadway. Two nights later, Dakotas loaded with supplies that included mules and ponies flew into the two strips; 62 transport aircraft flew into Broadway while twelve gliders were towed into Chowringhee, a new strip named

after Calcutta's main street. White City, Blackpool and Clydeside were familiar names given to other rough strips hacked through paddy fields and thick jungle growths, and on 23 March a Chindit Brigade was flown into yet another strip, code-named Aberdeen. It was over the latter strip that a Dakota was surprised by a Japanese Oscar fighter, which pressed home its attack so closely that it collided with the transport's tail unit, shed a wing and plunged to earth. The Dakota pilot was awarded 'one destroyed' and landed his own aircraft safely.

These Chindit operations, undertaken at the height of the Imphal-Kohima crisis, proved to be an important preliminary to the Allied summer offensive, which was sustained by a total of 23 British and American transport squadrons. This would not have been possible without complete air supremacy, established over the battle zone by the RAF's Spitfires and at longer ranges by Mustangs of the USAAF. These formidable aircraft struck several telling blows against the dwindling Japanese Army Air Force that summer; on one occasion, they destroyed 31 Japanese aircraft on the ground at Don Muang, near Bangkok, after a flight of 780 miles to the target. Enemy airfields were also attacked frequently by RAF Liberators, and the results of this sustained offensive were apparent when, at the end of the monsoon season, the effective Japanese air strength in Burma had been reduced to only 125.

Meanwhile, the 14th Army had forged down the Chindwin River, supported all the way by the tactical and transport squadrons. While the advance continued, RAF Liberators concentrated on severing rail links throughout the theatre, which they accomplished with considerable success. These long-range operations were sustained by the Liberators of Nos 159, 160 and 356 Squadrons, which were joined by No. 358 Squadron at the end of the year. Another Liberator squadron, No. 200, carried out long-range maritime patrols over the Bay of Bengal in conjunction with the Catalinas of No. 205 Squadron, carrying out numerous attacks on enemy shipping and shore installations. From mid-1944, most of the long-range squadrons in SEAC also undertook special operations in support of guerrilla forces operating in enemy-occupied territories.

In parallel with the 14th Army's offensive in central Burma, that of XV Corps in the Arakan was also gaining momentum. A major breakthrough was made on 2 January 1945, when Hurricane pilots of No. 20 Squadron, patrolling over Akyab, reported some inhabitants signalling that the enemy had pulled out. The island was subsequently occupied without opposition and turned into a secure base for further operations along the coast; Spitfires were flown in for air defence, and on 3 January these shot down five out of six Oscars that attempted to attack the Allied amphibious force engaged in landing personnel and stores.

With Akyab in Allied hands, the next step was to land a force on the Burmese mainland at Myebon, to the south-east. This objective was assaulted by the 3rd Commando Brigade under cover of a smoke-screen laid by Hurricanes, which then provided close support in conjunction with USAAF Mitchells. In all, Allied bombers and fighter-bombers flew 1,150 sorties in support of the landing, dropping 750 tons of bombs. On 21 January, Ramree Island was also captured, the landing being covering by RAF Spitfires and Thunderbolts, P-38 Lightnings of the USAAF and Hellcats of the Fleet Air Arm.

The capture of Ramree was an important step forward, because it provided an ideal forward base from which to supply the 14th Army by air in its offensive through the central Burmese plains. The indications were that the Japanese intended to make a firm stand at the major crossing points on the Irrawaddy, expecting that the 14th Army would engage in pitched battles at these places. Instead, the Allies had other plans. While the bulk of the 14th Army assaulted the Irrawaddy, IV Corps, under Lieutenant General Sir Frank Messervy, would carry out a great outflanking movement designed to trap the Japanese forces in the plain south of Mandalay. The primary objective was the seizure of Meiktila, and when this was in sight Messervy's corps would be reinforced by a British brigade airlifted in by US transports.

The assault succeeded; Meiktila was captured, with its vital airfield, and the Dakotas began flying in reinforcements and supplies, often under very heavy fire. On 20 March 1945, for example, seven Dakotas were destroyed on the ground by Japanese artillery. Meiktila Airfield was defended by 400 men of the RAF Regiment, who established a ten-day pattern of operations; they would hold the airstrip during the day to allow the transports to land and take off, permit the enemy to retake it at night (the Japanese excelled in night fighting on the ground) and then sweep the strip clear of enemy forces the next morning in time for the day's operations. This, incidentally, provided the only known occasion when an Air Traffic Controller leaned out of his tower to shoot an enemy with his pistol while continuing to control aircraft! It was at Meiktila that Sergeant N. Gerrish of the RAF Regiment earned the Military Medal. He was in charge of a rifle flight deployed on the airstrip when the enemy infiltrated at night. Although wounded early in the battle that developed, he took over a light machine gun, inflicting punishing fire on the enemy. When this weapon ran out of ammunition, he provided covering fire from another gun position, enabling his men to withdraw; his shooting was so effective that all were able to cross open ground and reach safety. To rejoin them Sergeant Gerrish finally had to make his way across the bullet-swept airstrip in full view of the enemy. His actions were instrumental in holding two companies of the Japanese and for their ultimate defeat, during which many of them were killed.

Meanwhile, in the north, Mandalay had fallen; its strongest defensive position, Fort Dufferin, was captured after great gaps had been blasted in its fortifications by Hurricanes, Thunderbolts and Mitchells. The slaughter of the hemmed-in Japanese on the Mandalay Plain now began, the fighter-bombers of No. 221 Group inflicting terrible casualties on the disorganized enemy columns. By the second week in April, Japanese resistance in Central Burma had been effectively smashed.

On 12 April 1945, the 14th Army began its march on Rangoon. In support of this, supply dumps in the area were heavily attacked by all available strategic bombers. The rapid capture of Rangoon was of extreme importance, for it had been decided that all US transport aircraft were to be withdrawn from the theatre for operations elsewhere at the beginning of June. On 1 May, an airborne force of Gurkhas was dropped on the plain near Bassein, south-west of Rangoon, and on the following day they were in the city; the Japanese had gone. The occupation of Rangoon was completed soon afterwards by a seaborne force of the 26th Indian Division.

The 14th Army's rapid advance towards Rangoon had by-passed strong pockets of Japanese, and much bitter fighting remained before these were eliminated. The casualties suffered by the enemy in this last phase of the campaign were appalling; on 21 July, for example, the Japanese tried to cross the Sittang River with up to 18,000 men and were attacked by every available squadron of No. 221 Group. In nine days the RAF flew over 3,000 sorties and killed 10,000 enemy troops.

It was the end. On 15 August, in the wake of two atomic bombs on their homeland, the Japanese accepted unconditional surrender in all theatres. The RAF transport and heavy bomber squadrons now turned their efforts to the repatriation of thousands of Allied prisoners from camps all over the theatre; and for many aircrews, the sight of these men, all starving and many diseased, brought home the truth of what the Japanese 'New Order in Asia' had really meant.

The Japanese left behind another grim legacy: armed nationalism in the Far East. Within weeks of the war's end, revolutionary elements in the Netherlands East Indies proclaimed the existence of the state of Indonesia, and skirmishing broke out with SEAC troops who were trying to establish order. When the rebels murdered Brigadier S.W.S. Mallaby, commanding the 49th Indian Infantry Brigade, it was decided to send the RAF into action against them. On 9 November, Mosquitos of Nos 84 and 110 Squadrons began armed reconnaissance flights, and later in the month they were joined by rocket-firing Mosquitos of Nos 47 and 82 Squadons. On 17 November, four Mosquitos of No. 47 Squadron attacked a rebel radio station at Kemajoran, and on 25 and 26 November aircraft of Nos 47 and 84 Squadrons attacked other radio stations at Soeramarta and Tagjakarta. Similar attacks were carried out by the Thunderbolts of No. 60 Squadron and the Spitfires of No. 155 Squadron. Later the squadrons operated in support of ground forces, attacking rebel road-blocks and strongpoints.

Operations against the rebel forces were completed in March 1946. For the RAF squadrons involved, the counter-insurgency operations in the East Indies had provided a foretaste of events that were to become a familiar pattern in the postwar years.

17

The RAF and the Atlantic Alliance
1945~68

World War Two had cost the Royal Air Force 70,253 personnel killed in action and 22,924 wounded. At its peak strength, at the end of the war in Europe, the Service had no fewer than 55,469 aircraft on charge, of which 9,200 were in first-line service. Cuts, however, had begun almost immediately, with the disbanding of many squadrons in the summer of 1945, and demobilization of personnel proceeded at a rapid rate thereafter. In May 1945, the RAF's personnel strength stood at 1,100,000; the target was the release of 742,000 by 30 June 1946, with further reductions to a total strength of 305,000 by the end of that year.

In terms of equipment, the RAF ended the war with some of the most advanced piston-engined types in the world. The only real innovation was the Gloster Meteor jet fighter, which on 7 November 1945 set a new world air speed record of 606 mph. Even this aircraft was based on a conventional design. This was not illogical; the Air Staff had consistently followed a policy throughout the war of developing more advanced versions of existing designs, rather than experimenting with new and radical ones, as a means of mass-producing aircraft that would wage a successful air war without fear of costly failure.

To analyse the RAF's equipment situation at the war's end, together with Air Staff thinking and the eventual adoption of new designs that would take the Service through into the 1960s, it is useful to examine the postwar development of each RAF Command in turn.

At the beginning of World War Two, Bomber Command had enjoyed an undisputed lead in the design of strategic bombers. When the conflict ended, that lead had been lost to the United States. The reason was a geographical one; the Americans needed a bomber that could cope with the vast distances of the Pacific, whereas the RAF's

requirement was for an aircraft that could deliver a big payload over medium ranges. The American answer was the Boeing B-29; the RAF's solution was the Avro Lincoln, developed from the well-tried Lancaster.

First deliveries of the Lincoln took place in the spring of 1945, when a Lincoln Flight was formed within No. 57 Squadron at RAF East Kirkby, Lincolnshire. In the immediate postwar years the type equipped 22 more Bomber Command squadrons. It became operational too late to see active service during World War Two, although plans had been made to send several squadrons to the Far East as part of 'Tiger Force' for operations against Japan. The Lincoln was to remain the mainstay of Bomber Command until the early 1950s, by which time the RAF's strategic bombing capability was so depleted that 87 B-29s were loaned to Bomber Command to bridge the gap until the service debut of new jet types.

The first of these was the English Electric Canberra, originally designed for the radar bombing role to Specification B.3/45. The first of four Canberra B.1 prototypes flew on 13 May 1949; problems with the radar bomb-aiming equipment, however, led to the redesign of the nose with a visual bomb-aiming station, and with this modification the fifth aircraft became the Canberra B.2, which

The de Havilland Hornet, which served in small numbers with Fighter Command after the war, proved highly effective as an anti-terrorist weapon in Malaya. It was the last—and the fastest—of the RAF's piston-engined fighters.

entered service with No. 101 Squadron in May 1951. By this time a photo-reconnaissance version, the Canberra PR.3, had also flown; basically a B.2 equipped with seven cameras, it entered service with No. 540 Squadron in 1953.

The Canberra B.2 was ordered into super-priority production, and by mid-1954 equipped 25 Squadrons of Bomber Command, replacing all but a few of the

The Avro Lincoln. A straightforward development of the Lancaster, the Lincoln remained the backbone of Bomber Command's strategic force until the early 1950s.

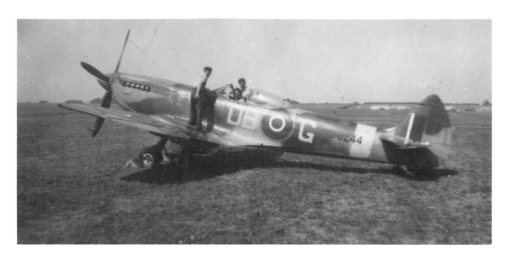

Spitfire LF.16Es of No. 63 Squadron at Hornchurch in 1946. No. 63 Squadron had disbanded on 30 January 1945, but on 1 September 1946 No. 164 Squadron was re-numbered No. 63. The Squadron retained its Spitfires until April 1948, when they were replaced by Meteor F.8s.

ageing Lincolns and the more modern, but still piston-engined, B-29 Washingtons. The next Canberra variant was the T.4 dual control trainer, which entered service with No. 231 OCU in 1954; it was followed by the B.5, a converted PR.3 intended for target marking, but only a few examples were built before it was superseded by the B.6, a version with more powerful Rolls-Royce Avon 109 engines. This version entered RAF service in 1954. Some B.6s were converted to B(I)6 standard by the addition of an underwing bomb armament and a 20mm cannon pack; the B(I)6 was an interim night interdictor, designed to fill much the same role as the RAF's night intruder Mosquitos a decade earlier. Another B.6 variant was the PR.7, designed for photographic reconnaissance at very high altitudes.

The Canberra's success story continued. The B(I)8 interdictor, which entered service with No. 88 Squadron in May 1956, featured some radical modifications, the most notable being an entirely redesigned fuselage nose and offset fighter-type cockpit, the navigator being 'buried' in the starboard fuselage. Another photo-reconnaissance variant, the PR.9, was developed from the B(I)8. The Canberra B.15 was a version of the basic B.6 with underwing hard points for bombs and rocket packs, and was designed for service in the Near and Far East, while the B.16, destined for service with the tactical squadrons in Germany, was similar except for its radar equipment. Several more Canberra variants were produced, including target facilities aircraft and target drones.

The Canberra, then, ushered Bomber Command into the jet age, and at the time of writing (in 1984) some variants are still in use in limited numbers. The Canberra, however, was a tactical strike aircraft; it had sufficient combat radius to reach targets in Eastern Europe, but not beyond, from bases in the UK, and in no sense did it form the basis of an effective strategic striking force.

The development of such a force resulted from the decision taken in 1947 by the British Government to produce nuclear weapons. Before that, however, the Air Staff had drafted a requirement for a British nuclear bomb and an aircraft capable of carrying it. The strategic jet bomber specification, B35/46, called for an aircraft capable of carrying a 10,000 pound store at 500 knots over a still-air range of 3,350 nautical miles, with a ceiling of 50,000 feet over the target. All the principal British aircraft companies tendered designs, and two received govern-ment backing: the Avro Type 698 and the Handley Page HP80. A third design, the Vickers Type 660, was much more conventional in nature than the other two and was at first rejected, but it was later decided to resurrect it as an insurance against the failure of the other two and in March 1948 a new specification, B.9/48, was written around it.

It was fortunate that this was so, for the Type 660—later named the Valiant—was to be the backbone of the RAF's nuclear strike force during the 1950s, and would pioneer the operational techniques of what was to be called the V-Force. The first Valiant flew on 18 May 1951, and the first production Va-liant B.1s began to enter service with No. 232 OCU at Gaydon, in Warwickshire in June 1955. The first squadron to equip with the Valiant was No. 138, also at Gaydon until July 1955, when it moved to Wittering.

The second squadron to receive Valiants was No. 543, which operated the B(PR)1 strategic reconnaissance version, but in 1956 three more Valiant bomber squadrons formed at Marham in Norfolk; these were Nos 148, 207 and 214 Squadrons, and in May 1956 No. 49 Squadron also reformed on Valiants alongside No. 138 at Wittering. A third Valiant wing, comprising Nos 7 and 90 Squadrons, was formed at Honington before

The Canberra was one of the British aviation industry's biggest success stories, and one of the RAF's longest-serving types. The aircraft seen here, T.19 WJ610, was originally built as a B.2, then converted to T.11, and finally to T.19. It served with Nos 85 and 100 Squadrons before being destroyed in a crash near West Raynham on 22 June 1972.

V-bomber squadrons carried out regular dispersal exercises, flying to different airfields in clutches of four aircraft. Crews are seen here leaving their Valiants at one such dispersal field—possibly Leeming, in North Yorkshire.

Three Valiant squadrons, Nos 49, 148 and 207, were assigned to NATO in 1960–61 for the tactical bombing role. Four aircraft are pictured here on Quick Reaction Alert (QRA) on an operational readiness platform angled into the runway at Marham, Norfolk.

the end of January 1957. The other squadron to be equipped with Valiants was No. 18, which used them in the electronic counter-measures role.

The Valiant had an impressive career as a strategic bomber. It was the first—and, until the Falklands campaign, the only—V-bomber to drop bombs in anger (see Chapter 20); it air-dropped prototype British nuclear and thermonuclear weapons; and it carried out regular overseas detachments, setting up several range and speed records in the process. By the time Valiant production ended in 1957, 108 aircraft had been built, plus three prototypes. Valiants also represented Bomber Command, with considerable success, at the USAF Strategic Air Command Bombing Competitions in the late 1950s

During 1960–61, three Valiant squadrons, Nos 207, 49 and 148, were assigned to the North Atlantic Treaty Organization in the tactical bombing role under the control of the Supreme Allied Commander Europe. For this task the Valiant could be armed with up to 21 1,000 pound conventional bombs or tactical nuclear weapons of American design.

Meanwhile, the two strategic bomber designs that had almost strangled the Valiant at birth had reached fruition. The first, the Avro 698, a bold delta-wing concept, first flew on 30 August 1952, and the first production aircraft—the Vulcan B.1—entered service with No. 230 OCU at Waddington in

January 1957. The first squadron to become operational on the Vulcan was No. 83 in July 1957, followed by No. 101 in October and No. 617 Squadron in May 1958. These three squadrons gradually assumed the role of spearhead of the British nuclear deterrent force in 1958–59; the blade of the spear, however, remained the Valiant force.

Meanwhile, in November 1957, the first production examples of the Handley Page design, the crescent-wing Victor B.1, had entered service with No. 232 OCU at Gaydon. The first two Victor squadrons, Nos 10 and 15, formed in April and September 1958, and a third, No. 57, in January 1959. Like the Vulcan, the Victor had been designed from

the outset to deliver its bombs from very high altitude, but in the late 1950s both designs were substantially modified to give them a better chance of survival at high altitude in a hostile SAM environment. The B.2 versions of both bombers were fitted with more powerful engines and ECM equipment, and in the Vulcan's case the wing was completely redesigned. Vulcan B.2s entered service with No. 83 Squadron in July 1960, the Squadron's B.1s being allocated to No. 44 Squadron; these were modified to B.1A standard with the addition of ECM gear. No. 617 Squadron also re-equipped with Vulcan B.2s from September 1961, and by the beginning of 1962 another squadron, No. 50, had reformed with B.1s and 1As.

The first Victor B.2 squadron, No. 139, formed at Wittering in February 1962, and in May it was joined by No. 100 Squadron. It had also been intended to equip Nos 9 and 12 Squadrons with Victors, and to arm the Vulcan and Victor B.2 squadrons with the American Skybolt air-launched IRBM. Skybolt, however, was cancelled, which dealt a severe blow to the RAF's plans to extend the life of the V-Force. It was fortunate that development had proceeded with the British-designed Blue Steel ASM; this had a range of only 100 nautical miles, but it would give the bomber an enhanced chance of survival against a strongly defended target.

Blue Steel became fully operational with No. 617 Squadron at Scampton in February 1963; the Squadron had actually had a limited operational status with the missile since the previous October, and had been ready to go into action with it at the time of the Cuban Missile Crisis. Blue Steel subsequently equipped two more Vulcan squad-

Valiants pioneered the operational use of air-to-air refuelling techniques. Here, an aircraft of No. 214 Squadron, Marham Tanker Wing, refuels two Lightning F.1 fighters in the early 1960s.

Vulcan B.1A of the Waddington Wing pictured in 1961 soon after receiving its ECM modifications.

Victor B.1s of No. 15 Squadron on QRA at Cottesmore, Rutland, in 1960.

rons, Nos 27 and 83, and two Victor squadrons, Nos 100 and 109. By the spring of 1964, therefore, Bomber Command had at its disposal five squadrons equipped with Blue Steel; of the other squadrons in the Medium Bomber Force, all tasked with free-fall bombing, Nos 9, 12 and 35 were at Coningsby with Vulcan B.2s, Nos 44, 50 and 101 were at Waddington with B.1As, and Nos 15, 55 and 57 Squadrons had Victors.

Of the Valiant squadrons, Nos 7, 18 and 138 had disbanded, Nos 49, 148 and 207 were assigned to NATO, and Nos 90 and 214 had been converted to the airborne tanker role, their principal task being to extend the range of the spearhead squadrons of the airborne deterrent force.

Only once, during its 12-year career, did it look as though the RAF's nuclear strike force might have to go into action, and that was during the Cuban Missile Crisis of 1962. While the crisis lasted, the whole of the V-Force was dispersed to airfields throughout the United Kingdom; such dispersal exercises, known as Kinsman or Micky Finn (dispersal without notice) were a regular feature of V-Force training, the bombers being dispersed in clutches of four. Unlike the USAF's Strategic Air Command, Bomber Command never maintained an airborne alert force; it relied on dispersal instead, and

in February 1962 the state of alert of the V-Force was further improved by the inauguration of the Bomber Command QRA (Quick Reaction Alert) plan, which initially involved one aircraft from each V-Force squadron being maintained in a fully armed condition, at a later date on operational readiness platforms at the ends of runways, prepared to scramble at a moment's notice. Such was the high state of V-Force QRA that, during the Cuban Crisis, the existing alert state would have been quite sufficient to get the V-Force off the ground in the event of an enemy attack; the only other precaution was to send all civilian personnel home and seal off the

bomber bases, using armed patrols to secure their perimeters.

In 1964, the growing sophistication of Soviet radar defences forced the V-Force to adopt low-level penetration tactics, and this proved too much for the Valiants; they were withdrawn from service in the bombing role after developing fatigue cracks. The Valiant tankers remained in service for a while longer until they were were replaced by Victor K.2s,

The Hawker Siddeley Blue Steel stand-off bomb. Blue Steel equipped Vulcans and Victors from 1963–1968 and was the spearhead of the RAF's deterrent until this was handed over to the Polaris submarines of the Royal Navy.

Close-up of a Meteor F.4 nose. Meteor F.4s of the RAF High Speed Flight set up new world air speed records in 1945–46.

which in 1984 were still operational with Nos 55 and 57 Squadrons.

The RAF maintained the strategic nuclear deterrent until 1969, when it was handed over to the Polaris submarines of the Royal Navy. The cancellation of Skybolt had effectively denied the RAF the chance to provide a deterrent into the 1970s, and cancellations elsewhere had written *finis* to other projects to which Bomber Command had looked forward at the beginning of the 1960s. There would be no supersonic strategic bomber to follow the Vulcan and Victor, although Avro had designed one, the Type 730, in the 1950s; ironically, both the Russians and Americans now have supersonic aircraft in the long-range strategic bombing role.

Any hopes that the Canberra would be replaced by a British-designed supersonic strike aircraft in the 1960s were also dashed by the cancellation, in 1965, of the English Electric (BAC) TSR-2, although the story behind its cancellation was long and complex. For example, although it possessed a superlative airframe, TSR-2's engines had a serious cold-start problem which seemed insurmountable, a major failing in an aircraft that would have been required to start up and roll very quickly under operational conditions. A plan to purchase 50 General Dynamics F-111 strike aircraft to replace the Canberra was also cancelled. By the beginning of 1968, the year in which sweeping changes in the structure of the RAF were to be implemented, the future of Bomber Command seemed very uncertain.

Fighter Command was not in much better shape. In the early postwar years, jet fighter development in Great Britain had lagged behind that of both the United States and the Soviet Union, both of whom had seized considerable quantities of German aviation research material relevant to high-speed flight—although in the USSR's case, the sudden appearance of the MiG-15 in 1948 was made possible by the naive action of Britain's Labour Government in shipping Rolls-Royce Nene turbojets to the Russians.

At the end of 1945, the bulk of Fighter Command's squadrons were still equipped with Spitfires, Tempests and Mosquitos, and it was not until 1946 that re-equipment with Gloster Meteor and de Havilland Vampire jet fighters really got under way. The first two RAF jet fighter squadrons, Nos 616 and 504, had re-equipped with Meteor F.3s early in 1945 and had taken them to join 2nd TAF in Belgium, where they carried out ground attack operations; 210 F.3s were built between 1944 and 1946, and equipped fifteen squadrons of Fighter Command. It was followed by the F.4, which served in large numbers and equipped 23 squadrons.

The RAF's other early jet type, the Vam-pire F.1, entered service with No. 247 Squadron in March 1946, and was subsequently joined by Nos 54 and 72 Squadrons to form the first Vampire Wing. Eleven squadrons in all received this variant, which was followed into service by the F.3. The major production version, however, was the FB.5, which was developed for ground attack and had strengthened wings to carry external stores. The Vampire FB.5 eventually equipped no fewer than 40 RAF squadrons at home and overseas. Its service career ran closely parallel to that of the Meteor F.8, which was basically an F.4 with a new high-speed tail unit, a lengthened forward fuselage, an additional internal fuel tank and a one-piece sliding cockpit canopy over a Martin-Baker ejection seat. From its appearance in 1948, the Meteor F.8 went on to equip 32 regular and eleven RAuxAF squadrons, becoming the mainstay of Fighter Command in the early 1950s.

Meanwhile, in 1946, the Ministry of Supply had at last shown an interest in the swept-wing formula, and two Specifications were prepared, each calling for the construction of a swept-wing research aircraft to investigate the transonic flight. The two companies involved were Hawker Aircraft and Supermarine, which respectively produced the Hawker P.1052 and the Supermarine 510. The Hawker design, which flew in 1948, showed such promise that at one point it was seriously considered placing the fighter in quantity production as a replacement for the Meteor; by that time, however, fighter designs of greater potential were on the drawing board, and the idea was abandoned.

The obvious need to find a replacement for the Meteor in the day-fighter role led to the issue, in 1946, of Air Staff Specification

Three Gloster Meteor T.7 two-seat trainers and an F.4 taking off from RAF Middleton St George in the early 1950s. The aircraft belong to No. 4 Flying Training School.

Vampire FB.5s of No. 608 Squadron, Royal Auxiliary Air Force, at RAF Thornaby in the 1950s. The RAuxAF was disbanded in 1957, but today is making a comeback; there are Auxiliary squadrons of the RAF Regiment, and a flying branch is being reconstituted to operate tactical support helicopters.

De Havilland Venom NF.3 of No. 141 Squadron. The Venom equipped five RAF night-fighter squadrons in the 1950s until it was replaced by the Gloster Javelin.

F.43/46. This was replaced by a new Specification, F.3/48, which conformed to the Air Staff's Operational Requirement 228. The requirement was a tough one; the aircraft that met it would have to be capable of reaching 45,000 feet six minutes after engine start and was to have a level flight speed of at least 547 knots at that altitude. Its rate of climb was not to be less than 1,000 feet per minute at 50,000 feet, and it was to have an endurance of one and a quarter hours.

Hawkers and Supermarine both submitted designs to F.3/48. The Hawker design, the P.1067, was to be fitted with a Rolls-Royce AJ65 turbojet and was to be armed with four 30mm Aden cannon; the Supermarine aircraft, the Type 541, was a straightforward development of the earlier Types 510 and 535. The Ministry of Supply, impressed by the Type 535, awarded Supermarine a production contract for 100 examples, which were to be built if the Type 541 and the Hawker P.1067 proved failures.

The P.1067 was the first to fly, in July 1951, and was followed by the prototype Supermarine 541 a fortnight later. Both aircraft had by this time been ordered into super-priority production for Fighter Command, a haste dictated by the Korean War, and had already been allocated names: the Hunter and the Swift.

The Supermarine Swift F.1 entered service with No. 56 Squadron, Fighter Command, in February 1954, five months before the Hunter went into service with No. 43 Squadron. In squadron service the Hunter, although it had its share of teething troubles, proved by far the better of the two designs and went on in its various marks to become a first-rate combat aircraft, although in fairness it should be stressed that the Swift's shortcomings were not the fault of the super Vickers-Supermarine design team. The problem lay in the fact that the Swift had been rushed into service as a panic measure when the Korean War hammered home the lesson that the RAF's current equipment was completely outclassed by that of the Russians, and it had simply not been possible to iron out all the snags. Both the Swift F.1 and F.2 were found to be quite unsuitable for their primary role of air interception, being prone to tightening in turns and suffering frequent high-altitude flameouts as a result of shock waves entering the air intakes when the cannon were fired. By February 1955 the Air Ministry had concluded that the Swift could not be relied upon to carry out its primary role and its time as a day fighter was at an end, the type being replaced by the Hawker Hunter in Fighter Command. Later, two squadrons of Swift FR.5s (Nos 2 and 79) were used in the tactical reconnaissance role in Germany from 1956 to 1961.

The first swept-wing transonic jet fighter to enter RAF service, however, was not of British design. It was the Canadair-built North American F-86E Sabre, 376 of which were supplied to the RAF in the autumn of 1953. They were ferried across the Atlantic in 'Operation Becher's Brook' by No. 147 Squadron. Although most were used by the squadrons of 2nd TAF in Germany, the Sabre also equipped two home-based squadrons of Fighter Command, Nos 66 and 92 at Linton-on-Ouse. The Sabre's RAF career was relatively short-lived, as it was replaced by the Hunter from the spring of 1956, but it filled a dangerous gap in the UK and NATO air defences.

In parallel with the specification that had led to the Hunter and Swift day fighters, the Air Ministry had also issued a specification, F.44/46, for a night and all-weather fighter. This underwent a number of changes and was eventually finalized in F.4/49; designs were submitted by the Gloster Aircraft Company and de Havilland, but both were to have a long, troubled development history.

In the meantime, Fighter Command's night-fighter force had to rely on aircraft developed from existing jet types, the Meteor and Vampire. The night-fighter version of the latter, the Vampire NF.10, entered service with three squadrons—Nos 23, 25 and 151—in 1951, replacing the Mosquito NF.36. In 1953, No. 23 Squadron became the first to receive the de Havilland Venom NF.2, developed from the fighter-bomber that then equipped the squadrons of 2nd TAF; Nos 33, 219 and 253 Squadrons

Twenty-two Hunters of Nos 111 and 43 Squadrons at the 1958 SBAC Show. This was the largest number of aircraft ever to indulge in formation aerobatics.

also received Venom NF.2s, but the principal Venom night-fighter variant was the NF.3, which equipped Nos 23, 89, 125, 141 and 151 Squadrons.

The Meteor night-fighter variants began with the NF.11, the prototype of which flew in May 1950. The nose was redesigned to take a large AI scanner and a two-seat tandem cockpit with full night fighting equipment. The NF.11 began to replace Mosquitos in the night-fighter squadrons in 1951, and thirteen squadrons were eventually equipped with it at home and abroad. Improved variants were the NF.12, NF.13 (for tropical service) and NF.14; 100 examples of the latter were built, and deliveries to the RAF were completed in 1955.

Meanwhile, one of the advanced all-weather fighter designs, the de Havilland DH 110, had fallen by the wayside after the second prototype broke up over Farnborough in 1952, although it was eventually to emerge as the Royal Navy's Sea Vixen. In 1953, the RAF decided to fill its all-weather fighter requirement with the Gloster design, the GA.5, and despite a series of accidents that slowed down development this aircraft was ordered into super-priority production as the Javelin FAW.1, deliveries beginning in February 1956 to No. 46 Squadron at Odiham. It was the beginning of a twelve-year operational career for the delta-wing Javelin, which was progressively developed up to the FAW.9, and the type equipped eighteen squadrons.

In the early 1950s, the Air Staff was considering a truly transonic successor to the Hunter and Swift—in other words, an aircraft that would reach a speed of Mach 1.5 in level flight. Hawker and Supermarine both submitted proposals, the P.1083 and the Type 545, but the promising Hawker project was cancelled in 1953 when the prototype was approaching completion, and the Supermarine 545 was cancelled in 1955. The failure of the Swift was partly the reason for the latter, but not all; by this time, the Air Staff had decided to put all its eggs into one supersonic basket by turning a manned supersonic research aircraft, the English Electric P.1, into a complete weapon system. In its new form, it flew in April 1957 as the P.1B; and as the Lightning, it eventually entered RAF service with No. 74 Squadron in June 1960.

The RAF therefore succeeded in bridging the gap from subsonic to supersonic at one stride, cutting out the transonic phase altogether. It was a formidable achievement, and the Lightning, which was to equip nine squadrons of Fighter Command, provided the RAF with a system that could outfly and outfight anything in the world for a decade.

The Lightning, in fact, was the sole survivor of the cancellations that swept through the British military aircraft industry following the Defence Review of 1957, much of which was based on the completely erroneous theory that manned combat aircraft would be replaced by missiles in the 1960s. Despite the chaos and disillusionment caused by this, Britain's aircraft designers rose to meet the demands of the future with their customary ingenuity, and nowhere was this more true than in the development of V/STOL. The year 1960 saw the first hover-

ing trials of the Hawker P.1127 V/STOL aircraft—eventually to reach fruition as the Harrier—and soon afterwards, in response to Specification NBMR-3, Hawkers began design of the P.1150, a supersonic variant which would have been capable of 1.7M. Its design, however, was overtaken by events fairly quickly. In mid-1961, the final version of the NBMR-3 specification was issued, and this required a supersonic jet V/STOL aircraft with a 250 nautical mile radius of action flying at 0.92M at low level, carrying a 2,000 pound weapon load following a rolling VTO of 500 feet to clear a 50-foot screen. The Air Staff Requirement called for a squadron of twelve to be in service by 1966.

The P.1150 was too small to meet this requirement, so Hawkers turned to a larger design, the P.1154. The design was promising and very advanced, but although NATO was interested in it, the RAF and the Royal Navy could not agree on a jointly acceptable version. In the end, the Navy opted for the Spey-powered McDonnell F-4 Phantom, and the RAF went on alone. Then the axe fell; in 1965, the P.1154 was cancelled, together with the TSR-2. The only bright spot was that its cancellation led directly to the development of the P.1127(RAF) which first flew eighteen months later, and which as the Harrier was to enter RAF service in 1969.

Britain's commitment to NATO in the post-war years brought new responsibilities for Coastal Command, which became responsible for the Eastern Atlantic area of the NATO Atlantic Command and also for the Channel Command. Coastal Command had ended the war with a miscellany of maritime patrol aircraft—Halifaxes, Lancasters, Liberators, Catalinas, Warwicks, Wellingtons and Sunderlands—in addition to the Mosquitos that equipped the anti-shipping strike wings; there had been an attempt to retain a torpedo-strike element after the war with the introduction of a Beaufighter development, the Brigand TF.1, but these aircraft equipped only Nos 36 and 42 Squadrons for a year in 1946–7 before they were converted as light bombers, and after that the Command's main tasks were clearly defined as trade protection, meteorological reconnaissance and search and rescue.

In 1946, in response to a requirement for a new long-range maritime patrol aircraft, Avro designed the Type 696 Shackleton. Originally designated Lincoln ASR.3, this flew for the first time in March 1949, powered by four Rolls-Royce Griffon engines, and was the first British aircraft to fly with contra-rotating propellers. The prototype was armed with two 20mm cannon in the nose, two cannon in a dorsal turret and two 0.5-inch machine guns in a tail turret, but the nose and tail armament was dropped on subsequent aircraft.

Seventy-seven production Shackleton MR.1s were ordered, the first entering service with No.120 Squadron at RAF Kinloss, Scotland, in April 1951. A Shackleton Operational Conversion Unit, No.236, was also formed at Kinloss. The next Shackleton squadrons to form were No.220, with MR.1As, which were slightly modified to simplify engine changes, this unit moving from Kinloss to St Eval in Cornwall in November 1951, and No. 224, which received its first aircraft in Gibraltar in August of that year. By the end of 1952, Nos 240 and 269 Squadrons were operating Shackletons from Ballykelly in Northern Ireland, and Nos 42 and 206 had joined No. 220 at St Eval, providing maritime coverage from Norway to mid-Atlantic, as far south as Gibraltar and westwards of Malta.

June 1952 saw the first flight of a new variant, the Shackleton MR.2, which had a ventral ASV radar 'dustbin' in place of the MR.1's chin radome, an elongated tail with an observation post and twin 20-mm cannon in the nose. First units to re-equip with the MR.2 were Nos 42 and 206 Squadrons, followed by Nos 220 and 204 Squadrons. Nos 37 and 38 Squadrons in Malta also received MR.2s, extending coverage to the whole of the Mediterranean with the ability to deploy rapidly east of Suez. Sixty-nine MR.2s were built, providing enough aircraft for the formation of another squadron, No. 228.

The next Shackleton variant, the MR.3, incorporated some radical design changes, with an altered wing shape and wingtip tanks that increased the total fuel capacity to 4,248 gallons. The mid-upper turret was deleted and the aircraft featured a tricycle undercarriage, improving its airfield performance.

By the end of 1957, Coastal Command's Shackletons were ranging world-wide, carrying out a wide variety of tasks—including oceanic survey and trooping—in addition to their usual maritime reconnaissance role. In 1958, fifteen squadrons were equipped with the type, as well as the Maritime Operational Training Unit at Kinloss, which operated a mixture of MR.1As and T.4s, the latter being modified MR.1s with dual controls. Only 34 Shackleton MR.3s were built for the RAF, but a further eight were delivered to No. 35 Squadron, South African Air Force. During the next four years, the remaining Shackleton MR.1s and 1As were progressively phased out and replaced by MR.2Cs, which were standard MR.2s brought up to

MR.3 equipment standard. Most of the MR.1s and 1As were modified as T.4s and served with MOTU until 1968, when they were replaced by surplus MR.2s.

In 1953, to augment its maritime patrol capability while the build-up of the Shackleton force continued, Coastal Command took delivery of 36 Lockheed P2V-5F Neptunes, which served with Nos 36, 203, 207 and 210 Squadrons as the Neptune MR.1. Sunderlands also continued in service until 1959, when the last examples were withdrawn from service with maritime squadrons in the Far East.

For Transport Command, a stern test came soon after the war when, in 1948, the Soviet Union imposed a blockade of the divided city of Berlin in an attempt to force out the occupying western powers. Tentative plans for the supply of the occupying forces in the event of such a blockade already existed, but something on a far greater scale was needed to keep the city above starvation level. The British and Americans acted with great speed, arresting and diverting aircraft

Representative RAF types, 1950–60, seen outside the air museum at RAF Cosford. Back row, top to bottom: two Shackleton MR.2s, Canberra, Comet C.2, Canberra, Shackleton MR.1, Varsity. Middle row: Tempest FB.6, two Chipmunks, Auster AOP.6, two Chipmunks, Mosquito. Front row: Lightning, Meteor NF.11, three Javelins, Meteor F.4, Hunter F.4.

movements all over the world so that in a few weeks the airlift, named Operation Plainfare, had built up to an estimated minimum requirement of 3,000 tons a day. In the winter of 1948–49, this rose to 5,000 tons daily, despite appalling weather and continual Soviet harassment.

At the height of the Berlin Airlift, RAF Transport Command used 40 Avro Yorks, 40 Dakotas and fourteen Handley Page Hastings transports, the latter aircraft making their operational debut. Ten Sunderlands of Coastal Command also joined the airlift from July to December 1948, alighting on Lake Havel in West Berlin. Aircraft and crews averaged two or more sorties a day, and many RAF crews exceeded 300 sorties to Berlin. Nevertheless, the British effort was considerably overshadowed by the American contribution, which amounted to some 200 C-54 Skymasters, and it was clear that—with the exception of the handful of Hastings aircraft—Transport Command's equipment was inadequate for the task in hand. The Hastings—an aircraft which, although not exactly designed for comfort, had a superb safety record—went on to become Transport Command's backbone in the 1950s, equipping fourteen squadrons. A similar number of units used the Vickers Valetta, developed from the civil Viking airliner, and this became a real workhorse on medium-haul routes.

In March 1956 the tactical transport squadrons of Transport Command began re-equipping with the Blackburn Beverley, which could carry 94 fully-equipped troops or a 29,000-pound payload. The Beverley served with Nos 30, 34, 47, 53 and 84 Squadrons until No. 46 Group's tactical force began re-equipping with the Lockheed Hercules in 1968.

In June 1956, No. 216 Squadron, RAF Transport Command, became the world's first jet transport squadron, equipping with eight Comet C.2s at RAF Lyneham. The RAF also acquired five Comet 4Cs at a later date. The Comets were used on high-speed, long-range mixed passenger and freight services. Another new type to join Transport Command in the 1950s was the Bristol Britannia C.1, which flew for the first time on 29 December 1958 and entered service with No. 99 Squadron in 1959, followed by No. 511 Squadron. Twenty-three Britannias were delivered, including three C.2s the latter differing from the C.1 in having only the forward section of its fuselage floor strengthened for heavy loads, being intended mainly for trooping.

In the early 1960s a V/STOL tactical jet transport, the Hawker Siddeley 681, was being developed for Transport Command, but this fell victim to the 1965 cancellations and the American Hercules was ordered instead. Other tactical squadrons were equipped, from 1966, with the Hawker Siddeley Andover CC.1, while in that year the Command received a heavy-lift capability with the introduction of ten Short Belfast transports into No. 53 Squadron. Also in 1966, No. 10 Squadron reformed at Brize Norton to operate VC.10s—the most aesthetically-appealing aircraft ever to serve with the Command—and began scheduled services to the Far East and the Persian Gulf with them in the spring of 1967. Completing Transport Command's line-up in the 1960s was the twin-boom Armstrong Whitworth Argosy, which equipped six squadrons starting in 1961.

For Transport Command, the most significant event in its postwar career was the re-formation, on 1 January 1960, of No. 38 Group as a specialised tactical group within the Command. With helicopters and tactical transport aircraft, and strike aircraft to provide fire support, it was No. 38 Group's responsibility to airlift and sustain British forces in emergency situations, a task which it has been developing and refining ever since. From the beginning, the squadrons of No. 38 Group were earmarked for assignment to NATO in time of war in accordance with British Government policy of giving increased support to the Alliance.

The sharp end of the RAF's contribution to NATO in the postwar era was the 2nd Tactical Air Force, later re-designated RAF Germany. The Vampire formed 2nd TAF's early jet equipment, but from 1952 the fighter-bomber squadrons standardised on the de Havilland Venom and air exercises were designed to practice mobility, with rapid deployment to other airfields in the NATO continental area. During big exercises, a complete Venom wing could be dispersed, sometimes operating from incomplete airfields, and from time to time 2nd TAF squadrons were detached to the Middle East for live bombing and rocket practice. The 2nd TAF squadrons regularly rotated to the UK to take part in air defence exercises. In addition to its fighter-bomber role the Venom was also used as a high-altitude interceptor, and proved quite capable of out-turning both the Sabre and the Hunter above 35,000 feet.

From 1953, ten fighter squadrons of 2nd TAF re-equipped with Sabres, but by 1956 these had received the Hunter F.4. The primary task of the 2nd TAF Hunter squadrons was border interception, and each Wing maintained a Duty Battle Flight at all times; this consisted of one squadron with a pair of Hunters on QRA and the rest at 15 minutes' readiness. High-level interception training was a regular feature, with either Hunter v Hunter or Hunter v Venom.

In 1957 the 2nd TAF Hunter squadrons began to receive the F.6, but several were disbanded soon afterwards. By the early 1960s the teeth of 2nd TAF remained the Hunter and the Canberra, and it was not until 1965 that Nos 19 and 92 Squadrons were deployed to Gutersloh, east of the Rhine, with Lightning F.2A fighters to police the northern half of the 30-mile-wide Air Defence Identification Zone along the border with East Germany. The RAF in Germany now formed one of four national 'wings' of NATO's Second Allied Tactical Air Force (Two ATAF), its area of responsibility covering 60,000 square miles. Operations within that area were largely dictated by the Royal Air Force, but, in the mid-1960s, the RAF's influence, although essential, was of a strictly limited variety. In 1967, for example, Two ATAF's only nuclear-strike and long-range attack capability was provided by the Command's Canberra force—and there were many who wondered whether, if the Canberras had been compelled to go to war, they would have suffered the same kind of attrition as the Fairey Battles in France 27 years earlier. Fortunately, it was never put to the test; and, after 1968, matters were to change appreciably for the better.

18

RAF Action Overseas
1948~71

The tenuous peace that followed the end of World War Two was only three years old when, in 1948, the Royal Air Force was compelled to take action in support of the Malay Government against a large-scale offensive by Communist Terrorists. At that time there were five RAF strike and reconnaissance squadrons in the area; Nos 28 and 60 with Spitfire FR.18s, No.81 with Mosquito PR.34s and Spitfire PR.19s, and Nos 205 and 209 with Sunderlands. There was also an Air Observation Post squadron, No. 656, with Austers. All these units were based on the Singapore airfields of Tengah, Changi and Seletar. There were two more airfields in the Malay Peninsula: Butterworth, which was used as an armament practice camp, and Kuala Lumpur. The latter was to become the principal base for the anti-terrorist operations, which received the code-name 'Firedog'.

In July 1948 the Spitfires of Nos 28 and 60 Squadrons moved up to Kuala Lumpur together with the Beaufighters of No. 45 Squadron, which arrived from Ceylon. In addition to their main equipment, all three squadrons also used Harvards to carry out the programme of air strikes, which began immediately. The Singapore-based Sunderlands were also active, cruising over terrorist areas of jungle for lengthy periods and dropping fragmentation bombs when targets were sighted.

In May 1949, No. 28 Squadron moved to Hong Kong, but in August the air strike force was strengthened with the arrival of No. 33 Squadron, equipped with Hawker Tempest F.2s. The Squadron set up its HQ at Changi, the Tempests being deployed to forward bases in Malaya on a rotational basis. In October, No. 45 Squadron began re-equipping with Bristol Brigand B.1 light bombers, more of which arrived in April 1950 with No. 84 Squadron from Habbaniyah. By this time Firedog operations were getting into their stride, the Far East Air Force (formed on 1 June 1949 from Air Command, Far East) was beginning to receive considerable assistance from other formations outside its normal sphere. From time

to time, Fleet Air Arm fighter-bombers en route for Korea joined in the air strikes, and early in 1950 six Lancaster GR.3s of Coastal Command were deployed from the United Kingdom to carry out bombing operations. They were followed, on 15 March, by the Lincolns of No. 57 Squadron from Waddington, which lent massive weight to the offensive; five Lincolns, flying in close formation, could lay 70 1,000-pound bombs on a very small area of jungle.

No. 57 Squadron stayed in Malaya until May 1950, when it was relieved by the Lincolns of No. 100 Squadron, and from then on Bomber Command detachments were a regular feature of Firedog. Jet bombers entered the scene in February 1955, when a flight of No. 101 Squadron's Canberra B.6s deployed to Tengah. For the bomber crews, operations over Malaya were not particularly exciting; they rarely saw their targets, their bombs being aimed generally at smoke markers dropped by the Austers of No. 656 Squadron—which at this time was one of the biggest squadrons in the RAF, with over 30 aircraft on charge. Target intelligence was the responsibility of No. 81 Squadron, which operated eight Mosquitos

The Royal Air Force did not send combat squadrons to serve in Korea between 1950 and 1953, Britain's air commitment being met by carrier strike aircraft of the Royal Navy. However, Sunderlands of Nos 88 and 209 Squadrons were detached to Iwakuni, Japan, on a regular basis to carry out reconnaissance patrols off the Korean Coast.

and five Spitfires and continued to use them even after it started on receive Meteor PR.10s in November 1953. The last operational Spitfire was withdrawn from the Squadron in April 1954, and the last operational Mosquito flight—which was also the Squadron's 6,619th Firedog sortie—was made by RG314 on 15 December 1955.

Strike sorties by jet aircraft against the CTs began on 26 April 1951, following the arrival of six Vampire FB.5s on 2 December 1960. These came by air, completing a journey of 8,850 miles; at that time, this was the longest delivery flight made by any jet aircraft. A total of 44 Vampire FB.5s were eventually sent out to FEAF, some going to No. 28 Squadron in Hong Kong and the remainder to No. 60 Squadron, which now had the dual task of carrying out anti-CT operations and providing air defence for Singapore; the Korean War was in progress, and there was always the possibility that this might escalate. In May 1952, the 41 surviving FB.5s were returned to the UK and replaced by tropicalised Vampire FB.9s.

The other RAF strike squadron in Malaya, No. 33, continued to use its Tempest F.2s until March 1951, when it began to re-equip with the de Havilland Hornet F.3 and F.4. The Hornet, a graceful and powerful development of the Mosquito, had earlier equipped Nos 19, 41, 64 and 65 Squadrons of Fighter Command before being replaced by the Meteor; in December 1951 they also re-equipped No. 80 Squadron in Hong Kong,

RAF fighter pilots were attached to No. 77 Squadron, RAAF, which flew Mustangs and Meteors in Korea. The photograph above shows RAF and RAAF pilots at Kimpo, No. 77 Squadron's base. No. 77 Squadron's Meteors, at first used in the fighter escort role, were outclassed by the MiG–15 but proved highly successful in the ground attack role. In the above right photograph the Squadron's Meteor F.8s are seen here in blast shelters at Kimpo.

and in March 1952 they replaced the Brigands of No. 45 Squadron.

The Hornet quickly earned itself the reputation of being Operation Firedog's most formidable strike aircraft. Its great combat radius meant that it could be used in conjunction with strikes made by Lincolns and Canberras, and it was a much more stable firing platform than either the Tempest or the Brigand. The last Brigand squadron, No. 84, disbanded on 20 February 1953, to reform in the transport role; during its Firedog operations, it had carried out over 2,000 sorties, dropping 1,883 tons of bombs on CT targets.

The Hornet remained the mainstay of anti-CT operations until April 1955, when a

Dakotas of the RAAF operated a regular freight and passenger service between Korea and Japan; RAF Transport Command Hastings and Valetta aircraft were also used on routes between Japan and various points in the Far East.

shortage of spares brought about the disbandment of No. 33 Squadron; it reformed six months later as a night-fighter squadron in Fighter Command. In May 1955, No. 45 Squadron re-equipped with Vampire FB.9s, and its Hornets—the RAF's last operational piston-engined fighters—were withdrawn. Later in 1955, Nos 45 and 60 Squadrons both re-equipped with Venom FB.1s. By this time, anti-CT operations were also being undertaken by the Lincolns of No.1(B) Squadron, RAAF, and the Venom FB.1s of No. 14 Squadron RNZAF; of the maritime squadrons, No. 88 had disbanded and No. 209 had merged with No. 205, which continued to use Sunderlands until it received Shackleton MR.1As at Changi in May 1958. The last two faithful Sunderlands were finally retired a year later.

The Communist offensive in Malaya, after ten years, was now showing signs of failing, permitting a reduction in the air units involved. In March 1957, No. 60 Squadron received the Venom FB.4 and went on with its Firedog commitment, but No. 45 Squadron disbanded to be reformed at Coningsby with Canberra B.2s the following November. It returned to Singapore immediately afterwards and became FEAF's first and only jet bomber squadron. In 1959, No. 60 Squadron relinquished its strike role and re-equipped

with Meteor NF.14 all-weather fighters, which continued in service until they were replaced by Javelin FAW.9s in 1961.

By the time Operation Firedog ended in October 1960, much of the offensive and defensive roles in Malaya had been assumed by the Australians and New Zealanders, with air strikes against the dwindling CT presence carried out by Canberras of No. 2 RAAF and No. 75 RNZAF Squadrons and the Sabres of Nos 3 and 77 Squadrons RAAF operating out of Butterworth. During the twelve-year war of attrition, ground forces had relied almost entirely on air support, with larger loads parachuted into jungle clearings from Valettas and Dakotas in all kinds of weather; light transport such as the Prestwick Pioneer had also rendered invaluable service in spotting, re-supplying outposts and patrols and carrying out casualty evacuation, and from 1953 helicopter operations had been undertaken by No. 194 Squadron, with Sikorsky Dragonflies. The squadron later re-equipped with Bristol Sycamores. The second helicopter squadron in Malaya was No. 155, which operated S-55 Whirlwinds from 1954; it was

Aircraft of No. 1913 Flight, RAF, were used for artillery spotting in Korea but were flown by Army pilots and observers. Here, an Auster AOP.6 and L–19 of No. 1913 Flight, RAF fly over the rugged Korean terrain.

Hunter FGA.9s of No. 20 Squadron carried out many armed patrols and rocket attacks on terrorist infiltrators during the period of the Confrontation. Two Hunters are pictured here on patrol off the Malaysian coast.

No. 66 Squadron used the twin-rotor Westland Belvedere helicopter in Malaysia and Borneo. The photograph shows troops embarking from a forest clearing. The Belvedere was used from 1962 to 1969, but was not a particularly successful design and suffered a number of technical problems.

subsequently amalgamated with No. 194 to form No. 110 Squadron, with both types of helicopter.

Finally, there was the role of the RAF Regiment. Six Field Squadrons, Nos 91–96, took part in the Malayan Emergency, and were credited with nineteen terrorists killed, 57 wounded and 300 captured, as well as with the destruction of 300 CT camps and supply dumps. Members of the RAF Regiment in Malaya won thirteen medals and 64 Mentions in Despatches.

Units of the RAF Regiment were active in Borneo, too, during the so-called 'Confrontation' with Indonesia that accompanied the creation of Malaysia out of the eleven former Malay States. In December 1962, there was an armed uprising in Sarawak when a group of Communist-inspired rebels seized the oil refinery at Brunei, and Malaysia requested the help of the British Government in restoring order. At this time, FEAF's air strength comprised No. 48 Squadron (Hastings) and No. 205 (Shackleton) at Changi; No. 224 Group, controlling FEAF's tactical transport component, including short-range fixed-wing and support helicopter squadrons, at Seletar; No. 60 Squadron (Javelins), No. 20 Squadron (Hunter FGA.9s), No. 45 Squadron (Canberra B.15s), No. 14 Squadron RNZAF (Canberra B[I]12s) and Canberra PR.7 reconnaissance aircraft of the RAF, all at Tengah. In addition, there were the Sabres and Canberras of the RAAF at Butterworth, and various naval air squadrons operating in the area.

One of the tactical transport units at Seletar was No. 34 Squadron, and its Beverleys were given the task of landing troops on an airstrip near Seria, a town near the oil refinery, as a first step to recapturing Brunei. Another Seletar-based squadron, No. 209, was to use its Twin Pioneers to land more troops on the other side. This operation was completely successful, as was the subsequent recapture of the objective. However, Indonesian hostility towards Malaysia remained, and in September 1963 Indonesian guerrillas began infiltrating Malaysian territory. A cease-fire agreement was negotiated in February 1964 but was never fully implemented on the Indonesian side, and at the request of the Malaysian Government RAF fighter units were placed on a high alert footing. The Javelins of No. 60 Squadron, reinforced by those of No. 64 Squadron in April 1965, maintained regular night and all-weather patrols over the Indonesian coastline after the Indonesians stated an intention to supply their guerrillas by air; Malaysian territory was declared an air identification zone and all unauthorized aircraft were threatened with interception. The main concern was that the Indonesians might use their Russian-built Tu-16 Badger jet bombers to attack Malaysian targets, but this never happened.

The Indonesians were left in no doubt that the British would do everything in their power to defend Malaysia's integrity. Detachments of V-Bombers, armed with conventional weapons, were deployed to Singapore, and a Royal Navy carrier task force was also deployed in the area. The Hunters of No. 20 Squadron, detached to Labuan and Kuching, carried out surveillance and CAP patrols, and from their main base at Tengah made rocket attacks on groups of suspected hostile troops in the swamps of Johore, on the southern end of the Malay Peninsula. With this pattern of operations British and Allied control of the area was firmly re-established, and the Confrontation came to an end in 1966.

The defence of protected territories in the Middle East area also required a major Royal Air Force commitment in the two decades after World War Two. To begin with, the British withdrawal from Palestine in May 1948, following the creation of the State of Israel, was not without its traumas; Egyptian aircraft strafed the airfield at Ramat David, where the Spitfire FR.18s of Nos 32 and 208 Squadrons were still based and caused some casualties to personnel and equipment, and in January 1949 four RAF Spitfires and a Tempest were shot down by the Israelis while carrying out a reconnaissance over northern Sinai.

Four years later, the RAF became involved in air actions against the Mau Mau terrorists in Kenya, who had embarked on a campaign of murder and intimidation against European settlers and their own fellow-countrymen. Anti-terrorist ground forces were soon mobilized, but apart from a few light aircraft of the Kenya Police Air Wing they were totally lacking in air support. In March 1953, therefore, No. 1340 Flight was formed at the Rhodesian Air Training Group, Thornhill, with four Harvards under Squadron Leader A. Trant; each Harvard was fitted with a Browning machine gun in the starboard wing and racks for eight 20-

pound anti-personnel bombs. In ten weeks of operations, No. 1340 Flight flew 183 offensive sorties, attacking 85 targets and expending 1,100 bombs and 69,000 rounds of ammunition. Later in 1953, Lincoln squadrons of Bomber Command also operated against the Mau Mau hideouts, and No.8 Squadron flew to Eastleigh, Nairobi, from Aden with its ground-attack Vampire FB.9s. Dakotas equipped with loudspeaker equipment made frequent sorties over the Mau Mau areas, exhorting the terrorists to give themselves up. The operational phase of the Kenya emergency ended in December 1956, by which time the Mau Mau had lost 10,572 killed and 2,633 captured.

Meanwhile, at the beginning of November 1956, as a consequence of the Arab-Israeli War that threatened the Suez Canal, Anglo-French forces had launched Operation Musketeer, a major combined operation designed to seize key points in the Canal Zone by means of air and sea landings. These were supported by British and French land-based and carrier-borne aircraft, the former operating from Malta and Cyprus, and the build-up of all forces had continued since August. By the third week of October, there were seventeen RAF bomber squadrons on Malta and Cyprus, equipped with either Canberras or Valiants; the RAF fighter elements included the Venom FB.4s of Nos 6, 32 and 73 Squadrons, all based on Akrotiri, the Meteor NF.13s of No. 39 Squadron, which moved from Luqa to Akrotiri early in October, and the Hunter F.5s of Nos 1 and 34 Squadrons, based on Nicosia. For long-range photo-reconnaissance there were the Akrotiri-based Canberra PR.7s of No. 13 Squadron, while the Shackletons of No. 37 Squadron carried out maritime reconnaissance from Luqa. RAF air transport units at Tymbou comprised the Valettas of Nos 30, 84 and 114 Squadrons and the Hastings of Nos 70 and 99 Squadrons; later, the Hastings of No. 511 and the Comet 2s of No. 216 Squadrons also operated out of this base.

Shortly before midnight on 31 October, Almaza airfield—one of the Egyptian Air Force's principal MiG-15 jet fighter bases—was target-marked by a pathfinder Canberra, dropping clusters of red TIs, and then bombed by Canberras of No. 10 Squadron. That night, three more airfields in the Nile Delta and eight in the Canal Zone were bombed by the Canberras of Nos 10 and 12 Squadrons and the Valiants of No. 148 Squadron. Two Egyptian Meteor NF.13 night fighters were sighted, one of which fired an inaccurate burst at a Valiant.

From daybreak on 1 November, the airfield attacks were continued by naval aircraft, and widespread raids by RAF Canberras and Valiants continued during the night. Once again the Egyptian airfields were the main targets, but Canberras of No. 27 Squadron made a precision attack on Radio Cairo's transmitters and knocked them out. The air offensive followed much the same pattern for 72 hours. Towards the end, the night bomber missions were carried out at medium level, which allowed greater bombing precision. Post-strike reconnaissance was carried out by the Canberra PR.7s of No. 13 Squadron, one of which was damaged by a MiG-15 on 1 November; another Canberra was shot down by a MiG-15 over Syria on a mission to photograph the build-up of MiGs and Il-28s on Syrian airfields.

By nightfall on 2 November, the Egyptian Air Force had virtually ceased to exist as a fighting force, most of its modern combat equipment having been destroyed or evacuated to neighbouring countries, and the Allied fighter-bombers were now released for attacks on other targets. On 3 November, they struck at every known military target, and by the end of the day enemy communications had been brought almost to a complete standstill. The only RAF loss was one Venom which hit the ground on a strafing run, killing its pilot. Air strikes continued on 4 November; the last two offensive operations were carried out by the Canberras and Valiants, one against coastal guns and radar installations near Alexandria and the other against Huckstep Barracks. Under cover of darkness, a lone Hastings dropped half a million leaflets on Cairo, urging the Egyptian Government to accept Allied ceasefire proposals.

On 5 November, the air-drop went in, the British paratroops being dropped on Gamil airfield by Hastings and Valetta aircraft. Nine aircraft were damaged by anti-aircraft fire, though none was lost. Fighter-bombers continued their support of the paratroops as the latter consolidated, and attacked targets ahead of the seaborne force that landed the next day. Part of the spearhead force of Royal Marines was flown ashore by Whirlwind and Sycamore helicopters of the Joint Experimental Helicopter Unit (JEHU), a combined Army and RAF venture. At midnight on 6 November, under intense political pressure in the United Nations and threats of military intervention by the Soviet Union, Great Britain and France agreed to a ceasefire.

There is no scope here to discuss the political implications of the Suez venture, or the loss of credibility that Britain and France suffered as a result of their ignominious withdrawal a few weeks later. Broadly, the concensus of world opinion was that Britain's day as a leading military power was over, and that she would never again be able to mount a major offensive operation.

Suez, 1956. The photographs show Valiant crews briefing and de-briefing on Malta before carrying out night attacks on targets in Egypt. The Suez operations revealed some problems with the Valiant's bomb release; bombs would 'float' in the airflow beneath the bomb-bay and accuracy was consequently impaired. A specially-fitted baffle cured the complaint.

Helicopters of the Joint Experimental Helicopter Unit carry Royal Marines into action at Port Said on 5 November 1956.

As events were to prove 26 years later, however, the concensus was wrong.

Elsewhere, returning to the immediate postwar years, the RAF in the Middle East was preoccupied with covering the withdrawal of British forces from various territories as well as with undertaking police actions where required. Palestine, mentioned earlier, was one example; another was Somaliland, which was handed back to Italy in 1950 as the result of a UN resolution. The withdrawal of British troops from this area was covered principally by the Tempests of No. 213 Squadron, detached to Mogadishu from No. 324 Wing at Khartoum.

Other squadron detachments involved in this operation came from No. 8 Squadron, Aden, and No. 84, Habbaniyah, both with Brigands. No. 8 was Aden's 'resident' squadron, and as such was responsible for internal security and tribal duties within the Aden Protectorates; it was a hard-worked unit, being called upon to send detachments of aircraft to reinforce other RAF units in East Africa and Iraq on frequent occasions.

In Iraq, the sole operational squadron at the end of the war was No. 249, which re-equipped with Tempest F.6 aircraft at Habbaniyah in 1947. No. 249 moved to Deversoir in Egypt in 1949 to join the Tempest Wing already there, and its place at Habbaniyah was taken by No. 84 Squadron. Reinforcement exercises were frequently practised, the Vampires of Nos 6 and 32 Squadrons flying up to Habbaniyah from the Canal Zone; these shows of strength were important, for the political situation in Iraq was highly unstable, and their importance increased

when No. 84 Squadron moved to Tengah in April 1950 to support the Malayan operations, leaving Habbaniyah completely dependent on rapid reinforcement from elsewhere. The speed with which such reinforcement could be carried out was demonstrated in 1951, when the Vampires and Brigands of Nos 6 and 8 Squadrons flew into Shaibah to cover a possible occupation of the Abadan oilfield, where European lives were at risk following political riots in Persia. A peaceful solution was found and the operation never took place, but the Persian Government lodged a strong protest with Iraq for allowing British aircraft to use her airfields for offensive operations, and from then on Iraqi resentment at the presence of RAF units on their territory continued to grow.

However, the RAF commitment in Iraq increased following the closure of the British bases in Egypt. In 1952, the resident squadrons at Habbaniyah were No. 683, with Vampire FB.9s, and No. 82 with four Lancaster PR.1s; the latter was a long-range photographic reconnaissance unit. RAF units in Jordan also came under the control of AHQ Iraq. Later in 1952, Habbaniyah was reinforced by the Vampires of No. 185 Squadron from Malta, and the two squadrons together formed No. 128 Wing. No. 185 Squadron disbanded in May 1953 and its place was taken by No. 73 Squadron, also from Malta. In February 1954, No. 6 Squadron began to receive the Venom FB.1, and No. 73 Squadron also re-equipped with these aircraft later in the year.

By the spring of 1955, talks were under way between the British and Iraqi Governments, their aim being to draw up a programme for the withdrawal of British forces from the Iraqi bases. The Royal Iraq Air Force was to move into the bases vacated by

the RAF, and was to be given all possible training and technical assistance. The handover ceremony at Habbaniyah took place on 2 May 1955; No. 73 Squadron was at armament practice camp in Cyprus at the time and it was decided to leave it there. No. 6 remained at Habbaniyah for the time being, and No. 32 Squadron flew up to Shaibah from the Canal Zone with its Venom FB.1s.

The original idea had been that the Iraqi bases would still be used by the RAF for reinforcement purposes as required by the Baghdad Pact, but Iraq withdrew from the Pact in 1959 and as a result all RAF personnel were pulled out of Habbaniyah on 31 May and from other Iraq bases in June. Relations with Iraq continued to deteriorate and reached an all-time low in 1961.

In Aden, No. 8 Squadron continued to use its Brigands until 1952, when they were replaced by Vampire FB.9s, and in the summer of 1955 the Squadron received its first Venom FB.1s, re-equipping with FB.4s at the end of the year. These aircraft, together with a flight of Meteor FR.9s, were heavily committed to operations against dissident tribesmen in the Trucial Oman area and the Western Aden Protectorate. From 1959, No. 8 Squadron began re-equipping with the Hunter FGA.9, and two years later, in the summer of 1961, the Squadron became involved in a major international crisis when Iraq laid claim to the oil-rich territory of the state of Kuwait and moved troops and armour up to the Kuwaiti border. Plans existed to reinforce the area if the Kuwait Government so requested; these involved the deployment of five British battalions in Kuwait, together with supporting armour. The deployment involved the large-scale diversion of Transport Command aircraft from other duties in the Middle East, and

assistance in this respect was also rendered by the newly-formed No. 38 (Tactical) Group. To provide air strike facilities, Canberra B(I)8s and B(I)6s of Nos 88 and 213 Squadrons were deployed to Sharjah from 2nd TAF in Germany; for air defence and close support, the Hunters of Nos 8 and 208 Squadrons were deployed to Bahrain. For No. 208 Squadron, this involved a flight of 2,300 miles from Nairobi, with a single stop at Khormaksar. Two squadrons of Beverleys also arrived at Bahrain, together with a detachment of Shackletons of No. 37 Squadron; the latter stood ready to drop flares over the frontier in the event of an Iraqi night attack.

As it was, the show of strength deterred Iraq from taking offensive action, and by 20 July 1961 the Kuwait crisis had been sufficiently defused to permit the withdrawal of the bulk of British forces from the area. For some time, however, the two Hunter squadrons operated on a rotation basis between Khormaksar and Bahrain in case of further outbreaks of trouble.

At the beginning of 1962 the two Hunter squadrons formed the offensive nucleus of the Khormaksar Strike Wing. During the year they were involved in carrying out air attacks on dissident villages; in October, following an Egyptian-backed coup in the Yemen and incursions by unidentified aircraft into the Western Aden Protectorate, they also flew CAP over the border area.

In 1963 there was a major rebellion in the Radfan, 35 miles north of Aden, where dissident tribesmen, supported by the Yemen, defied the Federal Government. A State of Emergency was declared, and early in 1964 security forces, backed up by the Khormaksar Strike Wing, carried out a large-scale operation known as 'Nutcracker' against the dissidents. The two original Hunter squadrons were now joined by a third, No. 43 from Cyprus; there was also a photographic reconnaissance flight with Hunter FR.10s, which produced hundreds of target photographs of the poorly-mapped Radfan area. In the months that followed the strike Hunters carried out many attacks with cannon and RPs on rebel strongpoints, the attacks being directed by Forward Air Control. On one occasion, on 1 May 1964, they were instrumental in extricating 40 troopers of 22 SAS Regiment who were pinned down by sniper fire deep inside enemy territory. In eighteen sorties, the Hunters fired 127 rockets and 7,000 rounds of ammunition against rebel targets, and the SAS men slipped away after dark. On the following day the Hunters provided effective close support for 45 Royal Marine Commando, strafing rebels so close to friendly troops that some of the latter were hit by spent shell cases as the Hunters flew low overhead. The major offensive phase of the operation was an assault on the rebel stronghold of Jebel Huriyah; this was preceded by heavy rocket and cannon attacks, and the casualties inflicted on the rebels by the Hunters were so severe that they were unable to defend the peak of the Jebel, which was occupied on 11 June.

Offensive action in the Radfan ended on 18 November 1964 with the capitulation of the rebels. During the height of the campaign, from 30 April to 30 June, the Hunter FGA.9s of the three squadrons involved had flown 527 sorties, launched 2,508 RPs and fired 176,092 cannon shells, while the Hunter FR.10s had flown 115 sorties and fired 7,808 cannon shells.

After their defeat in the Radfan, Yemeni and Egyptian subversive activities switched to the urban areas of Aden, and terrorism increased sharply after the British Government announced that South Arabia would be granted independence not later than 1968. By mid-1967, the Federal Government was fast losing control of the situation, and in August plans were implemented to withdraw the operational RAF presence from Aden to Muharraq. Nos 8 and 208 Squadrons accordingly left for this base, leaving No. 43 Squadron at Aden to cover the British withdrawal. Intensive flying continued in support of the South Arabian Army, the Hunters flying over 300 sorties in September and October 1967 before their task was taken over by Fleet Air Arm strike aircraft. The last Hunter ground-attack sorties by No. 43 Squadron were flown on 7 November 1967, more than three weeks after the Squadron had officially disbanded; it later reformed as a Phantom FG.1 unit in Strike Command on 1 September 1969. At the same time, the Hunter FR.10s of No. 1417 Flight went to Muharraq to join Nos 8 and 208 Squadrons. Their departure marked the end of 48 years of RAF presence in Aden.

At Muharraq, the Hunter squadrons combined to form an Offensive Support Wing, which remained in existence until 1971, when No. 208 Squadron disbanded, to be reformed later as a strike/attack unit with Buccaneer S.2As at Honington. No. 8 Squadron disbanded on 15 December 1971, to be reformed on New Year's Day as an airborne early warning unit at Kinloss with Shackleton AEW.2s. On the day of its disbandment, the Royal Air Force Ensign was lowered at Muharraq for the last time. Earlier in the year, a regular British presence on Singapore had also ceased with the disbandment of the Far East Air Force.

Step by step, after more than half a century, the Royal Air Force was coming home.

19

The RAF
1968~84

On 1 August 1967, RAF Transport Command was renamed Air Support Command and given greatly increased responsibility for the long-range strategic, and tactical, air support roles. It was the first step in an organisational restructuring programme designed to produce a more streamlined and effective Service in the light of Britain's reducing overseas commitments.

The next step came at 0001 hours on Tuesday, 30 April 1968, when Bomber and Fighter Commands stood down and were merged into the new RAF Strike Command. On 1 June 1968, Training Command was formed by the merger of Flying Training and Technical Training Commands, and on 1 January and 28 November 1969 Signals and Coastal Commands were absorbed into Strike Command to become No. 90 (Signals) Group and No. 18 (Maritime) Group. On 1 May 1972, No. 90 Group moved once again to become part of Maintenance Command, and on 1 September that year Air Support Command amalgamated with Strike to form a single multi-role operational command.

On its formation in 1968, Strike Command, with its HQ at High Wycombe, Buckinghamshire, had two Groups under its control—No.1 (Bomber) Group, which controlled the V-Bomber Force and the refuelling force of Victor tankers, and No. 11 (Fighter) Group which controlled the air defence squadrons of Lightning interceptors and Bloodhound SAMs and their associated ground environment of radars and communications, together with the Ballistic Missile Early Warning Station at Fylingdales, Yorkshire. The Command was also responsible for a third formation with Group status: the Central Reconnaissance Establishment, which co-ordinated reconnaissance forces operating from the United Kingdom. Strike Command's front line at that time consisted of Vulcan and Victor B.2s, some armed with Blue Steel, and the Lightning all-weather fighter, the latter having a flight refuelling capability provided by Victor tankers.

To ensure the efficient operation of the Force in a limited war situation, squadrons were regularly detached to overseas theatres to carry out conventional training in the operating environment. Great emphasis was placed on the ability to provide the necessary reinforcements in the shortest possible time, and the rapid deployment of Vulcans and Lightnings from the UK, backed by Air Support Command aircraft, was frequently exercised. On 21 November 1968, for example, eight Vulcans, supported by eleven Britannias, VC-10s and Hercules, staged the biggest ever reinforcement exercise to the Far East by the Westabout Route, across America and the Pacific, while on 6 January 1969 the RAF mounted its biggest air-to-air refuelling exercise to that date when ten Lightning F.6 aircraft of No. 11 Squadron, refuelled by Victor tankers from RAF Marham, deployed to the Far East for a four-week visit. During the two-way journey of 18,500 miles, 166,000 gallons of fuel were transferred in 228 air refuelling contacts.

Apart from tasks of overseas reinforcement, there were regular overseas training

A Vulcan twists away from the gunsight of an RAAF Mirage during joint exercises over Malaysia.

missions enabling air and ground crews to operate in areas and environments very different from those of their home bases. These ranged over both hemispheres and occasionally took the form of 'showing the flag' flights or participation in air displays throughout the British Commonwealth, the American continent or in any NATO or CENTO countries. On 16 June, 1969, to give one example, four Lightnings of No. 74 Squadron flew non-stop from RAF Tengah, Singapore, to Darwin, supported by Victor K.2 aircraft from RAF Marham.

The year 1969 saw the introduction into service of several new operational aircraft types. The first was the Phantom FGR.2, which became fully operational with No. 6 Squadron at RAF Coningsby on 6 May; the interceptor version, the Phantom FG.1, went into service later in the year with No. 43 Squadron, which reformed at RAF Leuchars on 1 September. On 22 September, No. 6 Squadron went to Cyprus for three weeks' training, and in doing so made the first Middle East deployment of RAF Phantoms the squadron having already deployed to Bruggen on 13 June 1969. On 1 October, the Hawker Siddeley Harrier V/STOL strike fighter—which had already captured public interest on both sides of the Atlantic by making the first city centre to city centre jet flight in history during the Trans-Atlantic Air Race of 1969—entered service with No. 1 Squadron at RAF Wittering, and also on 1

The Bloodhound 2 surface-to-air missile. The RAF began to equip with the Mark 1 version in 1958, but this was not air transportable and was restricted to UK deployment in defence of V-bomber bases. The Mark 2 has been widely deployed overseas; in 1984, it equipped Nos 25 and 85 Squadrons, with detachments at home and in Germany.

By 1969, the Vulcan's role as the spearhead of the British nuclear deterrent had been handed over to the Royal Navy's Polaris submarines. The airborne deterrent had not consisted entirely of manned bombers; from 1959–64, it was supplemented by 60 Thor intermediate-range missiles, operated by twenty reactivated RAF squadrons with three missiles each. The photograph shows Vulcan B.2 XM646 of No. IX Squadron landing at Waddington; this aircraft was scrapped at St Athan early in 1982.

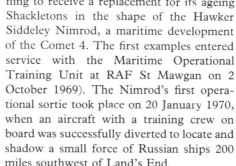

A Victor K.2 refuels a Phantom FGR.2. In December 1969, two Phantoms of No. 54 Squadron made a non-stop deployment to Singapore as a preliminary to Exercise *Bersatu Padu*, and long-range deployments with flight refuelling have been a regular feature of RAF Phantom operations ever since.

October No. 12 Squadron reformed at Honington with Buccaneer S.2 aircraft. The Buccaneer's service debut with the RAF was somewhat ironic; Blackburn Aircraft had offered it to the RAF in the early 1960s, but it had been rejected in favour of the TSR-2 and then the F-111. Neither of those aircraft had entered service, so the Buccaneer had been selected for the low-level strike role at long last. It was to prove a formidable addition to the RAF's offensive capability.

Coastal Command, too, was at last begin-ning to receive a replacement for its ageing Shackletons in the shape of the Hawker Siddeley Nimrod, a maritime development of the Comet 4. The first examples entered service with the Maritime Operational Training Unit at RAF St Mawgan on 2 October 1969). The Nimrod's first operational sortie took place on 20 January 1970, when an aircraft with a training crew on board was successfully diverted to locate and shadow a small force of Russian ships 200 miles southwest of Land's End.

A major Far East reinforcement exercise was planned for 1970, and as a preliminary to this two Phantoms of No. 54 Squadron, which had begun re-equipping with the type in September 1969, deployed non-stop to Singapore together with ten Lightning of No. 5 Squadron on 8 December 1969. The full deployment phase of the giant five-nation exercise in Western Malaysia, named Bersatu Padu, began on 12 April 1970 with the biggest exercise airlift ever carried out by Air Support Command. In ten days, VC-10, Britannia, Hercules and Belfast aircraft completed 4,538 flying hours, flew over 1,365,000 nautical miles and carried 2,265 passengers, 1,503,920 pounds of cargo, 350 vehicles and twenty helicopters. Later, on 19/20 May, Phantoms of No. 54 Squadron, during deployment to the Far East, established and then broke a new point-to-point record from the UK to Singapore. The best time, put up by two aircraft flying non-stop, was 14 hours 8 minutes 19 seconds.

The Hawker Siddeley Buccaneer S.2B gave the RAF a fast and effective low-level strike capability that helped to fill the gap created by the cancellation of earlier projects such as TSR-2.

The Anglo-French Jaguar entered RAF service in 1973 and subsequently re-equipped the tactical strike squadrons of RAF Germany as well as three squadrons of No. 38 Group.

Illustrating the importance of Strike Command's air defence role is this Soviet Tupolev Tu–95 Bear maritime reconnaissance aircraft, intercepted in the 'Faroes Gap' off north Shetland by Phantoms of No. 43 Squadron.

One of the most pressing concerns in the early 1970s was to re-equip the tactical strike squadrons of RAF Germany, which were still using Hunter FGA.9s and Canberra B(I)8s, with more modern aircraft, and as a first step No. 4 Squadron at Wildenrath began to receive Harriers on 1 June 1970. On 1 July, No. 14 Squadron became operational with the Phantom FGR.2 at RAF Bruggen, and in January 1971 No **XV** Squadron, which had reformed at Honington the previous October, moved to Laarbruch with Buccaneer S.2Bs From then on, the re-equipment of the RAF Germany squadrons proceeded at a steady rate, and as an additional defensive measure, Bloodhound SAMs were also deployed to key points in Germany, together with two squadrons of the RAF Regiment for airfield defence. Later in the 1970s, RAF Germany's tactical strike squadrons began to receive the Anglo-French Jaguar, which entered RAF service with the OCU at Lossiemouth in May 1973. The first squadron to re-equip with this type, on 29 March 1974, was No. 54, which was a ground attack and tactical reconnaissance unit in No. 38 Group; it was followed by Nos 6 and 41 Squadrons at Coltishall. The RAF Germany Phantom FGR.2 Squadrons re-equipped with the Jaguar from 1975.

By 1970, the RAF in the Near East was concentrated on two islands, Cyprus and Malta. The Headquarters of Near East Air Force was at Episkopi, while the main operational base of Akrotiri—the largest multi-role station in the RAF, and also the largest in physical size—operated offensive, defensive, transport and SAR forces. Early in 1969, two Vulcan squadrons, Nos 9 and 35, were deployed to Cyprus to form the NEAF Bomber Wing, with the task of supporting CENTO, and carried out numerous exercises during the next five years. The squadrons dispersed briefly in the summer of 1974, when Turkish forces invaded the northern part of Cyprus, then flew intensively on a variety of operational tasks, the Vulcans—among other

things—acting as airborne relay stations. The two squadrons left Cyprus in February 1975 and returned to the UK. The air defences in Cyprus at this time comprised the Lightning F.6s of No.56 Squadron, the Bloodhound Mk 2s of No. 112 Squadron, and the Bofors guns of Nos 27 and 34 Squadrons of the RAF Regiment. The resident squadrons on NEAF's other base, Luqa in Malta, were Nos 13 and 203, the former equipped with Canberra PR.9s and the latter

with Nimrods. Both remained there until 1977, when the British garrison withdrew from the island.

In 1978 the principal strike force of No.1 Group, Strike Command, was still six squadrons of Vulcan B.2s, totalling 85 aircraft. There were 24 Victor K.2 tankers with Nos 55

In 1984, the search and rescue detachments of No. 18 Group were mostly equipped with the Sea King HAR.3 helicopter. The photograph shows an aircraft of No. 202 Squadron.

The Puma was a valuable addition to the capability of No. 38 (Tactical) Group. Here, men of the RAF Regiment deploy from an aircraft of No. 230 Squadron.

Hunter FGA.9 of No. 54 Squadron seen during a No. 38 Group deployment on Exercise *Winter Express* in Norway.

and 57 Squadrons at RAF Marham, while long-range maritime radar reconnaissance was undertaken by Vulcan B.2(MRR) aircraft of No. 27 Squadron, Scampton. No. 39 Squadron, at Wyton, operated Canberra PR.9s in the high-altitude reconnaissance role, alongside the Nimrod R.1s of No. 51 Squadron, which for many years had been the RAF's electronic surveillance unit, and the Canberra T.17s of No. 360 Squadron, a joint services ECM training unit. Canberras were also used by Nos 7 and 100 Squadrons, providing target facilities training.

At Honington, the Buccaneer S.2As and S.2Bs of Nos 12 and 208 Squadrons, the former tasked with anti-shipping operations, were joined in 1980 by No. 216 Squadron, operating in a combat role for the first time since 1919; No. 216 was destined for the anti-shipping role at Lossiemouth, but was disbanded after only a short rebirth following the discovery of fatigue cracks in the wings of its Buccaneers, which were mostly ex-Royal Navy aircraft.

In No. 11 Group's air defence squadrons, the Phantom had gradually been taking over the interceptor role from the Lightning, and for this purpose, by mid-1978, it equipped Nos 23, 29, 43, 56 and 111 Squadrons and No. 228 OCU at Coningsby, Wattisham and Leuchars, while at Binbrook Nos 5 and 11 Squadrons still operated Lightnings in the air defence role. At RAF Leuchars, a major air defence base, anti-aircraft protection had received a boost in the shape of the Rapier surface to air missile, which had just become operational with No 27 Squadron of the RAF Regiment. The longer-range Bloodhound MK 2 SAM was deployed at Bawdsey, North Coates and West Raynham, under the

operational control of No. 85 Squadron. At Lossiemouth, airborne early warning was the responsibility of twelve Shackletons of No. 8 Squadron, which in 1984 was due to be replaced by the Nimrod AEW.3.

No. 18 (Maritime) Group of Strike Command, with responsibility for maritime reconnaissance and SAR over the North Sea, Atlantic and home waters, had four squadrons of Nimrod MR.1s—Nos 42, 120, 201 and 206—and these aircraft were later updated to MR.2 standard with the addition of more advanced navigation, search and sensory equipment. Helicopter search and rescue was the responsibility of Nos 22 and 202 Squadrons, with nine flights stationed around the coasts of the United Kingdom and operating in concert with similar flights of Royal Navy and USAF SAR helicopters. Equipment in 1978 was the Westland Wessex and Whirlwind, but the latter was later replaced by additional Wessex and by Sea King HAR Mk 3s.

The strike element of No. 38 Group,

Strike Command's tactical force, comprised the Harriers of No.1 Squadron at Wittering, together with No. 233 OCU, and the Coltishall-based Nos 6, 41 and 54 Squadrons, with Jaguar GR.1s. The Group's tactical helicopter force, based on Odiham, consisted of Nos 33 and 230 Squadrons, with Puma HC.1s, and No. 72 Squadron with Wessex HC.2s, all three providing transport helicopter detachments to Germany, Northern Ireland and elsewhere. Since 1977, the Group has maintained a Harrier and helicopter force in Belize, supported by units of the RAF Regiment, as an insurance against threatened invasion by Guatemala.

The disbanding of No. 46 Group in the 1970s resulted in all RAF transport elements coming under the operational control of No. 38 Group. These included the VC-10s of No. 10 Squadron and No. 241 OCU at Brize

A British Aerospace Hawk equipped with Sidewinder AAMs for airfield defence. Hawks fitted out in this way provide a valuable boost to UK air defences.

Tornado GR.1 of No IX Squadron, RAF Honington. The Tornado will be the RAF's principal strike aircraft into the 1990s. The aircraft in the photograph are carrying four 1,000 pound bombs, two fuel tanks and two ECM pods.

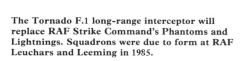

The Tornado F.1 long-range interceptor will replace RAF Strike Command's Phantoms and Lightnings. Squadrons were due to form at RAF Leuchars and Leeming in 1985.

Norton, the Hercules of Nos 24, 30, 47, 70 Squadrons and 242 OCU at Lyneham, Nos 32 and 207 communications Squadrons with Dominie, Andover and Devon aircraft and Gazelle helicopters, and the Queen's Flight. No. 1 Tactical Weapons Unit at Brawdy, also under the operational control of No. 38 Group and equipped initially with Hunters, re-equipped with Hawk T.1 aircraft from 1978; also equipped with Hawks was No. 2 TWU, which formed later and subsequently became established at RAF Chivenor. The Hawk has proved a highly versatile aircraft in RAF service, and some are equipped with AIM-9L Sidewinder, AAMs for short-range air defence.

In RAF Germany, by the end of the 1970s, Jaguars equipped Nos 2, 14, 17, 20 and 31 Squadrons, with Harriers equipping Nos 3 and 4 Squadrons, Buccaneers Nos XV and 16 Squadrons, and Phantom FGR.2s Nos 19 and 92 Squadrons. For air defence, RAF Regiment Rapier squadrons were deployed to the principal strike bases, together with the Bloodhounds of No. 25 Squadron. Apart from Germany, the RAF's permanent commitment overseas was reduced to Hong Kong, where the Wessex HC.2 helicopters of No. 28 Squadron operated from Kai Tak and

later from Sek Kong; RAF Hong Kong today comes under the operational control of Strike Command.

Another organisational change in the RAF's structure in recent years has been the amalgamation of flying training and maintenance units into a new formation, Support Command. This is responsible for the RAF College Cranwell, the Central Flying School, six flying training schools equipped with Jet Provosts, Hawks, Hunters, Dominies, Bulldogs, Jetstreams and a variety of helicopters; air experience flights; University Air Squadrons; air traffic control schools; gliding schools; technical training establishments; maintenance units and the school of firefighting. Also under Support Command's wing is the Battle of Britain Memorial Flight.

Such, broadly, is the picture of the Royal Air Force today. The Vulcans have gone, the surviving examples reduced to museum pieces or crash rescue training airframes, and the tanker force has been strengthened by the addition of No. 101 Squadron, with VC-10 tankers. One important development, however, remains to be mentioned.

Its name is Tornado, and it is the strike aircraft that will take the Royal Air Force through to the next century. Developed

jointly by the United Kingdom, Federal Germany and Italy, it is truly a NATO aircraft. Air and ground crews of all three countries are trained to operate it with the Tri-national Tornado Training Establishment at Cottesmore; it is in service with the Tornado Weapons Training Establishment at Honington, which is also the home base of No. 9 Squadron, the first to form on it. Other UK-based Tornado GR.1 units at the time of writing are Nos 27 and 617 Squadrons at Marham, while Nos XV and 16 Squadrons in Germany have also re-equipped with the type.

Tornado, described as the only aircraft in NATO capable of knocking out enemy armour from 50 feet at night and in sleet, is probably the best thing that has happened to the Royal Air Force since No. 19 Squadron received the first Spitfires in 1938. It has gone a long way towards offsetting the traumas of the 1960s, and would be a good point at which to close this history.

But there is one final chapter—one that illustrates only too well how the RAF, as a result of the drastic cuts of the 1960s, was forced to improvise in a time of crisis. In the summer of 1982, the Royal Air Force once again went to war.

Royal Air Force Order of Battle, July 1974

Sqn	Base	Aircraft	Group	Sqn	Base	Aircraft	Group
1	Wittering	Harrier GR.1, GR.1A, GR.3	38 Group	45	Wittering	Hunter FGA.9	38 Group
2	Laarbruch	Phantom FGR.2	RAFG	46	Thorney Island	Andover C.1	38 Group
3	Wildenrath	Harrier GR.1A, GR.3	RAFG	47	Lyneham	Hercules C.1	38 Group
4	Wildenrath	Harrier GR.1, GR.3	RAFG	48	Lyneham	Hercules C.1	38 Group
5	Binbrook	Lightning F.3, F.6	11 Group	51	Wyton	Canberra B.2	
6	Coningsby	Phantom FGR.2	38 Group			Comet C.2, R.2	
7	St Mawgan	Canberra TT.18, B.2	11 Group			Nimrod R.1	1 Group
8	Lossiemouth	Shackleton MR.2C, AEW.2	11 Group	53	Brize Norton	Belfast C.1	46 Group
9	Akrotiri	Vulcan B.2	NEAF	54	Lossiemouth	Jaguar GR.1	38 Group
10	Brize Norton	VC-10 C.1	46 Group	55	Marham	Victor K.IA, K.2	1 Group
11	Binbrook	Lightning F.3, F.6	11 Group	56	Akrotiri	Lightning F.6	NEAF
12	Honington	Buccaneer S.2, S.2B	1 Group	57	Marham	Victor K.1A, K.2	1 Group
13	Luqa	Canberra PR.9	NEAF	58	Wittering	Hunter FGA.9	38 Group
14	Bruggen	Phantom FGR.2	RAFG	60	Wildenrath	Pembroke C.1	RAFG
15	Laarbruch	Buccaneer S.2B	RAFG	70	Akrotiri	Hercules C.1	NEAF
16	Laarbruch	Buccaneer S.2	RAFG	72	Odiham	Wessex HC.2	38 Group
17	Bruggen	Phantom FGR.2	RAFG	84	Akrotiri	Whirlwind HAR.10	NEAF
18	Gutersloh	Wessex HC.2	38 Group		Nicosia		
19	Gutersloh	Lightning F.2, F.2A	RAFG	85	West Raynham	Canberra B.2, T.4, T.11, T.19	11 Group
20	Wildenrath	Harrier GR.1	RAFG	92	Gutersloh	Lightning F.2, F.2A	RAFG
21	Andover	Pembroke C.1	1 Group	98	Cottesmore	Canberra B.2, E.15	11 Group
22	St Mawgan	Whirlwind HAR. 10	18 Group	99	Brize Norton	Britannia C.1, C.2	46 Group
23	Leuchars	Lightning F.6	11 Group	100	West Raynham	Canberra B.2, E.15, T.19	11 Group
24	Lyneham	Hercules C.1	38 Group	101	Waddington	Vulcan B.2	1 Group
25	Wildenrath	Bloodhound 1, 2	RAFG	103	Tengah	Wessex HC.2	NEAF
26	Wyton	Basset CC.1	1 Group	111	Wattisham	Lightning F.3	11 Group
27	Waddington	Vulcan SR.2	1 Group	112	Episkopi	Bloodhound 2	NEAF
28	Kai Tak	Wessex HC.2	RAF	115	Cottesmore	Argosy E.1	1 Group
			Hong Kong	120	Kinloss	Nimrod MR.1	18 Group
29	Wattisham	Lightning F.3	11 Group	201	Kinloss	Nimrod MR.1	18 Group
30	Lyneham	Hercules C.1	38 Group	202	Leconfield	Whirlwind HAR.10	18 Group
31	Bruggen	Phantom FGR.2	RAFG	203	Luqa	Nimrod MR.1	NEAF
32	Northolt	Basset CC.1	1 Group	206	Kinloss	Nimrod MR.1	18 Group
		Andover CC.2		207	Northolt	Devon C.I, C.2	
		Whirlwind HCC.12, HC.10				Basset CC.1	
		HS.125 CC.1				Pembroke C.1	1 Group
33	Odiham	Puma HC.1	38 Group	208	Honington	Buccaneer S.2A	1 Group
35	Akrotiri	Vulcan B.2	NEAF	214	Marham	Victor K.1, K.1A	1 Group
36	Lyneham	Hercules C.1	38 Group	216	Lyneham	Comet C.4	46 Group
39	Wyton	Canberra PR.9	1 Group	230	Odiham	Puma HC.1	38 Group
41	Coningsby	Phantom FGR.2	38 Group	360	Cottesmore	Canberra T.4, T.17	1 Group
42	St Mawgan	Nimrod MR.1	18 Group	511	Brize Norton	Britannia C.1, C.2	46 Group
43	Leuchars	Phantom FG.1	11 Group	617	Scampton	Vulcan B.2	1 Group
44	Waddington	Vulcan B.2	1 Group				

20

Fortress Falklands ~ The Last Battle?

Early in April 1982, the British Government initiated Operation Corporate, a joint services undertaking to recapture the Falkland Islands from Argentina. The Royal Navy, with its carrier task force and Sea Harriers, was very much at the forefront of the operation; but only 28 Sea Harriers were available, and so No. 1 Squadron, No. 38 Group, was ordered to prepare for deployment to the South Atlantic with its Harrier GR.3s. Apart from some necessary modifications to the aircraft for carrier operations, this involved some hurried training in air combat techniques, for No. 1 Squadron was a ground attack unit and the Harriers had to be fitted with points for Sidewinder AIM-9L AAMs as well as IFF transponders. Nevertheless, work went ahead with surprisingly few snags, and preparations were made to ship a batch of Harriers to the South Atlantic aboard the container ship *Atlantic Conveyor*.

Right from the beginning of the operation, it was realised that the principal airfield on the Falklands, Port Stanley, would have to be neutralised in order to deny its use to Argentinian combat aircraft. This presented a major problem, for the nearest land base available to the RAF was Ascension Island, which was 4,000 nautical miles from the Falklands and consequently far outside the combat radius of any RAF aircraft—except one—which might reach Port Stanley with a worthwhile bomb load.

The exception was the Vulcan B.2. When the Falklands crisis developed, the Vulcan force was being run down at a rapid rate; what remained of it was concentrated at Waddington with Nos 44 and 50 Squadrons, two more units, Nos 9 and 101 Squadrons, being on the point of disbanding. No. 44 Squadron was tasked with offensive operations over the Falklands, the most experienced crews being selected from all four squadrons, and ten of the most airworthy Vulcans were picked from the aircraft pool. An air-to-air refuelling capability was restored on these, the necessary equipment being acquired from time-expired Vulcans at points throughout the UK and farther afield. Once the refuelling equipment had been installed,

the crews embarked on a three-week series of air refuelling exercises with the Victor K.2 tankers of the Marham Wing. The Vulcans were also modified to carry 21 1,000-pound bombs instead of their normal load of low-level retarded bombs, and a Carousel INS was fitted to help with long-range navigation. Later, the AN/ALQ-101D (Dash Ten) ECM pod was fitted to the Vulcans on the starboard underwing hard point that had originally existed for the carriage of the Skybolt missile. The port hardpoint was reserved for the carriage of the AS37 Martel anti-radar missile, but in the event the AGM-45A Shrike was used instead.

While these preparations were under way, aircraft of No. 38 Group were busily flying stores and equipment into Ascension Island's Wideawake Air Base. On 5 April, two Nimrod MR.1s of No. 42 Squadron arrived with their ground crews to begin long-range patrols in support of the Task Force, and on 12 April they were joined by detachments of Nos 120, 201 and 206 Squadrons, with better-equipped Nimrod MR.2s. On 18 April, six Victor K.2s of Nos 55 and 57 Squadrons also arrived on Ascension; one of these aircraft was fitted with cameras for the strategic reconnaissance role. Finally, at Odiham in Hampshire, seven Chinook helicopters of No. 18 Squadron were being fitted with radar warning receivers and other items of electronic equipment before joining the *Atlantic Conveyor* for the voyage south.

The first air reconnaissance of the disputed area was carried out on 20 April by a Victor captained by Squadron Leader John Elliott, supported by three tanker aircraft. The Victor made a radar search of 150,000 square miles of ocean in the South Georgia area before returning to Ascension after a flight lasting 14 hours 45 minutes. The aircraft had covered a distance of over 7,000 miles; it was the longest operational reconnaissance mission ever carried out, and was an essential preliminary to the successful re-occupation of South Georgia that took place five days later.

On the night of 30 April/1 May, Vulcan XM607, captained by Flight Lieutenant

Martin Withers and supported by eleven Victor Tankers, made the first 'Black Buck' sortie against the Falklands, dropping a stick of 21 1,000-pound bombs across the main runway at Port Stanley. There was no opposition, and one bomb impacted on the runway while the remainder caused considerable damage to adjacent aircraft and stores. The Vulcan recovered safely to Ascension after a flight of 15 hours 45 minutes. For his skill in completing this, the longest-range bombing operation in history, Flight Lieutenant Withers was awarded the DFC.

Soon after this mission, Port Stanley airfield was attack by nine Sea Harriers of Nos 800 and 801 Squadrons, Royal Navy. Attached to No. 801 was Flight Lieutenant David Morgan, RAF; his was the last Harrier to attack, and it was hit in the fin by a 20-mm shell. Despite this damage, Morgan recovered safely to the carrier HMS *Hermes*. Another RAF pilot with No. 800 Squadron was Flight Lieutenant Paul Barton, who on the morning of 1 May was flying CAP west of the task force with a second Sea Harrier flown by Lieutenant Commander John Eyton-Jones, RN. They made contact with six Argentine air force Mirages, but the latter were at high altitude and had no intention of coming down to engage the Harriers in a sea-level combat. After a few minutes, both sides headed for their respective bases, and it was left to the Harrier pilots of the Royal Navy to fight an inconclusive action against the Argentines later in the morning. In the afternoon, however, Flight Lieutenant Barton shot down a Mirage with a Sidewinder, achieving the first air-to-air kill of the conflict, and his wingman, Lieutenant Steve Thomas, RN, possibly destroyed another.

Also in the afternoon of 1 May, Sea Harriers of No. 800 Squadron engaged Argentine Dagger fighter-bombers that were attempting to attack Royal Navy forces which had been bombarding Port Stanley airfield; one of the enemy aircraft was destroyed by yet another RAF pilot, Flight Lieutenant Tony Penfold.

On the night of 3/4 May, Vulcan XM607, captained on this occasion by Squadron

Harriers and Sea Harriers on *Hermes* on a dark, wet South Atlantic morning. The Harriers offered great support capability, especially during the Argentine retreat. Towards the end of the fighting, No. 1 Squadron Harriers flew several missions using US-supplied laser guided bombs.

Above
Showing the problems RAF Harrier pilots had adapting to carrier operations, a GR.3 which fell off *Hermes'* side is manhandled back. After inspection, it was pronounced operational and flew a bombing mission, testimony to its rugged strength.

Leader R.J. Reeve, carried out Black Buck Two, the second bombing attack on Port Stanley airfield. On this occasion, the runway was not hit, though further damage was caused to nearby installations. A third mission, Black Buck Three, had to be cancelled because of unexpectedly strong headwinds en route.

Sea Harrier operations, hampered by a good deal of bad weather, continued throughout the first week in May. On the 4th, three Harriers mounted a heavy attack on the airstrip at Goose Green; one of the pilots involved was Flight Lieutenant Ted Ball, RAF, of No. 800 Squadron, who witnessed the destruction of the first Sea Harrier; flown by Lieutenant Nick Taylor, it was hit by 35mm fire and crashed in flames, killing its pilot.

On 9 May, after a week that had witnessed, among other actions, the sinking of the cruiser *General Belgrano* and the Type 42 destroyer HMS *Sheffield* and the accidental loss through collision—or so it was presumed—of two more Sea Harriers, Flight Lieutenant David Morgan was involved in an action between No. 800 Squadron and the Argentine trawler *Narwal*. The latter was in the Total Exclusion Zone, and so it was bombed and strafed by Morgan and the other Harrier pilot, Lieutenant Commander Gordon Batt. The *Narwal* was later boarded and her crew taken prisoner; she sank under tow the next day.

By 15 May, major reinforcements of men

and equipment were well on their way from Ascension to join the Task Force. The convoy routes were kept under constant surveillance by Nimrod MR.2 aircraft, now fitted with improvised flight refuelling equipment; on 15 May, an aircraft of No. 201 Squadron (Wing Commander David Emmerson), refuelling twice en route, flew to a point 150 miles north of Port Stanley, turned west until it was 60 miles off the coast of Argentina, then turned north-east to fly parallel with the coast, the crew making a visual and radar search of the areas near the major Argentine naval bases. The Nimrod recovered to Ascension after a flight of 19 hours 5 minutes, during which it had covered over 8,300 miles and broken the record previously set up by the Victor flight to South Georgia.

This reconnaissance confirmed that no major units of the Argentine Navy were at sea, but seven more similar flights were made during the days that followed. The original Nimrod had not been intercepted, but as an insurance against possible action by the Argentine fighters the Nimrods undertaking subsequent missions were armed with Sidewinder AAMs for self-defence.

One of the most important vessels in the reinforcement convoy heading south from Ascension was the *Atlantic Conveyor*. As well as large quantities of badly needed equipment, including just about every spare tent the Army could muster, she also carried seven naval helicopters, four Chinooks of

No. 18 Squadron, eight Sea Harriers of No. 809 Squadron and six Harrier GR.3s of No. 1 Squadron, the latter having joined at Ascension after a nine-hour flight from the UK. Four more Harriers of No. 1 Squadron were retained at Ascension to provide air defence and to act as replacement aircraft if needed. The transfer to the Task Force took place on 18 May, No. 1 Squadron's aircraft being assigned to HMS *Hermes*.

Soon after their arrival, it was decided to remove the Sidewinder launchers from the Harrier GR.3s and use them in the ground attack role. The first such sortie, on the afternoon of 20 May, was flown by Wing Commander Peter Squire and Squadron Leaders Robert Iveson and Jeremy Pook, the Squadron CO and flight commanders. The three Harriers attacked a fuel dump at Fox Bay, on West Falkland, with cluster bombs and recovered successfully to the carrier. On 21 May, Squadron Leader Pook, accompanied by Flight Lieutenant Mark Hare, took off to fly in support of the British amphibious assault in San Carlos Water; while Sea Harriers flew CAP, the two GR.3s were briefed to attack enemy helicopters in the Mount Kent area. They destroyed two Pumas and a Chinook on the ground, then Hare was hit by several bullets and returned to the carrier, covered by Pook.

Soon afterwards, two more Harrier GR.3s flown by Wing Commander Squire and Flight Lieutenant Jeff Glover were briefed to provide close air support for the forces in the landing area. While searching for defensive positions at Port Howard, Glover's aircraft was badly hit by ground fire; the pilot ejected and was taken prisoner.

Later in the day, during the bitter air battles that accompanied the Argentine air force's attempts to break up the British landings, Flight Lieutenant John Leeming, RAF, and Lieutenant Clive Morell of No. 800 Squadron engaged a pair of Skyhawks near Goose Green and destroyed both of them, Leeming using his 30mm cannon to achieve his kill. Almost all the combats took place at very low level—in most cases at about 50 feet—and the Harriers enjoyed a distinct superiority, the pilots being able to make full use of their vectoring in forward flight (VIFF) technique to get out of trouble or to pull the nose of their aircraft round a few more degrees to get into a good aiming position.

By nightfall on 21 May more than 3,000 troops and nearly 1,000 tons of stores had been placed ashore around San Carlos Water. Argentine air losses had amounted to five Skyhawks, five Daggers, two Pucaras and the helicopters knocked out by Pook and Hare; the British had lost two helicopters and Jeff Glover's Harrier GR.3, all victims of ground fire. In support of the day's operations, Wing Commander Emmerson of No. 201 Squadron flew the longest maritime reconnaissance sortie so far, his Nimrod covering 8,453 miles in a flight that lasted 18 hours 51 minutes.

On 22 May, the Harriers of No. 1 Squadron attacked the airfield at Goose Green, and on the following day they also bombed the strip at Dunnose Head on West Falkland, which was thought to be used by Argentine transport aircraft; in fact it was not, and the bombs caused some damage to local property. Soon after this, Flight Lieutenants David Morgan and John Leeming were flying CAP over Falkland Sound when they sighted three Pumas and an Augusta 109 helicopter flying up the coast. The two RAF pilots dived down to attack and one of the Pumas crashed and burned before a shot had been fired; the pilot may have gone out of control while trying to take evasive action. The other helicopters landed hastily; two were destroyed by Morgan and Leeming, the fourth by Sea Harriers of No. 801 Squadron.

Also on 23 May, No. 1 Squadron's Harriers carried out several armed reconnaissance sorties and made a three-aircraft attack on the airstrip at Pebble Island. The next morning, four Harrier GR.3s joined Sea Harriers in an attack on Port Stanley airfield with 1,000-pound retarded bombs. The airfield was attacked again on 25 May, but no

serious damage was caused. On this day, the *Atlantic Conveyor* was hit by an Exocet missile and sunk with the loss of most of her equipment, including all but one of No. 18 Squadron's Chinooks. The sole survivor went on to render astonishing service throughout the remainder of the campaign, flying well beyond its normal limitations.

On 26 May, the breakout from the San Carlos beachhead began, with Commando and Paratroop units setting out on the first stage of their advance on Port Stanley. No. 1 Squadron flew seven ground support sorties in the course of the day, one Puma being destroyed on the ground by Squadron Leader Pook. On 27 May, the Squadron's Harrier GR.3s operated in support of the paratroops' advance on Goose Green, and on one of these attacks the aircraft flown by Squadron Leader Bob Iveson was hit by 35mm fire and shot down. Iveson ejected and took refuge in an abandoned house; he managed to evade capture and joined up with friendly forces some time later. The day's Harrier attacks, which were heavy and very accurate, badly demoralised the enemy and played a major part in the subsequent British victory at Goose Green.

Bad weather curtailed air operations on 29 May, but on the next day, No. 1 Squadron made six sorties against targets near Mount Round, Mount Kent and Port Stanley. During one of these, Squadron Leader Pook's aircraft was hit and he had to eject over the sea; he was picked up by a Sea King after less than ten minutes in the water. Bob Iveson also returned to HMS *Hermes* on this day.

Meanwhile, on the night of 28/29 May, another Vulcan sortie, Black Buck Four, had been aborted when one of the Victor tankers went unserviceable before the penultimate fuel transfer. The mission was completed as Black Buck Five on the night of 30/31 May by Vulcan XM597 (Squadron Leader Neill McDougall); in conjunction with a Harrier attack on Port Stanley airfield the Vulcan launched three Shrike anti-radar missiles at targets identified by the AEO, with what result it was impossible to assess. Before 31 May ended, No. 1 Squadron's Harriers carried out seven ground-attack sorties in the area around Port Stanley, softening up the enemy in preparation for the final phase of the ground operation. By this time No. 1 Squadron was down to three Harriers, but on 1 June two replacement aircraft flown by Flight Lieutenants Murdo Macleod and Mike Beech landed on *Hermes* after a non-stop 8 hour 25 minute flight from Ascension, each aircraft supported by four Victor tankers.

Later in the day, Flight Lieutenant Ian

Mortimer, an RAF pilot with No. 801 Squadron, had a lucky escape when his Sea Harrier was hit by a Roland missile several miles south of Port Stanley; he ejected over the sea and spent nine hours in his dinghy before being picked up by a Sea King.

On the night of 2/3 June, Vulcan XM597, again captained by Squadron Leader McDougall, carried out Black Buck Six, launching two Shrikes at radar contacts. On the way home to Ascension, the Vulcan's refuelling probe fractured during a 'prod' at a Victor tanker and McDougall had to divert to Rio de Janeiro. The aircraft and crew were held at Rio for a week while diplomatic channels buzzed before being allowed to depart for Ascension.

On the morning of 5 June, the Harriers of No. 1 Squadron, together with Sea Harriers, began operations from a site at Port San Carlos, which considerably shortened the time it normally took them to reach their operational areas. By this time, essential spares were being airlifted to the task force by No. 38 Group's Hercules aircraft, which now had a flight refuelling capability and were consequently able to make the trip from Ascension; they had nowhere to land as yet, but they were able to make low-level supply drops.

On 8 June, the Argentine air force launched heavy attacks on British naval forces at Bluff Cove, hitting the landing ships *Sir Galahad* and *Sir Tristram* and causing heavy loss of life. Another enemy attack just before dusk was intercepted by Flight Lieutenant Dave Morgan and Lieutenant Dave Smith of No. 800 Squadron; the two pilots shot down three out of four Skyhawks with Sidewinders, Morgan claiming two of them.

On 9 June, No. 1 Squadron, now reinforced by two more Harrier GR.3s from Ascension, flew four sorties against enemy gun positions on Sapper Hill and Mount Longdon. Ground attack sorties against targets in the Port Stanley area continued the next day, and some Harriers were damaged by small-arms fire, although none seriously. The Squadron flew eleven sorties on 11 June, of which ten were ground-attack sorties against Argentine positions and the other a toss-bombing attack on Stanley airfield.

Early on 12 June, Flight Lieutenant Martin Withers carried out the last Vulcan operations against the Falklands, Black Buck Seven. This was a conventional bombing attack, the aircraft dropping a mixture of 1,000-pound HE and anti-personnel bombs, fuzed to burst in the air, on enemy troop concentrations around Port Stanley. The operation was held to be a partial success. In the course of the day, No. 1 Squadron's Harriers flew six ground attack sorties against enemy positions around Sapper Hill; one aircraft, flown by Flight Lieutenant Murdo Macleod, was hit by small-arms fire bullets, creating a severe fire risk; he nevertheless managed to recover safely to HMS *Hermes*.

By 13 June, forward air controllers were in position on the hills around Port Stanley, and this enabled No. 1 Squadron to use laser-guided bombs to good effect against the Argentine forward positions. Several direct hits were scored on enemy artillery positions; this was a credit to the skill of the pilots involved, none of whom had previously had experience with laser-guided weapons. The next day saw the surrender of the enemy garrison in Port Stanley, and although the Sea Harriers continued to fly CAP for some time, No. 1 Squadron ceased offensive operations. The battle for the Falklands was over.

As this book is being written, the Falkland Islands are being turned into a major military base, its air defence assured by a squadron of Phantoms. At a later date these may be replaced by Tornado F.2s; the first squadrons of this new long-range interceptor are due to enter service in 1985.

The Royal Air Force has seen active service since the Falklands Campaign; in 1983, Buccaneers were deployed to Cyprus to fly reconnaissance and, if necessary, strike missions in support of the British element of the peace-keeping force in the Lebanon. But it may be that the Falklands War was the last major conflict in which the RAF will ever be called upon to fight.

Royal Air Force Order of Battle, 1 July 1984.*

Sqn	Base	Aircraft	Group/Command	Sqn	Base	Aircraft	Group/Command
1	Wittering	Harrier GR.3, T.4, T.4A	38 Group	51	Wyton (including EWAU)	Andover C.I Nimrod R.1	1 Group
2	Laarbruch	Jaguar GR.1, T.2	RAFG	54	Coltishall	Jaguar GR.1, T.2	38 Group
3	Gutersloh	Harrier GR.3, T.4	RAFG	55	Marham	Victor K.2	1 Group
4	Gutersloh	Harrier GR.3, T.4	RAFG	56	Wattisham	Phantom FGR.2	11 Group
5	Binbrook	Lightning F.3, F.6, T.5	11 Group	57	Marham	Victor K.2	1 Group
6	Coltishall	Jaguar GR.1, T.2	38 Group	60	Wildenrath	Pembroke C.1	RAFG
7	Odiham	Chinook HC. 1	38 Group	63 (Shadow Sqn)	Chivenor	Hawk T.1	38 Group
8	Lossiemouth	Shackleton AEW.2	11 Group	64	Coningsby	Phantom FGR.2	11 Group
9	Honington	Tornado GR.1	1 Group	70	Lyneham	Hercules C.1, C.3, K.1, C.1P	38 Group
10	Brize Norton	VC-10 C.1	38 Group	72	Aldergrove	Wessex HC.2	38 Group
11	Binbrook	Lightning F.3, F.6, T.5	11 Group	79 (Shadow Sqn)	Brawdy	Hawk T.1 Hunter F.6A, T.7, FGA.9 Jet Provost T.4	38 Group
12	Lossiemouth	Buccaneer S.2A, S.2B Hunter T.7	1 Group	84	Akrotiri and Nicosia	Wessex HC.2	RAF Cyprus
14	Bruggen	Jaguar GR.1, T.2	RAFG	85	West Raynham and detachments	Bloodhound 2	11 Group
15	Laarbruch	Tornado GR.1	RAFG	92	Wildenrath	Phantom FGR.2	RAFG
16	Laarbruch	Tornado GR.1	RAFG	100	Wyton	Canberra B.2, T.4, E.15, TT.18	1 Group
17	Bruggen	Jaguar GR.1, T.2	RAFG	101	Brize Norton	VC10	1 Group
18	Gutersloh	Chinook HC.1	RAFG	111	Leuchars	Phantom FG.1	11 Group
19	Wildenrath	Phantom FGR.2	RAFG	115	Benson	Andover C.1, E.3, E.3A	38 Group
20	Bruggen	Jaguar GR.1, T.2	RAFG	120	Kinloss	Nimrod MR.2	18 Group
22	Finningley and detachments	Wessex HC.2	18 Group	151 (Shadow Sqn)	Chivenor	Hawk T.1	38 Group
23	Stanley	Phantom FGR.2	11 Group	201	Kinloss	Nimrod MR.2	18 Group
24	Lyneham	Hercules C.1, C.3, K.1, C.1P	38 Group	202	Finningley and detachments	Sea King HAR.3	18 Group
25	Wyton and detachments	Bloodhound 2	11 Group	206	Kinloss	Nimrod MR.2	18 Group
27	Marham	Tornado GR.1	1 Group	207	Northolt Wyton detachment	Devon C.2	38 Group
28	Sek Kong	Wessex HC.2	RAF Hong Kong	208	Lossiemouth	Buccaneer S.2A, S.2B Hunter T.7	1 Group
29	Waddington	Phantom FGR.2	11 Group	230	Gutersloh	Puma HC.1	RAFG
30	Lyneham	Hercules C.1, C.3, K.1, C.1P	38 Group	234 (Shadow Sqn)	Brawdy	Hawk T.1	38 Group
31	Bruggen	Jaguar GR.1, T.2	RAFG	360	Wyton	Canberra T.17	1 Group
32	Northolt	Andover C.1, CC.2 HS.125 CC.1, CC.2, CC.3 Gazelle HT.3, HCC.4	Transport and Communications	617	Marham	Tornado GR.1	1 Group
33	Odiham	Puma HC.1	38 Group				
38 (Shadow Sqn)	St Mawgan	Nimrod MR.1, MR.2	18 Group				
41	Coltishall	Jaguar GR.1, T.2	38 Group				
42	St Mawgan	Nimrod MR.1, MR.2	18 Group				
43	Leuchars	Phantom FG.1	11 Group				
47	Lyneham	Hercules C.1, C.3, K.1, C.1P	38 Group				

*Compiled from published sources

Unit	Base	Aircraft	Group/Command	Unit	Base	Aircraft	Group/Command
226 OCU	Coningsby	Jaguar GR.1, T.2	38 Group	2 TWU	Chivenor	Hawk T.1	38 Group
228 OCU	Coningsby	Phantom FGR.2	11 Group	1 FTS	Linton-on-Ouse	Jet Provost T.3A	Support
231 OCU	Wyton	Canberra B.2, T.4	1 Group				
232 OCU	Marham	Victor K.2	1 Group	2 FTS	Shawbury	Gazelle HT.3	Support
233 OCU	Wittering	Harrier GR.3, T.4, T.4A	38 Group			Wessex HU.5	
236 OCU	St Mawgan	Nimrod MR.1, MR.2	18 Group	3 FTS	Leeming	Bulldog T.1	Support
237 OCU	Honington	Buccaneer S.2A, S.2B	1 Group			Jet Provost T.3A, T.5A	
		Hunter F.6A, T.7, T.8B		4 FTS	Valley	Hawk T.1	Support
240 OCU	Odiham	Puma HC.1	38 Group	6 FTS	Finningley	Jet Provost T.5	Support
		Chinook HC.1				Dominie T.I	
241 OCU	Brize Norton	VC-10 C.1	38 Group			Jetstream T.1	
242 OCU	Lyneham	Hercules C.1, C.3, K.1, C.1P	38 Group	7 FTS	Church Fenton	Jet Provost T.3A, T.5A	Support
Andover Training Flight				RAFC	Cranwell	Jet Provost T.5A	Support
	Benson	Andover C.1, E.3	38 Group	CATCS	Shawbury	Jet Provost T.4	Support
Lightning Training Flight				Flying Selection Squadron			
	Binbrook	Lightning F.3, F.6, T.5	11 Group		Swinderby	Chipmunk T.10	Support
Lightning Augmentation Flight				SARTF	Valley	Wessex HC.2	18 Group
	Binbrook	Lightning F.3, F.6, T.5	11 Group	The Queen's Flight			
Tri-national Tornado Training Establishment					Benson	Andover CC.2	38 Group
	Cottesmore	Tornado GR.1	1 Group			Wessex HCC.4	
Tornado Weapons Conversion Unit				C in C AFNE Flight			
	Honington	Tornado GR.1	1 Group		Fornebu	Andover C.1	RAF Norway
1 TWU	Brawdy	Hawk T.1	38 Group	1 PRU	Wyton	Canberra PR.9	1 Group
		Hunter F.6A, T.7, FGA.9					
		Jet Provost T.4					

Index

Adam, Flt Lt M. J. 29
Addison, AC E. B. 98
Addison, Observer Officer Roger, MC 14
Ahmed, Sheikh 21
Alexander, Field Marshal 90, 105–6
Ali, Rashid 77–8
Allenby, Gen Sir Edmund 17–18
Amanullah, Amir 22
Anderson, Flt Lt W. F. 14
Arrowsmith, Cpl V. 46
Atcherley, Wg Cdr R. L. R. 51
Aten, Capt Marion 13
Auchinleck, Gen Sir Claud 54, 88
Austin, Plt Off. 106

Bader, Wg Cdr Douglas 85
Balfour, R, MP 30
Ball, Flt Lt Ted 155
Barker, Maj W. G. 12
Barnett, S. R. 29
Barratt, Air Marshal 55–6, 59
Barton, Flt Lt Paul 154–5
Bateson, Wg Cdr Bob 108
Batt, Lt Cdr Gordon 155
Beech, Flt Lt Mike 156
Benn, Sgt 71
Bennett, Gp Capt D. C. T. 97
Bentley, Plt Off 53
Biard, Capt H. C. 29
Billotte, Gen. 59
Bishop, Capt W. A. 9–10
Blacker, Lt Col L. V. S. 29
Blount, AVM 48, 55, 60
Blue Steel 135, 148
Boardman, Russell 28
Bock, Gen Fedor von 55
Boothman, Flt Lt J. W. 30

Bowen, AVM Webb 27
Bowhill, ACM Sir Frederick 45, 80, 82
Bowyer, Fg Off 57
Boyd, AVM O. T. 41
Bradley, AVM J. S. T. 41
Braham, Wg Cdr J. R. D. 101
Brand, AVM Sir Quintin 66, 68
Brereton, Lt Gen L. H. 120
Briggs, Fg Off Denis 82
Broadley, Flt Lt Alan 108
Brooke-Popham, ACM Sir Robert *87*
Brophy, Fg Off G. P. 113
Broughall, Gp Capt S. 127
Brown, Capt A. Roy 7
Brown, Grp Capt L. O. 77
Brown, Sgt W. 25
Bryson, Flt Lt Oliver 13
Buerling, Plt Off George F. 89
Buglass, Sgt 101
Bunker, Plt Off 54
Burges, Sqn Ldr G. 79
Burnett, AM Sir Charles 41
Burns-Thompson, Flt Lt 14

Cadbury, Maj Egbert 11
Calder, Sqn Ldr C. C. 120
Camm, Sydney 40, 113
Campbell, Lt C. H. Noble 11
Campbell, Fg Off Kenneth, vc 81
Carey, Plt Off 57
Carey, Wg Cdr Frank 126–7
Carr, Maj Charles R. 13
Carter, Flt Lt 57
Cave-Brown-Cave, Grp Capt 27
Churchill, Sir Winston 19, 31, 57, 62, 85, 87
Clydesdale, Sqn Ldr Lord 29

Cochrane, Flt Lt Ralph 26
Collishaw, Air Cdre Raymond 13–14, 72–3
Coningham, AVM Arthur 27, 88
Cowan, Adm 14
Cowles, Fg Off 54
Craig-Adams, Plt Off 52
Crockett, Sgt W. 25
Cronin, Fg Off Edward J. 14
Cross, Sgt 101
Cross, Sqn Ldr K. B. B. 54
Cruickshank, Fg Off J. A., vc 110
Culley, Lt Stuart 11
Culliford, Flt Lt S. G. 107
Cunliffe-Lister, Sir Philip 38
Cunningham, Flt Lt John 71

d'Albiac, Air Marshal J. H. 99
Daley, Capt Bill 14
Dallas, Maj Roderick 8–9
Dashwood, Fg Off E. J. 23
Davis, Wg Cdr Reg 124
Dawson, AVM Graham 88
Day, Fg Off A. H. 14
Day, Wg Cdr H. M. A. 48
Dean, Fg Off 113
Deere, Grp Capt A. C. 85
Dempsey, Gen 116
Dickson, Capt W. F. 11
Donald, Sqn Ldr D. G. 14, 15, 35
Donaldson, Sqn Ldr E. M. 66
Doorman, Adm Karel 126
Doran, Flt Lt K. C. 46–7
Dowding, ACM Sir Hugh 41, 57–8, 60, 64, 70
Drummond, Plt Off 54
Dunlap, Wg Cdr M. V. 49
Dunsterville, Maj Gen L. C. 16
Dunwoodie, Sgt 78

Eden, Rt Hon Anthony, MP 38
Edwards, Wng Cdr H. I., VC 86
Ellington, ACM Sir Edward 37–8
Elliot, Fg Off William 14
Elliott, Sqn Ldr John 154
Elliott, AVM William 107
Embry, Flt Lt Basil 26
Emmerson, Wg Cdr David 155–6
Eschwege, Rudolf von 16
Esmonde, Lt Cdr Eugene, VC 95
Eyton-Jones, Lt Cdr John, RN 154

Faisal, Prince 18
Falkson, Plt Off 53
Farquhar, Sqn Ldr A. D. 47
Ferte, AM Sir Philip Joubert de la 82
Fonck, Rene 10
Ford, Sgt 57
Forrest, Sgt 52
Frogley, Fg Off S. G. 14
Frost Fg Off 54

Garland, Fg Off Donald, VC 56–7
Gayford, Sqn Ldr O. R. 28
Geddes, Sir Eric 31
Gee 94–6
Genders, Plt Off G. E. 91
Georges, Gen 55
Gerrish, Sgt N., MM 132
Gibson, Wg Cdr G. P., VC 63, 98
Glover, Flt Lt Jeff 155–6
Gordon, Grp Capt Robert 22
Goring, Reichsmarschall Hermann 63–4, 70
Grand Slam 120
Grant-Ede, Plt Off 52–3
Gray, Sgt Tom, VC 56–7
Graziani, Marshal 72–4
Greenslade, Fg Off Norman 14
Greig, Flt Lt D. d'Arcy 29
Griffiths, Wng Cdr J. F. 47

H₂S 97
Halley, Capt Robert 22, 25
Hare, Flt Lt Mark 155–6
Harris, AM Arthur T. 26, 87, 96–7
Harrod, Flt Lt E. J. 107
Hassan, Mohammed bin Abdullah 22
Hatchett, Fg Off J. R. 14
Hayter-James, Fg Off N. C. 23
Held, Unteroffizier Alfred 47
Herrtage, Fg Off 78
Hillman, Sgt R. W. 81
Hitler, Adolf 37–8, 43, 70–1, 120
Hodgkinson, Sgt 71
Holywell, Sgt Jack 62
Hornell, Flt Lt D. E., VC 110
Houston, Lady 29–30
Hull, Flt Lt C. B. 52–3
Humphreys, Sir Francis 23
Hunter, AC H. J. F. 125

Inglis, Lt D. C. 9
Iveson, Sqn Ldr Robert 155–6

Jacobs, Flt Lt H. 101
Jacobsen, Plt Off 54
Jameson, Flt Lt 54
Jenkins, Flt Lt N. H. 28
Jones-Williams, Sqn Ldr A. G. 28

Kain, Fg Off Edgar James 48–9
Kazakov, Alexander 13
Keith, Fg Off D. N. 102
Kellett, Wg Cdr R. G. 28, 47
Kemal, Mustapha 19
Kerim Fattah Beg 19
Kesselring, FM Albert 64, 70, 103–5
Khan, Mirza Ali 24
Kinkead, Maj Marcus 13–14
Kitchener, Sgt 53
Knight, Fg Off 54

Lack, Sgt 101
Lawrence, Col T. E. 17–18

Learoyd, Flt Lt R. A. B., VC 67
Leckie, Capt Robert 11
Leeming, Flt Lt John 156
Leigh, Sqn Ldr 109
Leigh-Mallory, AVM Sir Trafford 67, 99, 111
Letchford, Sgt F. 47
Lindbergh, Charles 28
Linke, Maj 12
Lloyd, AVM Sir Hugh P. 90
Lloyd, Sqn Ldr I. T. 35
Lockwood, Flt Lt Jimmy 124
Longcroft, AC C. A. H. 36
Longmore, ACM Sir Arthur 27, 41, 72–3, 75
Lord, Flt Lt D. S. A., VC 116
Loveitt, Flt Sgt Raymond 82
Lutjens, Admiral 82
Lydekker, Lt, RN 53

McCudden, Maj James B. 9
McDougall, Sqn Ldr Neill 156
McEwen, Brig Gen Norman 25
MacGregor, Plt Off 53
McIntyre, Flt Lt D. F. 29
MacLaren, Maj A. S. C. 25
MacLeod, Flt Lt Murdo 156–7
MacNamara, Plt Off 52
McPherson, Fg Off A. 46
Mahmoud, Sheikh 19–20
Mai-Maevsky, Gen 14
Malan, Sqn Ldr A. G. 66, 84
Mallaby, Brig S. W. S. 132
Maltby, AVM P. C. 124
Manning, Grp Capt E. R. 126
Mannock, Maj Edward, VC, DSO, MC 9
Mason, Fg Off Lloyd 13
May, 2nd Lt W. R. 7
Mee, Fg Off 54
Meintjes, Major 27
Mercer, Fg Off Howard, MC 14
Messervy, Maj Gen Sir Frank 129, 131
Milligan, Sgt 53
Mills, Flt Lt 52
Milne, Lt Gen G. F. 16–17
Mitchell, Fg Off 48
Mitchell, Obs Off John 14
Mitchell, Reginald J. 29–30, 41
Montgomery, FM Sir Bernard L. 90
Moore, Grp Capt M. 54
Morell, Lt Clive 156
Morgan, Flt Lt David 154–6
Mortimer, Flt Lt Ian 156
Mould, Plt Off 48
Mountbatten, Adm Lord Louis 128–9
Mullis, Sgt W. 81
Mulock, Lt Col R. H. 8
Mussolini, Benito 106
Mynarski, Plt Off A. C., VC 112–13

Nagumo, Adm 128
Nettleton, Sqn Ldr J. D., VC 96
Nicholetts, Flt Lt E. 28
Nicolson, Flt Lt J. B., VC 68

O'Connor, Gen 73–4
Oboe 97–98, 118
Operations: Abigail 83; Becher's Brook 138; Black Buck 154–6; Corporate 154–6; Crusader 88; Diadem 105; Dragoon 105; Dynamo 60; Exodus 121; Firedog 142–3; Glimmer 112; Gomorrah 98; Husky 102; Manna 107, 121; Market 114–115; Market Garden 114; Millennium 96; Musketeer 145; Nickel 45–7, 49; Nutcracker 147; Plainfare 140; Strangle 105; Taxable 112; Thursday 130; Torch 91; Varsity 120
Orlebar, Sqn Ldr A. H. 30

Park, AVM Sir Keith 60, 63, 66, 68, 90
Parnall, Plt Off 53
Pattle, Flt Lt M. T. St. J. 75
Phillipson, Sgt J. 71
Pickard, Grp Capt P. C. 108
Pierse, ACM Sir Richard 84, 87, 128, 130
Pink, Wg Cdr R. C. M. 22–23
Pinkerton, Flt Lt G. 47

Playfair, AVM P. H. L. 48, 59
Pohl, Gen Ritter von 105
Polando, John 28
Pook, Sqn Ldr Jeremy 155–6
Pulford, AVM C. W. H. 27, *87*, 124
Purdy, Plt Off 53

Ramshaw, Flt Lt Jack *87*
Reeve, Sqn Ldr R. J. 155
Reynolds, Fg Off G. W. H. 91
Reynolds, LAC 57
Richards, Plt Off 52
Richey, Fg Off Paul 49
Richthofen, Manfred von 7
Riley, Fg Off 52–53
Rommel, Gen Erwin 77, 88–9, 91
Rothermere, Lord 38
Rundstedt, FM von 119

Salisbury, Lord 31–33
Salmond, AVM Sir Geoffrey 22–3, 26
Samson, Wg Cdr C. R. 27
Sanders, Gen Liman von 17
Sassoon, Sir Philip 27–8
Saundby, Flt Lt Robert 26
Scarf, Flt Lt A. S. K., VC 124
Schneider, Jacques 29–30, 35, 41
Scott, Wg Cdr C. L. 27
Scott, Sgt J. P. 81
Shackley, Flt Sgt 54
Simmons, Fg Off H. E., MC 14
Simms, Sgt 57
Simon, Sir John 38
Singer, Grp Capt N. C. 127
Skalski, Sqn Ldr Stanislaw 93
Skybolt 135–136, 154
Slatter, Air Cdre L. H. 75
Smart, Capt B. A. 11
Smart, AVM H. G. 77
Smith, Sgt 78
Smith, Flt Sgt A. E. 25
Smith, Lt Dave 156
Smith, Capt Ross 25
Sperrle, Gen Hugo 64, 70
Squire, Wg Cdr Peter 155–6
Stainforth, Flt G. H. 30
Steel, AM Sir John 41
Stephens, Plt Off 57
Stevens, Sqn Ldr E. E. 47
Stevens, Flt Lt R. P. 71
Stevenson, AVM D. F. 126
Stewart, Flt Lt 54
Stilwell, Gen 128
Stumpff, Gen Hans Jurgen 64
Suckling, Fg Off Mike 81
Swain, Sqn Ldr F. R. D. 29

Tait, Wng Cdr J. B. 118
Taylor, Lt Nick 155
Taylor, Sgt 54
Tedder, ACM Sir Arthur 88, 111
Tennant, Lt Col 16
Thomas, Fg Off Norman 56
Thomas, Lt Steve, RN 154
Thompson, Cdr, RN 46
Thompson, Sqn Ldr J. M. 66
Trant, Sqn Ldr A. 144
Trenchard, ACM Sir Hugh 7–8, 19, 30–1, 34–6
Trigg, Fg Off L. A., VC 109–10
Trollop, Capt J. L. 6

Vigerie, Gen d'Astier de la 55
Vigors, Flt Lt Tim 124
Vincent, Air Cdre S. F. 125, 130

Waghorn, Fg Off H. R. D. 29
Wallis, Sir Barnes 120
Warships: *Admiral Scheer* 46–7, 120; *Altmark* 49; *Argus* 14, 79; *Ark Royal* 82; *Atlantic Conveyor* 154–6; *Bismarck* 81–2; *Eagle* 89; *Emden* 47, 120; *Furious* 89; *General Belgrano* 155; *Glorious* 51–4; *Gneisenau* 46, 49, 51, 54, 81; *Graf Spee* 49, 81; *Hermes* 128, 154–6; *Hipper* 49, 120; *Hood* 81; *Konigsberg* 51; *Lancastria* 62; *Leipzig* 47, 51;

Lutzow 81–2; *Nurnberg* 47; *Pamyat Azova* 15; *Prince of Wales* 81, 124; *Prinz Eugen* 81–2; *Repulse* 124; *Scharnhorst* 46, 49, 51, 54, 81, 86; *Sheffield* 155; *Sir Galahad* 156; *Sir Tristram* 156; *Tirpitz* 94; *Victorious* 82; *Vindictive* 14–15
Watson-Watt, Robert 64
Wavell, FM Sir Archibald 73, 128
Webster, Flt Lt S. N.
Welter, Oberleutnant 120
Whall, Sgt 52
Wilkie, Plt Off 54
Williams, Flt Lt 53
Wilson. Lt Col A. T. 26
Window, 98, 112
Withers, Flt Lt Martin 154, 156
Woollett, Capt H. W. 7
Wooton, Sqn Ldr 101
Worsley, Flt Lt O. E. 29

Zeppelin 11, 64

AIRCRAFT

Aicha: D3A (Val) 128
Airco: DH.4 11, 13, 16; DH.6 11; DH.9 13–14 17–19, 22–3, 27
Airspeed: Horsa 102, 115–16; Oxford 41, 77
Albatros: D.III 7, 10, 14, 16
Armstrong Whitworth: Albemarle 102, 114–15; Argosy 141; Atlas 35; Siskin 21, 33; Whitley 39, 45–51, 55–6, 58, 62, 67, 83, 106
Avro: 504 41; 652 41; Andover 152; Anson 41, 45, 61; Bison 35; Cadet 124; Lancaster 84, 94, 96–8, 112–13, 116–120, 133, 139, 142, 146; Lincoln 133, 139, 142–3, 145; Manchester 84, 94, 96; Shackleton 139–140, 143–5, 147, 149, 151–2, 154; Tutor 41; Vulcan 134–7, 148, 150–1, 155–6; York 140

BAC: VC-10 141, 148–9, 151–2
Blackburn: Beverley 141, 144; Blackburn 35; Buc-caneer 147, 149–152, 156; Dart 35; Griffin 14–15; Iris 27; Perth 41; Skua 51
Boeing: B-17 Fortress 86–87, 108, 110, 126; B-29 Washington 133–4
Boeing-Vertol: CH-47 Chinook 152, 154, 156
Boulton Paul: Defiant 61, 64, 71; Sidestrand 34
Brewster: Buffalo *87*, 124–7
Bristol: 138A 29; 142 38; F.2B 22–3, 33, 35; Beaufighter 71, 79–80, 91, 101–102, 105, 107, 128, 139, 142; Beaufort 80–1, 90, 94–5, 108, 128; Bisley 91; Blenheim 22, 24, 38, 41, 43, 46–9, 51, 55–9, 61, 71–8, 83–6, *87*, 95, 99, 124–8; Bombay 26, 72; Brigand 139, 142–3, 146; Britannia 141, 148–9; Bulldog 40, 152; Fighter 11, 17–20, 22, 27; Scout 16–17; Sy-camore 143, 145

Caproni: Ca3 10 72
Consolidated: Catalina 80–2, *87*, 108, 110, 125, 128, 131, 139; Liberator 106–8, 110, 120, 128, 131, 139
Curtiss: H.4 11; P-40 series 78, 88, 90–1, 93, 102–105, 107, 126–8; Hawk 48

Dassault: Mirage 154
De Havilland: DH.9A 8, 13, 19–23, 26–7, 33–4; DH.10 22, 26, 34; Comet 141, 145, 149; Devon 152: Dominie 152; Hornet 142–3; Mosquito 96–8, 101–2, 108, 110–11, 113, 116–20, 132, 134, 137, 139, 142; Rapide 48; Sea Vixen 139; Tiger Moth 41, 124; Vampire 137–8, 141–6; Venom 138–9, 141, 143, 145–6
Dewoitine: 520 78
Dornier: Do 17 48, 53, 56–7, 63–4, 66, 68, 71; Do 26 53, 63
Douglas: A-4 Skyhawk 156; C-54 Skymaster 141; Boston 95, 98–9, 111; Dakota 102, 107, 112, 114, 116, 120, 127–32, 143, 145

English Electric: Canberra 133–4, 137, 141–6, 150–1; Lightning 104, 131, 139, 141, 148–51
English Electric: TSR-2 137, 139, 149

Fairey: IIID 27, 35; IIIF 21, 27; Albacore 90; Battle 38, 43, 47–8, 55–7, 59, 61–62, 80; Fawn 34; Flycatcher 35; Fox 34; Fulmar 128; Hendon 39; Monoplane 28; Swordfish 52, 79, 82, 90, 94–5
Felixstowe: F.3 35; F. 5 35; H.12 11
Fiat: CR.32 72; CR.42 73; G.50 Falco 72, 75
Focke-Wulf: Fw 190 85, 92–3, 99, 101, 108, 116; Fw 200 80
Fokker: D. VII 12, 14, 16; E.III 16; Triplane 7, 9, 13, 16

General Aircraft: Hamilcar 115
General Dynamics: F-III 137, 149
Gloster: Gamecock 33; Gauntlet 40; Gladiator 40, 43, 47–8, 51–5, 59–60, 72–3, 75–79; Grebe 31, 33; Javelin FAW.9 143–4; Meteor 113, 133, 137–9, 142–3, 145–6
Gloster-Napier: Floatplane 29; Mk III, IV and VI 29
Gotha: 11
Grumman: Hellcat 131

Halberstadt: 16
Handley Page: HP.80 134; 0/400 8, 17, 25–6; V/1500 8, 22, 25–6; W.8b 34; Halifax 83–4, 86, 95, 97–8, 102, 106–7, 110, 114–20, 139; Hampden 39–40, 46–7, 49, 51, 56, 58, 63, 67, 83, 86, 94–5; Harrow 38–39; Hastings 140–1, 144–5; Heyford 39; Hinaidi 23, 27, 34, 39; Hyderabad 34; Jetstream 152; Victor 135–7, 148, 150, 154–6
Hanoveraner: 12
Hawker: Audax 41, 72, 77; Demon 40; Fury 40; Hardy 22, 41, 72; Hart 27, 38, 41; Hawfinch 40; Hector 41; Hind 38; Horsley 34; Hunter 138–9, 141, 144–6, 150, 152; Hurricane 15, 40–3, 47–9, 53–5, 57–64, 66–8, 70–3, 76–7, 79, 84, 88–91, 99, 102, 107, 124–32; Tempest 113, 117, 120, 137, 142–4, 146; Typhoon 99, 108, 112–14; Woodcock 33
Hawker-Siddeley: Andover 141; Harrier 139, 148–9, 151, 154–7; Hawk 142; Nimrod 149–51, 154–6
Heinkel: He III 47–9, 52–5, 57, 60, 67, 71, 78; He 115 49, 52, 54, 67, 71
Henschel: Hs 126 57
Hunting: Jet Provost 152

IAe: Pucara 156
IAI: Delta Dagger 154–6
Ilyushin: Il-28 145

Junkers: Ju 52 53, 55, 93, 103; Ju 87 'Stuka' 53–54, 57, 61, 63–4, 66–8, 77, 79, 90; Ju 86P-2 91; Ju 88 47, 51, 53–4, 57, 64, 66–8, 71, 79, 102; Ju 90 52–3

Lockheed: 14 41; Hercules 141, 148–9, 151, 156; Hudson 41, 45, 49, 51, 58, 61–3, 80, 82, *87*, 96, 107–8, 124–8; P2V-5F Neptune 140; Ven-tura 98, 101, 107

Macchi: C.200 78
McDonnell-Douglas: F-4 Phantom 139, 147–52, 157
Martin: Baltimore 91, 107; Maryland 78–9, 81, 111
Martinsyde: G.102 16–17; S.1 16–17
Messerschmitt: Bf 109 47–9, 55, 59–61, 63–4, 66–8, 71, 76–9, 85–6, 103, 105; Bf 110 47, 49, 52–3, 57, 59–60, 64–8, 71, 76–9, 86, 101, 116; Me 163 93; Me 262 120; Me 323 93
MiG: MiG-15 137; 145
Miles: Magister 41; Master 41
Mitsubishi: Ki46 *Dinah* 128; A6M Zero 124–6

Nakajima: Ki27 126; Ki43 *Oscar* 127, 131
Nieuport: 17 13–14
North American: Harvard 41, 142, 144; Mustang 99–100, 104, 107–8, 112–13, 116–118, 131; Mitchell 107, 111, 131–2; F-86E Sabre 138, 141, 143–4
Northrop: N-3PB 80–1

Panavia: Tornado 152, 156

Parnall: Panther 35
Pfalz: 10, 14, 18
Prestwick: Pioneer 143

Republic: Thunderbolt 112, 130–2
Royal Aircraft Factory: BE.2c 11, 16–17; BE.2e 17; BE.12 16; Fe.2b 11; RE.8 7–8, 12, 16–18; SE.5 and SE.5A 9, 16–18

Saro: London 41
Savoia Marchetti: S.79 79
Scottish Aviation: Twin Pioneer 144
SEPECAT: Jaguar 150–1
Short: Belfast 141, 149; Rangoon 21–2, 41; Sea-plane 14–15; Singapore III 22, 41; Stirling 68, 83, 86, 97, 112, 114–16, 120; Sunderland 41, 45, 49, 51, 72, 76, 79–80, 82, 108, 139–40, 142–3
Sikorsky: Dragonfly 143
Sopwith: 2F1 Camel 7, 11–15; 7F1 Snipe 8, 12–13, 19–20, 31, 33; Cuckoo 30; 1½–Strutter 13–16
Spad: 13–14
Staaken: R.VI 11
Supermarine: S.5 and S.6 series 29, 30, 41; Scapa 41; Seafire 104; Southampton 27, 35; Spitfire 41–2, 47, 60–1, 63–4, 66–8, 70–1, 81, 85–6, 89–91, 93, 99, 101–5, 107–8, 110, 112–13, 116–18, 128–9, 131–2, 137, 142, 144, 152; Swift 138–9; Walrus 110
Supermarine-Napier: S.4 29

Taylorcraft: Auster 142
Tupolev: Tu-16 *Badger* 144

Vickers: Bullet 17; Valentia 22, 26, 72–3; Valetta 141, 143; Valiant 134–6, 145; Vernon 19–20, 26; Victoria 20–3, 26; Vildebeest 41, *87*, 124–6; Vimy 19, 26, 33–4; Vincent 22, 75; Virginia 28, 39; Warwick 139; Wellesley 28, 38–9, 72, 74–5; Wellington 39, 46–7, 49, 51, 55, 58, 61–2, 73, 75, 77, 79, 83–4, 86, 90, 94, 96–7, 102, 106–8, 139
Vultee: Vengeance 128–9

Waco: Hadrian 102, 115, 130
Westland: PV.3 29; Gazelle 152; Lysander 41, 43, 48, 55, 58–60, 72–3, 76–8, 107; Sea King 151, 156; Wallace 29; Walrus 35; Wapiti 21, 23–4, 27, 34, 41; Wessex 151–2; Whirlwind 86, 143, 145, 151
Westland/Aerospatiale: Puma 151, 155

I have received assistance from many quarters in the preparation of this book; there is not space enough to mention the dozens of people who have delved into their files or their memories to bring to light half-forgotten snippets of invaluable information. I should, however, like to thank the following in particular for their help:

Air Commodore Henry Probert, RAF (Ret'd) and the staff of the Air Historical Branch, Ministry of Defence, (RAF); Mrs D. Blackwell; George Blows; Ron Chappell; J. Cowie; Albert Holmes; Major W.K. Ison (Ret'd); Group Captain L.B.B. King, RAF (Ret'd); Jim Kyle; George E. Leak; A.J. Lynch; Major R.B. Schofield (Ret'd); K.A. Simmons; E.J. Sparkes; Mrs E. Swinerd; Mrs H.E. Thomas; Betty Webber; Flight Lieutenant Reg Wheatley, RAF (Ret'd); and A. Wilson.